LINCOLN
and the
PATRONAGE

A. Lincoln.

From a photograph by C. S. German, Springfield, Ill., February 9, 1861, now in possession of The Lincoln National Life Insurance Company, Fort Wayne, Ind.

LINCOLN
and the
PATRONAGE

By **HARRY J. CARMAN**
and
REINHARD H. LUTHIN

GLOUCESTER, MASS.
PETER SMITH
1964

PREFACE

ABRAHAM LINCOLN will always present an attractive subject for reading, discussion, and research. The more one studies him and his career the more one becomes convinced that both require further study. The early accounts of his career were either highly laudatory or bitterly denunciatory. After his tragic death criticism softened and with passing decades the real Lincoln increasingly gave way to the legendary Lincoln. Mistakes and weaknesses were ignored or forgotten, and the martyred President became more and more the object of adulation and deification. Nor is this to be wondered at, for in the hearts of the American people Lincoln, more than any other man, has long been regarded as the savior of the Union and the symbol of the pioneer and of American democracy. Largely as a consequence, by far the greater part of the innumerable biographies, novels, poems, essays and scenarios which have been written about him portray the deified Lincoln. This book belongs in a different category. Operating upon the thesis that only by recourse to source material is it possible to separate the false from the true, the legendary from the real, the authors of this volume have attempted to analyze Lincoln's policy in distributing the public offices, government contracts, and other political favors during his presidency.

From the early days of the Republic our federal government has in practice been dominated by political parties, the party in power, to all intents and purposes, becoming the government itself. The very structure of our Federal system, with its legal separation of powers and its division of legislative authority between Congress and the states, makes party government indispensable. And of the several sources of party strength none, perhaps, is more important than patronage in the form of jobs, contracts, and sundry favors, large and small. Indeed, if one would fully understand the administration of any one of that long line of executives who have occupied the White House, one cannot ignore the "spoils system." Lincoln's administration was no exception. Confronted with a herculean task he, perhaps more than any of his predecessors in the presidency, had need for competent and trusted aides and for the backing of unified public support. Patronage was one means of procuring them.

This volume represents an effort to set forth in detail the extent and influence of patronage at a critical period in American history. If in the process we shed light on the real Lincoln our labors will be doubly repaid. Wherever possible we have let the documents speak for themselves, though in so doing we have tried to avoid being cataloguers.

For aid and encouragement in preparing this volume the authors are especially indebted to their colleagues, Professors Allan Nevins and Samuel McKee, Jr., of Columbia University. Professor Dwight C. Miner, of Columbia University, and Professor Charles C. Tansill, of Fordham University, have placed at our disposal their extensive bibliographical knowledge. Generous aid came also from four eminent Lincoln scholars: Professor James G. Randall, of the University of Illinois, who read the entire manuscript; Dr. Paul M. Angle, of the Illinois State Historical Library, Springfield; Dr. Harry E. Pratt, of the Abraham Lincoln Association, Springfield, Illinois; Dr. Louis A. Warren, of the Lincoln National Life Foundation, Fort Wayne, Indiana. Dr. Elizabeth Cometti, of the Women's College of the University of North Carolina, Dr. Stephen G. Chaconas of Brooklyn College, Dr. Raymond Walters, Jr., Mr. Alfred W. Bedingfield, Mr. Arthur J. Alexander, and Dr. Francis Brown have contributed valuable criticism. Miss Helen O'Brien, Miss Carolyn Robinson, Mrs. Cathryne Barrett Carman, Miss Hildegard Luthin, and Miss Clotilde Luthin have been very helpful in the preparation of the manuscript. To them and to all others who have assisted in this enterprise we are grateful. For any errors of fact the authors alone are responsible.

H. J. C.
R. H. L.

Columbia University
January 4, 1943

CONTENTS

ILLUSTRATIONS

LINCOLN
and the
PATRONAGE

Chapter I

FACING THE ORDEAL

E VEN BEFORE the November election of 1860 had crowned the
Republican cause with success, the "folks back home" were
plying their Congressmen with requests for political favors. "In
the event that Mr. Lincoln is elected," wrote one aspirant to a
Pennsylvania member, "I will be an applicant . . . I have served
my party." [1] To another job seeker the election of Lincoln to the
presidency was "about a foregone conclusion." He wanted "some
consulship or something that I am capabil [sic] of filling and that
will pay. . . . I want a good paying office." [2] To a Massachusetts
Republican chieftain came the following: "As the approaching
political contest is likely to result in our favor, it is but fair under
the circumstances that those who have worked should be remuner-
ated, and lest you ever think us too candid in our avowal, we will
state why we believe it our due. . . ." [3] And these were typical
of the job-hunting communications which every Republican leader
received while the presidential contest was in progress. For many
the gigantic task of preserving the Union was lost sight of in the
mad scramble for office.

The quest for office was not confined to obscure men who claimed
to have labored in the interests of the party. The famous historian
John Lothrop Motley, for example, paused long enough in his
historical work to write home from the Netherlands:

I can have no doubt, writing a week before the election, of the success of the Republican party. . . . It has become necessary for me
to renew my researches in the archives of the Hague, and a protracted residence there will become almost indispensable. I have

1 James G. McQuaide to Covode, Oct. 16, 1860, John Covode Papers. Covode was
a Republican member of Congress from Pennsylvania.
2 William Larimer to Covode, Oct. 29, 1860. *Ibid.*
3 Benjamin B. Patton to Banks, Nov. 4, 1860, Nathaniel P. Banks Papers, Essex
Institute. (In volume marked "II, 1860.") Banks was the Republican governor of
Massachusetts.

thought, therefore, that the new government might be willing to give a literary man, who has always been a most earnest Republican, ever since that party was organized, the post of minister at the court of the Hague.[4]

No sooner was the news of Lincoln's election known than the rush of office seekers began in earnest. Indeed, a scant three weeks after the verdict at the polls the Republican state chairman of New Hampshire lamented: "The offices are now sought for with avidity, and a rush to reap where they have not sown is made by every slippery politician in the Republican party." [5] "I wish there was an office for every deserving working Republican who desired it," bemoaned an Indiana congressman, "but alas! there will not be one for every fifty I fear. The applications are almost innumerable." [6] To another Hoosier Republican leader, who resided in Indianapolis, it seemed "as though everybody here who voted for Lincoln expects to get an appointment." [7] So did Republican voters elsewhere throughout the nation!

The 1860 election returns were scarcely in before Springfield, Illinois, home of the President-elect, quickly filled with an anxious and motley crowd. For three months Lincoln was besieged by a swelling army of office hunters.[8] Nor was there any respite for him during the first days in Washington. Here, too, he was hounded by swarms of would-be job holders, the majority of whom seemed apparently oblivious to the fate of the federal government and even of the Union itself. Jobs—political plunder—was the item uppermost in mind. To those who came to Springfield and to Washington must be added thousands who sent their request by mail or by those who waited or endeavored to wait upon Lincoln in person. As the job fever mounted, not only Lincoln but seemingly every Republican of prominence, depending upon his place in party councils, was deluged with requests and demands, moderate and extravagant. Of these some were accompanied with

[4] J. Lothrop Motley to Grinnell, Nov. 2, 1860, Lincoln Collection, John Hay Library, Brown University.

[5] Amos Tuck to Giddings, Nov. 26, 1860, Joshua R. Giddings Papers.

[6] Schuyler Colfax to Pratt, Dec. 7, 1860, Daniel D. Pratt Papers.

[7] Caleb B. Smith to Schouler (confidential), Dec. 1, 1860, William Schouler Papers.

[8] Fish, "Lincoln and the Patronage," *The American Historical Review*, VIII (Oct., 1902), 53.

appeals to pity and charity; others by claims for reward for party services. Some were even reinforced with bribes. Interestingly enough, the clamoring horde of office seekers which harried the President-elect was a representative cross section of the diverse elements responsible for the Republican victory. Once again, as at the Chicago convention which nominated Lincoln, idealists, who wanted to destroy every vestige of slavery, eastern manufacturers, western farmers, representatives of other economic groups, anti-slavery Democrats, ambitious young lawyers, hardened machine politicians, political drill sergeants, and hangers-on of every description curried favor.[9] As the pressure for jobs increased, little wonder that Lincoln, having contracted a slight attack of small-pox, should half seriously, half facetiously instruct his secretary to "tell all the office seekers to come at once for now I have something I can give to all of them." [10]

The techniques for winning consideration for public office were many. Some were clever, others clumsy; not all were new. The method used by Lucius E. Chittenden, a Vermonter, who had stumped pivotal Pennsylvania for the Republican standard bearers during the late campaign and who finally secured from Lincoln the post of register of the Treasury,[11] was employed to great advantage by others. Chittenden explained it frankly:

The praises which were the reward of my services in Pennsylvania naturally increased my estimate of the value of those services, so that when I returned to my law office I looked about to see what office would suitably reward me. I had been treading out corn for a month—the Republicans would not muzzle the ox that treadeth out the corn—the laborer was worthy of his reward, and I did not doubt that I should be strongly supported as a candidate for any place in my own state for which I might apply. . . .

I prepared letters to leading Republicans in all parts of the state. I am sure they were models. I put the whole responsibility upon my friends. Personally, I said, I was rather disinclined to take office—but my friends were so persistent—they insisted that I ought to receive some substantial reward—that my appointment would do credit to the state, to myself, and the party. I had decided to take their ad-

9 Ibid.
10 L. A. Warren, "Lincoln and Patronage," Lincoln Lore, No. 290 (Oct. 29, 1934).
11 The National Cyclopaedia of American Biography, XIII, 553.

vice. If the gentleman addressed agreed with them, would he kindly
furnish me with his written recommendation to the President for my
appointment? [12]

Evidence is conclusive that Lincoln found the patronage problem always most trying and at times almost overwhelming. As the
graver problem of secession became ever more threatening and
patronage questions continued to consume precious moments and
energy, he complained that he felt like a man who was filling
offices in one end of his house while the other was burning down.[13]
Circumstances, for which he was in no way responsible, made his
task extremely difficult. Lincoln became President of the United
States at a time when the spoils system flourished. The movement
which was finally to eventuate in a measure of civil service reform
was hardly yet in its infancy.[14] Public offices were still regarded
as a fund from which the most deserving party workers were to
be paid for their services. With each change in administration
came a new crop of officeholders. Whatever may have been his
innermost thoughts about this practice Lincoln outwardly did not
oppose it prior to his election to the presidency. In any event, the
Republican victory of 1860 was so pronounced that it was bound
to have far-reaching consequences for those in public office.[15]

Moreover, Lincoln knew that he headed a party composed of
diverse elements and without tradition. Indeed, several months
before the Republican National Convention assembled at Chicago
in 1860, a future Republican governor of Massachusetts wrote
to one of the North's foremost Republican editors:

To the policy and conduct of Mr. Buchanan's administration there
must be opposition, and the Republican organization is the only
one which presents a force and front. Made up of somewhat diverse
antecedent fellowships and association, we can nevertheless move on
harmoniously in solid column.[16]

[12] Chittenden, *Recollections of President Lincoln and His Administration*, pp.
17–18.
[13] Ward H. Lamon, *Recollections of Abraham Lincoln*, p. 212.
[14] Fish, *The Civil Service and the Patronage*, p. vii.
[15] Fish, "Lincoln and the Patronage," *The American Historical Review*, VIII
(Oct., 1902), 53.
[16] A. H. Bullock to Samuel Bowles, Oct. 6, 1859, Banks Papers, Illinois State
Historical Library. Bowles was editor of the *Springfield* (Mass.) *Republican*.

A party of "diverse antecedent fellowships and association" it most certainly was. The Chicago convention was a heterogeneity of delegates representing varied groups, more often than not hostile to each other and brought together by a common opposition to the intrenched Democratic administration and policies of President James Buchanan. Among the delegates at Chicago were former antislavery Whigs, as Judge David Davis, of Illinois, and Caleb B. Smith, of Indiana; erstwhile Free Soil Democrats, as Norman B. Judd, of Illinois, and Preston King, of New York; German-born leaders, as Carl Schurz, of Wisconsin, and Gustave Koerner, of Illinois; abolitionists, as Joshua R. Giddings, of Ohio, and John A. Andrew, of Massachusetts; conservative Union-lovers, as Francis P. Blair, Sr., and his two sons, Frank. P. Blair, Jr., of Missouri, and Judge Montgomery Blair, of Maryland; politically minded reformers, as Horace Greeley, editor of the New York *Tribune;* protective-tariff devotees, as Joseph Casey, of Pennsylvania, and Thomas H. Dudley, of New Jersey; and antislavery men from border-slave regions, as Alfred Caldwell, of Virginia, and George D. Blakey, of Kentucky.[17]

Then there was a bogus "Texas" delegation recruited from a Michigan town, pretending to represent the Lone Star State.[18] A unique delegation at the convention was that representing far-away Oregon, three of whose five delegates were not residents of that state. The time and expense required to travel from Oregon to Chicago necessitated enlisting the services of eastern Republicans as "proxies," one of whom was Horace Greeley.[19] Well could one Democratic critic caustically describe the Chicago convention:

Probably no deliberative body ever came together, even in France, during the old revolutionary period, composed of such miscellaneous

[17] The roster of delegates to the Republican National Convention, which assembled at Chicago on May 16, 1860, is printed in full in Halstead, *Caucuses of 1860,* pp. 123–28.

[18] Detroit *Free Press,* May 29, 30, 31, June 3, 1860; Detroit *Daily Tribune,* June 20, 1860; *Springfield* (Mass.) *Republican,* May 29, 1860.

[19] Horace Greeley of New York, Franklin Johnson of New York, and Eli Thayer of Massachusetts represented Oregon. For Greeley, see Greeley to Chase, Aug. 5, 1860, Salmon P. Chase Papers, Historical Society of Pennsylvania. For Johnson, see *Dictionary of American Biography,* X, 99–100; Johnson, "Nominating Lincoln," *The Companion,* Feb. 8, 1917. For Thayer, see *Dictionary of American Biography,* XVIII, 402–4; F. P. Rice, "The Life of Eli Thayer."

and incongruous elements. There were Free Soil Whigs in the largest proportion, and with them Free Soil Democrats, Native Americans, and foreign adventurers; abolitionists and their life-long opponents; those for saving the Union, and those for dividing it; professed conservatives and the most thorough-going radicals; sentimentalists and ideologists; "economists and calculators"; a sprinkling of delegates pretending to represent some sort of constituency in two or three of the border slave states; and to crown all, Mr. Horace Greeley of the New York *Tribune* as an accredited deputy from the somewhat distant regions of Oregon.[20]

The geographic regions and the political antecedents of the leading contenders for the presidential nomination at Chicago in 1860 were almost as varied as those of the delegates: Abraham Lincoln, the Illinois antislavery Whig; Senator William H. Seward, the New York antislavery Whig; Judge Edward Bates, the Missouri Old Line Whig; Governor Salmon P. Chase, the Ohio Free Soil Democrat; Senator Simon Cameron, the Pennsylvania opportunist, and successively Democrat and Know-Nothing before affiliating with the Republicans, and always a staunch protectionist in his tariff views; Supreme Court Justice John McLean, the Ohio conservative Whig; Judge William L. Dayton, the New Jersey conservative Whig; and Senator Benjamin F. Wade, the Ohio antislavery Whig. Considerations of expediency lumped together under the term "availability," desire for victory over the Democrats in November, and the shrewd maneuvers of Lincoln's managers, Republican State Chairman Norman B. Judd, of Illinois, Judge David Davis and others, resulted in the nomination of Lincoln as the Republican standard bearer. To balance the ticket geographically and politically, Senator Hannibal Hamlin, a Maine ex-Democrat, was chosen as the vice-presidential candidate.[21]

In the campaign that followed four presidential candidates contended for the glittering prize: Lincoln; Senator Stephen A. Douglas, the "Northern" Democrat; John C. Breckinridge, the "Southern" Democrat; and John Bell, the "Constitutional Union-

[20] George Lunt, *The Origins of the Late War,* p. 353.
[21] For Lincoln's nomination for the presidency, consult Baringer, *Lincoln's Rise to Power.*

ist." Even with four entries in the field Lincoln received a majority of the electoral vote.[22]

The groups who contributed to Lincoln's triumph in 1860 almost defy analysis, so numerous and varied were they. Among the more important were: (1) The antislavery Whigs, who seized upon the sectional issue for political reasons or because they sincerely believed that the southern-planter interests would either politically ruin the nation or cause disunion. (2) Free Soil Democrats, particularly in the Northwest, who feared extension of Negro slavery into their territory or who had severed their allegiance with the Democratic party when the administrations of Presidents Franklin Pierce and James Buchanan disregarded their section's interest in favor of the South.[23] (3) Disgruntled Democrats, with no pronounced opinions on the sectional controversy, who had broken with the dominant faction of their party because they were disappointed in their many quests for public office or else detested Buchanan and other Democratic chieftains on personal grounds.[24] (4) Certain Know-Nothing groups who disliked the Democrats for party reasons or because of the latter's coddling of the Irish vote. (5) German-born naturalized citizens who hated the southern slave-plantation system, feared competition with Negro labor, and wanted free land.[25] (6) Homestead and internal-improvement people in general.[26] (7) Protective-tariff advocates, particularly in Pennsylvania, who opposed the Democrats because

[22] For a general account of the campaign, see Fite, *The Presidential Campaign of 1860.*

[23] See especially Stoler, "The Influence of the Democratic Element in the Republican Party in Illinois and Indiana, 1854–1860."

[24] John W. Forney was one of the most conspicuous of this type. See Auchampaugh, "John W. Forney, Robert Tyler and James Buchanan," *Tyler's Quarterly Historical and Genealogical Magazine*, XV (Oct., 1933), 71–89; Auchampaugh, *James Buchanan and His Cabinet on the Eve of Secession*, p. 36.

[25] Donnal V. Smith, "The Influence of the Foreign-Born of the Northwest in the Election of 1860," *The Mississippi Valley Historical Review*, XIX (Sept., 1932), 192–204; Carman and Luthin, "Some Aspects of the Know Nothing Movement Reconsidered," *The South Atlantic Quarterly*, XXXIX (April, 1940), 213–34; New York *Herald*, Dec. 9, 1860. Cf. Schafer, "Who Elected Lincoln?" *The American Historical Review*, XLVII (Oct., 1941), 51–63.

[26] Rayback, "Land for the Landless; The Contemporary View"; George M. Stephenson, *The Political History of the Public Lands from 1840 to 1862*, pp. 221–39; *Zachariah Chandler: An Outline Sketch of His Life and Public Services by the Detroit Post and Tribune*, pp. 164–71.

of their free-trade tendencies.[27] (8) Groups in favor of a Pacific railroad.[28] (9) Those who wanted a daily overland mail and who believed that the Buchanan administration was favoring southern routes.[29] (10) Certain Union-minded conservative men in the border states, who believed that the regular Democratic party under Pierce and Buchanan was becoming an instrument of pro-slavery interests and a force for secession and who hoped to conservatize the Republican party from within.[30]

Only a few years before these numerous factions and groups had hewn at one another's heads; they had come together in the recent campaign like Highland clans to battle the common foe.[31] The leaders of these various factions were still jealous of one another and often openly hostile. Lincoln realized that public jobs wisely distributed were the cement he must use to hold the Republican party together. In a letter to Seward, shortly after his elevation to the presidency, he set forth his policy in these words: "In regard to the patronage, sought with so much eagerness and jealousy, I have prescribed for myself the maxim 'Justice to all.' " [32] Commendable in itself, the carrying out of such a generous policy was to be fraught with many obstacles.

27 Pitkin, "The Tariff and the Early Republican Party"; Eiselen, *The Rise of Pennsylvania Protectionism*, pp. 255–64.

28 Clark, *Leland Stanford*, pp. 164–65; Ellison, *California and the Nation, 1850–1869*, chap. viii.

29 Nettels, "The Overland Mail Issue during the Fifties," *The Missouri Historical Review*, XVIII (July, 1924), 521–34.

30 W. E. Smith, *The Francis Preston Blair Family in Politics*, Vol. I, chaps. xxv, xxvi; "The Diary of Edward Bates, 1859–1866," ed. by Howard K. Beale, *Annual Report*, American Historical Association, IV (1930), 60 ff.

31 Dunning, "The Second Birth of the Republican Party," *The American Historical Review*, XVI (Oct., 1910), 56.

32 Lincoln to Seward, Dec. 8, 1860 ("Private and Confidential"), William H. Seward Papers.

Chapter II

LINCOLN FORMS HIS CABINET

OVERSHADOWING all of Lincoln's patronage problems was that of selecting a cabinet. The public waited in eager anticipation, since the list of the new President's advisers would, it was thought, reveal the character of his administration. Newspaper correspondents the country over vied with each other in furnishing lists of prospective appointments, claiming to have the "best authority" for what proved to be mere rumor and conjecture.[1]

There was no dearth of contenders for the few coveted places in Lincoln's inner council. Among those eager for Cabinet positions were United States Senator Simon Cameron, of Pennsylvania;[2] Caleb B. Smith[3] and Congressman Schuyler Colfax,[4] both of Indiana; Congressman Thaddeus Stevens, of Pennsylvania;[5] Republican State Chairman Norman B. Judd, of Illinois;[6] Republican National Committeeman Amos Tuck, of New Hampshire;[7] and Cassius M. Clay, of Kentucky.[8] Among those vigorously supported for a cabinet post by their followers were Governor Salmon P. Chase, of Ohio;[9] Judge Montgomery Blair[10] and Congressman Henry Winter Davis,[11] both of Maryland; Gideon

[1] L. A. Warren, "Cabinet Building in 1861," *Lincoln Lore,* No. 464, Feb. 28. 1938; New York *Daily Tribune,* Nov. 10, 1860; Cincinnati *Daily Gazette,* Nov. 14, 1860.

[2] Pratt, "Simon Cameron's Fight for a Place in Lincoln's Cabinet," *Bulletin of the Abraham Lincoln Association,* No. 49 (Sept., 1937); Meneely, *The War Department, 1861,* pp. 66–74.

[3] Caleb B. Smith to David Davis, Jan. 13, 1861, David Davis Papers.

[4] Schuyler Colfax to ———, Jan. 11, 1861, Logan U. Reavis Papers.

[5] Thaddeus Stevens to S. Stevens, Feb. 10, 1861, Thaddeus Stevens Papers; McClure, *Old Time Notes of Pennsylvania,* I, 452–53.

[6] N. B. Judd to Lyman Trumbull, Jan. 3, 1861, Lyman Trumbull Papers.

[7] Amos Tuck to Giddings, Nov. 26, 1860, Joshua R. Giddings Papers; Amos Tuck to Yates, Dec. 21, 1860, Richard Yates Papers.

[8] C. M. Clay to Andrew, Jan. 16, 1861, John A. Andrew Papers.

[9] Hiram Barney to William Cullen Bryant, Jan. 17, 1861, Bryant-Godwin Papers.

[10] Frank P. Blair, Jr. to Frank P. Blair, Sr., Dec. 23, 1860, Francis Preston Blair Papers; W. E. Smith, *The Francis Preston Blair Family in Politics,* I, 514.

[11] Whitney, *Lincoln the President,* p. 15.

Welles, of Connecticut;[12] Governor Nathaniel P. Banks[13] and
Charles Francis Adams,[14] both of Massachusetts; United States
Senator Jacob M. Howard, of Michigan;[15] and Fitz Henry
Warren, of Iowa.[16]

The very day after Lincoln received assurances of his election
as President, he communicated with Vice President-elect Hannibal
Hamlin of Maine, requesting that they meet in Chicago.[17] Accordingly, in late November, the victorious candidates met in Chicago
and proceeded to Lake View, the home of Lincoln's friend Judge
Ebenezer Peck. Here Lincoln confided to Hamlin his plan of
forming a Cabinet that would unify the followers of Senator William H. Seward, of New York, Judge Edward Bates, of Missouri,
Governor Salmon P. Chase, of Ohio, and Senator Simon Cameron,
of Pennsylvania—his late chief rivals for the Republican presidential nomination. Seward, Senator Charles Sumner, of Massachusetts, and Judge William L. Dayton, of New Jersey, were those
most prominently mentioned for the secretaryship of state. Lincoln's first choice was Seward, for he believed that circumstances—
Seward's major position in the Republican party and his prestige as the Empire State's most distinguished leader—dictated
his selection to head the Cabinet. Lincoln and Hamlin discussed
other names for Cabinet posts: Chase, Cameron, and James Guthrie, of Kentucky, for the Treasury portfolio. Chase held a conspicuous position among the Free Soil-Democratic element of the
Repubican party; Cameron came from pivotal Pennsylvania,
second in importance to New York; Guthrie was a resident of
a border-slave state and it was thought, therefore, that were he
in the cabinet the border states might not leave the Union. Lincoln
seems to have favored Chase from the first, while Hamlin, himself
a former Democrat, also leaned toward the Ohioan. Other names

[12] James Dixon to Trumbull, Nov. 13, 1860, Trumbull Papers.
[13] George S. Boutwell to Banks (copy), March 8, 1861, Nathaniel P. Banks
Papers, Essex Institute.
[14] *Charles Francis Adams, by His Son Charles Francis Adams*, p. 143.
[15] Henry Waldron to Howard, March 2, 1861, Jacob M. Howard Papers, Burton
Historical Collection, Detroit Public Library.
[16] Angle, *Lincoln, 1854–1861*, p. 367.
[17] Lincoln to Hamlin, Nov. 8, 1860, in John G. Nicolay and John Hay (eds.),
Complete Works of Abraham Lincoln, Gettysburg ed., VI, 68. (Hereafter cited as
Complete Works of Abraham Lincoln.)

considered in a general way for Cabinet posts were Bates, Caleb B. Smith, Schuyler Colfax, Montgomery Blair, Henry Winter Davis, Charles Francis Adams, and Governor Nathaniel P. Banks. Gideon Welles, of Connecticut, Kenneth Raynor, of North Carolina, and Emerson Etheridge, of Tennessee, were also mentioned. Throughout the discussion Lincoln emphasized two points: First, in conformity with his policy of "justice to all," he stressed the importance of recognizing both the Whig and the Democratic elements of the Republican party; and secondly, the desirability of having representatives from the slave states in his Cabinet. The interview between Lincoln and Hamlin closed with the understanding that Hamlin should not only "sound" Seward on the secretaryship of state, but should be permitted to name the New England representative in the Cabinet family.[18]

Hamlin, still holding his seat in the United States Senate, proceeded from Chicago to Washington for the convening of Congress in early December (1860). In Washington he approached Senator Preston King, Seward's not-too-affable colleague from New York. King suggested that Hamlin approach Seward directly.[19] Accordingly, Hamlin dispatched a note to Lincoln on December 4: "I have had an interview with Mr. King in relation to the position and desire of Governor Seward, and Mr. King prefers that I should confer directly with the governor [Seward]. On the whole, is that not the appropriate method? It seems to me so. . . . Shall I confer with the governor directly, and ask him what are his wishes and desires?"[20]

In his reply under date of December 8, Lincoln virtually placed the matter in the hands of Hamlin and United States Senator Lyman Trumbull, of Illinois:

[18] Hamlin, *The Life and Times of Hannibal Hamlin*, pp. 367–70. Thurlow Weed substantiates the story that Lincoln allowed Hamlin to select the New England member of the Cabinet. See *Autobiography of Thurlow Weed*, p. 614. For Lincoln's reasons for preferring Seward, see John Nicolay, MS Notes, printed in "Diary of Edward Bates, 1859–1866," ed. by Howard K. Beale, *Annual Report,* American Historical Association, IV (1930), 166 n.

[19] Senator King told John Bigelow that when he was approached by Hamlin with Lincoln's invitation to Seward to enter the Cabinet, he (King) consulted with Seward. King then suggested to Hamlin that he approach Seward directly. See John Bigelow Diary, MS, May 8, 1861.

[20] Hamlin to Lincoln, Dec. 4, 1860, in Hamlin, *The Life and Times of Hannibal Hamlin,* p. 371.

Yours of the 4th was duly received. The inclosed to Governor Seward covers two notes to him, copies of which you find open for your inspection. Consult with Judge Trumbull; and if you and he see no reason to the contrary, deliver the letter to Governor Seward at once. If you see reason to the contrary, write me at once.[21]

Meanwhile, William Cullen Bryant, editor of the New York *Evening Post*, and other leaders of the anti-Seward wing of New York Republicans had waited upon Senator Trumbull as he passed through the metropolis en route from Illinois to Washington. They requested that Trumbull inform Lincoln that it would be most unwise to appoint Seward to the Cabinet, especially in view of the fact that Seward's political backers, notably Thurlow Weed and his henchmen, had been deeply implicated in legislative corruption.[22] Trumbull, unfriendly to Seward and Weed, dispatched a note to Lincoln to the effect that Seward was undesirable. The President-elect, however, apparently was not deeply impressed by the New Yorkers' hostility toward Seward, for he answered Trumbull firmly:

Yours of the 2nd is received. I regret exceedingly the anxiety of our friends in New York, of whom you write; but it seems to me the sentiment in that state which sent a united delegation to Chicago in favor of Gov. Seward ought not and must not be snubbed, as it would be, by the omission to offer Gov. S. a place in the Cabinet. *I will myself take care of the question* of "corrupt jobs" and see that justice is done to all our friends of whom you wrote as well as others.

I have written to Mr. Hamlin on this very subject of Gov. S. and requested him to consult fully with you.

He will show you my note and enclosures to him; and then please act as therein requested.[23]

In Washington, Hamlin, as directed by Lincoln, consulted with Trumbull, and the two agreed that Hamlin should deliver the two enclosures to Seward.[24] One enclosure was a formal invitation

[21] Lincoln to Hamlin (Private), Dec. 8, 1860, in *Complete Works of Abraham Lincoln*, VI, 75–76.

[22] White, *The Life of Lyman Trumbull*, pp. 139–40.

[23] Lincoln to Trumbull (Private), Dec. 8, 1860, in *ibid.*, p. 141. This letter is printed also in *Uncollected Letters of Abraham Lincoln*, comp. by Gilbert A. Tracy, p. 170.

[24] Hamlin, *Hannibal Hamlin*, p. 372.

to Seward to accept the State portfolio. The other letter from Lincoln informed the New York senator: "It has been my purpose, from the day of the nomination at Chicago, to assign you, by your leave, this place in the administration." [25] Seward was evidently bewilderingly surprised at Lincoln's magnanimity and, after reading, is quoted as saying to the Vice President-elect: "This is remarkable, Mr. Hamlin. I will consider the matter, and, in accordance with Mr. Lincoln's request, give him my decision at the earliest practicable moment." [26] In a letter dated December 13 Seward thanked Lincoln for the proffer and added: "You will readily believe that coming to the consideration of so grave a subject all at once, I need a little time to consider whether I possess the qualifications and temper of a Minister, and whether it is in such a capacity that my friends would prefer that I should act, if I am to continue at all in the public service. . . .   Without publishing the fact of your invitation, I will reflect upon it a few days with your leave, and then give you my definite answer. . . ." [27] Seward also took occasion to express agreement with Lincoln on his policy of recognizing all Republican elements: "Whatever may be my conclusion you may rest assured of my hearty concurrence in your views in regard to the distribution of the public offices as you have communicated them." [28]

While Seward pondered over Lincoln's proffer of the State portfolio, Hamlin gave thought to the selection of the New England member of the Cabinet. There were several possibilities. Charles Francis Adams, of Massachusetts, son of one President of the United States and grandson of another, was eliminated since he was a Whig.[29] "I need a man of Democratic antecedents from New England," wrote Lincoln to Hamlin, "I cannot get a fair share of that element in without. This stands in the way of Mr. Adams. I think of Governor Banks, Mr. Welles, and Mr. Tuck. Which of them do the New England delegation prefer?

[25] The originals of these two notes from Lincoln to Seward, dated Dec. 8, 1860, are in the possession of Mr. W. H. Seward, of Auburn, N.Y. Both were examined by the authors of this volume. Copies of them are printed in *Complete Works of Abraham Lincoln*, VI, 76–77.

[26] Carroll, *Twelve Americans*, p. 154.

[27] Seward to Lincoln (copy), Dec. 13, 1860, Seward Papers.

[28] *Ibid.*

[29] *Charles Francis Adams, by His Son Charles Francis Adams*, p. 143.

Or shall I decide for myself?" [30] Hamlin had no desire to have
Lincoln interfere, inasmuch as the latter had given him practically a free hand in the selection of a New Englander. Nathaniel
P. Banks, governor of Massachusetts and former Democrat, was
pressed by certain Bay State Republicans.[31] But Hamlin detested
Banks as a "trimmer in politics" whose appointment would not
be satisfactory to New England. Consequently Banks was eliminated from consideration.[32] Amos Tuck, Republican national
committeeman from New Hampshire, was most anxious for a
Cabinet position; [33] indeed, he even visited Lincoln in Springfield; [34] but Hamlin was cold to the prospect. Hamlin's choice
narrowed down to Gideon Welles, of Connecticut.

Welles had been a Democrat throughout most of his political
life, serving in state offices. He had had limited experience in the
Navy Department during the Mexican War as Chief of the Bureau of Provisions and Clothing.[35] He was one of the founders
of the Connecticut Republican party [36] and had been a delegate
to the Chicago Convention, where he opposed Seward's nomination.[37] Moreover, he had powerful backers for a place in the Cabinet. Among them was James Dixon, Connecticut's Republican
United States Senator. Apparently knowing that Hamlin's support would be indispensable for any New Englander to gain
entrance into the Cabinet, Dixon, a week following the election,
had written to Trumbull suggesting Welles for the Postmaster-
Generalship. "Mr. Welles may truly be said to represent the democracy of New England—very much as Mr. Hamlin himself
does. . . . I lay this matter before you, knowing that Mr. Lincoln
will consult you with regard to the formation of his Cabinet." [38]

[30] Lincoln to Hamlin, Dec. 24, 1860, in *Complete Works of Abraham Lincoln*,
VI, 86–87.
[31] Geo. S. Boutwell to Banks (copy), March 8, 1861, Banks Papers, Essex Institute.
[32] Hamlin, *Hannibal Hamlin*, p. 370.
[33] Amos Tuck to Giddings, Nov. 26, 1860, Giddings Papers; Amos Tuck to Yates,
Dec. 21, 1860, Yates Papers.
[34] Angle, *Lincoln, 1854–1861*, p. 366.
[35] Paullin, "President Lincoln and the Navy," *The American Historical Review*,
XIV (Jan. 1909), 286–87.
[36] Trumbull, *The Memorial History of Hartford County, Connecticut, 1633–
1884*, I, 609, 619; Noonan, *Nativism in Connecticut, 1829–1860*, pp. 235, 239.
[37] Baringer, *Lincoln's Rise to Power*, p. 233.
[38] James Dixon to Trumbull, Nov. 13, 1860, Trumbull Papers. Welles also had

Dixon and Hamlin soon had their heads together in Washington, whence Dixon dispatched a letter to Welles. In it the Connecticut Senator informed Welles that Hamlin had told him that Lincoln desired Welles's views on the fugitive-slave law. Wrote Dixon: "Mr. Hamlin . . . then said Mr. Lincoln & himself agreed that the fugitive-slave law must be executed in good faith—that your name had been the subject of conversation between him & Mr. Lincoln, as a proper person for one of his Cabinet . . . that an agreement between yóu & him on that point was indispensable. . . ." [39] Dixon ended his message to Welles with these words: "He [Hamlin] gave me to understand that in his judgment, your appointment was more probable than that of any other man in New England. Still nothing was understood to be decided." [40] Welles, as soon as he finished reading Dixon's letter, assured Dixon by mail that he was "sound" on the fugitive-slave law: "Yours of the 3rd inst. I received last evening. . . . I am very free to say I think the [fugitive-slave] law itself obnoxious in many respects, and susceptible of great and beneficent improvement. But a law-abiding citizen cannot do otherwise than submit to it, however repulsive may be its details, and a public officer must obey and faithfully execute it." [41]

While Welles was under consideration, other groups were pressing favorites for Cabinet posts. The Blair family was conspicuous. One hardly ever spoke of this Blair or that Blair; usually they were referred to as "the Blairs." Francis P. Blair had been a power in the Democratic party ever since he had been "Old Hickory's" right arm during the early 1830s, and his transfer to the camp of the Republicans had not in the least dimmed his forceful personality. One son, Frank Blair, Jr., was the most powerful Republican leader in Missouri, while his other son, Judge Montgomery Blair, reigned in the impotent Republican party of Maryland. The Blairs had supported Edward Bates, of Mis-

---

the backing of William Cullen Bryant. See Godwin, *A Biography of William Cullen Bryant*, II, 153.

[39] James Dixon to Welles, Dec. 3, 1860, Gideon Welles Papers, Library of Congress.

[40] *Ibid.*

[41] Welles to James Dixon (copy), Dec. 5, 1860, Welles Papers, Library of Congress.

souri, for the Republican presidential nomination, but when Lincoln won out had campaigned for him.

Usually the Blairs were not far distant when patronage was being dispensed by victorious candidates whom they had supported.[42] No more than a week after the election returns were in, Senator King, of New York, divulged that "our friends the Blairs would like to have Judge Montgomery Blair made Attorney General."[43] December 11 found Frank Blair in Springfield conferring with Lincoln.[44] Blair came away from Lincoln's home supremely confident. To his father he reported: "I have thought also that I should probably be able to get elected to the Speakership of the next House of Representatives, if the Judge gets into the Cabinet, of which I have no doubt at all."[45] And Lincoln himself almost decided that a place should go to Montgomery Blair. Toward the end of December the President-elect in a letter to Trumbull concluded: "I expect to be able to offer Mr. Blair a place in the cabinet; but I can not, as yet, be committed on the matter, to any extent whatever."[46]

Lincoln himself took the initiative in his search for Cabinet possibilities. Aside from desiring Seward in his councils, Lincoln most wanted a member from the border-slave states. When in Chicago for his appointment with Hamlin, he had requested his friend Joshua F. Speed, of Kentucky, to meet him there. Speed did so, and in the course of the interview the President-elect spoke of Guthrie, of Kentucky, as a suitable choice for Secretary of War. Lincoln commissioned Speed to see Guthrie, but to be cautious, in order not to give him the advantage of the tender of a Cabinet appointment to be declined by an insulting letter.[47] "I did see Mr. Guthrie," Speed related, "and never tendered him any office for I was not authorized to do so."[48]

In the hope of mollifying southern opinion, Lincoln finally de-

[42] For a scholarly account of the Blairs' long political lives, see W. E. Smith, *The Francis Preston Blair Family in Politics.*

[43] Preston King to Trumbull, Nov. 15, 1860, Trumbull Papers.

[44] Angle, *Lincoln, 1854–1861,* p. 363.

[45] Frank P. Blair, Jr. to Frank P. Blair, Sr., Dec. 23, 1860, Francis Preston Blair Papers.

[46] Lincoln to Trumbull, Dec. 24, 1860, in *Uncollected Letters of Abraham Lincoln,* comp. by Tracy, p. 173.

[47] J. F. Speed to Ward H. Lamon, June 24, 1872, in Ward H. Lamon, *Recollections of Abraham Lincoln, 1847–1865,* p. 286.

[48] *Ibid.*

cided to ask John A. Gilmer, of North Carolina, to accept a Cabinet post; in December he wrote Gilmer inviting him to Springfield. By the end of the month, however, Gilmer had not shown up and Lincoln complained: "He has neither come, nor answered me." [49] Lincoln thereupon requested Seward to write Gilmer, and the New York Senator did so. "As yet, I have no word from Mr. Gilmer, in answer to my request for an interview with him," [50] wrote Lincoln on January 3, 1861. As late as January 12 Lincoln desired Gilmer: "I still hope Mr. Gilmer will, on a fair understanding with us, consent to take a place in the Cabinet." [51] The secession of North Carolina from the Union ended all hope of securing the North Carolinian. Gilmer appears to have been the only man invited by Lincoln to take a post in his Cabinet who failed to accept. Most of the contenders for places in Lincoln's inner council were not invited.

Lincoln did succeed in securing the services of a border-slave state leader—Edward Bates. Next to Seward, the aged Bates was Lincoln's most formidable contender for the Republican presidential nomination at the Chicago Convention. Virginia-born, a former slave owner and resident of slaveholding Missouri, Bates had risen high in state politics as a Whig and had gone into retirement years before, only to reappear as a presidential possibility in 1859–60. In all matters a die-hard conservative, he never became a bona-fide Republican. In response to an invitation from Lincoln, Bates arrived in Springfield on December 15. Lincoln informed him that since the day of his nomination for President he had planned to offer Bates a Cabinet post. During this interview, Lincoln tendered Bates the Attorney Generalship, at the same time expressing regret that he could not offer Bates the State Department portfolio.[52] Apparently Bates had not lifted a hand to acquire one of the coveted prizes. On December 18—three days after his interview with Bates—Lincoln suggested to the Missourian:

Let a little editorial appear in the "Missouri Democrat" in about these words:

[49] Lincoln to Seward ("Private"), Dec. 29, 1860, Seward Papers.
[50] Lincoln to Seward ("Private"), Jan. 3, 1861, *ibid.*
[51] Lincoln to Seward ("Private"), Jan. 12, 1861, *ibid.*
[52] John Nicolay, MS Notes, in "Diary of Edward Bates, 1859–1866," ed. by Howard K. Beale, *Annual Report, American Historical Association, IV (1930),* 166 n.–167 n.; also pp. 164–65.

"We have the permission of both Mr. Lincoln and Mr. Bates to say that the latter will be offered, and will accept, a place in the new cabinet, subject, of course, to the action of the Senate. It is not yet definitely settled which department will be assigned to Mr. Bates."

Let it go just as above, or with any modification which may seem proper to you.[53]

Bates caused Lincoln's request to be complied with, and on December 21 an announcement appeared in the St. Louis *Democrat* to the effect that Bates had accepted Lincoln's invitation to membership in the Cabinet.[54] His appointment to be one of Lincoln's councilors was not received with too much enthusiasm. He was born during Washington's administration, clung tenaciously to the past, and became a die-hard Old Line Whig. Notwithstanding his spotless integrity, there were many who agreed with the noted Chicago editor, Joseph Medill, that Bates was "a fossil of the Silurian era—red sandstone, at least—and should never have been quarried out of the rocks in which he was imbedded." [55]

Meanwhile, Seward was still trying to make up his mind about the Department of State. To this end he consulted with his political Warwick and lifelong friend, Thurlow Weed. Weed, who had managed Seward's fight for the Republican presidential nomination, had been heartbroken when his favorite lost the prize to a little-known Illinois lawyer. But he was too practical, too much the party man to think of bolting the Republican ticket. Lincoln's managers, not unmindful of the huge bloc of New York electoral votes, made certain to court Weed's favor. Much of the flirtation with the Weed following was conducted by Lincoln's staunch friend, Judge David Davis, one of the small clique of Illinois Republicans primarily responsible for Lincoln's nomination.[56] Associated with Judge Davis was his Bloomington fellow townsman friend, Leonard

[53] Lincoln to Edward Bates (confidential), Dec. 18, 1860, in *Complete Works of Abraham Lincoln*, VI, 83.

[54] St. Louis *Democrat*, Dec. 21, 1860, clipped in New York *Herald*, Dec. 25, 1860.

[55] Joseph Medill to Schuyler Colfax, undated, in Hollister, *Life of Schuyler Colfax*, p. 200.

[56] For Davis's and Swett's tireless work in securing Lincoln's nomination, see Baringer, *Lincoln's Rise to Power*, pp. 193, 227, 230–39, 266–67, 277; Baringer, "Campaign Technique in Illinois—1860," *Transactions of the Illinois State Historical Society*, 1932, pp. 229, 233, 236.

Swett.[57] At Davis and Swett's urging, Weed had visited Lincoln in Springfield following the convention, and during the campaign the Davis-Swett wing of the Illinois Republicans coöperated with Weed in planning campaign strategy and raising funds for electing Lincoln.[58] While the campaign still raged, Weed, Davis, and Swett, according to Gideon Welles, met in conference at Saratoga, New York, a meeting which was allegedly attended by Senator Simon Cameron, of Pennsylvania, himself a disappointed Republican presidential aspirant. Then and there it was agreed, Welles asserted, that the Seward-Weed-Davis-Swett-Cameron combination should be the controlling element in the new administration; that any possible influence of Governor Chase, of Ohio, a leader of the Democratic faction of the national Republican party, should be curtailed and that Cameron should be supported for Secretary of the Treasury in preference to Chase.[59]

It so happened that Seward, Weed, Davis, and Swett were all former Whigs, while the opportunist Cameron, although nominally a former Democrat, had consorted during his career with Whigs and other groups of various political hues during the years before the formation of the Republican party.[60] To complicate matters in an era of strong past-party loyalties, the "Democratic," or anti-Weed wing of the New York Republican party, led by William Cullen Bryant, Hiram Barney, George Opdyke, and David Dudley

[57] Horace White, associated in editing the Chicago *Press & Tribune* at the time, wrote: "Swett, it may be remarked, was the *Fidus Achates* of David Davis at all times." See White, *The Life of Lyman Trumbull,* p. 144.

[58] Davis to Weed, Sept. 11, 1860, Thurlow Weed Papers, University of Rochester Library; *Autobiography of Thurlow Weed,* pp. 334, 602; Swett to Weed, July 4, 1860, Davis to Weed, Aug. 24, 1860, printed in Barnes (ed.), *Memoir of Thurlow Weed,* pp. 298–300.

[59] "Comment Upon the Autobiographical Sketch of Thurlow Weed Relating to the Formation of Lincoln's Cabinet," MS, undated, Gideon Welles Papers, New York Public Library; MS, undated, by Gideon Welles, Illinois State Historical Library; "Letters of Gideon Welles, 1860–1871," *The Magazine of History,* Extra No. 105 (1924), pp. 28–29; *Diary of Gideon Welles,* II, 389–90. For the close coöperation between Seward, Weed, Davis, Swett, and Cameron in the months following Lincoln's election see Seward to Cameron, Nov. 15, 1860; Davis to Cameron, Feb. 8, July 30, 1861, Simon Cameron Papers; Weed to David Davis, Feb. 20, 1861, David Davis Papers.

[60] For Cameron's various "deals" with other political parties, see Geary, *A History of Third Parties in Pennsylvania, 1840–1860,* pp. 111, 173; McClure, *Old Time Notes of Pennsylvania,* I, 92–100, 267–73; Hewitt, "The Know Nothing Party in Pennsylvania," *Pennsylvania History,* II (April, 1935), 78–79.

Field, was closely allied to Chase.[61] Similarly the "Democratic," or anti-Davis, anti-Swett wing of the Illinois Republican party, led by Republican State Chairman Norman B. Judd, State Treasurer William Butler, and Senator Trumbull, was also allied with Chase.[62] The feud within the Illinois Republican ranks had started even before the Chicago Convention, when Davis had backed his friend Swett for the party's gubernatorial nomination in preference to Judd.[63] The feud became more bitter following Lincoln's election by reason of the fact that Judd, who had been quite as influential as Davis and Swett in securing Lincoln's nomination for President,[64] wanted a Cabinet seat. Moreover, the ambitious Judd had the backing of Republican groups around Chicago, his home city, who were opposed to the Bloomington junta of Davis and Swett.[65]

In the bitter, complex controversy waged by the Seward-Weed-Davis-Swett-Cameron combination against the Chase-Judd-Trumbull forces, another annoying factor entered, namely, the commitments made by Lincoln's managers at the Chicago Convention. Here Davis and others are supposed to have promised Cameron's managers that the Pennsylvania leader would receive a Cabinet position if his Pennsylvania delegates would switch to Lincoln. These same spokesmen also promised Caleb B. Smith, of Indianapolis, a Cabinet post if the Hoosier delegation would go for Lincoln.[66] Meanwhile, an anti-Smith faction of Indiana Re-

---

[61] Chase to Geo. Opdyke (copy), Jan. 9, 1861, Salmon P. Chase Papers, Historical Society of Pennsylvania; D. V. Smith, "Salmon P. Chase and the Election of 1860," *Ohio Archaeological and Historical Quarterly*, XXXIX (July, 1930), 527, 533–34; Brummer, *Political History of New York State during the Period of the Civil War*, pp. 18–19, 128–29.

[62] Judd to Trumbull, Feb. 17, 1861; Butler to Trumbull, Feb. 13, 1861, Trumbull Papers.

[63] David Davis to Dummer, Feb. 20, 1860, Henry E. Dummer Papers.

[64] For Judd's work in securing Lincoln's nomination, see Baringer, "Campaign Technique in Illinois—1860," *Transactions of the Illinois State Historical Society*, 1932, pp. 208–10, 218, 233; L. O. Leonard, "Norman B. Judd," *Rock Island Magazine*, XXI (May, 1926), 33–34. John M. Palmer, one of the small Illinois group primarily responsible for Lincoln's nomination, wrote: "Undoubtedly, Judge David Davis and Norman B. Judd contributed most to the nomination of Mr. Lincoln." See *Personal Recollections of John M. Palmer*, p. 81.

[65] White, *The Life of Lyman Trumbull*, p. 148; Harry E. Pratt, "David Davis, 1815–1886," p. 82; Caleb B. Smith to Schouler (Confidential), Dec. 1, 1860, William Schouler Papers.

[66] For the agreements by Davis to give Cabinet posts to Cameron and Smith, see

publicans were backing Congressman Schuyler Colfax, of South Bend, for the Postmaster Generalship.[67] Dr. Harry E. Pratt, biographer of Davis, writes:

Now that he was elected, would Lincoln fulfill the pledges made at the convention? Having made them, Davis insisted that they be kept, so much so that he annoyed Mr. Lincoln. . . . Caleb B. Smith very much wanted the cabinet position promised him at the Chicago convention. He wrote two long letters to Davis, refuting charges of double-dealing, dishonesty and want of business capacity made against him by the Schuyler Colfax followers and by Murat Halstead in the *Cincinnati Commercial.* Davis wrote him to get the members of the Ohio legislature to sign an endorsement and send it to Lincoln. This was done.[68]

Smith himself was supremely confident that he would emerge victor over Colfax. To a Massachusetts political crony he confided at this time: "I should not decline a seat in Mr. Lincoln's Cabinet, and although I have no promises from any one authorized to speak for Mr. L. I have reason to believe that a place will be offered me. I am *very confident* that if a place is offered to any person from Ind. it will be offered to me. I do not wish to be P. M. Genl. but if I go into the Cabinet, would much prefer the Interior Department." [69] Colfax, furious at the efforts being made in Smith's behalf, started a sniping correspondence against his fellow Hoosier.[70]

The first move by Lincoln in cutting through the entanglement of promises and intrigues was to invite Weed to visit him at Springfield. Davis and Swett, not Lincoln, wrote a joint letter inviting the Albany politician to come.[71] Weed accepted, and stopped off at Bloomington, home of Davis and Swett, before going on to Spring-

Herndon's Life of Lincoln, ed. by Angle, p. 381, Gresham, *Life of Walter Quintin Gresham,* I, 110–11; II, 565–66.

[67] Godlove S. Orth to Colfax, Nov. 20, 1860, Colfax-Orth Papers; Hollister, *Life of Schuyler Colfax,* pp. 174–75; Harbison, "Lincoln and Indiana Republicans, 1861–1862," *Indiana Magazine of History,* XXXIII (Sept., 1937), 278–79.

[68] Pratt, "David Davis, 1815–1866," p. 82.

[69] Caleb B. Smith to William Schouler (confidential), Dec. 1, 1860, William Schouler Papers. John D. Defrees, another Indiana leader was ambitious for Cabinet honors. See John D. Defrees to Weed, Jan. 16, 1861 ("Confidential"), Thurlow Weed Papers, University of Rochester Library.

[70] Colfax to unnamed correspondent, Jan. 11, 1861, Logan U. Reavis Papers.

[71] Leonard Swett, quoted in Barnes, *Memoir of Thurlow Weed,* p. 293; Davis and Swett to Weed, Dec. 10, 1860, in *ibid.,* pp. 301–2.

field. Two days later Weed, in company with Davis and Swett, proceeded to the Illinois capital. At the conference with Lincoln on December 20, the formation of the Cabinet was discussed. The President-elect suggested Chase for Secretary of the Treasury, on the ground that a former Democrat should receive second place in the Cabinet inasmuch as Seward, a former Whig, was to have first place. To this Weed dissented, maintaining that Chase had been an abolitionist rather than a Democrat and that, if the Treasury Department were to go to a former Democrat, Cameron would be the ideal appointment.[72] That the old divisions between Whig and Democrat were still alive within the victorious Republican party of 1860 was apparent at this conference. Weed's approval of Bates and Caleb B. Smith, ex-Whigs, as possible Cabinet selections and his disapproval of Chase, Welles, and Montgomery Blair, ex-Democrats, for Cabinet portfolios were very evident.[73] One reason why Weed opposed Blair may have been because David Davis was pressing his cousin, Henry Winter Davis, another Marylander, for the Cabinet.[74]

More intimate details regarding Weed's conference with Lincoln, in which Davis and Swett participated, are lacking and perhaps may never be known. Certain it is, however, that Weed returned home convinced that Seward must accept the proffered State Department portfolio. The tension was temporarily eased when, several days after Weed's return from Springfield, Hamlin met Seward in New York City and satisfied himself that Seward would accept Lincoln's invitation.[75] On December 28 Seward dispatched his decision to Lincoln: "I have, after due reflection, and with much self distrust, concluded that if I should be nominated to the Senate for the office of Secretary of State, and the nomination should be confirmed, it would be my duty to accept the appointment." [76]

[72] Harry E. Pratt, "Simon Cameron's Fight for a Place in Lincoln's Cabinet," *Bulletin of the Abraham Lincoln Association,* No. 49 (Sept., 1937), pp. 5-6.

[73] Barnes, *Memoir of Thurlow Weed,* pp. 293-94.

[74] Whitney, *Lincoln the President,* p. 15; New York *Herald* Nov. 24, 1860.

[75] Hamlin to Trumbull (Private), Dec. 27, 1860, Trumbull Papers.

[76] Seward to Lincoln (copy), Dec. 28, 1860, Seward Papers. Weed wrote an editorial declaring that Seward had accepted the Secretaryship of State, publishing it in his Albany *Evening Journal.* See Albany *Evening Journal,* clipped in New York *Herald,* Jan. 10, 1861.

Weed's conference with Lincoln not only assured Seward's acceptance of the State Department post; it likewise brought to the fore the question of Cameron's appointment, and the Pennsylvanian proved to be Lincoln's thorniest patronage problem.

After Weed's visit to Springfield, Swett journeyed to Pennsylvania to consult with Cameron. In a telegram to Joseph Casey, a lieutenant of Cameron,[77] dated December 26, 1860, Swett wrote from Chicago: "I come tonight. It is very important I should see Cameron immediately." [78] Swett arrived in Harrisburg, Cameron's chief center of operations, on December 28, and wrote Cameron: "Last week I was at Springfield, and had an interview with Mr. Lincoln. He requests me to come to see you, and invite you to visit Springfield, as soon as you could conveniently do so, in order that he might have an interview with you." [79] Gideon Welles always maintained that Swett was unauthorized by Lincoln to invite Cameron, and that Davis, Swett, and Weed conspired to get Cameron to Springfield.[80]

Cameron turned up in Springfield a few days following Swett's visit to Harrisburg and secured an interview with Lincoln. He remained at the Lincoln residence "until a late hour." [81] For weeks Lincoln had been receiving letters from Pennsylvania urging Cameron's appointment to the Cabinet; some were from Pennsylvania leaders not too friendly to Cameron, who saw a chance to secure Cameron's Senate seat were he elevated to the presidential councils. Among this group was David Wilmot, who declared that Lincoln, in justice to himself and to Cameron and his followers, ought to tender Cameron the headship of the Treasury.[82] Lincoln was amazed: "I also find letters here from very strong and unexpected quarters in Pennsylvania, urging the appointment of General Cameron to a place in the Cabinet." [83] The pressure on Lincoln

[77] Casey had been one of Cameron's managers in Cameron's struggle for the Republican presidential nomination. See Jos. Casey to Cameron, Jan. 28, May 7, 1860, Cameron Papers.

[78] This telegram is among the Cameron Papers.

[79] Leonard Swett to Cameron, Dec. 28, 1860, Cameron Papers.

[80] *Diary of Gideon Welles*, II, 390.

[81] Angle, *Lincoln, 1854–1861*, p. 366.

[82] Wilmot to Cameron, July 28, 1860; Cameron to B. R. Petriken, Dec. 11, 1860, Cameron Papers; Hamlin to Trumbull (Private), Dec. 27, 1860, Trumbull Papers.

[83] Lincoln to Hamlin, Nov. 27, 1860, in *Complete Works of Abraham Lincoln*, VI, 72.

was not without result, for under date of December 31 he handed Cameron the following: "I think fit to notify you now, that by your permission, I shall, at the proper time, nominate you to the U. S. Senate, for confirmation as Secretary of the Treasury or as Secretary of War—which of the two, I have not yet definitely decided—Please answer at your own earliest convenience." [84]

On his return from Springfield and while en route to Washington, Cameron stopped off at Harrisburg long enough to inform his lieutenants that Lincoln had tendered him a place in the Cabinet and that he had accepted; [85] to a few trusted friends he even showed Lincoln's written invitation to him. [86]

The Seward-Weed-Davis-Swett-Cameron combination seemed to be firmly intrenched. Seward was in the Cabinet; so, also, was Cameron.

Perturbed by the turn of events, the opponents of this combination resolved to give fight. Cameron's tarnished past was made the basis for immediate attack. In 1838 President Van Buren had appointed Cameron commissioner to settle the claims of the Winnebago Indians in Wisconsin. Cameron's administration of this trust produced a substantial scandal. Besides other irregularities Cameron had given to the red men depreciated notes on his own bank—all of which brought against him the first of many charges of dishonorable dealing and earned for him the derisive sobriquet of the "Great Winnebago Chief." [87] Indeed, "Cameron" and "corruption" became synonymous terms. [88] In 1860 one of Cameron's caustic critics declared that if Cameron had his just deserts,

[84] Lincoln to Cameron, Dec. 31, 1860, Cameron Papers.

[85] A correspondent at Harrisburg on Jan. 2 sent word: "Gen. Cameron passed through this city, on his way to Washington from Springfield. He only stopped while the cars were changed—say half an hour or more. During that time he saw several of his friends. These all unite in declaring that he communicated to them the fact that he had been appointed to a seat in the Cabinet, and that he had accepted. . . . This announcement has taken Gen. Cameron's opponents very greatly by surprise." See Philadelphia *North American and United States Gazette,* Jan. 3, 1861.

[86] Another correspondent at Harrisburg on Jan. 4 wrote: "The friends of Mr. Cameron say that they saw a promise of the appointment over Mr. Lincoln's signature." See Cincinnati *Daily Gazette,* Jan. 5, 1861.

[87] Ida M. Street, "The Simon Cameron Indian Commission of 1838," *Annals of Iowa,* VII (July–Oct., 1905), 115–39, 172–95; *Report and Collections of the State Historical Society of Wisconsin,* VII (1873–76), 394–96; "Execution of Treaty with the Winnebagoes," *Executive Document* No. 229, 25th Cong., 3d sess., serial no. 345.

[88] Mueller, *The Whig Party in Pennsylvania,* p. 117.

ALARMING APPEARANCE OF THE WINNEBAGO CHIEF; CAMERON AT SPRINGFIELD

From *Vanity Fair*, III (Feb. 2, 1861), 55.

Cameron.—"You've sent for me, and I've come. If you don't want me, I'll go back to my wigwam."

he would be serving out a sentence in the penitentiary instead of serving in the United States Senate.[89]

In no state was Cameron's unsavory reputation better known than in his own Pennsylvania, and his foes there readily capitalized on his spotted political record. In 1855 Cameron and Andrew G. Curtin had opposed each other in a tight race for United States Senator—and the Cameron forces always claimed that Curtin had not abided by an alleged deal, whereby he was to support Cameron for the senatorship in return for which Cameron would use his influence to have Curtin appointed secretary of state for Pennsylvania.[90] With the passing years the feud between Cameron and Curtin became more bitter. In 1860 the Cameronians had endeavored without success to prevent Curtin's nomination for governor; the Curtinites, on the other hand, had succeeded in blocking united Pennsylvania support for Cameron in his presidential aspirations. Curtin, to the chagrin of the Cameron forces, won the governorship in 1860, and his followers continued their warfare against Cameron.[91] Curtin had played a major role at the Chicago Convention, not only by opposing Cameron at every turn but by insistently reminding the delegates that Seward, if nominated, could not carry Pennsylvania.[92] Republican State Chairman Alexander K. McClure, Curtin's chief lieutenant, claimed that Seward joined in pressing Cameron's appointment to the Cabinet chiefly to punish Curtin for having defeated Seward's nomination at Chicago.[93] John A. Allison, another anti-Cameron leader, asserted:

While Genl. C. was endeavoring to make the impression upon Mr. Lincoln's mind, that he owed everything to him and his friends, he succeeded in making Mr. Seward *believe* that had it not been for the interference of Gov. Curtin at Chicago, the [Pennsylvania]

[89] John A. Morton to Thompson, March 26, 1860, Richard W. Thompson Papers. See also Saml. Galloway to Covode, Dec. 22, 1860, John Covode Papers.

[90] Jas. W. Brisbin to Covode, Nov. 28, 1859, Covode Papers.

[91] McClure, *Old Time Notes of Pennsylvania*, I, 198–99, 387–99.

[92] Baringer, *Lincoln's Rise to Power*, pp. 195, 224, 273–75.

[93] McClure, *Old Time Notes of Pennsylvania*, I, 408. That Seward was grieved at Curtin for his opposition at Chicago was indicated by a letter written by E. Peshine Smith, chief Rochester lieutenant of the Seward-Weed organization, to Henry C. Carey during the campaign of 1860: "I wish to God we could elect Lincoln & let Pennsylvania go against him. Especially do I wish that Curtin might be beaten, if we could afford it. *He* deserves it." See Smith to Carey, Sept. 25, 1860, Henry C. Carey Papers.

delegation would have in accordance with the Genl's wishes, cast its vote for Mr. Seward after they had complimented him (the Genl). . . .[94]

It is easy to understand, therefore, why the Curtin faction of Keystone State Republicanism should move at once when it learned of Cameron's appointment. McClure sent Lincoln a telegram of protest. The President-elect replied by inviting McClure to come to Springfield at once. Curtin's chief aide lost no time in journeying to Illinois. McClure, in his conference with Lincoln, emphatically declared that the appointment of Cameron would be a misfortune to the party in Pennsylvania. Lincoln was obviously disturbed and McClure left Lincoln, conscious that he had impressed him.[95]

Opposition to Cameron came not alone from the Curtinites of Pennsylvania. Other groups outside of the Keystone State now joined the anti-Cameron forces. Joseph Medill, Charles H. Ray, and Horace White, who edited and published the influential Chicago *Press & Tribune*, wanted no part of the wily Pennsylvanian. To give him a place in the Cabinet would, they declared, be catastrophic. Moreover, they wanted Chase in the Cabinet to offset the Cameron-Seward influence.[96] Ray and Medill, according to the latter's biographer, were fearful that Weed, Cameron, and Caleb Smith would get control of the Cabinet.[97] White, equally apprehensive, protested to Senator Trumbull: "If I am incorrect in supposing that Mr. C. defrauded the Winnebago half-breeds of $66,000 about the year 1832, I am *not* mistaken in believing that his general reputation is *shockingly bad*. . . . For my part I wish that Albany and Harrisburgh were in the bottom of the sea."[98] At this time—the closing days of December 1860—the Judd-Trumbull, or anti-Davis, anti-Seward, anti-Cameron faction of Illinois Republicans, received support from Vice President-elect Hamlin, who had no love for Cameron. On December 27 Hamlin

[94] John A. Allison to Trumbull, June 4, 1861, Trumbull Papers.
[95] *Old Time Notes of Pennsylvania,* I, 408; McClure, *Lincoln and Men of War-Times,* pp. 41–42, 140–41.
[96] Tracy Elmer Strevey, "Joseph Medill and the *Chicago Tribune* during the Civil War Period," p. 93.
[97] *Ibid.*
[98] Horace White to Trumbull (Private), Jan. 10, 1861, Trumbull Papers.

wrote to Lincoln protesting against Cameron's possible appointment.[99] Apparently Hamlin's letter reached Lincoln or was read by him shortly *after* the latter had on December 31 handed Cameron the written invitation to join the Cabinet family.

Unquestionably Lincoln was in a tight spot. After prolonged and troubled meditation, he dispatched a letter to Cameron, withdrawing his offer of a Cabinet place.[100] "Since seeing you," the letter to the Pennsylvania Senator began, "things have developed which make it impossible for me to take you into the cabinet. You will say this comes of an interview with McClure; and this is partly, but not wholly, true. The more potent matter is wholly outside of Pennsylvania; and yet I am not at liberty to specify. Enough that it appears to me to be sufficient." [101] The forces "outside of Pennsylvania" probably referred to the activity of the anti-Davis, anti-Swett faction of Illinois Republicans and to the attitude of the Vice President-elect. The letter then continued: "And now I suggest that you write me declining the appointment, in which case I do not object to its being known that it was tendered you. Better do this at once, before things so change that you cannot honorably decline, and I be compelled to openly recall the tender. No person living knows or has an intimation that I write this letter." [102] Lincoln added the postscript: "Telegraph me instantly on receipt of this, saying, 'all right.' " [103] Cameron did not comply with Lincoln's request. In fact, he did not even acknowledge Lincoln's letter withdrawing the Cabinet offer, for he had no intention, as we shall see, of yielding.

While waiting for Cameron's answer, Lincoln apparently was pressed by Judd and his friends for a Cabinet place. Davis, determined that Judd should get nothing, won the day, for Lincoln in due time intimated that the Republican state chairman would not be invited to a seat. Judd wrote to Trumbull dejectedly:

99 Hamlin to Trumbull (Private), Dec. 27, 1860, *ibid.* "Cameron," wrote Hamlin to Trumbull, "has got *all* the politicians for him, who want his place and they are *pressing him upon Lincoln.* All our friends in W. [Washington] should take hold to prevent it, or it may be done and if so, we will be in a sad position. There will be that odor about it that will damn us as a party. . . ."

100 This was on Jan. 3, the same day that McClure had left Springfield.

101 Lincoln to Cameron (Private), Jan. 3, 1861, in *Complete Works of Abraham Lincoln,* VI, 91–92.

102 *Ibid.*   103 *Ibid.*

Do not come to Springfield unless you are sent for by us. As for myself I am substantially played out. I have no word from Lincoln since my return [to Chicago]. . . . He never had a truer friend than myself—and there was no one in whom he placed greater confidence till circumstances embarrassed him about a Cabinet appointment. Or in my own language he is trimming and wants to get rid of me. The truth is that every appliance that the band could control have been brought against me even including female influence for the last month—whilst my friends have been content to rely upon justice and propriety and I suppose it will be so to the end of the chapter—and not content with finally placing me in the position of a ruined man, my friends are to be restrained in the use of the patronage. . . .[104]

Some evidence exists to indicate that the "female influence" mustered into service against him, of which Judd complained, was that exerted by Mrs. Lincoln. She wrote at least one letter to Davis, urging him to advise Lincoln not to take Judd, whom she disliked with feminine intensity, into the Cabinet.[105]

In addition to the influence which the future First Lady might have exerted in opposing Judd, there were other considerations which were working against the Chicagoan, namely the promise to give Caleb B. Smith a Cabinet seat made by Davis at the Chicago Convention. In the latter half of January Alexander H. Conner, Republican state chairman of Indiana, led to Springfield a small body of pro-Smith Hoosier Republicans, including Judge William T. Otto and R. K. Coffin. Their purpose was "to counteract the pressure of Illinois politicians to supplant Smith by Judd." [106] Conner's friend and law partner, William P. Fishback, wrote to his brother on this occasion:

[104] Judd to Trumbull, Jan. 3, 1861, Trumbull Papers.

[105] Mary Lincoln to Davis, Jan. 17, 1861, in Harry E. Pratt, "David Davis, 1815–1886," *Transactions of the Illinois State Historical Society*, 1930, pp. 168, 168 n. Gideon Welles wrote later: "Mrs. Lincoln has the credit of excluding Judd of Chicago from the Cabinet." See *Diary of Gideon Welles*, II, 390. Henry B. Stanton, a New York Republican leader, wrote in later years that Mrs. Lincoln was "suspected of communicating her wishes in respect to the composition of the Cabinet" to Davis. See Henry B. Stanton, *Random Recollections,* p. 221. Yet the evidence that her efforts were sufficient to influence Lincoln's action definitely in the matter of appointments is not conclusive.

[106] New York *Herald,* Jan. 20, 1861. Conner subsequently was appointed postmaster of Indianapolis by Lincoln. It was Judge William T. Otto, who served as an Indiana delegate at large to the Chicago Convention, who told Mrs. Matilda

Conner went (last evening) on a pilgrimage to the *Republican Mecca,* where Old Abe is now dispensing favors. There was a determination and promise on the part of Mr. Lincoln to give Mr. C. B. Smith a place in his *Cabinet*—for some reason the matter has been reduced from a supposed certainty to a perplexing probability or, more properly perhaps an improbability. Certain pecuniary advantages to the Law firm of Conner & Fishback are somehow remotely connected with the appointment of Mr. S. to the Department of the Interior & we of course feel a little anxious about it. I think the upshot of the quarrel between the friends of *Colfax* & *Smith* will result in Indiana being left entirely bare of Cabinet honors.[107]

On reaching Springfield, Conner and his group consulted with Davis and other opponents of Judd. Word came from an observer on the scene that the "leaders of the anti-Judd forces are all here, and co-operate with the Indiana delegation in favor of Smith." [108] The Hoosiers remained in Springfield for several days; that their activities were closely watched is evident from the following news despatch:

The Indiana agitators for Smith are still here. They have formed a sort of offensive and defensive alliance with the anti-Judd men from this State, now concentrated here in full force under the leadership of Judge Davis, Kellogg, Governor Yates and others. Judd himself is here, and leads his partisans in person. The strife for supremacy is fierce, and a source of great tribulation to the President-elect. A decisive battle is expected to be fought within the next forty-eight hours.[109]

Finally Judd left for his Chicago home,[110] and his opponents took leave of Springfield also.

Destiny favored Smith over Judd. Lincoln's close friend Jesse W. Fell—essentially neutral in the Davis-Judd Republican fac-

---

Gresham (wife of the later Secretary of State of the United States, Walter Q. Gresham), that David Davis promised Caleb B. Smith a Cabinet place in return for support for Lincoln at the Convention. See Gresham, *Life of Walter Quintin Gresham,* I, 110–11.

[107] William P. Fishback to his brother, "Tip," Jan. 19, 1861 (Photostat), Miscellaneous Papers, Indiana State Library, Indianapolis. The original of this letter is supposed to be in the possession of Mrs. Charles D. Herron, of Washington, D.C., the daughter of Mrs. H. J. Milligan, of Indianapolis.

[108] New York *Herald,* Jan. 21, 1861.

[109] *Ibid.,* Jan. 26, 1861.   [110] *Ibid.*

tional fight in the President-elect's own state—had suggested to Lincoln that Illinois had her share of glory and patronage in the President; that neither Judd nor Davis should go into the Cabinet; that Cabinet places should go to Indiana and Pennsylvania, for "such a disposition of favors was a good deal spoken of at Chicago, in a quiet way, though of course no improper pledges—so far as I know or believe—were asked—as I am very sure they were not, and could not be given." [111] Judd's followers did not surrender easily, but the odds were against them.[112] For Lincoln had almost definitely decided to take Smith. Soon Leonard Swett was writing an associate confidentially: "Tell Smith what I know, that it was through the Illinois fight and Judge Davis that Judd went out and he went in." [113]

In deciding on Smith the President-elect not only had to discard Judd, he likewise had to forsake Smith's fellow Hoosier, Schuyler Colfax. Lincoln's partiality for Smith was based in part on long acquaintance; they had served together in Congress some fifteen years earlier. Then too, Lincoln fully appreciated Smith's services at the Chicago Convention; Colfax, on the other hand, had supported Bates for the presidential nomination. Shortly after the convention Lincoln had expressed his appreciation to Smith: "I am indeed, much indebted to Indiana; and, as my home friends tell me, much to you personally." [114]

Nevertheless Colfax's followers, determined, if possible, to divert Lincoln from Smith and to snare the Cabinet prize for their favorite, crowded into Springfield for interviews with the President-elect.[115] When Lincoln finally did definitely take Smith into the Cabinet, he sought to salve Colfax's feelings with this written mes-

[111] Fell to Lincoln, Jan. 2, 1861, Jesse W. Fell Papers. The authors of this volume are deeply indebted to Dr. Harry E. Pratt for permission to examine a copy of this letter in his possession.

[112] A newspaper correspondent wrote from Springfield in Jan.: "The partisans of N. B. Judd of this State, who are now assembled around their leader at this point, are working with might and main to secure the place informally tendered to Caleb B. Smith, of Indiana, for him. The jealousy of rival Republican chieftains from this State paralizes, however, their efforts to some extent." See New York *Herald,* Jan. 17, 1861.

[113] Lamon, *Recollections of Abraham Lincoln, 1847–1865,* p. 318.

[114] Lincoln to C. B. Smith, May 26, 1860, in *Complete Works of Abraham Lincoln,* VI, 21.

[115] New York *Herald,* Jan. 30, 31, 1861.

sage: "When you were brought forward I said, 'Colfax is a young man, is already in position, is running a brilliant career and is sure of a bright future in any event; with Smith, it is now or never.' " [116] It is of passing interest that Colfax within a decade was to reach the vice-presidency of the United States.

At about the time that Judd was being shelved by Lincoln as a Cabinet possibility, Chase arrived in Springfield in answer to Lincoln's long-expected invitation. On January 5, the day after his arrival, he had a "long interview" with the President-elect.[117] Lincoln asked the Ohioan whether he would be able "to accept the appointment of Secretary of the Treasury without, however, being exactly prepared to make you that offer." This was a strange request indeed—but not so strange considering Lincoln's desire to conciliate divers factions. Chase replied that the offer must first be made, adding that since Seward was to receive first place in the Cabinet he would certainly not refuse out of pique. He also informed Lincoln that he "wanted no position, least of all a subordinate one." [118]

Chase's term as governor of Ohio had just expired and he had been elected to the United States Senate. He was probably sincerely reluctant to forsake the august body of Congress unless Lincoln should ask him as a personal favor to enter the Cabinet. In letters to friends Chase clearly expressed his feelings: "Mr. Lincoln & I understand each other. . . . I must consider my duty to the cause with as little admixture of personal feeling as may be possible. My reluctance to take any place is great." [119] And in a letter to Sumner: "The supposition that Mr. L. has tendered me the Treas'y Dept. is erroneous. When I was in Springfield the propriety of my taking it was talked of, but nothing decided on either

[116] Lincoln to Colfax, March 8, 1861, in *Complete Works of Abraham Lincoln,* VI, 187.

[117] Angle, *Lincoln, 1854–1861,* p. 366.

[118] D. V. Smith, "Salmon P. Chase and the Election of 1860," *Ohio Archaeological and Historical Quarterly,* XXXIX (1930), 535. Chase felt that in Lincoln's estimation he was subordinate to Seward. His feeling in this respect may have been due to the fact that he had been informed that Thurlow Weed had already discussed Cabinet appointments as well as minor places with Lincoln. Seè H. B. Stanton to Chase, Jan. 7, 1861, Chase Papers, Library of Congress; and Chase "Diary and Correspondence," Jan. 2, 1861, *Annual Report,* American Historical Association, Vol. II (1902).

[119] Chase to Robert Hosea, Jan. 16, 1861, Chase-Hosea Papers.

side. Should Mr. L. finally think it important that I leave the
Senate for the Cabinet & ask me to do so, I shall feel that a very
principal responsibility is imposed on me. My reluctance to do so
is extreme." [120]

Chase apparently feared that not only was he second to Seward
in Lincoln's estimation, but that the new Cabinet would be dominated by Seward. Unquestionably the anti-Weed faction of New
York Republicans shared this point of view.[121] "You know,"
penned one of this faction to Chase, "that Mr. Weed has been at
Springfield. . . . No particular men *by name* were distinctly mentioned by Mr. Weed, but his line of remark drifted directly towards
Seward & Cameron." [122] Upon his return home from Springfield,
Chase corresponded with George Opdyke, an anti-Weed leader
in New York. He confided to Opdyke the result of his conference
with the President-elect: "Mr. Lincoln . . . told me that he had
offered the post of Secy. of State to Mr. Seward . . . that Mr.
S. had accepted. . . . I can only say that if you and those who
concur with you as to the proper financial & economical policy of
the Administration expect that these views be properly represented
in the Cabinet, two or three gentlemen fully possessed of them
should at once visit Mr. Lincoln & discuss everything & unreservedly with him." [123] Chase wanted a place in the Cabinet if for no
other reason than to combat Seward. He was virtually giving Opdyke carte blanche in deciding with Lincoln whether he should go
into the Cabinet. The "proper financial & economical policy"
meant that free-trade sentiments should be represented in Lincoln's inner council; many Pennsylvanians had opposed Chase's
nomination for president because he had offended protectionist
sentiment in the Keystone State.[124]

[120] Chase to Sumner, Jan. 23, 1861, Charles Sumner Papers.

[121] D. V. Smith, "Salmon P. Chase and the Election of 1860," *Ohio Archaeological
and Historical Quarterly*, XXXIX (1930), 535.

[122] H. B. Stanton to Chase, Jan. 7, 1861, in "Diary and Correspondence of Salmon
P. Chase," *Annual Report*, American Historical Association, II (1902), 490.

[123] Chase to George Opdyke (copy), Jan. 9, 1861, Chase Papers, Historical Society of Pennsylvania.

[124] John A. Gurley to Chase, April 13, 1860 (Private), Chase Papers, Library of
Congress. "Chase has a record which many think would not read well in Pa., especially that chapter directed to the subject of a discriminating tariff. I think no man
can carry Pa. unless he really is or can make the masses there believe he is right on
this question." Robert F. Payne to Wade, March 1, 1860, Benjamin F. Wade Papers.

Opdyke himself was being considered as a Cabinet possibility. In December the anti-Weed Republican leaders had met in Albany and indulged in the wishful thought that Lincoln might be prevailed upon to drop Seward and appoint either Opdyke or James S. Wadsworth as the New York representative in the Cabinet.[125] When Opdyke received the letter from Chase telling of the result of Lincoln's interview, he needed no urging. He at once consulted with several of his associates among the New York anti-Weed Republicans, including Judge Hogeboom, David Dudley Field, Hiram Barney, and James H. Van Alen. Inevitably advocacy of Chase's appointment to the Treasury Department and opposition to Cameron became one and the same. Cameron, of course, had not divulged the fact that Lincoln had informed him that it was impossible to take him into the Cabinet. Van Alen, in a letter to Senator Trumbull of January 8, outlined the Chase men's plans:

Honest men of all parties were shocked by the rumor of Cameron's app't to the Treasury. This eve'g Messrs. Judge Hogeboom & Opdyke leave for Springfield and Messrs. Field & Barney for Wash'n to make their urgent protest against the act. These are respectable & intelligent citizens and their representations should be heeded. Mr. Cameron stands before the country as the prominent & completely characterized representative of what honest men most fear & hate. . . .

I have written Mr. Lincoln and forwarded from Congressional Documents extracts in relation to Simon Cameron's action as Commissioner to settle the claims of the Winnebago Indians. . . .[126]

While enroute to Springfield, the anti-Weed delegation stopped in Columbus to consult with Chase. No one has ever revealed what occurred at this conference, but Opdyke, Barney, and Hogeboom left Columbus determined to press on Lincoln Chase's appointment to the Treasury Department. Arriving in Springfield the three had an interview with Lincoln on January 16. Lincoln received them cordially, but politely informed them that no further appointments would be made until he reached Washington for the inaugu-

---

[125] H. B. Stanton to Chase, Dec. 7, 1860, in "Diary and Correspondence of Salmon P. Chase," *Annual Report, American Historical Association*, II (1902), 487–88.

[126] James H. Van Alen to Trumbull, Jan. 8, 1861, Trumbull Papers.

ration. He did indicate, however, that if the Pennsylvanians could be placated, he expected to name Chase as Secretary of the Treasury. Failing in their efforts to persuade Lincoln to appoint Chase at once, the delegation returned to New York.[127] One observer in Springfield reported: "Mr. Barney and his friends have been here today; they go home not wholly satisfied." [128] Barney confided to William Cullen Bryant the result of their mission to Columbus and Springfield:

Mr. Lincoln has invited to his Cabinet only three persons to wit— Mr. Bates, Mr. Seward & Mr. Cameron. All these have accepted. In regard to the latter named however Mr. Lincoln became satisfied that he had made a mistake and wrote him requesting him to withdraw his acceptance or decline. Mr. C. refused to answer the letter and was greatly offended by it. He however authorized a mutual friend to telegraph and he did so—that Mr. C. would not on any account occupy a seat in his Cabinet. Mr. Lincoln has thus a quarrel on his hands which he is anxious to adjust satisfactorily before he proceeds further in the formation of his Cabinet. He is advised from Washington not to conclude further upon the members of his Cabinet until he reaches Washington. . . . We tried to change this purpose but I fear in vain. He has not offered a place to Mr. Chase. He wants and expects to invite him to the treasury department. But he fears this will offend Pennsylvania & he wants to reconcile the republicans of that state to it before it is settled. He thinks Mr. Chase should be willing to let the matter stand so and leave the option with him (Mr. L.) of taking him when he can do so without embarrassment. . . .

He wants to take Judd; but this selection will offend some of his friends and he does not decide upon it. Wells [*sic*] of Connecticut is his preference for New England—Blair of Maryland is favorably considered. . . . Caleb B. Smith of Indiana is urged upon him and he may have to take him instead of Judd. Caleb is almost as objectionable as Cameron, & for similar reasons. . . . What he [Lincoln] will ultimately do after reaching Washington no one not even himself can tell. He wants to please & satisfy all his friends.[129]

[127] D. V. Smith, "Salmon P. Chase and the Election of 1860," *Ohio Archaeological and Historical Quarterly*, XXXIX (1930), 535–36; Angle, *Lincoln, 1854–1861*, p. 368.

[128] C. H. Ray to Trumbull, Jan. 16, 1861, Trumbull Papers.

[129] Hiram Barney to William Cullen Bryant, January 17, 1861, Bryant-Godwin Papers.

This report from Barney inspired Bryant to send an urgent appeal to Lincoln in an endeavor to cause the President-elect to act at once: "The only occasion for delaying is the hope of satisfying Mr. Cameron and his friends. . . . One thing, however, is perfectly clear—that, by losing the chance of securing the services of Mr. Chase in the Treasury department, both the country and the Republican party will lose infinitely more than the administration could possibly suffer from the enmity of Mr. Cameron and his adherents." [130]

Bryant, Barney, Opdyke, and the anti-Weed Republican leadership now acquired the support of Horace Greeley in pressing Chase for the Cabinet.[131] The famed New York *Tribune* editor was at this time at swords' points with Seward and Weed, his former political partners, and had been, ever since the latter two had neglected to give him public office.[132] Greeley was only too happy to hurl a political bomb at Seward, whose presidential candidacy he had violently opposed at the Chicago Convention.[133] Moreover, Greeley was Schuyler Colfax's mentor and staunch friend,[134] and Colfax's rival for a Cabinet seat, Caleb B. Smith, was in communication with Judge Davis seeking aid against Colfax.[135] Colfax, meanwhile, had become the anti-Weed Republicans' choice for the Indiana member of the proposed Cabinet.[136] Greeley now placed the tremendous power of his *Tribune* behind Chase's candidacy for the Cabinet.[137] Moreover, Greeley's assistant editor, Charles A. Dana, used his persuasive powers on Chase to accept a Cabinet post should it be tendered.[138]

[130] Bryant to Lincoln, Jan. 21, 1861, in Godwin, *A Biography of William Cullen Bryant*, II, 151–52.

[131] Henry B. Stanton, *Random Recollections*, p. 220.

[132] Horace Greeley to Seward (copy), Nov. 11, 1854, Seward Papers.

[133] Ralph R. Fahrney, *Horace Greeley and the Tribune in the Civil War*, chap. I, pp. 69–70. Greeley himself had been recommended to Lincoln for a Cabinet post by John W. Forney. See Forney, *Anecdotes of Public Men*, II, 422.

[134] For the close friendship between Greeley and Colfax, see Greeley to Colfax, Feb. 18, 24, 1859; Feb. 3, 1860, Greeley-Colfax Papers; W. H. Smith, "Schuyler Colfax: Whig Editor, 1854–1855," *Indiana Magazine of History*, XXXIV (Sept., 1938), 262–65.

[135] Caleb B. Smith to Davis, Jan. 13, 1861, David Davis Papers.

[136] H. B. Stanton to Chase, Nov. 30, 1860, in "Diary and Correspondence of Salmon P. Chase," *Annual Report*, American Historical Association, II (1902), 486.

[137] New York *Daily Tribune*, Jan. 7, 14, 1861.

[138] Chase to Charles A. Dana, Nov. 10, 1860, in "Diary and Correspondence of Salmon P. Chase," *Annual Report*, American Historical Association, II (1902), 292.

The pressure on Chase to accept a Cabinet appointment, if offered by Lincoln, was terrific. Congressman Elihu B. Washburne, of Illinois, implored the Ohioan: "Cameron will *not* have a place in the cabinet. . . . The country demands your services in the Treasury department. . . . I tell you it is *now* a necessity that you should go into the cabinet if Lincoln has tendered you a place." [139] The Free Soil-Democratic element within the Republican party was emphatic in prevailing on Chase. "It is our only hope," [140] said Senator Sumner, of Massachusetts, in his appeal to Chase. Congressman Francis E. Spinner, of New York, sent urgent word to the Ohioan: "Intrigues are again in progress to place a particular man at the head of the Treasury Department— The country is alarmed at the mere suggestion. . . . For God's sake, and the country's . . . , save the party and the great cause that brought it into being." [141] Vice President-elect Hamlin was also active.[142] Moreover, on January 23, Frank Blair, a former Democrat, turned up in Springfield to press his brother Montgomery Blair's claim to a Cabinet post, and word came that "the presence of a man of Frank Blair's nerve and enthusiasm has a happy influence on the tone of feeling here. The friends of Mr. Judd are taking fresh heart every day. . . . His chances brighten as Smith's and Cameron's fade." [143] Chase, sincerely reluctant to leave the Senate and willing to go into the Cabinet only if it appeared that the Seward-Cameron influence would prevail, finally consented: "If obliged to decide it at all I hope to lay personal considerations to myself out of the scales." [144] The probability that Chase would accept a Cabinet offer if tendered by Lincoln moved the anti-Weed Republicans of New York to more strenuous activity: David Dudley Field journeyed to Albany to induce

[139] E. B. Washburne to Chase, Jan. 10, 1861, in *ibid.*, p. 491.

[140] Chas. Sumner to Chase, Jan. 19, 1861, in D. V. Smith, "Salmon P. Chase and the Election of 1860," *Ohio Archaeological and Historical Quarterly*, XXXIX (1930), 536.

[141] F. E. Spinner to Chase, Jan. 22, 1861, in "Diary and Correspondence of Salmon P. Chase," *Annual Report*, American Historical Association, II (1902), 493.

[142] Henry B. Stanton, *Random Recollections*, p. 220.

[143] Cincinnati *Daily Gazette*, Jan. 24, 1861.

[144] Chase to Gen. James T. Worthington, Jan. 14, 1861, Lincoln Collection, John Hay Library, Brown University.

Lieutenant Governor Campbell, who was hostile to Weed, to write to Lincoln recommending Chase.[145]

Weed watched these pro-Chase, anti-Cameron developments closely and reported the activity to Judge Davis by mail.[146]

Greatly troubled, Lincoln sought to find a way out of the Cameron predicament by requesting Republican State Chairman Thomas H. Dudley, of New Jersey, to ask Henry C. Carey, of Philadelphia, to write to him (Lincoln) regarding Cameron's possible appointment to the Cabinet.[147] Carey, a prominent leader of the Quaker City, needed no urging. In a letter to Lincoln, Carey expressed his opinion of Cameron in no uncertain terms:

There exists throughout the State an almost universal belief that his fortune has been acquired by means that are forbidden to the man of honor. . . . There stand on the records of the courts, and but a very few years old, charges that would, if proved, involve the commission of serious crime. . . . Most of our well-disposed fellow citizens . . . look upon him as the very incarnation of corruption. . . . His appointment would be a signal to all the vultures of the Union to flock around the Treasury. . . . He is, therefore, the first choice of all the political gamblers of the State.[148]

William Cullen Bryant was no less outspoken. On February 5, 1861, he wrote Lincoln as follows:

I wrote to you yesterday in regard to the rumored intention of giving Mr. Simon Cameron, of Pennsylvania, a place in the Cabinet. I had not then spoken much with others of our party, but I have since heard the matter discussed, and the general feeling is one of consternation. Mr. Cameron has the reputation of being concerned in some of the worst intrigues of the Democratic party. His name suggests to every honest Republican in the State no other associations than these. At present, those who favor his appointment in this State are the men who last winter so shamefully corrupted our Legislature. If he is to have a place in the Cabinet at all, the Treasury department is the last of our public interests that ought to be committed to his hands.

In the last election, the Republican party did not strive simply for

---

[145] Weed to Davis, Jan. 20, 1861, David Davis Papers.   [146] *Ibid.*
[147] Henry C. Carey to Lincoln, Jan. 7, 1861 (copy), Carey Papers.
[148] *Ibid.*

the control, but one of the great objects was to secure a pure and virtuous administration of the Government. In the first respect we have succeeded; but, if such men as Cameron are to form the Cabinet, we shall not have succeeded in the second.[149]

This communication should, it would seem, have settled Cameron's fate as far as the Cabinet was concerned; and criticism of Lincoln for failure to drop Cameron from all consideration forever may well be justified. The fact of the matter is, however, that the President-elect had "kicked out" Cameron from his tentative Cabinet, but the Pennsylvanian refused to remain "kicked out." As late as February 4—one month after Lincoln withdrew his Cabinet offer to Cameron—Thaddeus Stevens wrote a close associate: "Genl. Cameron . . . informed me that he is offered a place in the Cabinet." [150] McClure's explanation sheds light on Cameron's tactics: [151]

Lincoln's letter to Cameron tendering him the Cabinet appointment had been shown to some confidential friends whose enthusiasm outstripped their discretion, and they made public the fact that Cameron was an assured member of the new Cabinet. The second letter from Lincoln to Cameron, recalling the tender of a Cabinet office, was not made public, and doubtless was never seen beyond a very small and trusted circle of Cameron's associates; but it soon became known that Lincoln regarded the question as unsettled, and that led to exhaustive efforts on both sides to hinder and promote Cameron's appointment. Sanderson, who had made the compact at Chicago with Davis for Cameron's appointment, was sent at once to Springfield to enforce its fulfillment. . . .

The temper of those Cameron leaders who knew of Lincoln's withdrawal of the Cabinet offer to Cameron, was at fever heat. One of them, Joseph Casey, informed Cameron that a heavy counter attack had been launched against the Chase forces:

J. P. S. [John P. Sanderson] left at 3 o'clock this morning for Springfield. *Cowan* goes with him. The feeling here [in Harrisburg] is intense. I put your declination on the ground, that the manner in which you have been thrust aside from the Treasury Department

[149] Godwin, *A Biography of William Cullen Bryant,* II, 152.
[150] Thaddeus Stevens to S. Stevens, Feb. 4, 1861, Thaddeus Stevens Papers.
[151] McClure, *Abraham Lincoln and Men of War-Times,* pp. 143–44.

is indicative of a feeling towards you, & of policy to be pursued which left you no honorable alternative but to decline.

The members of the Legislature through their Speaker telegraphed to Lincoln this morning insisting upon your retention in the Treasury & protesting against Chase's appointment as a man of free trade antecedents.

If it is made there will be resolutions denouncing it nearly unanimously, & instructing our Senators to vote against his confirmation. It will inevitably alienate Penna. from Mr. Lincoln's administration —once and forever and they better understand it now than hereafter —when it is too late to repair the mischief.[152]

Written protests against Chase's possible appointment, on the ground that he was a low-tariff man, poured into Springfield from Pennsylvania.[153]

In early January Sanderson had consulted Edgar Cowan, who had just been elected to the United States Senate from Pennsylvania. The gist of Sanderson's conversation with Cowan was at once forwarded to Cameron: "I had a two hours interview with Cowan to-day, & he is highly pleased with your own behavior & will cordially & fully cooperate with you. He will write to Lincoln at once. I gave him the points to write about. . . . He said further that he would go out to see him [Lincoln] but desired to go quietly & unknown." [154]

On January 12 or 13 Sanderson, accompanied by Senator Cowan, arrived in Springfield.[155] In the interview with Lincoln, Sanderson complained that the President-elect's letter to Cameron revoking the Cabinet appointment was offensively blunt and needed explanation, as it gave no reason whatever for the sudden change in Lincoln's judgment. Swett also had sent a letter, informing Lincoln of Cameron's wounded feelings. Lincoln was pretty adamant, however, and refused to go along with Sanderson's and Cowan's plea to appoint Cameron to the Treasury Department. Failing this, the Cameron spokesmen suggested that Lincoln send Cameron a conciliatory note. Accordingly on January 13—the very day that Sanderson and Cowan left Springfield

[152] Joseph Casey to Cameron, Jan. 11, 1861 (Private), Cameron Papers.

[153] Jno. A. Hiertand to Cameron, Jan. 14, 1861 (*Private*), Cameron Papers.

[154] J. P. Sanderson to Cameron, Jan. 8, 1861, Cameron Papers.

[155] Angle, *Lincoln, 1854–1861*, p. 367; New York *Daily Tribune*, Jan. 14, 1861.

for home—Lincoln wrote a "private and confidential" letter to Cameron apologizing for the brusqueness of his letter of January 3 and giving assurance that he "intended no offense." In his letter to the Pennsylvanian the President-elect enclosed a new letter, antedated January 3, which he suggested that he (Cameron) should accept as the original of that date. In this new January 3 letter (written on January 13) Lincoln declared to Cameron: "With much pain I now say to you that you will relieve me from great embarrassment by allowing me to recall the offer." The explanatory letter in which the antedated letter was enclosed gave Cameron only this assurance: "If I should make a Cabinet appointment for Pennsylvania before I reach Washington, I will not do so without consulting you. . . ." In the antedated letter Lincoln informed Cameron: "I now think I will not definitely fix upon any appointment for Pennsylvania until I reach Washington." [156]

Meanwhile the Illinois wing of the anti-Weed, anti-Davis, anti-Cameron movement was quite as busy as its New York allies. In mid-January (1861) Charles H. Ray, of the Chicago *Press & Tribune*, took up the burden of stimulating pro-Chase, anti-Cameron sentiment. To his friend, Governor John A. Andrew, of Massachusetts, Ray pleaded: "We here—I mean Mr. Lincoln's original friends, especially among the Radical Democrats—are doing what we can to get Mr. Chase into the Cabinet as a counterbalance to the schemers who hang upon the skirts of Mr. Seward." [157] The Massachusetts chief executive accordingly dispatched a letter to Lincoln urging the dropping of Cameron and the appointment of Chase. In this communication Andrew said that all the better elements of the Republican party opposed Cameron's appointment.[158] Ray also cautioned the Republican Members of Congress: "This Cameron business may be brought to a dead halt, if you gentlemen of the Senate and House will take a little responsibility in the matter and speak out. . . . Mr. Lincoln is hesitating and doubtful. He sees the error into which he has fallen; and would, I have no doubt, be glad to recede; but . . .

[156] Lincoln to Cameron, Jan. 3, 1861, enclosed in Lincoln to Cameron, Jan. 13, 1861, in *Complete Works of Abraham Lincoln*, VI, 96–97; McClure, *Abraham Lincoln and Men of War-Times*, p. 144.

[157] C. H. Ray to Andrew, Jan. 17, 1860, John A. Andrew Papers.

[158] Andrew to Ray (copy), Jan. 23, 1861, *ibid.*

he hears only from that Cameron and Weed gang. . . . Mr. Chase has expressed himself strongly in favor of Judd and quite as strongly in opposition to Cal. Smith, in a letter to Lincoln. Mr. Barney directs me to say that he saw the letter." [159] State Treasurer Butler, another of the Judd (or anti-Davis) Illinois faction, followed Ray in an appeal to the Republican Members of Congress: "If Mr. Cameron is out of the way Mr. Chase will be Secretary of the Treasury, a thing Mr. Lincoln much desires." [160]

In Indianapolis Caleb B. Smith, too, became alarmed at the activities of the Greeley-Chase-Judd-Colfax group and wrote to Davis urging the necessity for increased pressure on Lincoln in behalf of Cameron.[161] It was not surprising, then, to witness another Cameron emissary, Alexander Cummings, trekking to Springfield in late January.

For years Cummings had been Cameron's bosom friend and trusted adviser in Philadelphia. He had edited the Philadelphia *Bulletin* and had been active in Cameron's unsuccessful campaign for the Republican presidential nomination in 1860. In the latter year Cummings had started the New York *World*,[162] which at once became Cameron's mouthpiece in the metropolis. In early January (1861) the *World* came out ardently for the Seward-Weed-Cameron-Smith cause in a two-column editorial entitled "Mr. Lincoln's Cabinet." Seward's appointment as Secretary of State, ran this editorial, is "as suitable geographically as it is in every other respect"; Bates's appointment "meets universal approval"; Gideon Welles would not be as desirable as Senator Fessenden of Maine; Henry Winter Davis (cousin of Judge David Davis) should be preferred over Montgomery Blair. As for Cameron he was more "fitly" qualified for the Treasury Department than any other.[163] Soon afterwards a long eulogistic biography of Weed, penned by Cummings, appeared in the *World*.[164] Cummings further assured his readers "that Messrs. Seward, Cameron and Bates will be in it [the Cabinet] is settled, and it is under-

[159] C. H. Ray to Trumbull, Jan. 16, 1861, Trumbull Papers.
[160] William Butler to Trumbull, Feb. 13, 1861, *ibid.*
[161] Caleb B. Smith to Davis, Feb. 5, 1861, David Davis Papers.
[162] F. Hudson, *Journalism in the United States from 1690 to 1872,* pp. 182–83, 667–68.
[163] New York *World,* Jan. 9, 1861.   [164] *Ibid.,* Jan. 21, 1861.

stood that Indiana will be represented by Caleb B. Smith. . . . Depend upon it that Mr. Cameron will be in the Cabinet and in the Treasury department." [165]

Cummings was in Springfield on January 21 and urged on Lincoln the desirability of accepting Cameron.[166] Thurlow Weed was reported to have started for Springfield at the same time as Cummings, but apparently changed his mind.[167] Unsuccessful in his efforts to induce the President-elect to appoint Cameron, Cummings returned to New York, where he joined Weed in assailing Horace Greeley for the latter's ambitions to succeed to Seward's Senate seat.[168]

The end of January saw Lincoln's Cabinet no nearer completion than it had been in December. The situation was aptly summarized in the words of a Springfield observer:

The number of able, enlightened, patriotic and deserving statesmen who are willing to take places in Old Abe's Cabinet is perfectly astonishing, and somewhat bothers the veteran rail splitter. Out of all the timber offered to him he has accepted only two sticks—Mr. Seward and Mr. Bates—the latter a fine antique. Lincoln sticks fast upon the rock where Cameron has landed him. Cameron has enough of the Highland blood in him not to give up Old Abe's letter offering the Cabinet appointment, and so things are stuck fast. Meantime we have an immense amount of timber lying about loose. . . . Between the various factions, Old Abe is in danger of being torn to pieces, and the prospects of the country, under his administration, are not over and above encouraging.[169]

And Lincoln's law partner, William H. Herndon, viewing the discomfiture of Lincoln at this time, sympathized: "Lincoln is in

---

[165] New York *World,* Jan. 22, 1861.   [166] New York *Herald,* Jan. 26, 1861.

[167] Cincinnati *Daily Gazette,* Jan. 26, 1861. That Seward was fully aware of Weed's movements is evidenced by the following letter sent to Weed by Seward on Jan. 21 from Washington: "Cameron's appeals to me not for a Cabinet place but for some relief from his awkward position seemed to me so reasonable, and the consequences of a feud if it was not obtained so fearful, that I consented to advise your going [to Springfield]. But on Saturday the story was around that you had gone to Springfield to oppose Chase and instantly there was a commotion about my ears. . . ." Seward to Weed, Jan. 21, 1861, Weed Papers, University of Rochester Library.

[168] New York *World,* Feb. 2, 8, 9, 13, 1861.

[169] New York *Herald,* Jan. 23, 1861.

a fix. Cameron's appointment to an office in his Cabinet bothers him. If Lincoln do [sic] appoint Cameron, he gets a fight on his hands, and if he do [sic] not he gets a quarrel deep-abiding, & lasting. . . . Poor Lincoln! God help him!" [170]

Toward the end of January Lincoln designated February 11 as the day of his departure for Washington, and made known his desire for "utmost privacy" during his remaining days in Springfield.[171] Nevertheless, both factions of Republicans were working frantically under cover, although the number of visits to Lincoln decreased. The disappointed Judd was now doing his utmost for Chase,[172] and his ally, State Treasurer Butler, was urging Senator Trumbull to do something to ward off Cameron.[173] Chase, through his press organs, the Columbus *Ohio State Journal* and the Cincinnati *Commercial*, was waging unrestricted editorial warfare against Cameron.[174]

The Davis-Swett-Cameron-Weed-Caleb B. Smith bloc was by no means idle. Judge Davis assured Cameron, by "confidential" letter under date of February 8: "I have just returned from Springfield. Mr. Lincoln has invited me to accompany him on his trip. . . ." And in a postscript: "Every effort that mortal man could make has been made by me—Keep the spirits of your friends up. *Dont relax effort until the end.* . . . Write me at Albany if necessary, care Thurlow Weed." [175] Leonard Swett, recovering from illness in Pittsburgh, was doing all he could for the Cameron cause.[176]

According to schedule, Lincoln and his party left Springfield for Washington on February 11. In the party was Judd,[177] but by the time the President-elect's private train had reached Indianapolis, Davis was aboard.[178] From Buffalo, Judd, apparently keeping his eyes and ears open every minute of the day, sent word to Senator Trumbull in Washington: "My object in writing you

---

[170] W. H. Herndon to Trumbull, Jan. 27, 1861, Trumbull Papers.
[171] Angle, *Lincoln, 1854–1861*, p. 370.
[172] Judd to Trumbull, Feb. 17, 1861, Trumbull Papers.
[173] William Butler to Trumbull, Feb. 13, 1861, Trumbull Papers.
[174] Geiger to Cameron (Confidential), Feb. 7, 1861, Cameron Papers.
[175] D. Davis to Cameron (Confidential), Feb. 8, 1861, Cameron Papers.
[176] Leonard Swett to Cameron, Feb. 5, 1861, Cameron Papers.
[177] New York *Daily Tribune*, Feb. 12, 1861.   [178] *Ibid.*, Feb. 16, 1861.

now is to say in confidence that I believe I know what will happen, and that if the Treasury is offered to Gov. Chase he must accept." [179]

Also in the President-elect's party was Ward H. Lamon, friend and former law partner of Lincoln. Lamon was likewise a close friend and fellow townsman of Judge Davis [180] and at this time was in close touch with both Davis and Swett.[181] The selection of Lamon to accompany Lincoln to Washington was most gratifying to Caleb B. Smith, whose chief lieutenant, John P. Usher, wrote Lincoln: "It affords me much satisfaction to hear that you have invited our excellent friend W. H. Lamon to accompany you to Washington." [182]

What happened when the President-elect's party reached Albany—the abode of Weed—is perhaps better related by Lamon himself:

On arriving at Albany, N.Y., Mr. Thurlow Weed asked me where Mr. Lincoln was going to be domiciled in Washington until he was inaugurated. I told him Messrs. Trumbull and Washburne [who were pressing Chase for the Cabinet] had provided quarters for him; that they had rented a house on Thirteenth or Fourteenth Street, N.W., for his reception. . . . Mr. Weed said, "It will never do to allow him to go to a private house to be under the influence of State control. He is now public property, and ought to be where he can be reached by the people until he is inaugurated." We then agreed that Willard's Hotel would be the best place. . . .[183]

One of the motives for Weed's concern for Lincoln's comfort may be gleaned from the language of the Albany politician's letter to Mr. Willard, proprietor of Washington's famous hostelry:

DEAR WILLARD,—

Mr. Lincoln will be your guest.

In arranging his apartments, please reserve nearest him apart-

---

[179] Judd to Trumbull, Feb. 17, 1861, Trumbull Papers.

[180] Clint C. Tilton, "Lincoln and Lamon: Partners and Friends," *Transactions of the Illinois State Historical Society,* 1931, pp. 178–83.

[181] Leonard Swett to Lamon, Feb. 25, 1861; David Davis to Lamon, March 30, 1861, in Ward H. Lamon, *Recollections of Abraham Lincoln, 1847–1865,* pp. 313–14, 317.

[182] J. P. Usher to Lincoln, Feb. 4, 1861, in *ibid.,* p. xxv, n.

[183] Lamon, *Recollections of Abraham Lincoln, 1847–1865,* p. 34.

ments for two of his friends, Judge Davis and Mr. Lamon.

Truly yours,

THURLOW WEED.

Mrs. Lincoln and one son accompany him.[184]

From Albany the Lincoln party proceeded along the Hudson to New York City. The anti-Weed Republicans in the metropolis now had ambitious plans of excluding not only Cameron from the Cabinet but likewise Seward.[185] But this attempt was to prove abortive. Judge Davis occupied the first barouche with Lincoln in the welcoming ceremonies at City Hall.[186] On February 20 Weed, who had come down from Albany, breakfasted with Lincoln at the home of the merchant, Moses H. Grinnell, for years a follower of the Seward-Weed organization.[187] To the impartial observer it appeared as if the Davis-Weed-Cameron-Caleb B. Smith interest was in the ascendant in the President-elect's affections.

From New York the Lincoln party continued on to Philadelphia, and Davis, Lamon, and Judd, still in the entourage, enjoyed the crowd's plaudits.[188] It was in the City of Brotherly Love that the Cameron lieutenants cornered Lincoln. Already a Cameron leader had advised the Pennsylvania Senator that he had no doubt that by the time the President left the borders of the Keystone State he would have "come to the *unalterable* determination to adhere to his first impressions in reference to yourself." [189] In the Continental Hotel in Philadelphia the Cameronians conferred and pleaded in Cameron's behalf. The state of Pennsylvania, they asserted, was a unit in favor of Cameron's appointment. Even

[184] Weed to Willard, in *ibid.* On Lincoln's arrival in Washington, the New York *Herald* correspondent there reported that the apartments for Lincoln at Willard's Hotel were prepared for him "at short notice." The correspondent added: "It seems that the letter of the Illinois delegation [in Congress], announcing that they had engaged Mr. Smoot's house, on Franklin Row, did not reach Mr. Lincoln, and he ordered rooms to be engaged for him at Willard's, the only place in Washington that approaches a first-class hotel." See New York *Herald*, Feb. 23, 1861.

[185] Bigelow to Hargreaves, Feb. 21, 1861, John Bigelow Papers.

[186] New York Daily *Tribune*, Feb. 20, 1861. In the first barouche in addition to the President-elect and Judge Davis were Judge Harris, Colonel Sumner of the United States Army, and Alderman Cornell.

[187] *Ibid.*, Feb. 21, 1861; "The Diary of a Public Man," *The North American Review*, CXXIX (1879), 137–38.

[188] Philadelphia *North American and United States Gazette*, Feb. 22, 1861.

[189] W. Hutchins to Cameron (Confidential), Feb. 19, 1861, Cameron Papers.

Curtin, Carey, and McClure, they declared, had buried the hatchet and had lined up for the Pennsylvanian. In Harrisburg more pressure was exerted for Cameron. In fact, it seemed as though the opposition was engaged in a losing fight. Yet Lincoln was not swept off his feet. He expressed pleasure that the Republican factions in Pennsylvania now saw eye to eye, but frankly stated that the question of Cameron's appointment would not be settled until after he reached Washington. As events were to prove, he had apparently come to the conclusion that despite the pressure of the Cameron supporters, Chase must have a place in his official council.[190]

Lincoln suddenly abandoned the balance of his scheduled journey when a plot to assassinate him was uncovered and, as a consequence, he proceeded incognito with Lamon from Harrisburg to Washington, reaching the national capital early in the morning of February 23. He went at once to the Willard.[191] The office seekers were close on his heels.

When Lincoln reached Washington he had definitely selected only two members of his Cabinet—Seward and Bates.[192] He had almost decided on Smith and Welles and he definitely wanted Chase, despite the opposition of the Pennsylvanians. The Postmaster Generalship lay between Montgomery Blair and Henry Winter Davis. The President-elect apparently was still uncertain about Cameron, though he was more favorably disposed toward him, largely on the basis of what he had seen and heard in Philadelphia and Harrisburg. The Colfax followers had lost heart in their efforts to block Smith's appointment. Welles's chances were somewhat clouded by a last-minute boom for Governor Banks of Massachusetts. Strenuous efforts were made by Banks's followers to have Welles dropped. Lincoln listened favorably to the proposal, but Vice President-elect Hamlin, still nursing animosity toward Banks, insisted on Welles, and Lincoln complied. Welles was soon assured of a place—the Postmaster Generalship, it was then believed.[193]

[190] J. Hazlehurst to Cameron, Feb. 22, 1861; T. J. Coffey to Cameron, Feb. 22, 1861; Samuel A. Purviance to Cameron, Feb. 23, 1861, Cameron Papers.
[191] Angle, *Lincoln, 1854–1861*, p. 373.
[192] New York *Daily Tribune*, March 4, 1861.
[193] Boston *Commonwealth*, Feb. 27, 1869; New York *Herald*, Feb. 26, 1861; Geo.

The Blair family, perceiving the activity of Judge David Davis and Governor Hicks, of Maryland, in favor of Henry Winter Davis, shifted into high gear for Judge Montgomery Blair. Lincoln had arrived in Washington on February 23 at 6 A.M. By afternoon of the same day the venerable Frank Blair and his son Montgomery called on Lincoln.[194] The Blairs were actively co-operating with the anti-Seward, anti-Weed men of New York.[195] Weed, back again in Washington, supported the candidacy of Henry Winter Davis over any of the Blairs, and so did the New York *World*.[196] Somewhat uncertain of success, the Blairs appealed to Congressman Henry L. Dawes, of Massachusetts, to bring pressure on Lincoln. The elder Blair, one of the most experienced living politicians, and his son Frank, Jr., finally prevailed. Henry Winter Davis was dropped from consideration; Montgomery Blair was chosen.[197]

There still remained the question of Cameron and Chase. Lincoln wanted the Ohioan, but he still felt that it was politically expedient to conciliate the Pennsylvania element. David Dudley Field, Hiram Barney, and other anti-Weed Republicans were in Washington, violently opposing Cameron's appointment and insisting that Chase be taken into the Cabinet. Ohio members of Congress circulated a petition in Chase's favor.[198] Leaders of the Free Soil Democratic element of Massachusetts also waited on Lincoln in favor of Chase.[199] On the other hand, the opposition was formidable. Not only did Weed and his lieutenants oppose Chase, but so, too, did United States Senator Benjamin F. Wade, of Ohio.[200] Moreover, there was ever lurking behind the scenes

S. Boutwell to Banks (copy), March 8, 1861, Nathaniel P. Banks Papers, Essex Institute.

[194] New York *Herald*, Feb. 24, 1861. For the efforts of certain groups, including Judge Davis, in behalf of Henry Winter Davis, see Whitney, *Lincoln the President*, p. 15; New York *Herald*, Feb. 26, 1861; New York *World*, March 4, 1861; Cincinnati *Daily Gazette*, March 2, 1861.

[195] "The Diary of a Public Man," *The North American Review*, CXXIX (1879), 261.

[196] W. E. Smith, *The Francis Preston Blair Family in Politics*, I, 514.

[197] *Ibid.*, pp. 514–15.   [198] New York *Herald*, Feb. 26, 1861.

[199] J. Z. Goodrich to Andrew, Feb. 25, 1861, Andrew Papers.

[200] New York *Daily Tribune*, March 7, 1861; J. Z. Goodrich to Andrew, Feb. 25, 1861, Andrew Papers. "The fight . . . between the friends of Chase and Cameron," wrote a newspaper correspondent, "is most terrific. Greeley is furious. This morn-

in Willard's Hotel the portly figure of David Davis. An observer wrote:

Judge Davis, of Illinois, is already recognized as a power behind the throne, and is almost as much sought after as Mr. Lincoln himself. His apartments are steadily crowded with place-seekers, high and low. His influence is known to have done most towards putting Cameron and Smith in the Cabinet, and papers bearing his endorsement are considered gilt-edged in the place-market. . . . The Judd faction look decidedly blue at the prevalence of their rivals.[201]

By the close of February Lincoln had decided on a solution for his Cabinet troubles: He would take both Chase[202] and Cameron[203] into his Cabinet; with this in mind, he sent for Cameron. The latter declared at first that he could consider no other portfolio than the Treasury. Lincoln suggested the Interior and, finally, the War Department, which Cameron accepted.[204]

With his Cabinet complete, the harassed President-elect breathed a bit more easily. On the last day of February informal word came from Washington that Seward would be Secretary of State, Chase Secretary of the Treasury, Cameron Secretary of War, Montgomery Blair Secretary of the Navy, Caleb B. Smith Secretary of the Interior, Gideon Welles Postmaster General, and Edward Bates Attorney General.[205] This was Lincoln's Cabinet as finally formed—except that Blair was to be Postmaster General and Welles Secretary of the Navy.

One more obstacle Lincoln had to surmount before all was settled—the opposition of Seward and his friends to Chase's appointment. A delegation of Seward followers called on Lincoln on March 2 and pointed to the incongruity of both Seward and Chase sitting in the same Cabinet. Seward would not wish it; in

---

ing he told a member of Congress that Mr. Lincoln had sold out to Seward and the New York brokers." New York *Herald*, Feb. 28, 1861.

[201] New York *Herald*, Feb. 28, 1861.

[202] Cincinnati *Daily Gazette*, March 1, 1861.

[203] One correspondent claimed: "The appointment of Senator Cameron to the Secretaryship of the Treasury is a fixed fact. . . . The impressions received by the President-elect at Harrisburg, and the representations of Senator Seward, brought about this termination of the protracted squabble." See New York *Herald*, Feb. 27, 1861.

[204] New York *Daily Tribune*, March 2, 4, 1861.

[205] New York *Herald*, March 1, 1861.

fact his New York friends would not tolerate it, they argued. Lincoln, who had listened intently, then explained his ambition to form a Cabinet that would have the entire nation's confidence; that he respected and admired both Seward and Chase and had hoped to have them both in his service. However, the President-elect added, a change could be made if absolutely necessary. How would it be to have Chase as Secretary of the Treasury and William L. Dayton, of New Jersey, as Secretary of State, and Seward as Minister to England? This was more than the delegation bargained for and they withdrew with convenient speed, leaving the decision in Lincoln's hands.[206]

There is some evidence to indicate that the delegation to Lincoln was inspired by Seward or Weed or possibly by both. For on the very day of the delegation's visit, March 2, Seward sent Lincoln a letter withdrawing his consent to enter the Cabinet because of "circumstances" which had occurred since his original acceptance of the State portfolio.[207] Instead of accepting Seward's decision, the President-elect on March 4, Inauguration Day, asked the New York Senator to reconsider. "The public interest, I think," he wrote Seward, "demands that you should; and my personal feelings are deeply enlisted in the same direction—Please consider, and answer by 9 o'clock, A.M. tomorrow." [208] Seward reconsidered while Lincoln was being inaugurated. On March 5 he sent Lincoln another letter rescinding his declination and accepting the post of Secretary of State.[209] As he wrote to his wife: "At all events I did not dare to go home, or to England, and leave the country to chance." [210]

At twelve o'clock on Monday, March 4, 1861, the Democrats had a majority in the Senate presided over by Vice President John C. Breckinridge, of Kentucky. At one o'clock the same day the Republicans had a Senate majority, and on the dais sat Vice President Hamlin, a Maine Republican. So many secessionists

---

[206] "The Diary of a Public Man," *The North American Review,* CXXIX (1879), 271–73.

[207] Seward to Lincoln (copy), March 2, 1861, Seward Papers.

[208] Lincoln to Seward, March 4, 1861, Seward Papers.

[209] Seward to Lincoln (copy), March 5, 1861, Seward Papers. See also John Bigelow Diary, MS, March 27, 1861.

[210] Seward to Mrs. Seward, March 8, 1861, in F. W. Seward, *Seward at Washington as Senator and Secretary of State,* II, 518.

had left to follow their states out of the Union that Lincoln knew the upper chamber would confirm the nominations for his Cabinet. Accordingly when the Senate reassembled on Tuesday morning Lincoln laid before it the names of the following:

William H. Seward of New York for Secretary of State·
Salmon P. Chase of Ohio for Secretary of the Treasury
Simon Cameron of Pennsylanvia for Secretary of War
Gideon Welles of Connecticut for Secretary of the Navy
Caleb B. Smith of Indiana for Secretary of the Interior
Montgomery Blair of Maryland for Postmaster General
Edward Bates of Missouri for Attorney General.[211]

Probably no president of the United States was ever beset with greater difficulties in choosing his chief advisers than was Lincoln. Elected by a new party which was a composite of many mutually suspicious groups, it was quite impossible for him to select a cabinet of like-minded men. He was virtually compelled to give all the main elements in the party cabinet representation. This he did with great sagacity.That those selected were unable to work in harmony, as we shall see, should not surprise us. Circumstances over which Lincoln had no control forced him to form a cabinet unique in our political history. His presidential headaches, however, were just beginning.

[211] Seward to Mrs. Seward, pp. 517–18; Whitney, *Lincoln the President,* p. 1.

Chapter III

TO THE VICTORS

THE ARDUOUS TASK of cabinet-making was far from completed
before Lincoln was beset with a swarm of office seekers.
Indeed, Washington became a veritable mecca for patronage
mongers bent upon securing consulships, Indian agencies, postmasterships, or anything else in the gift of the appointing power.
Those who witnessed the rush of job hunters could not easily forget the spectacle.[1] Wrote home a Michigan Congressman: "The
City is overwhelmed with a crowd of rabid, persistent office-seekers
—the like never was experienced before in the history of the Government."[2] An Indiana member reminisced later: "I met at every
turn a swarm of miscellaneous people, many of them looking as
hungry and fierce as wolves, and ready to pounce upon members
[of Congress] as they passed, begging for personal intercessions,
letters of recommendation, etc. During my stay in Washington
through the months of March and April, there was no pause in
this business. . . . The scuffle for place was unabated."[3] One of
Lincoln's Cabinet in a letter to his son declared that "the rush
for office is overwhelming."[4] James R. Doolittle, Republican
United States Senator from Wisconsin, his nerves frayed by appeals of patronage hunters, gave vent to the written outburst: "I
am sick and nauseated with this miserable, selfish clamoring for
appointment to office. I sometimes wish I had never recommended
a man."[5] And the eccentric Count Adam Gurowski, viewing the

<hr>

[1] Aldrich, "At Lincoln's First Inauguration," *Annals of Iowa,* Series III, VIII
(April, 1907), 45; Hay, "Life in the White House in the Time of Lincoln," *The
Century Magazine,* Nov., 1890, p. 33; Speech of Representative Charles W. Willard,
of Vermont, April 17, 1872, in *Congressional Globe,* 42d Congress, 2d Session,
p. 2513.

[2] Henry Waldron to Howard, March 2, 1861, Jacob M. Howard Papers.

[3] Julian, *Political Recollections, 1840 to 1872,* pp. 193–94.

[4] Edward Bates to Barton Bates, March 22, 1861, Edward Bates Papers.

[5] Sellers, "James R. Doolittle," *The Wisconsin Magazine of History,* XVII
(March, 1934), 297–98.

scene, confided to his diary in this same month of March 1861, his impressions:

What a run, a race for offices. This spectacle likewise new to me.
The Cabinet Ministers, or, as they call them here, the Secretaries, have old party debts to pay, old sores to avenge or to heal, and all this by distributing offices, or by what they call it here—patronage. Through patronage and offices everybody is to serve his friends and his party, and to secure his political position. Some of the party leaders seem to me similar to children enjoying a long-expected and ardently wished for toy. . . . They, the leaders, look to create engines for their own political security, but no one seems to look over Mason and Dixon's line to the terrible and with lightning-like velocity spreading fire of hellish treason.[6]

That the members of Lincoln's Cabinet bickered over the allotment of jobs to their followers and favorites was apparent. "They are squabbling around me, in a quasi Cabinet council," said Attorney General Bates in a letter to an associate, "about the distribution of loaves & fishes." [7]

For the most part Lincoln permitted his Cabinet officers to choose their chief aides. Seward selected his son Frederick as Assistant Secretary of State.[8] The younger Seward in later years claimed that all clerks in the State Department loyal to the Union were retained by his father.[9] Nevertheless, the names of at least two of Seward's political associates from New York appear on the departmental roster—his campaign biographer, George E. Baker, and his publisher, James C. Derby.[10] It is to Seward's credit, however, that he retained the veteran William Hunter as chief clerk. For years Hunter had been the personification of the State Department, having been appointed first by John Quincy

[6] *Diary of Adam Gurowski*, I, 16–17.

[7] Edward Bates to Broadhead, March 26, 1861, James O. Broadhead Papers.

[8] F. W. Seward, *Reminiscences of a War-Time Statesman and Diplomat, 1830–1915*, p. 139.

[9] F. W. Seward, *Seward at Washington as Senator and Secretary of State*, II, 520.

[10] *Register of Officers and Agents, Civil, Military, and Naval, in the Service of the United States on the Thirtieth September, 1861* . . . , page 1. (Hereafter cited as *U. S. Official Register, 1861*.) See also Derby, *Fifty Years among Authors, Books and Publishers*, pp. 477–80; George E. Baker to Seward, Aug. 2, 1852, Seward Papers.

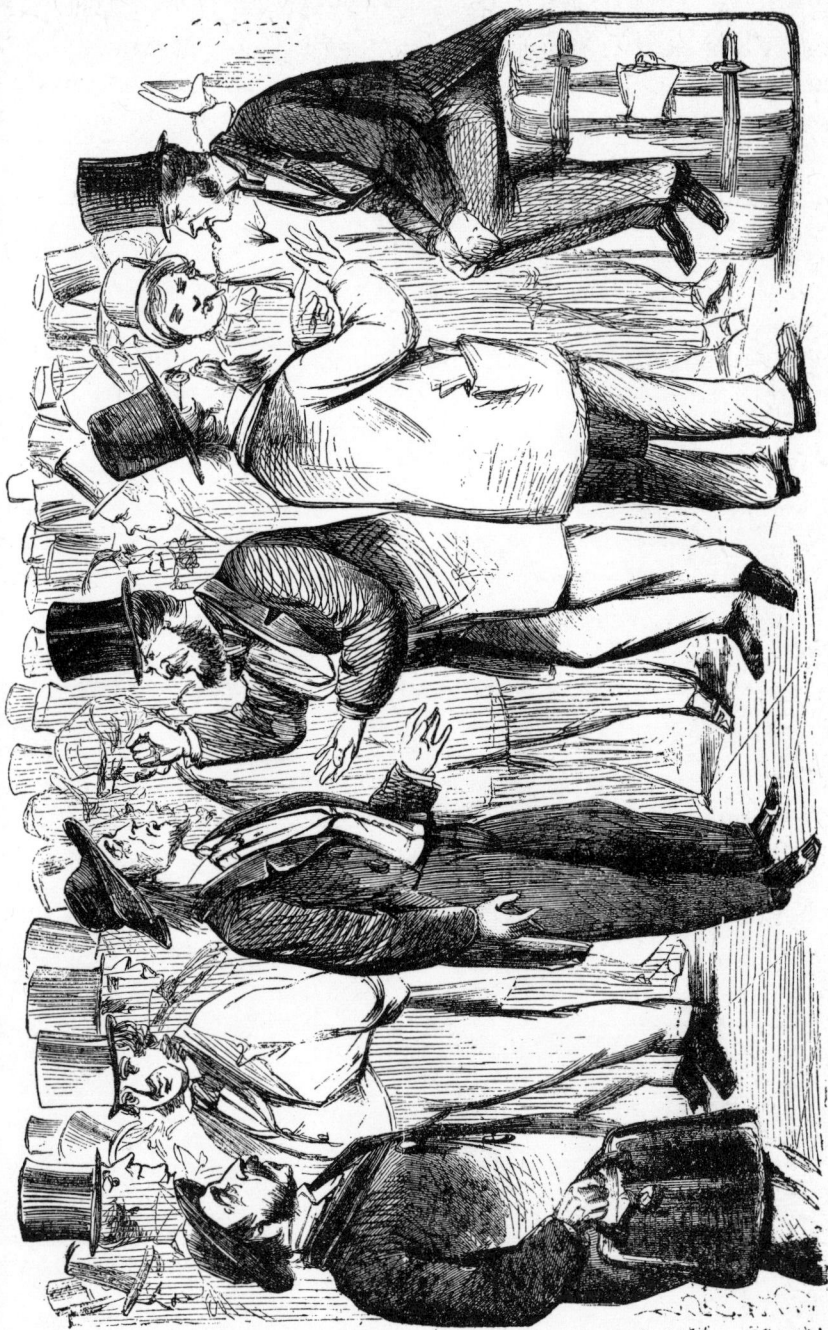

OFFICE SEEKERS AT WASHINGTON

From *Harper's Weekly*, V (March 16, 1861), 176.

Adams and having been retained by each succeeding Secretary of State.[11]

Cameron, in distributing the War Department offices, lived up to his reputation as a spoilsman. There being at the time no post of Assistant Secretary of War, Cameron gave to his faithful henchman, John P. Sanderson, the most desirable position at his disposal, the chief clerkship of the War Department. At the Chicago Convention Sanderson had extracted from Lincoln's managers the promise of a Cabinet position for Cameron in return for Pennsylvania's vote. For this deal Sanderson was handsomely rewarded.[12] As far as the subordinate positions in the War Department were concerned, Cameron early intimated that he expected them to be vacated and to be filled by others, who, as the New York *Tribune* put it, "had not enjoyed the flesh-pots." [13] Undoubtedly there was justification for the removal of War Department clerks disloyal to the Union or suspected of secessionist tendencies. That many were removed for party rather than patriotic reasons, however, was evident when the military officers in charge of the several bureaus of the department joined with General Winfield Scott, Chief of Staff, in remonstrating against wholesale dismissals.[14] The mismanagement, extravagance, and corruption of the department while Cameron was at its head were indices of his own incompetence and dishonesty and of the inexperience and shortcomings of his favorites whom he placed in office.[15]

The other Cabinet officers were not slow in expressing their gratitude to their followers. Blair tendered the First Assistant Postmaster General's position to John A. Kasson, a founder of the Iowa Republican party, who had spent years in St. Louis with Frank Blair and had supported the Blair family's plans to have Bates nominated for president. Kasson also had the support of

11 F. W. Seward, *Seward at Washington*, II, 519.

12 Meneely, *The War Department, 1861*, p. 108; Philadelphia *North American and United States Gazette*, March 22, 1861; J. P. Sanderson to Cameron, Oct. 1, 1860, Cameron Papers.

13 New York *Daily Tribune*, March 23, 1861.

14 Philadelphia *Press*, March 28, 1861.

15 Meneely, *The War Department, 1861*, chap. x; Shannon, *The Organization and Administration of the Union Army, 1861–1865*, pp. 55–73.

Senator Grimes, of Iowa.[16] Attorney General Bates selected as his Assistant Attorney General, Titian J. Coffey, a Pennsylvania Republican who in his youth had read law in Bates's office in St. Louis and in 1860 had worked to line up Keystone State support for Bates for president.[17] Moreover, Bates was able to place his son Richard on the government pay roll as a clerk in the Department of Justice.[18] Secretary of the Navy Welles brought with him to Washington his political associate, William Faxon, who had aided him in organizing the Republican party of Connecticut. Welles made Faxon chief clerk of the Navy Department.[19] Lincoln interfered in Welles's department to the extent of having Welles appoint as Assistant Secretary of the Navy the competent naval man Gustavus Vasa Fox. Lincoln well realized the necessity of giving Welles a strong right bower versed in naval affairs.[20]

Secretary of the Interior Smith, next to Cameron, seems to have administered his department less competently than any other Cabinet member. Smith selected John P. Usher, a political colleague in Indiana politics, as his right-hand man, and made him Assistant Secretary of the Interior. Usher was an ardent Lincoln man and had taken the stump in behalf of Lincoln in the presidential campaign.[21] Smith found the rush for clerk's jobs in the Interior Department most trying, and he complained: "I am annoyed by the applications for Clerkships. The number is ten times greater than all the Clerkships in the Department." [22] But Smith, a veteran

[16] "John A Kasson, an Autobiography," *Annals of Iowa,* Series III, XII (July, 1920), 349–50; Louis Pelzer, "The History of Political Parties in Iowa from 1857 to 1860," *The Iowa Journal of History and Politics,* VII (April, 1909), 214–16.

[17] "The Diary of Edward Bates, 1859–1866," ed. by Howard K. Beale, *Annual Report,* American Historical Association, IV (1930), 107, 107 n., 182; McClure, *Old Time Notes of Pennsylvania,* I, 374; Philadelphia *Press,* March 8, 1861.

[18] New York *Herald,* April 11, 1861; *U. S. Official Register, 1861,* p. 189; O. Bates, *Bates, et al., of Virginia and Missouri,* p. 76.

[19] Trumbull, *The Memorial History of Hartford County, Connecticut,* I, 96, 606, 609–10; Noonan, *Nativism in Connecticut, 1829–1860,* p. 235.

[20] Paullin, "President Lincoln and the Navy," *The American Historical Review,* XIV (Jan., 1909), 289–90; *Confidential Correspondence of Gustavus Vasa Fox, Assistant Secretary of the Navy, 1861–1865,* ed. by Thompson and Wainwright, I, 3–46.

[21] *President Lincoln's Cabinet, by Honorable John P. Usher . . . with a Foreword and Sketch of the Author by Nelson H. Loomis,* pp. 5–7. Usher was active in the Indiana Republican party. See Seeds, *History of the Republican Party of Indiana,* I, 25.

[22] Caleb B. Smith to R. W. Thompson, April 13, 1861, Lincoln Cabinet Collection.

party wirepuller of many years' standing, was able to handle the situation. Among the Interior Department clerks appointed was Walter Corwin, son of Smith's old Whig party associate "Tom" Corwin.[23] By the end of March a Washington reporter informed his paper that "the Secretary of the Interior's administration of that Department has been very pleasing, thus far, to his numerous friends." [24] It was not long before Smith was pushing an unsavory scheme, engineered by speculators, to colonize Negroes in Central America.[25]

The most competent appointments of subordinates made by any member of Lincoln's original Cabinet seem to have been made by Chase. For his Assistant Secretary of the Treasury Chase chose George Harrington, whose long experience in the Treasury Department under other administrations peculiarly qualified him for the added responsibility of planning a financial program for a nation about to be plunged into civil war.[26] However, by 1860 Harrington had become a strong disciple of Republican doctrine and had served as a delegate from the District of Columbia to the convention that nominated Lincoln for President.[27] Chase, with Lincoln's help, prevailed upon a Democrat, John J. Cisco, Assistant Treasurer at New York—who had served with distinction under Presidents Pierce and Buchanan—to continue in his position, despite the fact that Cisco had opposed Lincoln's election and was reluctant to accept Chase's proffer.[28] Another excellent appointment by Chase was that of Elisha Whittlesey, of Ohio, as First Comptroller of the Treasury. Whittlesey, a former Whig, had served under President Taylor in the same position and had even been continued by President Pierce, a Democrat.[29] Whittlesey's selection for the position, through which checks were issued in payment of government services, was lauded even by the Demo-

23 Cincinnati *Daily Gazette*, March 13, 1861.

24 *Ibid.*, March 29, 1861.

25 For Smith's vigorous support of the Chiriqui colonization scheme and its irregular character, see Caleb B. Smith to R. W. Thompson, Oct. 25, 1861, Richard W. Thompson Papers; J. P. Usher to R. W. Thompson, Dec. 26, 1861, Lincoln Cabinet Collection; *Diary of Gideon Welles*, I, 123, 150 ff.

26 Seward, *Seward at Washington*, II, 525; Cincinnati *Daily Gazette*, March 13, 1861.

27 Halstead, *Caucuses of 1860*, p. 128.

28 Field, *Memories of Many Men and of Some Women*, pp. 166–67, 253–54.

29 *The National Cyclopaedia of American Biography*, XIV, 523.

cratic press. His appointment, commented the New York *Herald*, "is rather unwelcome news to the sharks hereabouts, who expect to fatten off this administration." [30] James Madison Cutts, a Democrat and Stephen A. Douglas's father-in-law, whom Buchanan had appointed as an auditor in the Treasury Department in an effort to pacify Douglas, was promoted to the second comptrollership.[31] Still another creditable act on the part of Chase was his insistence on retaining the Democrat, James W. Taylor, of Minnesota, unusually gifted special Treasury agent, whose duties were to investigate reciprocal trade relations between the United States and Canada. Chase, a personal friend of Taylor, stood firm in his decision to continue him in his position, despite the efforts of an influential Minnesota Republican, Lieutenant Governor Ignatius Donnelly, to have Taylor dismissed and himself appointed.[32]

Despite Secretary Chase's independent, comparatively nonpartisan policy, his department was heavily loaded with political appointments. Francis E. Spinner, elected to Congress as an antislavery Democrat in 1854, had bolted his party to vote with the Republicans in the sharp contest for Speaker of the House of Representatives and had vigorously supported Lincoln in the recent campaign. He was rewarded with the Treasurership of the United States.[33] Lucius E. Chittenden, Vermont Republican who had rendered yeoman service by stumping Pennsylvania for Lincoln and Hamlin, had solicited a federal job and was made Register of the Treasury.[34] Lincoln prevailed on Chase to select his friend Nathan Sargent as Commissioner of Customs. By way of explanation, the President said: "I have felt myself obliged to refuse the post-office at this place [Washington] to my old friend Nathan Sargent, which wounds him, and consequently me, very deeply. He now says there is an office in your department, called the 'Com-

[30] New York *Herald*, March 30, 1861.

[31] Milton, *The Eve of Conflict: Stephen A. Douglas and the Needless War*, pp. 255–56, 255 n., 271–72; *U. S. Official Register, 1861*, p. 16.

[32] Blegen, "James Wickes Taylor: A Biographical Sketch," *Minnesota History Bulletin* (Nov., 1915), I, 155–58, 161, 171–72; Franklin F. Holbrook, "The Early Political Career of Ignatius Donnelly, 1857–1863," p. 71.

[33] Hartley, "General Francis E. Spinner, The Financier," *Magazine of American History*, XXV (March, 1891), 186–87, 192, 195; *Dictionary of American Biography*, XVII, 460.

[34] Chittenden, *Recollections of President Lincoln and His Administration*, pp. 17–18; *The National Cyclopaedia of American Biography*, XIII, 553.

missioner of Customs,' which the incumbent, a Mr. Ingham, wishes
to vacate. I will be much obliged if you agree for me to appoint Mr.
Sargent to this place." [35] Chase complied with the President's
wishes and Sargent—an old Whig who years before had written for
the cause of Whiggery under the nom de plume "Oliver Oldschool"
—was thus able to continue his residence at the National Capital.[36]

Other loyal Republicans found berths inside the staunch pillars
of the Treasury, among them John C. Underwood, of Virginia,
who was awarded the post of Fifth Auditor of the Treasury. Underwood, organizer of the infant Republican party of Virginia, had
been a delegate to the Chicago Convention.[37] James Pollock, former
Governor of Pennsylvania and a warrior against the Democrats
for years, was made Director of the United States Mint at Philadelphia.[38] Lincoln, when hard-pressed on one occasion, requested
Pollock to find employment for one who needed a job. "You must
make a job for the bearer of this," wrote the President, "make
a job of it with the collector and have it done. You *can* do it for
me and you *must*." [39]

Politically and financially, the collectors of the customs posts
were among the most important at the disposal of the Administration. Particularly was this true of the collectorships of the great
American seaports. That at the metropolis of the Empire State
was the most lucrative.[40] "There is no situation in the U. States
which enables the incumbent to exert such influence (and at the
same time do his duty) as the Collectorship of New York," [41] one
political observer had written in the 1840's; to another this position

35 Lincoln to Chase, May 10, 1861, in *Complete Works of Abraham Lincoln*, VI,
269.
36 *New Letters and Papers of Lincoln*, ed. by Angle, p. 257; *The New England
Historical and Genealogical Register*, XXIX (1875), 323–24; *U. S. Official Register,
1861*, p. 24.
37 John C. Underwood to Pratt, May 31, 1860, enclosed in Pratt to A. H. Conner,
June 9, 1860, Daniel D. Pratt Papers; Lanman, *Biographical Annals of the Civil
Government of the United States*, p. 436; *U. S. Official Register, 1861*, p. 19.
38 Philadelphia *Press*, April 20, 1861; Freeze, *A History of Columbia County,
Pennsylvania*, pp. 134–38.
39 Lincoln to James Pollock, Aug. 15, 1861, in Ida M. Tarbell, *The Life of
Abraham Lincoln*, II, 344.
40 Goebel, *William Henry Harrison*, pp. 374–75; Bonney, *A Legacy of Historical
Gleanings*, II, 147–54; Salmon, "History of the Appointing Power of the President," *Papers of the American Historical Association*, I, No. 5 (1886), 84 n.–85 n.
41 Silas E. Burrows to General Van Rensselaer, Jan. 21, 1841, in Bonney, *A
Legacy of Historical Gleanings*, II, 148.

was "second only in influence to that of Postmaster-General." [42]
Under the caption "Fat Offices of New York," Horace Greeley's
Tribune informed its readers in 1860 that ranking first in importance and revenue was the collectorship, with its fixed salary of
$6,340, and some $20,000 more in the form of "pickings and
fees." [43] Before Lincoln's first administration had run its four
years, the Surveyor of the Port estimated the number of employees
in the New York Custom House at 1,200 and the assessment on
their salaries for political party purposes at 2 percent.[44]

Over the award of the New York collectorship a bitter fight was
waged between the Seward-Weed wing and the Bryant-Barney
forces, allied to Chase and now openly supported by Greeley. The
two New York factions had crossed swords in early January when,
in party caucus, Littlejohn, candidate of the Seward-Weed interests, had defeated Lucius Robinson for the party's nomination for
the speakership of the state assembly. "His [Thurlow Weed's]
friends," declared an Albany observer, "have made the rural members [of the Assembly] believe that Thurlow is to be the person
that will deal out the soup for New York, and every person who is
expecting to share in the good things of Lincoln's administration
from the Empire State, must apply through him and at his favor.
Upon this point and this alone, was Mr. Littlejohn nominated and
Mr. Robinson defeated." [45] Complaint to Lincoln by the anti-
Seward-Weed faction that Weed was giving the impression that
he was to be the chief distributor of federal jobs for New York
had brought forth a mild rebuke from the President-elect:

. . . As to the matter of dispensing patronage, it perhaps will
surprise you to learn that I have information that you claim to
have my authority to arrange that matter in New York. I do not
believe that you have so claimed; but still so some men say. On that

[42] *The Private Correspondence of Henry Clay*, ed. by Colton, p. 448.

[43] New York *Daily Tribune*, Dec. 29, 1860.

[44] See testimony of Rufus Andrews in Weed-Opdyke suit in New York *Herald*,
Dec. 30, 1864.

[45] New York *Herald*, Jan. 3, 1861. A New Yorker wrote Governor Andrew of
Mass.: "Mr. Littlejohn is re-elected Speaker of our Assembly. That is a decided
snub to the Tribune. The seeming contest between him & Mr. Robinson was really
one for *dominion* between Mr. Weed & Mr. Greeley." See E. Howland to Andrew,
Jan. 1, 1861, John A. Andrew Papers.

subject you know all I have said to you is "Justice to all," and I have said nothing more particular to any one. I say this to reassure you that I have not changed my position.

In the hope, however, that you will not use my name in the matter, I am,

Yours truly,

A. LINCOLN [46]

Weed's chagrin that he could not control the entire patronage game must have been great indeed. Apparently it was of no greater proportions, however, than Greeley's disgust for the tactics of Weed and his followers. "The thieves hunt in gangs," wrote Greeley in March, 1861, "and each helps all the rest. Three quarters of the post-offices will go into the hands of the corruptionists." [47]

Years later Charles A. Dana, long associated with Greeley in editing the New York *Tribune*, expressed in no uncertain terms the fears of the anti-Weed leaders:

Some of the Republican leaders of New York who had been instrumental in preventing Mr. Seward's nomination to the presidency, and in securing that of Mr. Lincoln, had begun to fear that they would be left out in the cold in the distribution of the offices. General James S. Wadsworth, George Opdyke, Lucius Robinson, T. B. Carroll, and Henry B. Stanton were among the number of these gentlemen. Their apprehensions were somewhat mitigated by the fact that Mr. Chase, to whom we were all friendly, was Secretary of the Treasury. But, notwithstanding, they were afraid that the superior tact and pertinacity of Mr. Seward and of Mr. Thurlow Weed, Seward's close friend and political manager, would get the upper hand. . . . Accordingly, several of them determined to go to Washington, and I was asked to go with them.

I believe the appointment for our interview with the President was made through Mr. Chase.[48]

Lincoln assured them, Dana asserted, that one side should not gobble up everything. "Make out a list of places and men you

---

[46] Lincoln to Thurlow Weed, Feb. 4, 1861, in *Complete Works of Abraham Lincoln*, VI, 104-5.

[47] Greeley to B. Brockway of Watertown, N.Y., March 12, 1861, Horace Greeley Papers, Library of Congress.

[48] Dana, *Recollections of the Civil War*, pp. 2-3.

want," Lincoln told them, "and I will endeavor to apply the rule of give and take." [49]

The Greeley-Bryant-Barney-Chase faction pressed George Opdyke, defeated Republican candidate for mayor of New York, for Collector. The Seward-Weed group backed the merchant Simeon Draper, but were willing to take the banker Richard M. Blatchford if Draper were unacceptable.[50] Much to Seward's and Weed's embarrassment, however, Lincoln bestowed the New York collectorship on Hiram Barney, one of the principal anti-Weed leaders and bosom friend of Chase. The hand of the Secretary of the Treasury was clearly seen in the selection.[51] Rufus Andrews and Henry B. Stanton, two radicals who had given loyal service to the Republican organization, were named as Barney's subordinates.

In some respects Barney had a thankless task, for at once he was besieged by applicants for places. Indeed the New York Custom House became a miniature Washington as hundreds of eager office seekers aggressively thronged its rotunda; besides, Barney did not dismiss Democrats fast enough to satisfy certain New York City and Brooklyn Republicans, who soon began agitating for his removal.[52]

The rivalry between the two New York Republican factions came to the fore again in the appointment of Naval Officer of New York—next to the Collector's job the juiciest of plums in the Custom House. Lincoln attached vital importance to this office.[53] William Cullen Bryant and his *Evening Post* associate, Parke Godwin, affiliated with the anti-Weed faction, were backing Isaac Henderson for the post of Naval Officer.[54] Henderson traveled to Washington a few days after the inaugural, but returned to New

[49] Dana, *Recollections of the Civil War,* p. 3. When advised by General Wadsworth that the anti-Seward-Weed delegation would be unable to remain in Washington, but would leave a list "with Mr. Carroll," the President replied: "Let Mr. Carroll come in tomorrow, and we will see what can be done."

[50] New York *Herald,* Feb. 25, 1861.

[51] Greeley's *Tribune* commented: "The appointment of Hiram Barney as Collector was foreshadowed when Mr. Chase as one of the Cabinet was announced." See New York *Daily Tribune,* March 12, 1861.

[52] Brummer, *Political History of New York State during the Period of the Civil War,* pp. 136, 136 n, 137.

[53] Lincoln referred to the New York Naval Office as "so high an office." See Lincoln to Chase, May 18, 1861, in *Complete Works of Abraham Lincoln,* VI, 274.

[54] John Bigelow Diary, MS, Jan. 22, 26, 1861.

York very disheartened from his first expedition as an office hunter.[55] Evidently, Lincoln—still practicing his "Justice to all" policy—was determined not to give to the anti-Weed Republicans both the collectorship and the naval office. The close of March saw no appointment of Naval Officer. United States Senator Preston King was tenacious in pushing Philip Dorsheimer, a German-American leader, for the place. Weed, who was in Washington, watched developments with an eagle eye and finally came forward with a compromise candidate in the personage of John Bigelow, formerly associated in editing the *Post*, but who, unlike Bryant and Godwin, had supported Seward for president. At length Lincoln tired of the factional bickering, made an appointment of his own choice for Naval Officer—George Dennison, who was being pressed for the position by an Illinois friend. Chase opposed Dennison's selection, but Lincoln was firm. To the Secretary of the Treasury he explained: "I believe I have told you fully what it was, and is, that pressed me to appoint him: the urgent solicitation of an old friend who has served me all my life, and who has never before received or asked anything in return." [56]

Despite the fact that Chase's friend Barney had the coveted collectorship, the Seward-Weed faction emerged the victor in receiving the lion's share of Treasury offices in New York—notwithstanding Lincoln's expressed determination to remain impartial in the contest between the two Empire State factions. The interests of the Seward followers in New York State were apparently better protected by their leader than were those of his opponents by Chase.[57] Unquestionably Seward and Weed had a distinct advantage over Chase, for the majority of New York's representatives in Congress belonged to the Seward-Weed faction. By a gradual development through the decades Congress had established a strong claim to dictate many appointments.[58] Lincoln was fully aware of this fact and seems to have made it a uniform practice to discuss appointments not only with Cabinet officials but with

55 *Ibid.*, March 8, 14, 1861.

56 Lincoln to Chase, May 18, 1861, in *Complete Works of Abraham Lincoln*, VI, 274. Henderson was subsequently made Naval Agent, in which post his record was most corrupt.

57 Brummer, *Political History of New York State during the Period of the Civil War*, p. 137.

58 Riddle, *Recollections of War Times, 1860–1865*, p. 18.

Republican members of both the Senate and the House. He apparently had no desire to flout the traditional practice of "senatorial courtesy," nor did he try to avoid the time-honored custom of heeding the wishes of representatives, as far as most offices were concerned.[59]

Chase fully appreciated that in the matter of the New York patronage Seward had the whip hand. Under date of March 27, 1861, we find him informing Seward—probably reluctantly—that the appraisership at New York was vacant and inquiring "Which of the applicants do you prefer?" [60] Two weeks earlier Chase had indicated in correspondence with John Bigelow that the New York appointments were only "very partially" under his control. "The President desires," he wrote, "that all the Republican interests be consulted & in doing so it is necessary to make other concessions." [61] The rivalry that characterized even the minor appointments for New York provided Lincoln with opportunity to indulge in a bit of humor. On one occasion he wrote Chase: "Ought Mr. Young to be removed, and if yea, ought Mr. Adams to be appointed? Mr. Adams is magnificently recommended; but the great point in his favor is that Thurlow Weed and Horace Greeley join in recommending him. I suppose the like never happened before, and never will again; so it is now or never. What say you?" [62]

Only less important than the Treasury patronage in New York was that in New England; the grand prize of that region was the Collectorship of the Port of Boston.[63] This was handed to John Z.

[59] Fish, "Lincoln and the Patronage," *The American Historical Review*, VIII (Oct., 1902), 59. The circumstances surrounding the appointment of the postmaster in Providence, R.I., were probably typical of Lincoln's policy in distributing less important offices. Governor William Sprague, of Rhode Island, recommended a candidate, but Lincoln would not consider him, since the position must go to a man recommended by the majority of Members of Congress. Lincoln added: "I follow the rule in this case." See Lincoln to Governor William Sprague, May 10, 1861, in *Complete Works of Abraham Lincoln*, VI, 270.

[60] F. Bancroft, *The Life of William H. Seward*, II, 356 n. In 1862 Chase wrote that he spent much time discussing New York appointments with Weed. See "Diary and Correspondence of Salmon P. Chase," *Annual Report*, American Historical Association, II (1902), 62.

[61] Chase to Bigelow, March 11, 1861, in Bigelow, *Retrospections of an Active Life*, I, 349.

[62] Lincoln to Chase, May 8, 1861, in *Complete Works of Abraham Lincoln*, VI, 268-69.

[63] For the powerful influence wielded by the Collector of Boston, see Darling, *Political Changes in Massachusetts, 1824-1848*, pp. 60-63, 67-69, 176-83, 195-97,

Goodrich, manufacturer of woolens and Republican state chairman of Massachusetts.[64]

The job of Naval Officer at Boston, the next most desirable government gift in New England, went to Amos Tuck, graduate of Dartmouth, Republican state chairman of New Hampshire, and an unsuccessful aspirant for a Cabinet seat.[65] Both Goodrich and Tuck were former Whigs, and it was a source of envy to the former Free Soil Democrats that both the best positions in New England should go to leaders of Whig antecedents. One Massachusetts Republican who had received his baptism in the Democratic party complained to Chase: "The [Congressional] Delegation have had *their* choice in Mr. Goodrich, an old Whig—never a Free Soiler. The President had *his* choice in Mr. Tuck for naval officer, an old Whig. . . . Though it [the Treasury] is your department, you have not had *your* choice." [66]

The rush for jobs in the Boston Custom House was staggering, and Governor Andrew, besieged by office hunters, gave out the statement: "I scarcely know what to do under the terrible trial and pressure on me of those who are led to believe that some thing from me would gain their wishes with Mr. Goodrich. . . . The Collector is wholly independent of me." [67] Andrew managed to obtain for his brother a job in the Custom House.[68] Another lucrative Treasury position in Massachusetts was that of Assistant Treasurer at Boston paying $4,000 per year; this went to Ezra Lincoln, a Bay State Republican leader who had aided in steering part of the Massachusetts delegation to Lincoln at the Chicago Convention.[69]

In Pennsylvania the Collector of the Port of Philadelphia wielded

214–15; Howe, *The Life and Letters of George Bancroft*, I, 224, 236; C. Hudson, "Life, Services, and Character of Levi Lincoln."

[64] Case, *The Goodrich Family in America*, pp. 172–73; *The National Cyclopaedia of American Biography*, IX, 557.

[65] Corning, *Amos Tuck*, pp. 83–85, 90–92; Everett S. Stackpole, *History of New Hampshire*, III, 332.

[66] Unknown person to Chase, April 11, 1861, in Fish, "Lincoln and the Patronage," *The American Historical Review*, VIII (Oct., 1902), 59.

[67] Andrew to James A. Fox, March 30, 1861 (copy), John A. Andrew Papers.

[68] Pearson, *The Life of John A. Andrew*, I, 171 n.

[69] Ezra Lincoln to Weed, June 2, 1860, Weed Papers, University of Rochester Library; *U. S. Official Register, 1861*, p. 22; Merriam, *The Life and Times of Samuel Bowles*, I, 139.

more influence than probably any other federal officer in the state.[70] There was an early and mad scramble between the Cameron and Curtin factions for the collectorship, and the rival candidates, chief of whom were David Taggart, Thomas Webster, Jr., former Governor Pollock, and Morton McMichael, spent their time between Philadelphia, Harrisburg, and Washington in quest of the prize.[71] The Pennsylvania appointments were not awarded until after the middle of April, but early in the month word came from Washington that "Willard's Hotel is crowded with Pennsylvanians attracted here by the approaching distribution." [72] From Harrisburg came the report: "General Cameron, Governor Curtin, Col. A. K. McClure, Senator Finney, and many of the leading Republican politicians of the State, have either gone or are on their way to Washington. These *indices* show clearly that the final determination of the Pennsylvania appointments is fast approaching." [73] Secretary Chase, not Cameron nor Curtin, had his way in filling the collectorship. Chase's selection was William B. Thomas, a wealthy Philadelphia flour manufacturer and one of the old antislavery faction who had been a leading organizer of the Keystone State Republican party.[74]

A warm contest was waged for Naval Officer of the Port of Philadelphia between Dr. Edward Wallace and Dr. Diller Luther, both of Reading, and P. C. Ellmaker and J. W. Pomeroy, both of Philadelphia. McClure, Curtin's lieutenant, backed Pomeroy.[75] Lincoln himself decided in favor of Wallace for the Naval Office— paying $5,000 per year,[76] primarily because he was related to Mrs. Lincoln by marriage.[77] Cameron was placated by being given a voice in the appointments to the Custom House, as is shown by

[70] Mueller, *The Whig Party in Pennsylvania*, pp. 161–62, 177.

[71] Philadelphia *Press*, Feb. 28, March 7, 16, 1861; Philadelphia *North American and United States Gazette*, March 28, 1861.

[72] Philadelphia *Press*, April 2, 1861.

[73] Philadelphia *North American and United States Gazette*, April 3, 1861.

[74] Scharf and Westcott, *History of Philadelphia, 1609–1884*, I, 719, 720, 722 n.; II, 2224; McClure, *Old Time Notes of Pennsylvania*, I, 454; Philadelphia *Press*, April 20, 1861; Winslow, *Biographies of Successful Philadelphia Merchants*, pp. 78–80.

[75] Philadelphia *Press*, March 7, 28, April 4, 1861.

[76] *U. S. Official Register, 1861*, p. 62.

[77] McClure, *Old Time Notes of Pennsylvania*, I, 454–55; Philadelphia *Press*, April 20, 1861.

Lincoln's letter to the newly appointed Naval Officer: "I now . . . at the urgent request of Gen. Cameron also, earnestly solicit you to appoint Col. John C. Myers, of your own city, the deputy Naval officer. You will personally oblige me by doing this, besides smoothing things which otherwise might be a little rough." [78]

Baltimore was another major American seaport. To this $6,000 collectorship Lincoln named Henry W. Hoffman, a prominent Cumberland lawyer. Hoffman had figured in an early 1860 "deal" whereby Henry Winter Davis, Maryland "Know-Nothing" Congressman, cast the deciding vote for the election of William Pennington, a New Jersey Republican, as Speaker of the House of Representatives, in return for which Hoffman became Sergeant at Arms.[79] Francis S. Corkran, a Baltimore Republican and delegate to the Chicago Convention, became Naval Officer at $5,000 yearly.[80]

F. S. Evans, a preacher and a staunch Maryland campaigner for Lincoln, sought the office of Deputy Naval Officer at the Baltimore Custom House.[81] Lincoln requested Corkran to make the appointment, but Corkran did not readily comply with the President's request. Nettled, Lincoln at once dispatched the following communication to Corkran:

I am quite sure you are not aware how much I am disobliged by the refusal to give Mr. F. S. Evans a place in the Custom-House. I had no thought that the men to whom I had given the higher offices would be so ready to disoblige me. I still wish you would give Mr. Evans the place of Deputy Naval Officer.[82]

When the obstinate Corkran still hesitated in caring for Evans, Lincoln communicated with Chase: "I have been greatly—I may say grievously—disappointed and disobliged by Mr. Corkran's refusal to make Mr. Evans deputy naval officer, as I requested him

[78] Lincoln to Dr. Edward Wallace, April 18, 1861, Lincoln Collection, Illinois State Historical Library.
[79] Scharf, *History of Western Maryland*, II, 1400; *U. S. Official Register, 1861*, p. 64. For the "deal" between Davis and the Republicans involving Hoffman, see Indianapolis *Daily State Sentinel*, Feb. 7, 1860; *Congressional Globe*, 36th Cong., 1st Sess., pp. 641, 650, 663; Greeley to Colfax, Nov. 6, 1859, Greeley-Colfax Papers.
[80] Baltimore *Sun*, April 27, 1860; *U. S. Official Register, 1861*, p. 65.
[81] Nelson (publisher), *History of Baltimore, Maryland*, p. 126.
[82] Lincoln to F. S. Corkran, May 6, 1861, in Angle (comp.), *New Letters and Papers of Lincoln*, pp. 271–72.

to do. A point must be strained to give Mr. Evans a situation." [83]
Whatever may have been Corkran's thought about the matter, he
finally yielded, and Evans became Deputy Naval Officer of Baltimore.[84]

In California, with its port of San Francisco, the Republican
party, as in many other states, was rent into factions largely over
the struggle for spoils. One major faction was led by Lincoln's old
Illinois friend, Edward D. Baker, who had gone to California and
there organized the Republican party. He had then proceeded to
Oregon, where, after performing a similar service, he had been
chosen United States Senator. Shortly after the inaugural, in
which the Oregon Senator played an important role, Lincoln, who
was to receive a delegation of Californians respecting appointments, invited Baker to breakfast with him. Baker accepted and
in the course of conversation it was evident that he hoped to dictate
all federal appointments for California. No sooner did Lincoln
give audience to the waiting California delegation than Baker's
right to be heard on the matter of California patronage was immediately challenged in his presence. The anti-Baker faction was
led by James W. Simonton, one of the editors of the San Francisco
Bulletin.[85] Simonton and his followers left with the President the
following memorandum, signed by thirty-five Republican leaders
of California:

TO HIS EXCELLENCY THE PRESIDENT OF THE UNITED STATES:—

The undersigned Republicans of the State of California respectfully and earnestly protest against the interference of the Hon.
E. D. Baker, Senator from Oregon, with the Federal appointments
in the State of California. *First*—Because some of the appointments
which Col. Baker desires would be very unacceptable to the party
in our State, and would be most injudicious and most prejudicial
to the public interests. *Secondly*—Because California is able and
willing to represent herself; and to attach her as an appendage to

---

[83] Lincoln to Chase, May 6, 1861, in *Complete Works of Abraham Lincoln*, VI,
266.

[84] *U. S. Official Register, 1861*, p. 65.

[85] Shutes, "Colonel E. D. Baker," *California Historical Society Quarterly*, XVII
(Dec., 1938), 303–18; Kennedy, *The Contest for California in 1861: How Colonel
E. D. Baker Saved the Pacific States to the Union*, p. 203; San Francisco *Daily
Evening Bulletin*, April 16, 1861.

Oregon would be to demoralize our party, and to expose us to the certainty of defeat in the next and subsequent elections.
Washington, March 28, 1861.[86]

The fight was now on in earnest and a furious struggle was waged over Baker's determination to place his own men in the key California positions: F. B. Folger for Collector of the Port of San Francisco; Willard B. Farwell for Naval Officer; R. J. Stevens (Baker's son-in-law) for Superintendent of the Mint in San Francisco; Samuel H. Parker for Postmaster of San Francisco; J. C. Birdseye for Sub-Treasurer at San Francisco.[87] Both major factions remaining adamant, the matter was finally settled by the White House: Ira P. Rankin, an anti-Baker leader, received the much-sought-for collectorship.[88] Rankin had been a Whig, had joined the Republicans in 1856, and had become a candidate for Congress in that lean year. Five years later he was rewarded with the most coveted federal job on the Pacific Coast.[89] To offset the Rankin appointment Lincoln gave the desirable post of Naval Officer of the Port of San Francisco to Farwell, Baker's choice. Farwell was editor of the Republican organ, the San Francisco *Alta California*, and for a time Baker's private secretary.[90] R. J. Stevens, a recent convert to Republicanism, became Superintendent of the Mint in the Pacific coast's greatest city.[91] Samuel H. Parker, also a Bakerite, received the San Francisco postmastership.[92] To balance the Stevens and Parker appointments, the anti-Baker group secured the Sub-Treasurership for D. W. Cheeseman,

[86] San Francisco *Daily Evening Bulletin,* April 17, 1861.

[87] San Francisco *Daily Evening Bulletin,* April 16, 1861. Folger was not Baker's first choice for the collectorship. The Oregon Senator had turned to him after being unable to place J. C. Birdseye, of Nevada, in the post, and after him one of the Washburn brothers.

[88] San Francisco *Daily Evening Bulletin,* April 23, 1861.

[89] Phelps, *Contemporary Biography of California's Representative Men,* p. 61.

[90] San Francisco *Daily Evening Bulletin,* April 16, 23, 29, 1861; "Brief Biography of Willard Brigham Farwell," *Quarterly of the Society of California Pioneers,* I (1924), 28–29; John D. Farwell, *The Farwell Family,* I, 351; Swasey, *The Early Days and Men of California,* p. 289.

[91] San Francisco *Daily Evening Bulletin,* April 16, 17, 23, 1861; New York *Daily Tribune,* April 5, 1861. Lincoln was very reluctant to appoint Stevens. The President's inability to go back on an implied promise to Mrs. Stevens (Baker's daughter) that her husband would have the place, counted heavily in Stevens's favor.

[92] San Francisco *Daily Evening Bulletin,* April 17, 23, 1861.

a delegate-at-large to the Chicago Convention and member of the Republican state committee of California.[93] Charles Watrous, also an anti-Bakerite and a delegate to the Chicago Convention, who had been so instrumental in swinging the appointment of Rankin as Collector, was given the position of Special Agent of the Post Office Department for California and Oregon.[94] The anti-Baker faction was elated that it had secured the greatest of prizes, and its organ advised its followers: "We pray all good Republicans who are dead set for an office, to stick by the Custom House. . . . To the Custom House, then! On Mr. Rankin pin your hopes." [95]

The minor seaports went to collectors whose Republicanism was unquestionable. The collectorship at Providence was awarded to Charles Anthony, an important manufacturer and a relative of Republican United States Senator Henry B. Anthony, of Rhode Island.[96] The other principal federal appointment in Rhode Island, namely, the postmastership of Providence, went to Walter C. Simmons, son of Senator Anthony's colleague, Senator James F. Simmons.[97] To Governor Sprague of Rhode Island, who recommended another man, Lincoln explained: "I think I had a letter from you some time ago naming a person whom you would like to have appointed post-master at Providence. . . . There is a difficulty such as I have not surmounted in any other case. It is that a different man, Walter C. Simmons, is recommended by both the senators and both the old representatives of the State, and also by one of the new representatives." [98]

The distribution of the postmasterships for the thousands of cities, towns, and villages throughout the nation invited additional scrambles among various factions. Before the month of March, 1861, was over, 15,000 applications had poured into the Post Office Department.[99] Postmaster-General Blair let it be known that in distributing the fourth-class postmasters' jobs he would be guided by the wishes of Republican Congressmen where such existed,

[93] San Francisco *Daily Evening Bulletin*, April 17, 23, 1861.   [94] *Ibid.*
[95] *Ibid.*, May 17, 1861.
[96] *Representative Men and Old Families of Rhode Island*, III, 1510–11; *U. S. Official Register, 1861*, p. 47.
[97] Providence *Daily Journal*, May 14, 1861; New York *Daily Tribune*, May 14, 1861.
[98] Lincoln to William Sprague, governor of Rhode Island, May 10, 1861, in *Complete Works of Abraham Lincoln*, VI, 270.
[99] Cincinnati *Daily Gazette*, March 22, 1861.

and by Republican "bosslets" in those districts having Democratic representatives. Appointments to first- and second-class post offices in the larger cities or towns would be made, the Postmaster General said, in conformity with the wishes of the Republican United States Senators in whose state the post office was located.[100] New York's leading Republican journal was even more explicit as far as fourth-class postmasters were concerned:

The appointments of postmasters, with salaries less than $1,000 per annum, will be made upon the recommendations of the members of Congress in the different districts. Applications addressed to them will receive attention earlier than if sent to the Department, and save much delay and trouble.[101]

For many, such a notice was unnecessary, for already representatives were being swamped with requests. Congressman Albert G. Riddle, of Cleveland, wrote that the number of applications was "immense." Among the many requests that came to him was this sample:

Cleveland, March 5, 1861

DEAR SIR:

This is pure business between us. If you will recommend me for Postmaster and stand by me, I will give you $2,000, whatever the outcome.

Respectfully,[102]

Riddle declared that the author of this letter was a well-known and reputable business man, well connected, and of high standing in his church.[103]

Over the Cincinnati postmastership a lively fight was waged. Secretary of the Treasury Chase backed T. C. Day, United States Senator Wade of Ohio and Secretary of the Interior Smith (a former Ohioan) gave their support to Benjamin Eggleston. But Congressman Gurley, of the Cincinnati district, was firm for J. C. Baum.[104] Baum was named.[105]

Instances in which the wishes of Republican United States Sena-

[100] Philadelphia *North American and United States Gazette,* March 12, 1861; Pierce, *Memoir and Letters of Charles Sumner,* IV, 32.
[101] New York *Daily Tribune,* March 13, 1861.
[102] Riddle, *Recollections of War Times, 1860–1865,* p. 21.
[103] *Ibid.*
[104] Cincinnati *Daily Gazette,* March 12, 14, April 1, 1861.
[105] *U. S. Official Register, 1861,* p. 306.

tors prevailed were those regarding the post offices in Cleveland and Boston. Senator Wade was consulted regarding the appointment of Edwin Cowles, editor of the Cleveland *Leader*, as postmaster at Cleveland, which lay in the general vicinity of his home, the Western Reserve region of Ohio.[106]

A spirited three-cornered contest was waged over the Boston post office. United States Senator Charles Sumner, a Bostonian, considered the office as being within his sphere of control. Sumner insisted that it go not to one of the three major aspirants, but to John G. Palfrey of Cambridge, a strong antislavery man.[107] After much wrangling the last obstacle to Palfrey's appointment was removed when Palfrey telegraphed Sumner in Washington that if necessary he could change his residence from Cambridge to Boston in three days' time.[108] The struggle for even the lesser post offices in New England's leading commonwealth was intense. "The Massachusetts leaders," wrote one Boston historian, "accustomed to plead the 'Cause of Immortal Ideas' were now concerned with the dispensing of third-class postmasterships and minor clerkships." [109]

The post office in New York City was eagerly coveted. Its salary, a mere $2,000 yearly, was supplemented with a "commission upon the rent of boxes, and sundry fees and grabbings, which, united, make the place worth from five to eight thousand honest dollars per annum." [110] Seward's choice, William B. Taylor, received this prize. Charges were made that Taylor was a Democrat, but Thurlow Weed's Albany *Evening Journal* came to his defense with the statement that Taylor was a bona fide Republican, formerly a Whig.[111] The Seward-Weed influence was also felt in the selection of George Dawson, Weed's friend and editorial colleague on the Albany *Evening Journal*, as postmaster of Albany.[112] Postmaster-

106 Lincoln to Postmaster-General Blair, March 12, 1861, in Tarbell, *The Life of Abraham Lincoln*, II, 340; Riddle, *Recollections of War Times, 1860–1865*, pp. 20–24.

107 Pierce, *Memoir and Letters of Charles Sumner*, IV, 32. For Palfrey, see "John Gorham Palfrey," *Report of the Numismatic and Antiquarian Society of Philadelphia, 1881*, pp. 25–28; *Proceedings of the American Antiquarian Society*, New Series, I (1880–81), 160–61.

108 Pearson, *The Life of John A. Andrew*, I, 172 n.

109 *Ibid.*, p. 171.   110 New York *Daily Tribune*, Dec. 29, 1860.

111 *Ibid.*, March 14, 16, 1861.

112 Howell and Tenney (eds.), *History of the County of Albany, N.Y.*, p. 360; Barnes, *Memoir of Thurlow Weed*, p. 29.

General Blair complained frequently that Seward had too much to say about appointments in the Post Office Department.[113]

The postmasterships in the other important centers throughout the country occasioned a good deal of wrangling between contending factions, but in each case care was taken to select men who had performed services to the Republican party. In Philadelphia the post office was awarded to a staunch party man, Cornelius Walborn, after a wordy contest in Philadelphia and Harrisburg and a final decision in Washington.[114] The Harrisburg postmastership went to George Bergner, editor of Cameron's organ, the *Pennsylvania Telegraph*.[115] The postmastership of the city of Washington, the nation's political capital, was bestowed on Lewis Clephane. Few persons had given such untiring service to the party as Clephane, former business manager of the antislavery organ, the Washington *National Era*, whose pages had first run Harriet Beecher Stowe's *Uncle Tom's Cabin* serially before its appearance in book form. While still associated with the *National Era*, in disseminating antislavery propaganda, Clephane formed in 1855 a small club known as the Republican Association of Washington. Acting for this organization, Clephane prepared the "call" which was issued for the meeting of anti-Democratic leaders at Pittsburgh that in turn made arrangements for the first Republican National Convention in 1856. He likewise had rendered indefatigable service in support of the Lincoln-Hamlin campaign. Few influential leaders contested Clephane's right to the Washington post office, and Lincoln himself even refused the position to Nathan Sargent, whom he referred to as "my old friend," in order to reward Clephane.[116]

In the West, too, the party faithful received their share of important post offices. Alexander H. Conner, chairman of the Re-

113 Statement of John A. Kasson, First Assistant Postmaster-General during 1861–62, to Frederic Bancroft, in F. Bancroft, *The Life of William H. Seward*, II, 357, 357 n.

114 Philadelphia *Press*, March 7, 28, April 4, 22, 1861.

115 Egle, *History of the Counties of Dauphin and Lebanon in the Commonwealth of Pennsylvania*, p. 465; Philadelphia *Press*, March 19, 1861.

116 W. C. Clephane, "Lewis Clephane: A Pioneer Washington Republican," *Records of the Columbia Historical Society*, XXI (1918), 263–74; Crandall, *The Early History of the Republican Party, 1854–1856*, pp. 51, 53, 284. At the time of Lincoln's election Clephane was president of the "Wideawakes," the Republican Club of Washington. Lincoln asked Chase to take care of Sargent in the Treasury Department.

publican state central committee of Indiana, who in the preceding
January had journeyed to Springfield to press on Lincoln Caleb
B. Smith's selection as Secretary of the Interior, was made postmaster at Indianapolis.[117] Archibald W. Campbell, organizer of
the Republican party in Western Virginia, delegate to the Chicago
Convention and editor of the Wheeling *Intelligencer*—one of the
few "Black Republican" journals in a slave state—was appointed
postmaster at Wheeling.[118] The post office in Detroit was filled by
William A. Howard, erstwhile Republican Congressman from
Michigan, who had done much missionary work for the party as
chairman of the Kansas Investigating Committee of Congress.
Howard in 1860 was also chairman of the Republican state central
committee of Michigan.[119]

The Chicago post office was tendered to John L. Scripps, associated in editing the Republican "bible" of Illinois, the Chicago
Press & Tribune. Scripps also had written a campaign biography
of Lincoln.[120] In the words of Scripps's daughter: "After the
election of Mr. Lincoln the Chicago postoffice was offered to the
Chicago *Tribune* and because of my father's work for the Lincoln
campaign, the honor of becoming Chicago's eleventh postmaster
was bestowed upon him." [121] St. Louis was another large center
in the West, and its post office was awarded to Peter L. Foy, associated with the Blair interests in editing the *Missouri Democrat*.
Foy had aided Frank Blair and B. Gratz Brown in building the
infant Republican party of Missouri.[122] The Des Moines, Iowa,
postmastership was given to the editor John Teesdale, whose paper,

[117] A. H. Conner to Pratt, April 23, June 15, July 26, 1860, Daniel D. Pratt
Papers; Seeds, *History of the Republican Party of Indiana*, I, 31; New York *Daily
Tribune*, April 10, 1861.

[118] Ambler, *West Virginia: Stories and Biographies*, pp. 237–38; New York
Daily Tribune, March 22, 1861, *U. S. Official Register, 1861*, p. 166.

[119] "The Death of Governor William A. Howard," *Michigan Pioneer Collections*,
IV (1881), 128; Crandall, *The Early History of the Republican Party, 1854–1856*,
pp. 204, 280, 282.

[120] Dyche, "John Locke Scripps, Lincoln's Campaign Biographer," *Journal, Ilinois
State Historical Society*, XVII (1924–25), 343–46. John Locke Scripps was a cousin
of James E. Scripps, one of the founders of the Scripps newspaper chain. See
Dictionary of American Biography, XVI, 519.

[121] *Ibid.*, p. 349.

[122] Stevens, "Lincoln and Missouri," *The Missouri Historical Review*, X (Jan.,
1916), 66. For Foy's services to the Republican party, see C. J. Corwin to "the
Editor," Feb. 29, 1860, John F. Snyder Papers; St. Louis *Daily Missouri Republican*, March 11, 1860.

the *Iowa State Register*, became the leading Republican paper in the Hawkeye State.[123] Teesdale had been exceedingly active in the campaign of 1860.[124] As for the San Francisco post office, that had gone, after angry wrangling between the Baker and the anti-Baker factions, to a follower of Senator Baker—a sound Republican—Samuel H. Parker.[125]

The Department of the Interior was another rich storehouse of jobs. The Secretary of the Interior, although not possessing as much patronage as the Postmaster General, nevertheless had several thousand positions at his disposal. And in the hands of Caleb B. Smith this department was utilized fully for party purposes. The five most lucrative jobs at his command were the Commissioner of Patents, Commissioner of Indian Affairs, Superintendent of Public Printing, Commissioner of Pensions, and Commissioner of the General Land Office.

In two of these, Patents and Indian Affairs, Secretary Smith succeeded in placing his own friends. David P. Holloway, a Republican editor of Indiana, was made Commissioner of Patents after a keen struggle. His chief contender for the position was George G. Fogg of New Hampshire, Secretary of the Republican National Committee. Smith insisted that it go to Holloway. Fogg's friends in the United States Senate held up Holloway's confirmation; Lincoln was able to settle the controversy only by appointing Fogg as Minister to Switzerland.[126]

The job of Commissioner of Indian Affairs went to Smith's friend William P. Dole, formerly of Indiana but then of Illinois. There is some evidence of an incomplete nature to indicate that Dole figured in the deal by which the Indiana delegates at the Chicago Convention were swung to Lincoln for the Republican presidential nomination, in return for which Lincoln's manager, Judge David Davis, promised a Cabinet position to Smith.[127] On this point the historian of Lincoln's nomination writes:

[123] Gue, *History of Iowa,* IV, 259–60.
[124] *Annals of Iowa,* IX (April, 1909), 52–53.
[125] San Francisco *Daily Evening Bulletin,* April 23, 1861.
[126] Cincinnati *Daily Gazette,* March 23, 1861; New York *Herald,* March 14, 29, 1861. For Holloway, see *Biographical History of Eminent and Self-made Men of the State of Indiana,* II, 277; Seeds, *History of the Republican Party of Indiana,* I, 20.
[127] Baringer, *Lincoln's Rise to Power,* pp. 214–15.

Indiana's 26 votes were for sale in exchange for two offices, Secretary of the Interior and Commissioner of Indian Affairs. Lincoln badly needed these votes. . . . Davis readily promised that in President Lincoln's cabinet Caleb B. Smith of Indiana should run the Interior Department, and William P. Dole manage the pesky redskins. Lincoln had, at least by inference, approved these deals by his letter to Delegate Allen of Indiana arranging the early conference. . . . Too, the Lincoln cause was aided by William P. Dole, Indian Commissioner-designate of the hypothetical President Lincoln. Dole, one time Indiana leader, had moved to Paris, Illinois, was now a delegate from the Seventh Illinois District along with Lincoln's friend Thomas Marshall of Charleston. He made a perfect liaison agent.[128]

Certain it is that Judge David Davis, several days following Lincoln's inauguration, was in Washington urging on Lincoln Dole's claims to the Indian commissionership.[129] Dole received the post.[130]

Over the post of Superintendent of Public Printing a spirited rivalry ensued between three Republican editors—John D. Defrees of Indiana, James H. Barrett of Ohio, and S. P. Hanscom of Massachusetts.[131] Defrees emerged the victor. For years a veteran Whig strategist, an expert party wirepuller, and former editor of the Indianapolis *Journal*, Defrees had used his rare organizing talents in the struggle against the Democrats, and had been one of a small group who started the Republican party of Indiana.[132] Defrees was, in the words of one student of Hoosier politics, "the wisest, shrewdest politician of the State." [133] He probably was— with the exception of Caleb B. Smith, whose faction of Indiana republicanism Defrees opposed. Barrett was salved by being awarded the position of Commissioner of Pensions. Editor of the Republican organ, the Cincinnati *Gazette*, Barrett had been an

---

[128] Baringer, *Lincoln's Rise to Power*, pp. 214–15.

[129] In early March, 1861, a Washington correspondent wrote: "Dole, of Illinois, is a prominent applicant for Commissioner of Indian Affairs. Judge Davis supports his claims." See New York *Herald*, March 8, 1861.

[130] *U. S. Official Register, 1861*, p. 81.

[131] Philadelphia *North American and United States Gazette*, March 12, 1861.

[132] Sulgrove, "John D. Defrees," *Indiana Magazine of History*, II (1905), 147–50; Sulgrove, *History of Indianapolis and Marion County, Indiana*, p. 239; Woollen, *Biographical and Historical Sketches of Early Indiana*, pp. 486–87; John D. Defrees to Weed, Aug. 25, 1860, Weed Papers, University of Rochester Library.

[133] Zimmerman, "The Origin and Rise of the Republican Party in Indiana from 1854 to 1860," *Indiana Magazine of History*, XIII (1917), 227.

Ohio delegate to the Chicago Convention and had served as the Buckeye State's representative on the Committee on Resolutions.[134]

The remaining financially desirable position in the Department of the Interior—the commissionership of the General Land Office —was given to James M. Edmunds, a business man who had served for several years as chairman of the Republican state central committee of Michigan.[135] The patronage under Commissioner Edmunds was only less than that in the Indian Bureau. The most rewarding jobs under the General Land Office were the various posts of surveyor general of public lands in the western regions. William D. Washburn, graduate of Bowdoin, agent for owners of vast Minnesota water-power rights and brother of the three Republican Congressmen—Israel, Jr., of Maine; Elihu B., of Illinois; and Cadwallader C., of Wisconsin—became surveyor general for Minnesota.[136] Mark Delahay, Lincoln's Kansas friend, received the appointment of surveyor general for Kansas and Nebraska.[137] Delahay was described by a contemporary as "an empty-headed, self-puffing, vain-glorious strut, who bases his pretensions on unsolicited campaign services of doubtful efficacy in Illinois and Indiana." [138] Later Delahay became a source of embarrassment to Lincoln by his misconduct as United States District Judge for Kansas, to which position the President appointed him subsequently.[139] For surveyor general for Oregon the Lincoln administration settled on B. J. Pengra, Republican editor and Lincoln presidential elector of Oregon.[140] The surveyor generalship for Washington Territory went to Anson G. Henry of Oregon, long a

---

[134] James H. Barrett to Chase, April 9, 1860, Salmon P. Chase Papers, Library of Congress; J. P. Smith, *History of the Republican Party in Ohio*, I, 106; *The National Cyclopaedia of American Biography*, XIII, 167.

[135] [Edmunds], *Memorial Discourse Delivered by Rev. Byron Sunderland, at the Funeral of Hon. James M. Edmunds, Tuesday, December 16, 1879*, pp. 5–6. (Copy in New York Public Library.)

[136] Warner and Foote, *History of Hennepin County and the City of Minneapolis*, p. 654; Folwell, *A History of Minnesota*, III, 84; Washburn, *Genealogical Notes of the Washburn Family*, pp. 47, 74.

[137] *Uncollected Letters of Abraham Lincoln*, comp. by Tracy, pp. 99, 103, 116–17, 134–35, 141–42, 176; *New Letters and Papers of Lincoln*, ed. by Angle, pp. 242–43.

[138] New York *Herald*, Dec. 9, 1860.

[139] *New Letters and Papers of Lincoln*, ed. by Angle, p. 243.

[140] Woodward, *The Rise and Early History of Political Parties in Oregon, 1843-1868*, pp. 168, 174; H. H. Bancroft, *History of Oregon*, II, 295 n., 458.

Whig, friend of Lincoln in the early Illinois days, and active in waging the Lincoln-Hamlin campaign in Oregon.[141] The commissionership of Public Buildings was bestowed on Benjamin B. French, a former New Hampshire Democrat, who had rendered valuable service to the Republican party and who subsequently became very intimate with the Lincolns.[142]

Of particular importance, in view of Europe's attitude toward the American Civil War, were the diplomatic and consular appointments. To these appointments we now turn our attention.

[141] Woodward, *The Rise and Early History of Political Parties in Oregon*, p. 91; Lincoln to A. G. Henry, Sept. 22, 1860, in *Complete Works of Abraham Lincoln*, VI, 57; *U. S. Official Register, 1861*, p. 77.

[142] Lanman, *Biographical Annals of the Civil Government of the United States*, p. 156; *The National Cyclopaedia of American Biography*, II, 345.

Chapter IV

THE DIPLOMATIC AND CONSULAR
APPOINTMENTS

DURING DEBATE in Congress in 1859 on the annual diplomatic and consular bill, an Alabama Member of Congress flatly charged:

Our whole mission system is one grand humbug. . . . It is intended more to provide places for placemen, and to extend the patronage of the executive department, than to enlarge the commerce of this country, or to cultivate friendly or social relations with other Governments.[1]

An Illinois Republican member even suggested that all diplomatic posts be abolished.[2] Had this suggestion been followed, Lincoln's task of placating the office seekers would have been more difficult. In 1861 United States government jobs in foreign lands relieved him of considerable embarrassment. At the outset of his administration he appeased the disappointed Judd by giving him the mission to Berlin. Judd's was the first appointment to a diplomatic post sent by Lincoln to the Senate for confirmation. It was sent on March 6, two days after the inauguration.[3] Nominations to other foreign posts were soon to follow.

In view of the armed intervention of England, France, and Spain in Mexico to collect on defaulted bonds from the Juarez government, Lincoln considered it imperative that the posts at London, Paris, Madrid, and Mexico City be filled immediately. Only a week following his inauguration he suggested to Secretary of State Seward that William L. Dayton, of New Jersey, be sent to England; John Charles Frémont to France; Cassius M. Clay,

[1] Representative Jabez L. Curry in *Congressional Globe*, 35th Cong., 2d Sess., p. 458.

[2] Representative Owen Lovejoy in *ibid.*, pp. 458–59.

[3] Edwards, *Sketch of the Life of Norman B. Judd*, p. 17; *U. S. Senate Executive Journal*, XI (1858–61), 291.

of Kentucky, to Spain; and Thomas Corwin, of Ohio, to Mexico. In this communication to his Secretary of State, Lincoln was careful to add: "This is suggestion merely, and not dictation." [4]

Seward did not concur with Lincoln on Dayton as the selection for London. For this most desirable of all diplomatic prizes, Senator Sumner of Massachusetts was being pressed by his friends.[5] Because of his subsequent intemperate anti-British feelings,[6] it was perhaps fortunate that the Massachusetts solon was not appointed to England. Seward had his own choice for London in his friend, Charles Francis Adams, also of Massachusetts. Adams, son of one president and grandson of another, had broken with the ruling Massachusetts "Cotton Whig" junta of Webster, Choate, and Winthrop during the late 1840's; and, with Sumner and others, formed the so-called "Conscience Whigs." He had repudiated Zachary Taylor as the Whig presidential candidate and had become Van Buren's running mate on the Free Soil ticket in 1848. Ten years later Adams had campaigned for Congress on the Republican ticket, giving the prestige of the Adams name to the new party. Following Lincoln's nomination he addressed Congress in a speech that was circulated as a campaign document, entitled "The Republican Party a Necessity." With Seward he had campaigned for Lincoln in the Northwest. His friends had pressed him for a Cabinet position, but Lincoln had recognized Welles, of Connecticut, as the New Englander in his inner council. Adams's education in Europe and his diplomatic training under his father, the venerable John Quincy Adams, qualified him for the all-important English post.[7]

Lincoln did not yield readily to the suggestion of Adams. His personal selection for London was Dayton, who had been an informidable rival for the Republican presidential nomination at the Chicago Convention. The day following Lincoln's abrupt entry

[4] Lincoln to Seward, March 11, 1861, Seward Papers.

[5] "Letters to Governor John A. Andrew in March 1861," *Proceedings of the Massachusetts Historical Society*, LXII (June, 1929), 209–10.

[6] See, for instance, Nevins, *Hamilton Fish: The Inner History of the Grant Administration*, pp. 149–75.

[7] *Charles Francis Adams, by His Son Charles Francis Adams*, chaps. i–vii; Blegen, "Campaigning with Seward in 1860," *Minnesota History*, VIII (June, 1927), 150–71; Reinhard H. Luthin, "Abraham Lincoln and the Massachusetts Whigs in 1848," *The New England Quarterly*, XIV (Dec., 1941), 622–623.

into Washington in February as President-elect, Dayton's friends including the Republican members of Congress from New Jersey, in a formal interview with Lincoln in his rooms at Willard's Hotel, urged their favorite's claims to a Cabinet place. But New York and Pennsylvania, key states politically, had dictated the selection of Seward and Cameron. There could not well be three Cabinet members of the seven from three contiguous states; geographically it was politically inexpedient. Accordingly Lincoln picked Dayton for England. Only after long persuasion by Seward did the President agree to appoint Adams to the Court of St. James's.[8] Somewhat embarrassed by the pressure for Adams, Lincoln did not forget Dayton; he found a way out by suggesting that Dayton might be named minister to France. This was done and the New Jerseyite sailed for Paris, notwithstanding his ignorance of the French language.[9]

Another major mission was that to Italy (or Sardinia), whose capital was at this time located at Turin. This place was given to George Perkins Marsh, of Vermont, whose friends strongly urged his claims. Marsh, a loyal Republican party man, was highly fitted for the position by education and linguistic training.[10] In fact, of all Lincoln's diplomatic representatives, Marsh and Adams were probably the two most eminently qualified.

A diplomatic post held in high regard was that of minister to Austria. This was bestowed on the "lame duck" Anson Burlingame, defeated Republican Congressman from Massachusetts. As a result of a caustic speech delivered in 1856 denouncing Congressman Preston Brooks, of South Carolina, for the latter's assault on Charles Sumner, Burlingame was challenged to a duel by Brooks. Burlingame formally accepted, but ingeniously named as the duelling ground the Canadian side of Niagara Falls, which Brooks could reach only by passing through northern territory highly hostile to him. Brooks therefore declined to go to Niagara and through his seconds sought a new site. Failing in this, largely because of inability to locate Burlingame, the duel was averted. Nevertheless, the publicity given by the Republican press to Bur-

[8] *Charles Francis Adams, by His Son Charles Francis Adams,* p. 144.
[9] Elmer, *The Constitution and Government of New Jersey . . . and Reminiscences of the Bench and Bar,* pp. 388–90.
[10] Marsh (comp.), *Life and Letters of George Perkins Marsh,* I, 427–28.

lingame's ostensible eagerness to meet the southern hot-blood on the field of honor in order to avenge Sumner gained for both him and the Republican party a wide popularity in the North. No mention was made of the elusive Burlingame's hiding place in Ohio.[11] Subsequently Burlingame gained further favor by stumping for Lincoln in the presidential campaign.[12] He was amply compensated by being appointed minister to Vienna.

By March 18—two weeks after his inauguration—Lincoln could write Seward:

Charles F. Adams to England, William L. Dayton to France, George P. Marsh to Sardinia, and Anson Burlingame to Austria. These gentlemen all have my highest esteem, but no one of them is originally suggested by me except Mr. Dayton. Mr. Adams I take because you suggested him, coupled with his eminent fitness for the place. Mr. Marsh and Mr. Burlingame I take because of the intense pressure of their respective states, and their fitness also. The objection to this course is that, locally they are so huddled up—three being in New England and two from a single state. I have considered this, and will not shrink from the responsibility. This being done leaves but five full missions undisposed of—Russia, China, Brazil, Peru & Chile. And then, what about Carl Schurz? or, in other words, what about our German friends?

Shall we put the card through, and arrange the rest afterwards? What say you?[13]

The problem of caring for Schurz, Wisconsin's influential German Republican leader, was most perplexing to Lincoln. "Next to the difficulty about Fort Sumter," one observer in Washington wrote, "the question as to what is to be done with Carl Schurz seems to bother the administration more than anything else."[14] Schurz, who later became a crusader for civil service reform, was, in 1861, an indefatigable office seeker, fully appreciative of his own efforts in swinging tens of thousands of German-born nat-

[11] Campbell, "Sumner-Brooks-Burlingame, or the Last of the Great Challenges," *Ohio Archaeological and Historical Quarterly,* XXXIV (Oct., 1925), 435–73.
[12] Springfield (Mass.) *Republican,* Sept. 20, 1860; H. Wilson to Sumner, Oct. 24, 1860, Sumner Papers.
[13] Lincoln to Seward, March 18, 1860, Seward Papers.
[14] New York *Herald,* March 19, 1861; Donner, "Carl Schurz as Office-Seeker," *The Wisconsin Magazine of History,* XX (Dec., 1936), 129.

uralized citizens to the Republican standard in the recent campaign.[15] To Republican members of the Wisconsin delegation in Congress, Schurz had expressed his wishes for a major diplomatic post. As a matter of fact he had journeyed to Washington in anticipation of an appointment, and from the national capital in mid-March had come word that he was "still working like a beaver for the Sardinian mission." [16] The close of March neared, and still the administration had offered him nothing. Lincoln, appreciative of Schurz's oustanding role in the campaign, was, at the outset, quite willing to give Schurz the ministership to Sardinia. But Seward opposed this, pointing to the unwisdom of sending a foreigner—particularly a former revolutionist in Germany—to a European court in such critical times. Great portions of the Republican and Democratic press, particularly in the East, took the same view.[17] Lincoln heeded Seward's advice and selected Marsh, of Vermont, as we have seen, for the post at Turin.

Still Lincoln knew that Schurz on almost every count had to be cared for. Western Republican leaders realized, too, that the party's existence depended in no small measure on the continued loyalty of German-born voters. Besides, Democratic newspapermen were making political capital out of the situation by reproaching the Republicans for their alleged Know-Nothing heritage. Certain German-language journals, too, intimated that Republican leaders, despite their late willingness to achieve national victory by German-American votes, were still tainted with nativism.[18] The man who was later to become one of the staunch advocates of civil service reform was experiencing at first hand the demoralizing effect of the spoils system.

[15] For the power of the German vote in the Northwest in swinging the election of Lincoln in 1860, see D. V. Smith, "The Influence of the Foreign-born Vote of the Northwest in the Election of 1860," *The Mississippi Valley Historical Review,* XIX (Sept., 1932), 192–204. See also New York *Herald,* Dec. 9, 1860. The New York *Daily Tribune* (March 11, 1861), declared: "We believe the speeches of no other man gained so many votes for Lincoln and Hamlin as did those of Carl Schurz."

[16] New York *Herald,* March 13, 1861.

[17] Donner, "Carl Schurz as Office-Seeker," *The Wisconsin Magazine of History,* XX (Dec., 1936), 127–36. (The New York *Tribune* was the only influential eastern newspaper to push Schurz's appointment for the Italian post.)

[18] *Ibid.,* pp. 127–36.

Finally Lincoln saw a way out: Cassius M. Clay, Republican leader of Kentucky, who had been instrumental in helping carry the state of Indiana for the Republicans in 1860 and who was highly regarded by Lincoln, had been appointed Minister to Spain, but had previously expressed a desire to go to Russia. Obviously Schurz, a former revolutionist, would be *persona non grata* in the reactionary empire of the czar. Why not name him to Madrid? Postmaster General Blair, appreciating the situation, dispatched a telegram to Clay informing him that it was important that Schurz should have a place in Europe. "I advise you," wired Blair, "to take Russia instead of Spain. You will make immense capital of it." [19] The posts at Madrid and St. Petersburg each paid $12,000 yearly.[20] Blair's brother Frank followed up the telegram to Clay with a lengthy letter appealing to the Kentuckian, on the strength of his dislike of Seward, to vacate the Spanish mission in favor of Schurz. The appeal to Clay bore fruit, for he complaisantly accepted the Russian mission—and Lincoln, greatly relieved, was able to present to Schurz a written memorandum: "I nominate Carl Schurz of Wisconsin to be Minister Plenipotentiary and Envoy Extraordinary to Spain." [21] Elated, Schurz immediately wrote his wife the glad tidings. "Seward's influence," said he, "has been defeated, and I am master of the battle field. . . . This outcome is better than the Turin mission would have been. It is a victory. Next to Mexico, Spain is the most important diplomatic post—and it is mine." [22] Parenthetically, it might be added that while in Russia Clay was accused of not conducting himself in conformity with diplomatic etiquette. Evidence in support of this charge, however, is not conclusive.[23] True, Bayard Taylor, First Secretary of the Legation in the Russian capital, wrote home: "Between ourselves, he [Clay] is much better suited to the meridian of Kentucky than of St. Peters-

[19] Montgomery Blair to Clay, March 26, 1861, in *ibid.*, p. 137.

[20] *U. S. Official Register, 1861*, p. 4.

[21] Donner, "Carl Schurz as Office-Seeker," *The Wisconsin Magazine of History*, XX (Dec., 1936), 137–38; W. E. Smith, *The Francis Preston Blair Family in Politics*, I, 515–16; Robertson, *A Kentuckian at the Court of the Tsars: The Ministry of Cassius Marcellus Clay to Russia*, pp. 33–35.

[22] Schurz to Mrs. Schurz, March 28, 1861, *Intimate Letters of Carl Schurz, 1841–1869*, ed. by Schafer, pp. 252–53.

[23] The charge rests upon mere newspaper report, and for this reason may be exaggerated. It appeared years later in the New York *Herald*, Jan. 16, 1872.

LINCOLN'S POLITICAL INDEBTEDNESS TO CARL SCHURZ

From Albert Shaw, *Abraham Lincoln*, New York, The Review of Reviews Corporation, 1929, p. 227.

Senator Seward stands at the left of the cartoon, next to Lincoln, who is supported by the
American Eagle. The man with the high hat is the Uncle Sam of that day. At the right is a
group of "adopted fellow-citizens"—Italian, French, Irish, German, and Negro. The German,
with a stein around his neck and a huge pipe in his hand, is Carl Schurz. Mr. Lincoln addresses
the group: "My dear friends, I cannot express to you in words how deeply I am obliged to
you for your generous votes. They have made me what I am. Without you I should have
remained what I was—nothing. My emotions overpower me, as you can easily perceive. Be
assured that I will do for you whatever *lies in my power!*"

burg." But Taylor was anxious to be Clay's successor and was writing Greeley for support in his ambitions.[24]

Meanwhile the mission to Mexico had been given to the veteran "Tom" Corwin of Ohio—an Old-Line Whig, who, during his long political lifetime in both Houses of Congress, had served as governor of his state and as secretary of the treasury in President Fillmore's cabinet. He had been a source of strength to the Republicans in taking the sting out of bona fide Republicanism in conservative territory.[25]

Other full diplomatic missions remained to be filled, namely, the Papal States, China, Brazil, Peru, and Chile. Through Seward's influence the American ministry to the Papal States was tendered to Rufus King, of Wisconsin. Scion of one of New York's first families and graduate of West Point, King in his youth had been associated with Seward's political partner, Thurlow Weed, in editing the Albany *Evening Journal*, and Seward as governor had appointed him state adjutant general in 1839. Later King removed West to Milwaukee to become editor of the *Sentinel and Gazette*, a Whig sheet. When the Republican party was organized King's journal became one of the first prominent Wisconsin papers to support the new party. King had favored Seward for the Republican presidential nomination in 1860, but when Lincoln was chosen King used all his influence, both personally and editorially, for the Republican standard bearer. Armed with letters from prominent Wisconsin Republicans, King had journeyed to Washington to seek the postmastership of Milwaukee, but Postmaster General Blair informed him that the position had already been given to another and that King himself had signed the successful applicant's petition! Seward then offered King the post of Minister Resident at Rome. King accepted and was about to embark with his family for the Holy See when news came of the fall of Fort Sumter. King took the first train to Washington, tendered his resignation, and received permission to join the volunteer army, of which he became brigadier general. At King's suggestion the post at Rome was given to his friend, Governor

24 Bayard Taylor to Greeley, July 5, 1862, Horace Greeley Papers, New York Public Library.

25 Morrow, *Life and Speeches of Thomas Corwin,* pp. 65–67; J. P. Smith, *History of the Republican Party in Ohio,* I, 92–93, 104.

Alexander W. Randall, of Wisconsin.[26] In the opinion of William J. Stillman, critical American consul at Rome, Randall was "a mere party hack; he knew nothing of diplomacy or good manners, or of any language but Western American." [27] Randall soon found himself in a most embarrassing position. Charged by Seward to use his post as a sort of diplomatic sounding board for the trend of European opinion and official attitude, he found himself handicapped by his lack of knowledge of Italian, French, or German. Unfitted by temperament and training for the task to which he had been assigned, unversed in the history of European politics, and nurturing a frontier dislike for the punctilio and etiquette of diplomatic intercourse, Randall sent in his resignation within a year.[28]

Meanwhile the Vienna government indicated that because of his sympathetic utterances in Congress in behalf of the Hungarian revolutionist Kossuth and the Italian revolutionists who were fighting Austria, Burlingame would be *persona non grata* at the Hapsburg court. Richard M. Blatchford, wealthy New York attorney, friend of Seward and Weed, and long a contributor to Whig and Republican campaign chests, sought the post.[29] Blatchford made known his wishes to Seward as follows:

I see the Senate have gone and the Austrian mission is unfilled. I do not want to embarrass you in that matter, but there are many reasons why the tender of that would afford me infinite gratification. I am sure you will bring it about if you can. If any man can be found who has contributed as much money and as much labor as I have to secure the triumph of the Republican party, *let him have the appointment.* Mr. Weed tells me that $3,000 which I advanced in one sum last October was sent by him to Mr. Lincoln's relative

[26] Charles King, "Rufus King: Soldier, Editor and Statesman," *The Wisconsin Magazine of History,* IV (1920–21), 372–76; Stock (ed.), *United States Ministers to the Papal States: Instructions and Despatches, 1848–1868,* pp. 237–40, 240 n., 258; Thompson, *A Political History of Wisconsin,* pp. 300–1.

[27] Stillman, *Autobiography of a Journalist,* I, 366.

[28] Baehr, "The American Mission to Rome," p. 20; Stock, "The United States at the Court of Pius IX," *The Catholic Historical Review,* New Series, III (April, 1923), 114.

[29] For Blatchford's financial contributions to Whig and Republican campaigns, see *Autobiography of Thurlow Weed,* pp. 476–80; and R. M. Batchford to Seward, June 22 (no year), Seward Papers, Vol. XVIII. For Blatchford's wealth, see Moses Y. Beach, *The Wealth and Biography of the Wealthy Citizens of the City of New York,* 1846 ed., p. 5.

Mr. Smith at Mr. Lincoln's suggestion for the purpose of carrying the Legislature of Illinois which was deemed in danger.[30]

Much as Seward would have liked to oblige his friend Blatchford with the post in Vienna, his hands were somewhat tied by other considerations. Even before election day in November, 1860, John Lothrop Motley, as we have noted, had written from Europe in quest of the ministership to Holland.[31] A year later found the famous historian in Washington, where he was still pulling wires for the Dutch post.[32] Unfortunately for Motley, the place at the Hague had already been given to James S. Pike, a Maine Republican leader, who, as the Washington correspondent for Greeley's New York *Tribune*, had for years carried on relentless warfare against the Democrats.[33] With the Hague post taken, Motley had to seek an opening elsewhere. Senator Sumner urged his appointment to Austria.[34] Despite Blatchford's desire and the opposition of those who claimed that Massachusetts was obtaining more than its just share, Seward yielded and gave the Vienna post to Motley. Oliver Wendell Holmes maintained that Motley "had no expectation of any diplomatic appointment when he left Europe," [35] and the assertion of the Motley family that Motley's great lofty patriotism and intense interest in the Civil War motivated his return to his native country appears to be far-fetched.[36] Seward finally found a place for Blatchford when the rustic Randall quit the post at Rome and Blatchford was named as his successor to the Court of Pope Pius IX. The remarks of Stillman, the American consul at Rome, concerning the new envoy

[30] R. M. Blatchford to Seward, Aug. 8, 1861, Seward Papers.

[31] J. Lothrop Motley to Grinnell, Nov. 2, 1860, Lincoln Collection, John Hay Library, Brown University.

[32] Philadelphia *Press*, March 20, 1861.

[33] Pike was born in Calais, Maine, and his correspondence with J. S. Stevens, editor of the *Kennebec Journal* in Augusta, Maine, indicates that Pike rendered considerable services in Maine to the Republicans in 1860. See "The Notebooks of James S. Pike, 1861–1862," ed. by H. A. Davis, pp. 2–6. See also Talbot, "James Shepherd Pike," *Collections and Proceedings of the Maine Historical Society,* Series II, 1 (1890), 251.

[34] Motley to his wife, Aug. 12, 1861, in *The Complete Works of John L. Motley,* ed. by G. W. Curtis, XVI, 199.

[35] Holmes, *John Lothrop Motley: A Memoir,* p. 102.

[36] *John Lothrop Motley and His Family: Further Letters and Records Edited by His Daughter and Herbert St. John Mildmay,* p. 96.

were very pointed: "Came another bed-warmer for General King, this one a New York politician, also a friend of Seward's, an ancient politician, who had recently married a young wife desirous of a stay in some European capital. . . . These at least were gentlefolk." [37] Blatchford remained ever grateful to Seward and when he finally relinquished the Rome mission he sent Seward the following note: "You are sacrificing your pecuniary interests whilst devoting your energies to your country. Accept of the enclosed check for $2,000. I have dated it March 2nd." [38]

The appointment of Burlingame to Austria gave Lincoln much perplexity. Burlingame had reached Paris when he learned that Emperor Francis Joseph's government had objected to him as too outspoken a champion of the Hungarian revolutionists and of Italian nationalism; while in Congress he had moved for American recognition of Sardinia as a first-class power. Burlingame was too important to be left uncared for. Seward solved the dilemma by offering him the mission to China. Burlingame accepted[39] and proved to be an extremely able man.

The mission to Brazil was another plum that went to a loyal Republican. Seward's influence was here felt once more. The post at Rio de Janeiro was handed to his long and intimate friend James Watson Webb, editor of the New York *Courier & Enquirer*, who had always supported Seward in his state and national ambitions. At first Webb had accepted the ministry to Turkey, but finally decided not to be "exiled" to the Porte on an inadequate salary. He was pacified by being offered the Brazilian post, which he accepted.[40] The Brazilian mission paid $12,000 annually,[41] while that at Constantinople paid but $7,500.[42] The vacancy thus created in Turkey was given, at the insistence of Secretary of War Cameron, to E. Joy Morris, Republican Congressman from a Philadelphia district and a protectionist.[43] Obviously Secretary Cameron wanted Morris taken care of, for Lincoln con-

[37] Stillman, *Autobiography of a Journalist,* I, 367.
[38] R. M. Blatchford to Seward, Feb. 17, 1864, Seward Papers.
[39] F. W. Williams, *Anson Burlingame and the First Chinese Mission to Foreign Powers,* pp. 14, 14 n.
[40] Hill, *Diplomatic Relations between the United States and Brazil,* p. 146.
[41] *U. S. Official Register, 1861,* p. 11.
[42] *U. S. Official Register, 1861,* p. 8.
[43] Philadelphia *Press,* March 25, 1861.

fided to Seward: "Gen. Cameron is anxious that E. Joy Morris shall be Minister to Constantinople, and if Gen. Webb has definitely declined it, why might not Mr. Morris be appointed? Pennsylvania is well entitled to the place, and Gen. C. thinks there is political reason for the appointment being made at once." [44] Morris had been chargé d'affaires to the Two Sicilies from 1850 to 1853. He served as Minister to Turkey with zeal and fidelity for almost ten years.

Peru and Chile were the only full missions that were unfilled. The post at Lima went to Rhode Island in the person of Christopher Robinson, a defeated Republican Member of Congress.[45] The Chilean position was offered to Thomas H. Nelson, a Terre Haute, Indiana, lawyer, who had ridden the circuit with Lincoln in the old days. One of the founders of the Hoosier State Republican party, Nelson had campaigned for Congress in the recent election, but had gone down to defeat. He solicited the ministry to Brazil, but when that post went to Webb he readily accepted the one to Chile.[46]

The minor diplomatic places were likewise reserved for Republican leaders and their favorites. A friend of Thurlow Weed, Henry S. Sanford, of Connecticut, but withal an experienced diplomat, was selected as minister to Belgium.[47] Bradford R. Wood, of Albany, New York, a founder of the Empire State Republican party, was appointed Minister to Denmark.[48] A follower of Cameron, Jacob S. Haldeman, of Pennsylvania, became Minister Resident to Norway and Sweden at the urging of the Secretary of War.[49] "Haldeman," complained an anti-Cameron leader, "does not possess a single qualification for such a place." [50]

---

[44] Lincoln to Seward, May 6, 1861, Seward Papers. For Morris, see Scharf and Westcott, *History of Philadelphia, 1609–1884*, I, 728; *Dictionary of American Biography*, XIII, 206.

[45] *Ibid.*, XVI, 38; Providence *Daily Journal*, April 4, 1861.

[46] Thomas H. Nelson to Pratt, Feb. 18, 1861, Daniel D. Pratt Papers; Bradsby, *History of Vigo County, Indiana*, pp. 877–78; Seeds, *History of the Republican Party of Indiana*, I, 28, 31.

[47] *Autobiography of Thurlow Weed*, p. 628; Barnes, *Memoir of Thurlow Weed*, p. 326; New York *Daily Tribune*, May 23, 1891; C. E. Sanford, *Thomas Sanford, the Emigrant to New England*, I (Part 2), 628–29.

[48] *The National Cyclopaedia of American Biography*, XII, 504.

[49] Lincoln to Seward, March 13, 1861, in *Complete Works of Abraham Lincoln*, VI, 191.

[50] John A. Allison to Trumbull, June 4, 1861, Trumbull Papers.

The post of minister to Switzerland went to George G. Fogg, secretary of the Republican National Committee, editor of the Concord, New Hampshire *Independent Democrat*, one of the best-known papers in New England, and a master strategist in mapping the Lincoln-Hamlin campaign.[51] Fogg's appointment resulted from his insistence on being appointed Commissioner of Patents in the Interior Department; but Secretary of the Interior Smith insisted that the position go to his friend and fellow Hoosier, David P. Holloway, and Lincoln followed Smith's advice. For a time Fogg's friends in the Senate, disgruntled, held up Holloway's confirmation. Peace was restored only by Lincoln's agreeing to give Fogg the Swiss mission, despite the efforts of Senator Sumner, chairman of the Senate Foreign Relations Committee, and others to have Lincoln retain the incumbent at Berne, Theodore S. Fay.[52] One of Fogg's admirers conceded: "Geo. G. Fogg, we know, is a good fellow, but he is not fitted at all for a *diplomatic* position, and *Fay* should never have been superceded [*sic*]. He is the best informed man on European history and diplomacy." [53]

Probably the strangest circumstances under which any foreign appointment was made by Lincoln were those under which James E. Harvey became minister to Portugal. On the day when Lincoln's Cabinet decided to send supplies to Major Anderson—besieged in Fort Sumter by the Confederate armed forces—Harvey, a native South Carolinian but then Washington correspondent for the Republican Philadelphia *North American*, sent a telegram to Governor Pickens, of South Carolina, at Charleston, notifying Pickens of this Cabinet secret; he did not put his name to the telegram, merely signing "A Friend." Harvey's telegram to the South Carolina governor was made possible by Seward, who had been in touch with three "peace" commissioners sent

---

[51] James O. Lyford, *History of Concord, New Hampshire*, II, 1034–35; *A Memorial of George Gilman Fogg: The Address of Rev. Augustus Woodbury, at the Funeral Services, Oct. 8, 1881*, pp. 3–4.

[52] Pierce, *Memoir and Letters of Charles Sumner*, II, 120 n.; IV, 27; Cincinnati *Daily Gazette*, March 23, 1861; New York *Herald*, March 29, 1861. Lincoln had assured Sumner that Fay would not be disturbed.

[53] Albert G. Brown, Jr. (private secretary to Governor John A. Andrew, of Massachusetts) to Andrew, March 28, 1861, "Letters to Governor John A. Andrew in March, 1861," *Proceedings of the Massachusetts Historical Society*, LXII (June, 1929), 211.

from the Confederate Government then sitting at Montgomery, Alabama, in efforts to bring about a peaceful solution between North and South. Arriving in Washington in the last days of February, the three commissioners visited Seward, and Seward assured them that it was the incoming Lincoln administration's intention to settle the issue amicably. On March 15 Seward informed the three Confederate emissaries that Fort Sumter would be evacuated before a letter from them could reach Montgomery— that is, within five days. The majority of Lincoln's Cabinet, however, contrary to Seward's views and promises to the Confederate envoys, reached a decision to provision and relieve Anderson's garrison at Sumter. Curiously enough, Seward communicated to Harvey the news that assistance would go to Sumter, perhaps believing that Harvey would transmit it to Governor Pickens.[54] The incident itself constitutes one of the unsolved riddles of American history.[55] Meanwhile, Harvey apparently talked with Seward about a diplomatic appointment, for on March 14, one month before the Confederate assault on Fort Sumter that precipitated the Civil War, Harvey wrote Seward a letter: "I enclose a *carte blanche* to dispose of me diplomatically. My application filed with the President was for Austria or Sardinia, but if there are difficulties in either or both I submit the case to your discretion."[56]

He then continued:

I cannot afford to go to the Hague . . . plainly because I am poor. . . .

Brussels or Lisbon would suit me but the former better on many accounts, & I think Pike would be satisfied with the change, though

[54] White, *The Life of Lyman Trumbull,* pp. 155–58.

[55] That Harvey was in close touch with Seward is evident from the following letter from Harvey to Seward: "I received a telegram from the Hon. A. G. Magrath, Secretary of State of South Carolina, this morning, stating in answer to an inquiry from me, that there was no truth in the rumor, that the State would oppose the voluntary withdrawal of Major Anderson, or demand a formal capitulation. I submitted it to the Secretary of War, & subsequently at his suggestion, to the President, who asked to retain it. I failed to find you before seeing either of the others." James E. Harvey to Seward, dated "Monday Night," Seward Papers, Vol. VI. John Bigelow, soon to be appointed United States consul in Paris, wrote in his diary on July 3, 1861: "Dined at Seward's. . . . Seward said Harvey telegraphed to South Carolina merely because he thought he was in honor bound to do so & that he and the President were in *pari-delicte*." See John Bigelow Diary, July 3, 1861.

[56] James E. Harvey to Seward, March 14, 1861, Seward Papers, Vol. III.

I have no knowledge on the subject. He is able to live anywhere.

If Costa Rica & Nicaragua are to be kept united in one mission, as they now are, the increased pay there would be an inducement for me to take that post if offered it. But it is the only one in Central or South America, unless Peru, that I would like. I made myself familiar with the whole Central American question during the two administrations of Taylor and Pierce.

These frank suggestions are all I have to offer. It is important to me, to have an early decision, & if it can be reached today, I will be greatly relieved. Your manifestations of kindness and interest have touched me deeply, & the future will tell whether they are remembered or forgotten.

[P.S.] My recommendations are on the President's table.[57]

Seward's decision to send Harvey quickly off to Portugal soon after Harvey's telegram to Governor Pickens roused a tempest. Seward's foe, Secretary of the Navy Welles, was especially bitter, practically accusing Seward of treachery.[58] There were violent repercussions in Congress too; and a Senatorial Committee, boiling with indignation that a "rebel" had been sent to Lisbon to represent the nation, called on Lincoln at the White House and demanded that Seward be ousted from the Cabinet.[59] Seward's connection with Harvey has never been completely unraveled and still remains in the words of one authority: "One of the most mysterious incidents of the time." [60]

The diplomatic positions in the Latin American republics proved outlets for faithful Republicans. That these sinecures to the south of the United States served as convenient berths to accommodate minor Republican leaders who were disappointed in their quest for other federal jobs within the country is illustrated in the circumstances that led to the appointment of envoys to Bolivia, Paraguay, and Nicaragua.

David K. Cartter, a Cleveland leader, had served as chairman of the Ohio delegation at the Chicago Convention. He was the tall man who jumped from his seat in the convention and clinched the Republican presidential nomination for the Illinois lawyer

[57] James E. Harvey to Seward, March 14, 1861, Seward Papers, Vol. III.
[58] *Diary of Gideon Welles,* I, 32 ff.; II, 248–49.
[59] White, *The Life of Lyman Trumbull,* p. 155.
[60] Horace White, quoted in *Political Science Quarterly,* XXVIII (Sept., 1913), 514.

in the stuttering words: "I-I a-a-rise, Mr. Chairman, to a-a-nounce the c-c-change of f-four votes, from Mr. Chase to Abraham Lincoln." [61] Cartter had been "especially attentive to Mr. and Mrs. Lincoln" when Lincoln's party passed through Cleveland en route to Washington; [62] following the inauguration he turned up in the national capital in quest of the governorship of Nebraska Territory, which was said to have been promised him.[63] But the latter position was finally awarded to another, and Cartter agreed to become Minister Resident to Bolivia because, it was alleged, he "wanted to see the Andes." [64] While in Bolivia, according to his biographer, "he travelled, neglecting his legation duties." [65]

Charles A. Washburn, of California, was also in Washington for Lincoln's inaugural. Born in Maine and the brother of three Republican Congressmen, Elihu B. Washburne, of Illinois, Israel Washburn, Jr., of Maine, and Cadwallader C. Washburn, of Wisconsin, he had gone to the Far West in 1850 where he became editor of Republican newspapers in San Francisco. In the campaign of 1860 he had been named elector at large from California and had brought the vote of that state for Lincoln to Washington.[66] Desirous of political advancement, he became an aspirant for the lucrative collectorship of the port of San Francisco [67] and in this ambition had the support of the "three brothers." [68] Unfortunately for himself, Washburn was a man of unstable temperament and of unsound party loyalty, for word came from Washington that "abundant evidence had been placed in the hands of Secretary Chase to satisfy him that it would be suicidal to make Washburn Collector at San Francisco." [69] Nevertheless, it was generally conceded, as one California leader in Washington put it, that "something must be done in charity for Mr. Washburn.

61 Baringer, *Lincoln's Rise to Power*, pp. 287–88; J. P. Smith, *The History of the Republican Party in Ohio*, I, 11–12, 104, 117.

62 New York *Daily Tribune*, Feb. 18, 1861.

63 Cincinnati *Daily Gazette*, March 27, 1861; New York *Daily Tribune*, March 21, 1861.

64 Curran, "David Kellogg Cartter," *Ohio Archaeological and Historical Quarterly*, XLII (Jan. 1933), 109.

65 *Ibid.*

66 Washburn, *Genealogical Notes of the Washburn Family*, pp. 47, 68; *National Cyclopaedia of American Biography*, V, 255.

67 San Francisco *Daily Evening Bulletin*, April 17, 1861.

68 *Ibid.*   69 *Ibid.*, April 23, 1861.

This every Californian here admits. . . . If Mr. Seward should indicate a disposition to give him some foreign appointment that would take him out of the country, there would be an end of the difficulty, for I don't think there is a Californian here who would not say *Amen!* to the proposition." [70]

Meanhile Washburn was becoming more insistent. "The most difficult man to dispose of," wrote the Washington correspondent of a San Francisco daily, "has been Charles A. Washburn. . . . He must have *something*. . . . The effort has been made to send him out of the country, on some foreign mission. That to Chile has been talked of; but in the present condition of national affairs, it is not deemed wise to send, to represent us abroad, any man whose infirmities of judgement or temper render him unsuccessful at home . . ." [71] Finally, Washburn was sent as Minister Resident to Paraguay.[72] There was little of a diplomatic nature to do in this small landlocked South American country, even though in 1865 it became embroiled in war with its neighbors. Consequently Washburn during his sojourn in Asunción devoted most of his time and energy to the preparation of a history of Paraguay.[73] Together with his three brothers in Congress and his brother William D., who was made surveyor-general of public lands of Minnesota, Charles A. Washburn made the fifth of the Washburn clan to go on the federal pay roll.

The post of Minister Resident to Nicaragua was likewise tendered to a Republican of comparative obscurity who proved a source of embarrassment in distributing federal jobs within the United States. Andrew B. Dickinson of Steuben County, New York, was a close political associate and friend of both Seward and Thurlow Weed; [74] Dickinson wanted to be marshal of the Northern District of New York. For this place, however, the Administration had other plans. Seward's tender to Dickinson of a choice of foreign missions if he would decline the marshalship in favor of Edward I. Chase, brother of the Secretary of the Treasury, was ac-

[70] San Francisco *Daily Evening Bulletin,* April 23, 1861.
[71] *Ibid.,* April 26, 1861.
[72] Washburn, *Genealogical Notes of the Washburn Family,* p. 68.
[73] Washburn, *History of Paraguay.* . . .
[74] F. W. Seward, *Seward at Washington as Senator and Secretary of State,* II, 33, 85, 224, 583; Barnes, *Memoir of Thurlow Weed,* p. 326; New York *Daily Tribune,* Feb. 4, 1861.

cepted, and Dickinson became Minister Resident to Nicaragua.[75]

The other diplomatic posts in Latin America went to loyal Republicans. The mission to the Argentine Confederation was given to a Cameron follower, Robert M. Palmer, speaker of the Pennsylvania state senate.[76] Henry T. Blow, a St. Louis merchant-capitalist, who had aided the Blairs in building the Republican party in Missouri, journeyed to Washington seeking the Chilean post, but he was given the one to Venezuela at the urging of the Blairs and Attorney General Bates.[77] The post of Minister Resident to Ecuador was tendered to and accepted by the influential German-American Republican leader of Cincinnati, Frederick Hassaurek.[78] "One of our best German Republican workers in America . . . of whose character you cannot be ignorant," [79] Lincoln wrote Seward in introducing Hassaurek. When Hassaurek received the Ecuadorian mission he is quoted as thanking the President "for appointing him to the highest position the administration had the power to give." (The capital of Ecuador, Quito, is between nine and ten thousand feet above sea level). Lincoln is said to have enjoyed the quip and to have repeated it to his Cabinet and friends.[80] Another German-American who was given a diplomatic post in Latin America was Charles N. Riotte, a leader among the antislavery Germans of Texas. Riotte became envoy to Costa Rica.[81] Elisha O. Crosby, a California Republican, was given the mission to Guatemala.[82] Hezekiah G. Wells, of Michigan, who had served as a Lincoln elector for his state in the late presidential cam-

[75] Henry B. Stanton, *Random Recollections*, pp. 223–25.

[76] *History of Schuylkill County, Pa.*, p. 298; New York *Daily Tribune*, March 23, 1861; Palmer, *Washington and the Union: Oration Delivered by Hon. Robert M. Palmer, Speaker of the Senate of Pennsylvania, at the Reception of President Lincoln at Harrisburg . . . on the 22d Day of February, 1861.*

[77] Hyde and Conard (eds.), *Encyclopaedia of the History of St. Louis*, I, 183; New York *Herald*, April 6, 1861; *Dictionary of American Biography*, II, 391–92.

[78] Bruncken, "German Political Refugees in the United States during the Period from 1815–1860," *Deutsch-amerikanische Geschichtsblätter*, IV (Jan., 1904), 50, 50 n.; J. P. Smith, *History of the Republican Party in Ohio*, I, 61, 104, 110, 124.

[79] Lincoln to Seward, March 14, 1861, in *Complete Works of Abraham Lincoln*, VI, 191.

[80] Faust, *The German Element in the United States*, II, 132 n.

[81] Biesele, *The History of the German Settlements in Texas, 1831–1861*, p. 199; "The Texas State Convention of Germans in 1854," *The Southwestern Historical Quarterly*, XXXIII (April, 1930), 255; Lanman, *Biographical Annals of the Civil Government of the United States*, p. 594.

[82] San Francisco *Daily Evening Bulletin*, April 17, 1861.

paign, was offered the post of minister to Honduras. Wells, however, declined, and the position remained temporarily unfilled.[83] The post of minister to Colombia went to Allan A. Burton, a Kentucky lawyer of Union proclivities.[84]

There were still a few missions in the Pacific to be disposed of— that to Japan and the commissionership to the Hawaiian Islands. The Chinese mission went, as we have observed, to Anson Burlingame, following his rejection by the Austrian government.

The American representative to Japan since 1858 had been the famous Townsend Harris, first United States minister to the then infant Far Eastern Empire. Creditably enough, Seward was reluctant to have him superseded. In July (1861), however, Harris asked to be relieved of his post on the ground of impaired health and advancing years. In October Lincoln accepted Harris's resignation with "profound regret." This left a vacancy.[85] Meanwhile one of the followers, of many years' standing, of the Seward-Weed organization, Robert H. Pruyn, of Albany, former speaker of the state assembly, had apparently been promised by Thurlow Weed the consulate at Liverpool. But Seward found it impossible to live up to Weed's promise. Greatly perturbed, Pruyn communicated to Weed:

Judge Harris [United States Senator from New York] . . . gives it as his opinion that Gov. Seward does not intend to give me the Liverpool consulship.

In this, however, he must be mistaken as you assured me more than a month ago that *it was mine*. . . .

You also said no Legislature had given you less uneasiness & more satisfaction than that of 1854, though during most of its session you were confined to your House. In the legislation of that session you were personally and politically largely interested. How much of its favorable results was due to me, you can say. For it I have received and asked nothing, scarcely thanks. . . .

[83] "Memorial of Hezekiah G. Wells," *Michigan Pioneer Collections*, VIII (1885), 170–71. However, Wells remained listed as Minister to Honduras. See *U. S. Official Register, 1861*, p. 10.

[84] Richard Collins, *History of Kentucky*, I, 358; *National Cyclopaedia of American Biography*, V, 534.

[85] Treat, *The Early Diplomatic Relations between the United States and Japan, 1853–1865*, p. 188.

When you informed me at Washington, the Liverpool appointment was *mine*, I wrote home to that effect. . . . I ask you to stand by me earnestly and with true & friendly zeal. . . .[86]

The consulate at Liverpool having gone to another, Pruyn was given the ministership to Japan.[87]

The selection for commissioner to the Hawaiian Islands was Thomas J. Dryer, of Oregon. Dryer, a traveling journalist, had started the Portland *Oregonian* as a Whig sheet in 1850, attacking the Democrats with vitriolic pen. In 1859 he steered the *Oregonian* into the Republican party, became a Lincoln elector in 1860 and carried the state's vote for Lincoln to Washington. He remained in the national capital in the hope of political compensation.[88] He was tendered the commissionership to Hawaii, but, when the question of his confirmation came before the Senate, his intemperate habits were cited against him. It was only after Dryer's friend and sponsor, Senator Baker of Oregon, staunchly pledged his "sacred honor" that Dryer was a sober man and that the charge of intemperance was untrue, that the Senate agreed to accept him for the Hawaiian post.[89]

The selection for the secondary positions in the United States legations abroad were characterized by quite as much partisan politics and personal favoritism as were the appointments to the first positions. At least three American ministers were instrumental in placing members of their families on the federal pay roll as subordinates in their legations: Clay at St. Petersburg had his nephew, Green Clay, as secretary of legation at $1,800 annually.[90] Corwin at Mexico City had his son, William H. Corwin, secretary of the legation at the same salary as Clay's nephew;[91] Dayton at

---

[86] Robert H. Pruyn to Weed, Aug. 12, 1861, Weed Papers, University of Rochester Library.

[87] Treat, *The Early Diplomatic Relations between the United States and Japan, 1853–1865*, pp. 189, 193–94.

[88] Woodward, *The Rise and Early History of Political Parties in Oregon, 1843–1868*, pp. 48, 58, 152, 168; Carey, *History of Oregon*, I, 517, 632 n., 640, 645; Lyman, *History of Oregon*, IV, 244, 280–81.

[89] San Francisco *Daily Evening Bulletin*, April 17, 1861.

[90] Robertson, *A Kentuckian at the Court of the Tsars: The Ministry of Cassius Marcellus Clay to Russia, 1861–1869, and 1863–1869*, p. 46; *U. S. Official Register, 1861*, p. 4.

[91] *Ibid.*, p. 9.

Paris had his son, William L. Dayton, Jr., as assistant secretary of legation at $1,500.[92] For first secretary of legation at Paris, Dayton had the son of his friend William Pennington, Republican Speaker of the House of Representatives in 1860.[93]

The most desirable secretaryship of legation was that at London. This went to Charles L. Wilson, a Republican editor of Chicago, friend of both Lincoln and Seward; in fact, Wilson had placed Lincoln in nomination for United States Senator against Stephen A. Douglas at the Illinois State Republican Convention of 1858.[94] Another Chicagoan received second place in the legation at Berlin—the German-born Herman Kreismann, organizer among the naturalized German voters for the Illinois Republican party; his knowledge of the Germanic tongue probably stood Minister Judd in good stead in the Prussian capital.[95] The post of secretary of legation at Brussels was awarded to the Minnesota leader, Aaron Goodrich, friend and supporter of Seward and delegate from St. Paul to the Chicago Convention.[96] William H. Fry, music editor of the great Republican journal, the New York *Tribune*, was rewarded with the secretaryship of legation at Turin.[97]

The numerous consulships in Europe, the Americas, and Asia proved to be virtual life-savers to Lincoln in caring for those who had been loyal to the party. It was apparent that these positions abroad were ardently sought by those who desired travel in foreign lands and by those who were disappointed in their quest for other positions. Wrote a Washington correspondent only a few days

[92] John Bigelow Diary, March 22, 1861; *U. S. Official Register, 1861,* p. 4.

[93] Shaw (comp.), *History of Essex and Hudson Counties, New Jersey,* I, 267; John Bigelow Diary, March 22, 1861.

[94] *The Biographical Encyclopaedia of Illinois of the Nineteenth Century,* p. 336; Bateman and Selby (eds.), *Historical Encyclopedia of Illinois,* I, 592–93; Beveridge, *Abraham Lincoln, 1809–1858,* IV, 207, 211, 235.

[95] *U. S. Senate Executive Journal,* XI (1858–61), 291: H. Kreismann to Washburne, May 13, 1860, Elihu B. Washburne Papers; H. Kreismann to Banks, April 2, 1859, Nathaniel P. Banks Papers, Essex Institute. (Erroneously inserted in volume of Banks Papers marked "II, 1858.")

[96] Smalley, *A History of the Republican Party . . . To Which Is Added a Political History of Minnesota from a Republican Point of View,* p. 343; J. F. Williams, *A History of the City of Saint Paul and of the County of Ramsey, Minnesota,* pp. 219–20.

[97] *Dwight's Journal of Music,* April 6, 1861, p. 3; *Baker's Biographical Dictionary of Musicians,* p. 282.

after Lincoln's inauguration: "The rush for office seems undiminished. The applications are so very numerous that not one in a hundred will succeed. There seems to be a general application for Consulships." [98] Such an idealistic worker in the antislavery vineyard as Ohio's Joshua R. Giddings, lately of Congress, was in Washington following Lincoln's induction as President in quest of "an earthly acknowledgment"—a diplomatic or consular post.[99] He left Washington with the $4,000 job of consul general to the British North American Provinces with headquarters at Montreal.[100] The eagerness for posts as consul is again illustrated by the strenuous efforts exerted by the attractive wife of John P. O'Sullivan, of California, to secure for her husband a consulate in Alexandria, Egypt.[101] John Bigelow, himself an energetic seeker after the consulate in Paris, wrote in his diary concerning his encounter with Mrs. O'Sullivan at one of Lincoln's receptions at the White House:

Walked around the grand salon once, twice or thrice with . . . Mrs. O'Sullivan who was the handsomest and the best dressed lady there. She is still solicitous for her husband's appointment as consul in the East. Coming out I took her on my arm to take leave. . . . After Mrs. O'S. had gone Nicolay [secretary to President Lincoln] came to me and asked who that lady was. I availed myself of the occasion to say what I could in favor of her application for a new consulate.[102]

The post at Alexandria did not go to O'Sullivan, for it was reserved for William S. Thayer, associated in editing the Republican New York *Evening Post*. Thayer was backed by his personal friend, Senator Sumner, who had become chairman of the Senate Foreign Relations Committee under the new organization of the Republican-controlled upper chamber of Congress.[103] O'Sullivan, however, received the consulate at Singapore.[104]

In addition to Singapore, there were other United States con-

---

[98] Cincinnati *Daily Gazette*, March 7, 1861.
[99] J. R. Giddings to his daughter, March 10, 1861, George W. Julian Papers.
[100] *U. S. Official Register, 1861*, p. 3.
[101] John Bigelow Diary, March 22, 1861.   [102] *Ibid.*, July 9, 1861.
[103] Pierce, *Memoir and Letters of Charles Sumner*, IV, 33; Bigelow, *Retrospections of an Active Life*, I, 131, 131 n., 172.
[104] *U. S. Official Register, 1861*, p. 3.

sulates in the Far East that were awarded to men who had exerted themselves to achieve Republican victory in 1860. There was, for instance, Hong Kong—one of the most important places in the East—which went to Horace N. Congar, editor of New Jersey's leading radical Republican newspaper, the Newark *Daily Mercury*. Congar had been a New Jersey delegate to the Chicago Convention, where he had favored Seward's nomination—a fact which the Secretary of State did not forget.[105]

The consulates carrying the largest salary in the whole service were those at London and Liverpool, each paying $7,500 yearly.[106] The post at the English metropolis—a consul generalship—was given to a former Whig and present Republican leader of Maine, Freeman H. Morse.[107] The consulate at Liverpool was sought by Lincoln's friend, Leonard Swett, partner of David Davis,[108] but it went to Thomas H. Dudley, of New Jersey. Dudley, chairman of the Republican State Executive Committee and delegate at large to the Chicago Convention, had framed the tariff plank favoring incidental protection to American manufactures—a plank which was so instrumental in carrying Pennsylvania for the Republicans in 1860. Moreover, Dudley had played a major role at Chicago in conciliating discordant factions and inducing them to support Lincoln for the presidential nomination.[109] Other major American consulates in the British Isles were Manchester, which was tendered to Henry W. Lord, a Pontiac, Michigan, leader and pioneer in organizing the Republican party in 1854, and an active stump speaker for Lincoln in 1860; [110] and Cardiff, Wales, awarded to Charles D. Cleveland, of Pennsylvania, an educator and warrior in the antislavery political fight ever since the days

105 Shaw, *History of Essex and Hudson Counties, New Jersey*, I, 283; Knapp, *New Jersey Politics during the Period of the Civil War and Reconstruction*, pp. 18, 26 n., 27.

106 *U. S. Official Register, 1861*, p. 2.

107 Hatch, *Maine: A History*, II, 329.

108 Leonard Swett to Weed, March 6, 1861, Weed Papers, University of Rochester Library.

109 Potts, "Biographical Sketch of the Hon. Thomas H. Dudley, of Camden, N.J.," *Proceedings of the American Philosophical Society*, XXXIV (1895), 107, 110–11; Charles Perrin Smith, "Personal Reminiscences."

110 Pontiac (Mich.) *Weekly Gazette*, Oct. 26, 1860; *Biographical Directory of the American Congress, 1774–1927*, II, 1238; Stocking (ed.), *Under the Oaks: Commemorating the Fiftieth Anniversary of the Founding of the Republican Party at Jackson, Michigan, July 6, 1854*, p. 54.

of the Liberty party.[111] As Consul at Cork, Ireland, Seward selected Patrick J. Divine, a Brooklyn Democrat—perhaps the only member of the opposition party to receive such a position. Divine's appointment caused resentment within the Brooklyn Republican organization and it publicly protested:

If he is a Republican, he must be a very recent convert; certainly, it will prove to be something entirely new to the Republicans of Brooklyn if he can claim to have ever rendered any service to the Republican party, or to have ever even once voted the Republican ticket. . . . It is sufficient to say that the Republican party in Brooklyn has not been strengthened by the selection of Mr. P. J. Divine.[112]

Of the American consulates in France, the two most profitable were those in Havre and in Paris. The Havre post paid $6,000 yearly while that at Paris yielded $5,000.[113] The Havre consulate was given to James O. Putnam of Buffalo, New York. Putnam had played an influential part in bringing the bulk of Know-Nothings into the camp of the Republicans; in 1860 he was a Republican elector at large for New York State and took the stump for Lincoln.[114] The Paris consulate was eagerly sought after. John Bigelow, late part owner of the New York *Evening Post*, was a candidate for the place. For a time Seward and Thurlow Weed backed their journalistic ally, Henry J. Raymond, editor of the New York *Times*. Bigelow, in Washington, consulted with Weed, and the latter then informed him that "Seward . . . had intended it [the Paris consulship] for Raymond but the *Times* had behaved so it was impossible. Some one sent the Prest. [President] an article containing a savage attack on him. He read it, called Seward's attention to it and made a remark which put it out of S's power to mention Raymond's name for anything to the Prest. [President]." [115] Seward and Weed were partial to Bigelow, who, unlike the other partners of the *Evening Post*, Bryant and Parke Godwin,

111 *The New England Historical and Genealogical Register,* XXV (1871), 389.
112 New York *Daily Tribune,* March 29, 1861.
113 *U. S. Official Register, 1861,* p. 4.
114 "James O. Putnam Memorial Evening," *Publications of the Buffalo Historical Society,* VI (1903), 632; E. Putnam, *The Putnam Lineage,* p. 319; *New Letters and Papers of Lincoln,* ed. by Angle, p. 251.
115 John Bigelow Diary, July 3, 1861.

had supported Seward for the Republican presidential nomination in 1860 and had published a letter urging Seward for the Cabinet when the Chase men were trying to exclude him.[116] Godwin himself had already urged Governor Banks, of Massachusetts, to use his influence in securing for him the Paris consulate,[117] but obviously Seward wanted no part of Godwin. Bigelow won out. En route to Europe he met on board ship A. W. Crawford, a Pennsylvania follower of Cameron who had been appointed consul at Antwerp, Belgium. That Bigelow was unimpressed by Crawford is evident: "Not much of an ornament to our national representation. Twice however, he has held forth on the merits of Mr. Cameron." [118]

Other important consulates in France were those at Marseilles and La Rochelle. George W. Van Horne, of Iowa, an earnest Republican, supporter of Frémont for President in 1856 and of Lincoln in 1860, received the consulate at Marseilles.[119] Thaddeus Hyatt, of use to the Republicans in rousing the northern people about "Bleeding" Kansas, was selected as consul at La Rochelle.[120]

Elsewhere on the Continent were numerous consulates for the Lincoln administration to distribute. Some were given to naturalized German leaders who had led their fellow countrymen into the Republican party. Writing a month after Lincoln's election, a Springfield, Illinois, correspondent who witnessed the job hunters' onslaught on Lincoln, wrote home:

In Ohio, Illinois, Indiana, Iowa and Wisconsin, native Republicans now openly acknowledge that their victory was, if not wholly, at least to a great extent, due to the large accessions they received in the most hotly contested sections from the German ranks. . . . That the Germans, as a rule, run less after office than the natives, no candid observer of political life will deny. But that all those among them that made themselves conspicuous by their efforts, both on the stump and otherwise, in behalf of Lincoln, are disinterested patriots, free from all yearning for office, can hardly be supposed. . . . Mr. Lincoln is disposed to be just to his German friends.[121]

[116] John Bigelow Diary, July 7, 1861; Bigelow, *Retrospections of an Active Life,* I, 339.
[117] Parke Godwin to Banks (Private), Dec. 13, 1860, Nathaniel P. Banks Papers, Essex Institute. (In Volume marked "II, 1860.")
[118] John Bigelow Diary, Aug. 30, 1861.
[119] *Annals of Iowa,* Series III, II (April, 1895), 78; Gue, *History of Iowa,* IV, 272.
[120] *Collections of the Kansas State Historical Society,* VII, 407 n.; XVI, 714.
[121] New York *Herald,* Dec. 9, 1860.

Schurz had been appointed minister to Spain, Hassaurek had been given the mission to Ecuador, Riotte that to Costa Rica, and Kreismann had been sent as secretary of legation to Berlin. In addition to these Lincoln cared for other German-born leaders by placing them in European consulates: Dr. George Edward Wiss, of Baltimore, delegate to the Chicago Convention, stump speaker for Lincoln and a Republican elector for Maryland, was chosen as Consul to Rotterdam. Wiss was a native of Bavaria.[122] George Schneider, also born in Bavaria, editor of the Chicago *Illinois Staats-Zeitung*, vigorous opponent of the Kansas-Nebraska bill and one of the earliest pioneers in starting the Republican party in Lincoln's home state, was appointed Consul at Elsinore, Denmark.[123] Theodore Canisius, Prussian-born, and for a time Lincoln's partner in publishing a German Republican newspaper to attract the Teutonic vote away from the Democrats, received the post of Consul at Vienna.[124] John P. Hatterscheidt, also Prussian-born, German Republican leader of Kansas and delegate to the Chicago Convention, was tendered the position of consul at Moscow.[125] Charles L. Bernays, a native of Hesse-Darmstadt, editor of the German Republican organ, the St. Louis *Anzeiger des Westens* and Missouri delegate to the Chicago Convention, became consul at Zurich.[126] Bernays' associate on the *Anzeiger*, Henry Boernstein, native of Hamburg, was appointed

[122] Baltimore *Sun*, April 27, 1860; Nelson (publisher), *History of Baltimore, Maryland*, p. 126; New York *Daily Tribune*, Nov. 19, 1860; *U. S. Official Register, 1861*, p. 5; Cunz, "The Maryland Germans in the Civil War," *The Maryland Historical Magazine*, XXXVI (Dec., 1941), 407–9.

[123] Arthur C. Cole, *The Era of the Civil War, 1848–1870*, pp. 25, 26, 123, 342; Bateman and Selby (eds.), *Historical Encyclopedia of Illinois*, I, 469; George Schneider, "Anti-Nebraska Republican Convention at Bloomington, Illinois, May 29, 1856," *Transactions of the McLean County Historical Society*, III (1900), 87–94; *U. S. Official Register, 1861*, p. 6.

[124] Barton, *The Life of Abraham Lincoln*, I, 416–18, 421–23; A. C. Cole, *The Era of the Civil War, 1848–1870*, p. 342; F. W. Scott, *Newspapers and Periodicals of Illinois, 1814–1879*, p. 324; Herriott, "The Premises and Significance of Abraham Lincoln's Letter to Theodore Canisius," *Deutsch-amerikanische Geschichtsblätter*, XV (1915), 181–254; *U. S. Official Register, 1861*, p. 6; Carman and Luthin, "Some Aspects of the Know Nothing Movement Reconsidered," *The South Atlantic Quarterly*, April, 1940, 232.

[125] *Collections of the Kansas State Historical Society*, VII, 537, 541 n.; X, 211, 640 n.; XI, 13; XVI, 714; Wilder, *Annals of Kansas*, p. 244; *U. S. Official Register, 1861*, p. 4.

[126] *Memoirs of Gustave Koerner*, II, 54, 66, 85; Hyde and Conard (eds.), *Encyclopedia of the History of St. Louis*, I, 142; *The Diary of Edward Bates, 1859–1866*, ed. by Beale, p. 146 n.; *U. S. Official Register, 1861*, p. 7.

consul at Bremen by Lincoln.[127] Other German-born naturalized American citizens who received consulates in Europe at Lincoln's hands—whose political activities the present authors have not succeeded in tracing—were: August L. Wolff, of Iowa, native of Lippe-Detmold, as consul at Basle; [128] August Alers, of California, born in Oldenburg, as consul at Brunswick; [129] Francis J. Klauser, of Ohio, born in Württemberg, as consul at Amsterdam.[130]

Other Republican leaders received consulates in Europe: William W. Murphy, who attended the first Republican state convention of Michigan in 1854, was appointed consul at Frankfort, Hanover, and Karlsruhe.[131] William H. Vesey, a political follower of Seward and Weed, became Consul at Aix-la-Chapelle.[132] Timothy Bigelow Lawrence, son of the late "Cotton Whig" leader Abbott Lawrence, of Massachusetts, was tendered the consul generalship at Florence.[133] Andrew J. Stevens, Republican National Committeeman from Iowa in 1860, was offered and accepted the consulate at Leghorn.[134] William J. Stillman, brother of a prominent Republican leader, endeavored to secure the consulate at Venice, but finally had to be satisfied with the post at Rome.[135] Venice was awarded to the future famous man of letters, William Dean Howells. In 1860 Howells had been assistant editor of the Republican organ, the *Ohio State Journal*, of Columbus, and had written a campaign biography of Lincoln.[136] In late summer, 1861, Howells turned up in Washington in quest of a consulate. From Washington he wrote his father:

I suppose you are anxious to hear from me, and my success in office-seeking. . . . I set to work at once. I found that the law did not

[127] Faust, *The German Element in the United States*, I, 530; II, 369; *U. S. Official Register, 1861*, p. 7.

[128] *U. S. Official Register, 1861*, p. 7.   [129] *Ibid.*, p. 7.   [130] *Ibid.*, p. 5.

[131] Stocking (ed.), *Under the Oaks: Commemorating the Fiftieth Anniversary of the Founding of the Republican Party at Jackson, Michigan, July 6, 1854*, pp. 23, 44; Curtis, *The Republican Party*, I, 183; *U. S. Official Register, 1861*, p. 5.

[132] Barnes, *Memoir of Thurlow Weed*, p. 326. Barnes is in error in stating that Vesey was appointed to Havre. See *U. S. Official Register, 1861*, p. 6.

[133] "Col. Timothy Bigelow Lawrence," *Proceedings of the American Antiquarian Society*, LII (1869), 12–14; Robert M. Lawrence, *The Descendants of Major Samuel Lawrence of Groton, Massachusetts*, p. 50.

[134] *Annals of Iowa*, Series III, IX, 265 n.; XVI, 208; *U. S. Official Register, 1861*, p. 7.

[135] Stillman, *Autobiography of a Journalist*, I, 97–98, 336.

[136] Howells, *Years of My Youth*, pp. 202–3; Stillman, *Autobiography of a Journalist*, I, 336, 370.

permit the increase of the pay of any but seaport consulates, and I found that Rome was worth but a trifle over $500, and very uncertain at that. So I went to see Mr. Nicolay, the President's private secretary. He said he would see if the Consulate at Venice were vacant. I should call again the next day. I called, the place was vacant, he thought I could have it. I am told by him that the President has signed my commission.[137]

The consul generalship at Constantinople went to a Maine Republican lawyer, Charles W. Goddard.[138]

Consulates in Latin America were allotted also to staunch Republicans: Havana went to Robert W. Schufeldt, scion of a leading New York family and favorite of the party leaders.[139] Vera Cruz was tendered to Mark H. Dunnell, former Congressman of Maine and a delegate to the Republican National Convention of 1856.[140] The consulship at Buenos Aires was awarded to Hinton Rowan Helper, author of *The Impending Crisis*, which had served as useful Republican literature in the campaign of 1860. Obviously the North Carolina firebrand could not well return to his native state and remain there in safety after the publication of his sweeping attack on the institution of slavery and slaveholders. Helper, wrote his Republican backers to Lincoln in June, 1861, "has done nobly and suffered for it." Helper informed Seward that he was "still anxiously waiting your action on my application for one of the lesser European consularships." Helper had the support of such advanced Republican leaders as Senator Sumner. He was finally cared for in the Argentinian consular post.[141]

The consular post at Rio de Janeiro was the cause of additional friction between Seward and Chase. Despite the fact that his department was probably administered with less partisanship than any other, Chase set out to procure his share of the spoils. With mathematical precision worthy of a financier, he computed that since his home state of Ohio had one-eighth of the nation's total

[137] William Dean Howells to William Cooper Howells, Sept. 7, 1861, in "Letters of William Dean Howells, 1857–1867," *The Bookman*, LXVII (May, 1928), 263.

[138] *Biographical Encyclopaedia of Maine of the Nineteenth Century*, pp. 352–53.

[139] Mackenzie, *Colonial Families of the United States of America*, V, 454; New York *Daily Tribune*, March 26, 1861.

[140] *The National Cyclopaedia of American Biography*, XI, 486.

[141] Barbee, "Hinton Rowan Helper," *Tyler's Quarterly Historical and Genealogical Magazine*, XV (Jan., 1934), 164–65; Pierce, *Memoir and Letters of Charles Sumner*, IV, 33.

population, it should receive one-eighth of the federal offices. He informed Seward, for whom he had little if any personal or political regard, that of the 269 vacancies in the State Department, Ohio's share should be 33. So far, Chase had asked for only 13, but what Ohioan had a more valid claim than he to the rest? When the appointment of his ardent follower and personal friend, Col. Richard C. Parsons, speaker of the Ohio assembly, to the London consulship had gone awry,[142] Chase in a veiled statement cautioned Seward: "I have not thought it respectful to go to the President about appointments in your department, except through you: others do and it seems not unsuccessfully." [143] Apparently Seward took heed, for Parsons was accommodated with the consulship in Brazil.[144]

There were other consular posts to be distributed in the Pacific. For example, the consular position at Honolulu. Alfred Caldwell, organizer of the Republican party in western Virginia, and chairman of the Old Dominion's delegation at the Chicago Convention, was the beneficiary of the post in Hawaii.[145]

In attempting to analyze the foreign appointments made by Lincoln it is hardly possible to become enthusiastic over the quality of material which political expediency forced him to accept. Only a few men—such as Adams at London, Marsh at Turin, Sanford at Brussels, Motley at Vienna, Schurz at Madrid, and Burlingame at Pekin—appear to have been qualified by diplomatic training, education, and knowledge of language to represent the United States abroad. Pike was a creditable literary appointment and gave a good account of himself. Of the consuls, John Bigelow at Paris was brilliantly able, and Howells was not without ability. Also some of the German-American Republicans, because of their knowledge of the Teutonic tongue and university training, were highly qualified. Of the others, practically all were political appointments and, as far as the consuls are concerned, one may almost

[142] D. V. Smith, *Chase and Civil War Politics,* p. 30. For Parsons, see Chase to R. C. Parsons, April 10, 1860, Chase Papers, Historical Society of Pennsylvania; George H. Porter, *Ohio Politics during the Civil War,* p. 30.

[143] Riddle, *Recollections of War Times, 1860–1865,* p. 23; Chase to Seward, March 20, 1861, in Smith, *Chase and Civil War Politics,* p. 30.

[144] Riddle, *Recollections of War Times, 1860–1865,* p. 23.

[145] Miller and Maxwell, *West Virginia and Its People,* II, 12–13.

agree with William J. Stillman, then American Consul in Rome, when he concluded:

In fact, with the exception of Adams, at London, and Marsh, at Turin, we had hardly a representative abroad, either consular or diplomatic, who was a credit to the country. As the war continued, the importance of being respected in Europe became more evident, and a change took place; but the few men of respectable standing who were in foreign countries representing the United States of America were appointed on account of political pressure, and not on their merits.[146]

Although diplomatic and consular positions in foreign lands constituted almost the entire patronage under Secretary Seward, the State Department had sundry other positions of a domestic nature under its jurisdiction. Principally there were the positions of governors of the seven territories. Only one of these gubernatorial appointments—that of Dr. Henry Connelly to the highest position in New Mexico—was not tinged with party politics.[147] The other six territorial governors were party wheel horses whose appointments were dictated by political expediency. William H. Wallace, appointed governor of Washington Territory, had been active as Whig and later as Republican in territorial politics.[148] William Gilpin, selected as governor of Colorado, had cast what was said to be the only Republican vote in his home county of Jackson, Missouri, and was pressed for the position by his friend Postmaster General Blair; moreover, Gilpin had accompanied Lincoln on the President-elect's journey from Springfield to Washington.[149] Alvin Saunders, of Iowa, appointed governor of Nebraska, had participated as a delegate in the first Republican convention of his home state and had been one of those most instrumental in lining up Iowa support for Lincoln's candidacy at the

---

[146] Stillman, *Autobiography of a Journalist*, I, 369–70.

[147] Twitchell, *Leading Facts of New Mexico History*, V, 71, 293, 293 n. Dr. Connelly was the first merchant to take a caravan through north Texas.

[148] Meany, *Governors of Washington, Territorial and State*, p. 23; H. H. Bancroft, *History of Washington, Idaho, and Montana*, pp. 71, 211, 217–18.

[149] H. H. Bancroft, *History of the Life of William Gilpin*, p. 43. For more biographical material on Gilpin, see H. H. Bancroft, *History of Nevada, Colorado, and Wyoming*, pp. 413, 414 n.; Baskin (publisher), *History of the City of Denver and Arapahoe County, and Colorado*, pp. 437–38.

Chicago Convention.[150] Dr. William Jayne, made governor of Dakota Territory, had been prominent in Republican politics in Lincoln's town of Springfield and was Republican state senator and brother-in-law of United States Senator Trumbull.[151] John W. Dawson, of Indiana, who received the governorship of Utah, had flitted from one party to another in Hoosier politics, but finally ended up as Republican, throwing the support of his paper, the Fort Wayne *Daily Times*, in favor of Lincoln's candidacy in the campaign.[152] Dawson did not remain long in his high position. Shortly after his arrival in Salt Lake City his unwelcome gallantries toward a lady of the city became known, and he was happy to flee; not, however, before a party of Brigham Young's Latter-Day Saints waylaid and soundly thrashed him.[153] Of Dawson the historian of the Mormon movement narrated:

He was the editor and publisher of a party newspaper at Fort Wayne, Indiana, a man of bad morals, and a meddler in politics, who gave the Republican managers in his state a great deal of trouble. The undoubted fact seems to be that he was sent out to Utah on the recommendation of Indiana politicians of high rank, who wanted to get rid of him, and who gave no attention whatever to the requirements of his office.[154]

For the remaining territorial governorship, that of Nevada, the Lincoln administration chose James W. Nye, political henchman and bosom friend of Seward, former commissioner of police of New York City, member of the strongly pro-Seward Empire State

---

[150] Sorenson, *The Story of Omaha,* pp. 548–49; Gue, *History of Iowa,* IV, 233; Herriott, "Iowa and the First Nomination of Abraham Lincoln," *Annals of Iowa,* Series III, VIII (July, 1907), 96, 111, 114.

[151] "Dr. William Jayne," *Journal of the Illinois State Historical Society,* IX (1916–17), 82–84, 93; "Doctor William Jayne, First Governor," *South Dakota Historical Collections,* I (1902), 118; New York *Herald,* March 25, 1861; Jayne to Trumbull, Jan. 17, 1861, Trumbull Papers.

[152] Brand, "History of the Know Nothing Party in Indiana," *Indiana Magazine of History,* XVIII (1922), 204, 273–74, 281, 284; Zimmerman, "The Origin and Rise of the Republican Party in Indiana From 1854 To 1860," *Indiana Magazine of History,* XIII (1917), 260, 369; Griswold, *The Pictorial History of Fort Wayne, Indiana,* I, 341. For Dawson's support of Lincoln, see Dawson's Fort Wayne *Daily Times,* May 19, June 26, 28, July 3, 1860. Files of this latter newspaper are in the Fort Wayne Public Library.

[153] Tullidge, *History of Salt Lake City,* p. 249; H. H. Bancroft, *History of Utah,* p. 604.

[154] William A. Linn, *The Story of the Mormons,* p. 537.

delegation to the Chicago Convention, who had later stumped with Seward for Lincoln in the Northwest.[155] Even before Lincoln's inauguration Nye had been in Washington to collect for his party services, according to a newspaper dispatch of February 26, 1861:

General Nye, who, it will be remembered, had sundry trials of skill in telling peculiar kinds of stories with Old Abe, in which there was a sort of drawn battle, has applied for every office in New York. He has applied for Collector, Postmaster, Surveyor, Naval Officer, Sub-Treasurer and Superintendent of the Assay Office, on the principle, probably, that by making a grab for all he will be likely to secure one.[156]

Nye must have been a picturesque character. Mark Twain, who knew him intimately at this very time in Nevada, described him as:

An old and seasoned politician from New York—politician, not statesman. . . . His eyes could outtalk his tongue, and this is saying a good deal, for he was a remarkable talker, both in private and on the stump. . . . He had been a stage-driver in his early days in New York or New England, and had acquired the habit of remembering names and faces, and of making himself agreeable to his passengers. As a politician this had been valuable to him. . . . By the time he had been Governor a year he had shaken hands with every human being in the Territory of Nevada, and after that he always knew these people instantly and at sight and could call them by name. . . .[157]

Midsummer of 1861 found most of the State Department patronage distributed. By this time the nation was engulfed in civil war.

155 Mack, *Nevada: A History of the State from the Earliest Times through the Civil War*, p. 221.
156 New York *Herald*, March 2, 1861.
157 *Mark Twain's Autobiography*, II, 305, 308–9.

Chapter V

NEPOTISM, JOURNALISTIC REWARDS, AND CABINET CHANGES

I DISLIKE to make changes in office as long as they can be avoided. It multiplies my embarrassments." [1]

Thus wrote Lincoln during his presidency. But the American political game as played in Lincoln's day—and before and ever since, with some modifications—demanded changes in public office, and still more changes.

Theoretically it was contended that the war for the Union had transcended political parties. No longer should the nation be divided among "Republican" and "Democrat" and "Constitutional Unionist." Henceforth, many preached, there would be only two parties—the party of the Union and the party of Disunion. Nevertheless, the number of Democratic federal officeholders displaced by Republicans in the year following the firing on Fort Sumter may be considered a criterion; party labels were still very important. In this connection let us examine that rich mine of government jobs, the New York Custom-house. That portion of the Democratic press which supported Lincoln's Unionist cause appealed to the President not to remove Democrats from office for partisan reasons, pleading that the traditional rule of "To the Victors Belong the Spoils" be abandoned for the war's duration. [2] This appeal was of little or no avail, for the struggle of Republicans for place continued unabated. Thirty-five inspectors were removed from the Custom House in late October, 1861. [3] Several days later came word that "the heads of the clerks under the last administration continue to drop off quietly." [4]

In the New York Post Office it was much the same story. In the

[1] Lincoln to W. Jayne, Feb. 26, 1864, in *Complete Works of Abraham Lincoln*, X, 20–21.

[2] New York *Herald*, June 10, 22, 1861.

[3] *Ibid.*, Oct. 20, 1861.   [4] *Ibid.*, Oct. 22, 1861.

spring of 1862 Lincoln made room for a Seward-Weed follower, Abram Wakeman, for postmaster of the metropolis. Wakeman, commented Horace Greeley, "is mere clay in the hands of the potter, Weed." [5] Wakeman's appointment was confirmed by the Senate in March,[6] and the following June he commenced a thorough purge of the remaining Democrats from the nation's largest post office.[7] Suggestions that key men in the office be spared in the interests of efficiency fell upon deaf ears; political reward rather than fitness for service prevailed.

Although political partisanship was apparently the major cause for removals by Lincoln, it was not the only one. Disloyalty to the Union was deemed sufficient justification for dismissal of federal employees. The war had little more than started before a Congressional committee under the chairmanship of Representative Potter, of Wisconsin, began an investigation of suspected Confederate sympathizers in the various departments.[8] By May, 1862, it was estimated that the Lincoln Administration had removed some five hundred allegedly disloyal government employees on the representations of the Potter Committee.[9] Postmaster General Blair was especially vigilant in discharging disloyal postmasters.[10] While the great majority of those whose services were thus terminated were probably guilty of disloyalty to the Union, there is no way of determining the relative number who were dismissed allegedly for Confederate sympathies but actually for partisan political reasons. With war-time hysteria mounting ever higher in Washington, it is logical to conclude that the Lincoln administration removed some persons unjustly. But of this there is no proof. Indeed, it is almost impossible to draw the line between support of the Union and support of the Lincoln administration. Loyalty to each became one and the same under the duress of war.

During the entire course of his administration Lincoln, in choosing men for newly created positions or to fill vacancies caused by death or resignation, followed the hidebound rule of his predecessors in consulting with Senators and Congressmen of his party

[5] Greeley to Chase, Feb. 10, 1864, Salmon P. Chase Papers, Historical Society of Pennsylvania.

[6] *U. S. Senate Executive Journal*, XII (1861–62), 148, 172.

[7] New York *Herald*, June 12, 14, 1862.   [8] New York *Herald*, Aug. 16, 1861.

[9] New York *Herald*, May 25, 1862.

[10] W. E. Smith, *The Francis Preston Blair Family in Politics*, II, 95.

before deciding on appointments to or removals from offices in which they were interested.[11] Thus under date of July 24, 1862, we find him writing to James Dixon, United States Senator from Connecticut: "The bearer of this, Mr. Bronson Murray, now resident in the fourth district of Connecticut, wishes to be collector for that district. He is my acquaintance and friend of some years' standing, whom I would like to oblige, but I should not like to appoint him against the wish of yourself and other Union friends there."[12] A few days earlier he wrote Chase to this effect: "Mr. Senator Doolittle informs me that the Wisconsin delegation have unanimously recommended persons for assessors and collectors throughout their State, and that the paper showing this is filed with you. If so, I am in favor of adopting their 'slate' at once, and so disposing of one State."[13] Again we find him seeking the approval of Senator J. S. Ten Eyck, of New Jersey, before appointing Dr. J. R. Freese provost marshal in that state.[14]

On at least one occasion Lincoln yielded to the wishes of a Member of Congress who wanted an important federal official in his state removed. In this instance John Conness, United States Senator from California and a Republican-Unionist, asked Lincoln to dismiss Postmaster Parker of San Francisco and thus make way for a Conness favorite. Lincoln felt bound to comply, even though the new appointee had neither the respect nor the confidence of the better element of the Golden Gate city.[15] At another time Lincoln consulted a member of the Senate before removing an official who had originally been appointed on that legislator's recommendation. To Senator John P. Hale, of New Hampshire, the President confided: "I believe that it was upon your recommendation that B. B. Bunker was appointed attorney for Nevada Territory. I am pressed to remove him on the ground that he does not attend to the office, nor in fact pass much time in the Territory. Do you wish to say anything on the subject?"[16]

[11] *Uncollected Letters of Abraham Lincoln,* comp. by Tracy, pp. 205-6, 209, 212; *Complete Works of Abraham Lincoln,* VII, 286, 290-91; X, 226.

[12] *Complete Works of Abraham Lincoln,* VII, 290-92.

[13] *Ibid.,* 286.   [14] *Ibid.,* X, 226.

[15] Thomas Brown to Chase (Private), Jan. 20, 1864, Chase Papers, Library of Congress.

[16] Lincoln to John P. Hale, June 9, 1863, in Tarbell, *The Life of Abraham Lincoln,* II, 368.

More often than not Lincoln gave his Cabinet members a voice in the matter of appointments; thus Seward's endorsement was usually required for a New York selection for the Treasury, and Welles's acquiescence was necessary for a Connecticut man to be chosen for Chase's department. Chase insisted on being consulted on Ohio choices for diplomatic missions and consular posts under Seward's jurisdiction. Bates's approval was usually a requisite for a Missouri office; and Blair controlled almost half of the federal offices in Maryland.[17]

Lincoln realized the value of support not only from Congress and Cabinet, but likewise from the governors of the loyal states. Accordingly he kept in communication with them when appointing officials whose duties would be performed in their respective states. Governor Oliver P. Morton, of Indiana, complained that he was not being consulted on the selection of brigadier generals;[18] despite the Hoosier governor's unfriendly attitude toward the national administration,[19] Lincoln asked him to telegraph recommendations.[20] On another occasion he assured Morton that "no appointment has been or will be made by me for the purpose of stabbing you."[21] To Governor David Tod, of Ohio, the President wrote: "I think your advice with that of others would be valuable in the selection of provost-marshals for Ohio."[22] A few months earlier he wired Gov. Francis H. Pierpont, of the western or "loyal" part of Virginia, to indicate clearly whether he wished "Ross and Richter, or any other two . . . and they shall be appointed."[23] And on at least one occasion Gov. Austin Blair, of Michigan, accompanied Senator Zachariah Chandler, of his state, to the White House, where they reached an agreement with Lincoln concern-

[17] D. V. Smith, *Chase and Civil War Politics*, pp. 30–31; "Diary and Correspondence of Salmon P. Chase," *Annual Report*, American Historical Association, II (1902), 59; M. Howard to H. W. Shipman, May 14, 1861, Gideon Welles Papers, Library of Congress; W. E. Smith, *The Francis Preston Blair Family in Politics*, II, 2.

[18] Foulke, *Life of Oliver P. Morton*, I, 154 n.

[19] Harbison, "Lincoln and Indiana Republicans, 1861–1862," *Indiana Magazine of History*, XXXIII (Sept., 1937), 283.

[20] Foulke, *Life of Oliver P. Morton*, I, 154 n.

[21] Lincoln to O. P. Morton, June 28, 1862, in Tarbell, *The Life of Abraham Lincoln*, II, 347.

[22] Lincoln to David Tod, March 9, 1863, in *ibid.*, p. 361.

[23] Lincoln to F. H. Pierpont (telegram), Oct. 23, 1862, in *Complete Works of Abraham Lincoln*, VIII, 67.

ing the Michigan appointments to the Treasury Department.[24]

Lincoln also did not overlook the opinion of Vice President Hannibal Hamlin in parceling out the federal offices, chiefly in New England. He consulted the Vice President before making up his Cabinet and selected Welles as Secretary of the Navy partly on Hamlin's approval. The Vice President vigorously upheld Maine's claim to jobs. According to Collector John Z. Goodrich, of Boston, Hamlin insisted "that Maine was entitled, *fairly* entitled, to some of the Boston Custom House patronage." [25] Goodrich replied that he was already harassed by New Hampshire leaders for more jobs, despite the fact that the Granite State had the Boston Naval Office (Amos Tuck occupied it) and other positions in the Custom House amounting to $16,000 yearly.[26] Hamlin heatedly replied that "the Naval Office & subordinates is [sic] enough for New Hampshire." [27]

To Republican Members of Congress as well as to his official family, Republican governors of the loyal states, and Vice President Hamlin—to all these Lincoln was gracious in caring for their relatives. Specific illustrations in this respect are not lacking: Senator Trumbull's brother was given a job in the Land Office,[28] and his brother-in-law, William Jayne, as we have seen, was made governor of Dakota Territory.[29] Moreover, as we have noted too, Charles A. Washburn and William D. Washburn, brothers of the famous Washburn Congressional trio, were named minister to Paraguay and United States Surveyor General for Minnesota respectively. Enoch J. Smithers, relative of Congressman Nathaniel B. Smithers, of Delaware, received a consulship in Turkey.[30] Every Cabinet officer had one or more of his family on the federal pay roll or received for them military promotions at some time during the war: Seward had three sons—Frederick was Assistant Secretary of State, Augustus was a paymaster in the Army, while

[24] "Diary and Correspondence of Salmon P. Chase," *Annual Report,* American Historical Association, II (1902), 61.

[25] J. Z. Goodrich to Fessenden, Aug. 27, 1861, William P. Fessenden Papers. Fessenden was then United States Senator from Maine.

[26] *Ibid.*   [27] *Ibid.*

[28] Lincoln to Stuart, March 30, 1861, in Tarbell, *The Life of Abraham Lincoln,* II, 340.

[29] *South Dakota Historical Collections,* V (1910), 116; *Journal of the Illinois State Historical Society,* IX (1916–17), 93.

[30] Milford (Del.) *Peninsular News and Advertiser,* Jan. 31, 1862.

William H. Jr. (running the family countinghouse in Auburn in 1861) became a lieutenant colonel of volunteers in 1862, then colonel, and in 1864 a brigadier general. Seward's nephew, George F., was assigned as consul, then consul general, at Shanghai, China.[31] Secretary Chase, after a tilt with Seward over the issue, succeeded in having Lincoln appoint his brother as United States Marshal for the Northern District of New York. Secretary Cameron's son, Major Brua Cameron, was stationed at Washington for some time as paymaster in the United States Army.[32] Secretary of the Navy Welles had a son, Thomas, for whom he secured quick promotion in the Army.[33] Attorney General Bates found a place in his own office for one son, secured Lincoln's personal appointment of another son to West Point, and helped obtain a promotion for still another son in the Army: later Bates found a comfortable appointment in the Navy for the son who had been in his office.[34] Secretary of the Interior Smith selected his son as librarian of the Interior Department.[35] Postmaster General Blair, besides helping to secure a promotion in the Army for his equally famous brother Frank, saw his brother-in-law, Gustavus V. Fox, made Assistant Secretary of the Navy.[36] Fox was a highly competent administrator. Vice President Hamlin had his brother, Elijah L. Hamlin, appointed commissioner under the reciprocity treaty between the United States and Canada.[37]

Lincoln himself was not entirely free from practicing nepotism. Mrs. Lincoln, as we have observed, added her influence to that of Norman B. Judd's opponents when the latter was being considered for the Cabinet. It may not be amiss to restate by way of emphasis that Mrs. Lincoln's relative by marriage, Dr. Edward Wallace, received the profitable Naval Office at Philadelphia. Another Wal-

[31] *Who's Who in America*, 1899–1900, p. 650; Lanman, *Biographical Annals of the Civil Government of the United States*, p. 378; *U. S. Official Register, 1861*, p. 118.

[32] Philadelphia *Inquirer*, Jan. 15, 1864.

[33] *U. S. Senate Executive Journal*, XIV (1864–66), 224; *Diary of Gideon Welles*, II, 71, 80, 82.

[34] "The Diary of Edward Bates, 1859–1866," ed. by Beale, *Annual Report*, American Historical Association, IV (1930), xiv.

[35] Baltimore *Evening Patriot*, March 8, 1861; Frankfort *Weekly Kentucky Yeoman*, March 15, 1861.

[36] *Confidential Correspondence of Gustavus Vasa Fox*, ed. by Thompson and Wainwright, I, 2.

[37] H. F. Andrews, *The Hamlin Family*, pp. 197, 344–46; *U. S. Official Register, 1861*, p. 13.

lace—Dr. William Wallace, of Springfield, married to her sister—
was cared for by Lincoln with a paymastership of volunteers.[38]
Still another family connection of the First Lady, her cousin Capt.
John B. S. Todd of Yankton, Dakota Territory, had a voice in determining federal appointments in his region; moreover, Lincoln
tendered Todd, a West Pointer, a commission as brigadier general
of volunteers.[39] A cousin of Lincoln who wanted the job of postmaster in Lincoln's home town of Springfield gave him some slight
annoyance. To his friend Stuart the President wrote in March,
1861:

Washington, March 30, 1861.

DEAR STUART:

Cousin Lizzie shows me your letter of the 27th. The question of
giving her the Springfield Post-office troubles me. You see I have
already appointed William Jayne a territorial governor and Judge
Trumbull's brother to a land office— Will it do for me to go on and
justify the declaration that Trumbull and I have divided out all
the offices among our relatives? Dr. Wallace you know, is needy, and
looks to me; and I personally owe him much.

I see by the papers, a vote is to be taken as to the Post-office.
Could you not set up Lizzie and beat them all? She, being here, need
know nothing of it, so therefore there would be no indelicacy on her
part.

A. LINCOLN [40]

For his son, Robert, Lincoln arranged that upon completion
of his studies at Harvard College in 1864 he attend the Harvard
Law School, after which he obtained for him a captaincy in the
adjutant-general's department.[41]

In distributing the federal offices Lincoln was likewise not unmindful of his old political and personal friends. There was, for
instance, the note which he wrote to Simeon Draper (whom he in
1864 appointed Collector of the Port of New York), regarding
his former colleague William A. Newell, of New Jersey: "Allow
me to introduce Gov. W. A. Newell of New Jersey— You know

---

[38] Sandburg and Angle, *Mary Lincoln, Wife and Widow*, pp. 38, 208, 208 n.
[39] *South Dakota Historical Collections*, I, 115–16; III, 127 n.; V, 115; XIII, 97.
[40] Lincoln to Stuart, March 30, 1861, in Tarbell, *The Life of Abraham Lincoln*,
II, 340–41.
[41] *U. S. Senate Executive Journal*, XIV, Part I (1864–66), 157, 159, 167; New
York *Times*, July 27, 1926; and F. L. Paxson's sketch in *Dictionary of American
Biography*, XI, 266–67.

him by reputation. He and I were in Congress together sixteen years ago— He is a true friend of the Union, and every way a reliable gentleman. Please hear him whenever he calls." [42] Another letter (published for the first time in June, 1940) penned by Lincoln to his Springfield friend and financial trustee, Robert Irwin, indicates the President's aim to do right by those whom he left behind in Illinois:

Private

Washington D.C.
March 20, 1861

ROBERT IRWIN, ESQ
MY DEAR SIR:

I am scared about your friend Dennison. The place is so fiercely sought by, and for, others, while, except what has come through you, his name is not mentioned at all, that I fear appointing him will appear too arbitrary on my part. I have made no appointment at the City as yet; but it has pained me that among the scores of names urged, his has not occurred once.

Your tired friend
A. LINCOLN [43]

Apparently Irwin was urging George Dennison for the remunerative and coveted post of Naval Officer in the New York Custom House. For Lincoln, as we have seen, appointed Dennison to that position.[44] Among Lincoln's intimate Illinois friends to whom he tendered appointments were Judge David Davis, to be Associate Justice of the United States Supreme Court; Norman B. Judd, to be Minister to Prussia; Gustave Koerner, Minister to Spain; Jackson Grimshaw, Collector of Internal Revenue for the Quincy (Illinois) District; Archibald Williams, United States District Judge for Kansas; [45] Ward H. Lamon, United States Marshal for the District of Columbia; and, as we have noted, Anson G. Henry as surveyor general for Washington Territory.

Then there was that most extraordinary character, Mark W.

[42] Lincoln to Simeon Draper, Sept. 8, 1864 (Photostat), Emanuel Hertz Photostats, Library of Congress.

[43] Lincoln to Robert Irwin (private), March 20, 1861, in " 'Your Tired Friend': A Newly Published Lincoln Letter," *The Abraham Lincoln Quarterly*, June, 1940, p. 102.

[44] *Ibid.*, pp. 104–5.

[45] Thomas, "Lincoln and the Courts, 1854–1861," *Abraham Lincoln Association Papers*, 1933, p. 97.

Delahay, probably Lincoln's most confidential friend in Kansas, who had preached the Lincoln gospel even before Lincoln had the least idea that he would be President.[46] Lincoln had consulted him on the Kansas appointments.[47] In 1861 Lincoln selected Delahay as United States Surveyor General for Kansas and Nebraska,[48] and in December, 1863, elevated him by nominating him to the Senate as Judge of the United States District Court for Kansas,[49] over the protest of the bar and press of the state.[50] "There is not a respectable lawyer in the State that is not absolutely shocked at the appointment," [51] protested one Kansas opponent of Delahay. Collector of Internal Revenue Jackson Grimshaw, of Quincy, Illinois, appealed to Senator Trumbull:

Will the Senate confirm that miserable man Delahay for Judge in Kansas. The appointment is disgraceful to the President who knew Delahay and all his faults, but the disgrace will be greater if the Senate confirms him. He is no lawyer, could not try a case properly even in a Justice's Court, and has no character. Mr. Buchanan in his worst days never made so disgraceful an appointment to the bench.[52]

After prolonged debate the Senate confirmed Delahay.[53] Undoubtedly it was the most disastrous of Lincoln's personal appointments. The President had reason to regret the selection, for so flagrant was Delahay's conduct on the federal bench in Kansas that impeachment proceedings were instituted. The testimony was so damaging that Delahay resigned.[54]

Besides Congress, his Cabinet, the loyal-state governors, Vice President Hamlin, his personal and political friends, Lincoln by means of jobs, contracts, and sundry favors cultivated those ultra-potent forces—the newspaper men. In the 1850's a well-known journalist had boasted: "No party could exist for a year" without

[46] *Uncollected Letters of Abraham Lincoln,* comp. by Tracy, pp. 99–100, 103–4, 116–17, 134–36, 140–42.

[47] Lincoln to M. W. Delahay, March 13, 1861, in *ibid.,* p. 176.

[48] *U. S. Official Register, 1861,* p. 77; *ibid.,* 1863, p. 102.

[49] *U. S. Senate Executive Journal,* XIII (1862–64), 314.

[50] John T. Morton to Trumbull, Nov. 16, 1863, Trumbull Papers.

[51] *Ibid.*

[52] Jackson Grimshaw to Trumbull, Dec. 3, 1863, Trumbull Papers.

[53] *U. S. Senate Executive Journal,* XIII (1862–64), 447.

[54] *New Letters and Papers of Lincoln,* ed. by Angle, p. 243.

the support of the press; [55] and Edward Everett, former President of Harvard College, who experienced political warfare as governor of Massachusetts and United States Senator, declared that "the newspaper press of the United States is, for good or evil, the most powerful influence that acts on the public mind." [56] Of all the journalistic fraternity who gave Lincoln's administration strong support, undoubtedly John W. Forney, of Philadelphia, received the largest rewards from the President.

For a time during the Pierce administration Forney, then a Democrat, had been a partner in the administration organ, the Washington *Union*, and in 1856 had aided in electing his friend James Buchanan President of the United States. He aspired to be editor of the *Union* and the recipient of the lucrative Congressional printing contracts—all of which Buchanan had promised him. But Forney's enemies blocked this. As recompense, Buchanan had them support him for United States Senator from Pennsylvania in 1857, but because of the split in the Democratic ranks that prize had been captured by the wily Simon Cameron. Meanwhile, Forney's friends were vigorously endeavoring to get him into the Buchanan Cabinet, but were blocked by southern opposition. Disgruntled, he openly accused Buchanan of never having truly appreciated his worth. When Buchanan and Senator Stephen A. Douglas clashed over Kansas and other issues, Forney supported Douglas with his Philadelphia *Press*, which he had established in 1857 contrary to Buchanan's wishes.[57] Early in 1860 the Republican majority in Congress had shrewdly capitalized on the Buchanan-Forney split and had elected Forney as Clerk of the House of Representatives. Forney returned the favor by continuing to blast Buchanan and his administration in the columns of the Philadelphia *Press*.[58] In the campaign of 1860 he

[55] Wilmer, *Our Press Gang*, p. 209.   [56] *Ibid.*, p. 64.

[57] Auchampaugh, "John W. Forney, Robert Tyler and James Buchanan," *Tyler's Quarterly Historical and Genealogical Magazine*, XV (Oct., 1933), 71–89; Auchampaugh, *James Buchanan and His Cabinet on the Eve of Secession*, p. 36.

[58] Philadelphia *Press*, Feb. 8, 27, 29, March 6, 17, 31, April 3, 20, 26, 1860. Buchanan was plainly nettled by Forney's defection and unquestionably made an effort to placate him. That he was unsuccessful is to be accounted for largely because he had to choose between Forney and the powerful Senator Slidell and his Southern allies. See Auchampaugh, "John W. Forney, Robert Tyler and James Buchanan," *Tyler's Quarterly Historical and Genealogical Magazine*, XV (Oct., 1933), 88.

indirectly helped Lincoln to carry the Keystone State's huge bloc of electoral votes by attacking the "pro-southern" or Buchanan democracy and openly supporting Douglas for President, thus widening the Democratic split.[59] Lincoln appreciated Forney's aid and, following his election as President, wrote the Philadelphia editor thanking him and tendering him his friendship.[60] During the first month of Lincoln's administration Forney and his Philadelphia *Press* lined up solidly behind the new President.[61]

Lincoln did not long let Forney's services go unrewarded. In March, 1861, when Forney failed of reëlection as Clerk of the House, the President called in person upon a number of Senators and thereby was instrumental, together with Charles Sumner and Schuyler Colfax, in having Forney chosen as Secretary of the Senate at $3,600 per year.[62] Moreover, in this same month of March, 1861, and before the outbreak of war, Lincoln tendered Forney's son a commission as lieutenant in the Marine Corps.[63] It was in the administration's award of advertising contracts, however, that Forney fared best. Although the establishment of the Government Printing Office in 1861 had eliminated the practice of letting out federal printing as a means of subsidizing the party press, there still remained the advertising awards of the various government departments. Fierce competition ensued for these contracts among party publishers and editors.[64] The *United States Official Register* for 1863 lists the following sums, large and small, paid to Forney personally or to his firm for advertising for the War Department alone in either the Philadelphia *Press* or his other newspaper, the Washington *Chronicle:* $112.50;

[59] S. L. Davis, *Pennsylvania Politics, 1860–1863,* pp. 113–14, 119, 134–35.
[60] Forney, *Anecdotes of Public Men,* I, 166.
[61] Philadelphia *Press,* March 21, 1861.
[62] *The Diary of Orville Hickman Browning, 1850–1864,* ed. by Pease and Randall, I, 481–82; Forney, *Anecdotes of Public Men,* I, 167; *Forty Years of American Journalism: Retirement of Mr. J. W. Forney from the Philadelphia "Press,"* p. 14; *U. S. Official Register, 1861,* p. 208.
[63] New York *Daily Tribune,* March 12, 1861.
[64] Sellers, "James R. Doolittle," *The Wisconsin Magazine of History,* XVII (March, 1934), 297. Wm. H. Councell, of the Easton (Maryland) *Gazette,* wrote to his Congressman: "I see that a notice for proposals to carry the United States mails, and their different routes laid down, are extensively advertised throughout the State. . . . I would like to have you drop a word in my favor, to Mr. Blair the Post Master General, in order that I may secure the job also of advertising these routes." See Councell to Creswell, Feb. 1, 1864, John A. J. Creswell Papers.

$161.24; $3.00; $150.00; $1,000.00; $137.77; $119.62; $467.46; $10.12; $58.02; $173.69.[65] From the State Department in two years there came to Forney the sum of $4,776.34 for advertising purposes.[66]

The Washington *Sunday Morning Chronicle* had been founded by Forney in 1861 as a weekly; in November, 1862, the *Daily Morning Chronicle* was started at the suggestion, it was afterwards said, of Lincoln, who feared the influence on the Army of the Potomac of Horace Greeley's anti-administration New York *Tribune*.[67] Ten thousand copies of the *Chronicle* went daily on government order to the Army of the Potomac, and it became the official mouthpiece of Lincoln's administration. Lincoln rendered the *Chronicle* further assistance by appointing one of its editorial writers, Daniel R. Goodloe, as one of the commissioners of emancipation in the District of Columbia. He also appointed one of Forney's brothers-in-law, William Reitzel, who was associated in the business management of the *Chronicle*, as a route agent for the Post Office Department.[68] Moreover, a cousin of Forney, who was also connected with the paper, was given a sinecure in the Interior Department to enable him to devote more time to the *Chronicle* and to take care of his salary.[69] Forney in turn rendered valuable service to the administration as a party tactician and stump speaker; he also proved a big factor in easing the Douglas Democrats of Pennsylvania, by slow degrees, into the Republican fold.[70] In all, Lincoln compensated him handsomely and when the war ended a Pennsylvanian who knew Forney well could write to an associate: "Forney by his *devotion* to Lincoln has made money, and is the proprietor of the 'organ' at Washington and the Press in Philada." [71]

[65] *U. S. Official Register, 1863*, pp. 197, 198.
[66] *U. S. Official Register, 1865*, p. 17.
[67] Washington *Sunday Chronicle*, Dec. 11, 1881, cited in Professor Roy F. Nichols's sketch of Forney in *Dictionary of American Biography*, VI, 527.
[68] Elwyn B. Robinson, "The Public Press of Philadelphia During the Civil War," p. 146.
[69] D. C. Forney to Cameron, April 23, 1863, Cameron Papers; *U. S. Official Register, 1861*, p. 74.
[70] S. L. Davis, *Pennsylvania Politics, 1860–1863*, pp. iv, 242–44, 291, 301.
[71] J. D. Hoover to Howell Cobb, Aug. 31, 1865, in Phillips (ed.), "The Correspondence of Robert Toombs, Alexander H. Stephens and Howell Cobb," *Annual Report*, American Historical Association, II (1911), p. 666.

There were other Philadelphia editors and publishers who received patronage from Lincoln's administration in return for support. Morton McMichael, proprietor of the strongly pro-Lincoln Philadelphia *North American*, received a generous amount of advertising, principally in the form of proposals for the coal, pork, beef, and other supplies needed to carry on the war. For such advertising in the *North American* McMichael received nearly five thousand dollars from the War Department in less than two years. It also published in its columns the laws passed by Congress. To this sum were added the sweets of office. James E. Harvey, Washington correspondent of the *North American*, was named by Lincoln as Minister to Portugal, under strange circumstances, as noted previously. Not long after Harvey's appointment to the Lisbon mission, the bonds between the *North American* and Lincoln's administration were strengthened by favors extended to four of McMichael's sons in the form of Army promotions or civil appointments.[72]

Still another pro-Lincoln organ of the Quaker City received its reward for loyalty—the *Evening Bulletin*. Its publisher, James S. Chambers, secured the position of Navy Agent. As an additional bit of the public pap the father of the *Evening Bulletin's* editor, at the age of seventy-three, was made Superintendent of Warehouses in the Customs service at Philadelphia, at $1,200 per year. Another having connections with this newspaper, Casper Souder, Jr., a reporter and owner of two shares in this journal, received appointment as Inspector of Customs at Philadelphia, with an official salary of $1,905. Furthermore, the *Evening Bulletin* received advertising contracts from the administration.[73]

Lincoln tried his utmost to enlist the support of the nation's most widely circulated Democratic newspaper, the New York *Herald*. For years James Gordon Bennett, the *Herald's* editor, had been a sworn foe of anything smacking of Republicanism; "abolitionists," he called all members of Lincoln's party. The *Herald*, with its large American and European circulation, was creating a public sentiment dangerous to the Lincoln adminis-

[72] Robinson, *"The North American: Advocate of Protection," The Pennsylvania Magazine of History and Biography*, LXIV (July 1940), 345, 350–53.
[73] Robinson, "The Public Press of Philadelphia during the Civil War," pp. 105–6.

tration both at home and across the Atlantic. After discussing the matter with his Cabinet, Lincoln commissioned Thurlow Weed to see Bennett and endeavor to persuade him to change the *Herald's* course by taking a more friendly attitude toward the administration.[74] Weed accordingly visited Bennett in New York where, in the course of conversation, Weed remarked that "Mr. Lincoln deemed it more important to secure the *Herald's* support than to obtain a victory in the field." [75] To what extent the adroit Weed influenced Bennett cannot be determined. But it is worth noting that Bennett himself soon afterward decided to make overtures to Lincoln. For this purpose he sought out Henry Villard, then a young syndicate writer in Washington. Villard's account of his interview with the *Herald* editor follows, in part:

I received a despatch from James Gordon Bennett asking me to come at once to New York. . . . After dinner he [Bennett] disclosed his true purpose in sending for me. First, he wanted me to carry a message from him to Mr. Lincoln that the *Herald* would hereafter be unconditionally for the radical suppression of the Rebellion by force of arms. . . . Secondly, he wanted me to offer to Secretary Chase his son's famous sailing yacht, the *Rebecca*, as a gift to the Government for the revenue service, and to secure in consideration thereof for its owner the appointment of lieutenant in the same service. The last wish I thought rather amusing, but I agreed to lay it before Secretary Chase, to whom I had ready access as the representative of the Cincinnati *Commercial*, his strongest supporter in Ohio.[76]

Villard's account of Bennett's desire that his son receive an officer's commission in the Revenue Service would seem to be correct. For in the historical collection of the Treasury Department is the following letter, which Lincoln wrote to Secretary Chase:

Executive Department
May 6, 1861.

HON. SEC. OF TREASURY
DEAR SIR:
    The Secretary of State this moment introduces to me Mr. James Gordon Bennett, Jr. who tenders to the U. S. service, a fine yacht

---

74 *Autobiography of Thurlow Weed*, pp. 615–16.   75 *Ibid.*, p. 617.
76 *Memoirs of Henry Villard*, I, 161–62.

of 160 tons burthen. If you allow him, which I ask for him, he will talk with you about putting some other vessels of the same class into the service. We send this subject to you because we believe these vessels may be made most available in the Revenue service.

Yours truly,

A. LINCOLN.[77]

It will be perceived that Seward was given the task of steering the younger Bennett to Chase, for the above letter carries the following endorsement:

President Lincoln in relation to the offer of James Gordon Bennett, Jr. to furnish his yacht for the Revenue Cutter Service.

May 6, 1861.

Commission as Third Lieutenant in Revenue Cutter Service sent to Mr. Bennett May 15, 1861.

W. H. S.[78]

The junior Bennett's yacht was not the *Rebecca,* as Villard stated, but the *Henrietta,* named after the young man's mother. The Treasury Department records show that the vessel was equipped with armament. Bennett's commission was dated May 14, 1861. The cutter cruised off the Long Island coast during 1861 and in the following February was reported at Port Royal, South Carolina. In April, 1862, she was withdrawn from service, and in the following month Lieutenant Bennett tendered his resignation, which was accepted. No glory appears to have been acquired, but ever after he dwelt upon the fact that he had served his country upon the sea.[79]

Lincoln continued to woo James Gordon Bennett, Sr. One officeholder, the erratic Count Adam Gurowski, even claimed that Lincoln read no newspaper except the New York *Herald;*[80] undoubtedly this was an exaggeration, for in all probability the President read other journals. When the *Herald* editor was relentlessly pounding Secretary of War Stanton over the shoulders of General Hunter for the latter's proclamation uttered at Harper's Ferry, freeing slaves, Lincoln wrote Bennett:

[77] Lincoln to the Secretary of the Treasury, May 6, 1861, in Seitz, *The James Gordon Bennetts: Father and Son,* p. 181.

[78] *Ibid.,* pp. 181–82.   [79] *Ibid.,* p. 182.

[80] *Diary of Adam Gurowski,* I, 81.

Private.

Executive Mansion,
May 21, 1862.

JAMES GORDON BENNETT, ESQ.

Dear Sir: Thanking you again for the able support given by you
through the *Herald* to what I think the true course of the country,
and also for your kind expressions toward me personally. I wish to
correct an erroneous impression of yours in regard to the Secretary
of War. He mixes no politics whatever with his duties; knew nothing
of General Hunter's proclamation; and he and I alone got up the
counter proclamation. I wish this to go no further than to you,
while I wish to assure you it is true.

Yours truly,
ABRAHAM LINCOLN [81]

Bennett's favorable policy toward the Lincoln administration
was of short duration, and he soon reverted to his critical attitude
toward the President; by early 1864, when the questions of Lincoln's renomination and reëlection were being considered, the
Herald was running editorials of which "Why General Grant Is
the Best Candidate for The Presidency" is an example.[82] To win
back the influential editor's support, Lincoln in February, 1865,
offered him the cherished post of Minister to France. But either
Bennett declined the proffer, or else Lincoln was assassinated before he could arrange the appointment.[83]

That Lincoln fully appreciated the power of the press and the
desirability of journalists and former journalists in federal posts
at home and abroad is evident from even a casual examination
of his appointments.[84] In fact, Lincoln seems to have chosen more
newspaper men for official positions than any of his predecessors
in the White House. At random may be named some two score
of publishers, editors, and ace correspondents who received fed-

[81] Lincoln to Bennett, May 21, 1862, in Seitz, *The James Gordon Bennetts: Father
and Son*, p. 187.
[82] New York *Herald*, Jan. 6, 1864.
[83] Lincoln to James Gordon Bennett, Feb. 20, 1865, in Seitz, *The James Gordon
Bennetts: Father and Son*, p. 193; *Diary of Gideon Welles*, II, 258; *Autobiography
of Thurlow Weed*, p. 619.
[84] Chauncey M. Depew quotes Lincoln as remarking in 1864: "No man, whether
he be private citizen or President of the United States, can successfully carry on
a controversy with a great newspaper, and escape destruction, unless he owns a
newspaper equally great, with a circulation in the same neighborhood." See Rice
(ed.), *Reminiscences of Abraham Lincoln by Distinguished Men of His Time*,
p. 436.

eral appointments at his hands. Among them were George G. Fogg, of the Concord (New Hampshire) *Independent Democrat*, Minister to Switzerland; [85] James F. Babcock, of the New Haven *Palladium*, Collector of Customs at the Port of New Haven; [86] George Dawson, of the Albany *Evening Journal*, postmaster at Albany, N.Y.; [87] Charles A. Dana, of the New York *Tribune*, Assistant Secretary of War; [88] James S. Pike, of the New York *Tribune*, Minister to Holland; [89] Bayard Taylor, of the New York *Tribune*, First Secretary of Legation in St. Petersburg; [90] William H. Fry, of the New York *Tribune*, First Secretary of Legation in Turin; [91] John Bigelow, of the New York *Evening Post*, Consul General at Paris; [92] Horace N. Congar, of the Newark *Daily Mercury*, Consul at Hong Kong; [93] Jacob R. Freese, of the Trenton *State Gazette*, Commissioner of the Board of Enrollment for the Second District of New Jersey; [94] George Bergner, of the Harrisburg *Telegraph*, postmaster in Harrisburg; [95] Russell Errett, of the Pittsburgh *Gazette*, paymaster in the Army; [96] John. S. Prettyman, of the Milford (Delaware) *Peninsular News and Advertiser*, Consul at Glasgow; [97] John F. McJilton, of the Baltimore *Patriot*, Surveyor of the Port of Baltimore; [98] James C. Welling, of the Washington *Na-*

[85] Lyford, *History of Concord, New Hampshire*, II, 1034–35.

[86] *Diary of Gideon Welles*, I, 81 n.; *U. S. Official Register, 1861*, p. 48; *ibid., 1863*, p. 67; *ibid., 1865*, p. 92.

[87] Howell and Tenney (eds.), *History of the County of Albany, N.Y.*, p. 360; Barnes, *Memoir of Thurlow Weed*, p. 29.

[88] Stone, *Dana and the Sun*, pp. 23–24; Shannon, *The Organization and Administration of the Union Army, 1861–1865*, II, 263.

[89] "The Notebooks of James S. Pike, 1861–1862," ed. by H. A. Davis, pp. 2–6.

[90] Beatty, *Bayard Taylor*, pp. 223–24; Hansen-Taylor and Scudder, *Life and Letters of Bayard Taylor*, I, 383–86.

[91] *Dwight's Journal of Music*, April 6, 1861, p. 3.

[92] John Bigelow Diary, July–Aug., 1861.

[93] Shaw, *History of Essex and Hudson Counties, New Jersey*, I, 283.

[94] Lincoln to Provost Marshal General, Sept. 27, 1864, Lincoln Letters, Photostats; Jacob R. Freese to Chase, Dec. 18, 1863, Chase Papers, Historical Society of Pennsylvania, Library of Congress.

[95] Egle, *History of the Counties of Dauphin and Lebanon in the Commonwealth of Pennsylvania*, pp. 465–66; *U. S. Official Register, 1863*, p. 591.

[96] *Biographical Directory of the American Congress, 1774–1927*, p. 948; *U. S. Senate Executive Journal*, XII (1861–62), 64; J. Cutler Andrews, *Pittsburgh's Post-Gazette*, pp. 147, 153.

[97] Milford (Del.) *Peninsular News and Advertiser*, Sept. 20, 1861; Nov. 28, 1862.

[98] Montgomery Blair to the President, undated (copy), Blair Papers, Library of Congress (in box marked "1864"); *U. S. Official Register, 1861*, p. 65.

tional Intelligencer, Assistant Clerk in the United States Court of Claims; [99] Archibald W. Campbell, of the Wheeling *Intelligencer*, postmaster in Wheeling; [100] Frederick Hassaurek, of the Cincinnati *Volksblatt*, Minister to Ecuador; [101] Victor Smith, of the Cincinnati *Commercial*, Special Treasury Agent and Collector of Customs at Puget Sound; [102] James H. Barrett, of the Cincinnati *Gazette*, Commissioner of Pensions; [103] William Dean Howells, of the Columbus *Ohio State Journal*, Consul in Venice.[104]

Those just named did not exhaust the list. Among others were Edwin Cowles, of the Cleveland *Leader*, postmaster in Cleveland; [105] John D. Defrees, of the Indianapolis *Journal*, Superintendent of Public Printing; [106] John W. Dawson, of the Fort Wayne *Times*, governor of Utah Territory; [107] John. L. Scripps, of the Chicago *Press & Tribune*, postmaster in Chicago; [108] Charles L. Wilson, of the Chicago *Daily Journal*, First Secretary of Legation in London; [109] George Schneider, of the Chicago *Illinois Staats-Zeitung*, Consul at Elsinore, Denmark; [110] David L. Phillips, of the Springfield *Illinois State Journal*, United States Marshal for the Southern District of Illinois; [111] Theodore Canisius, of the Springfield *Illinois Staats-Anzeiger*, Consul at Vienna; [112] Rufus King, of the Milwaukee *Sentinel*, Minister to the

[99] "The Diary of Edward Bates, 1859–1866," ed. by Howard K. Beale, *Annual Report*, American Historical Association, IV (1930), 26 n.

[100] Ambler, *West Virginia: Stories and Biographies*, pp. 237–38; New York *Daily Tribune*, March 22, 1861.

[101] Herriott, "The Conference at the Deutsches Haus, Chicago, May 14–15, 1860," *Transactions of the Illinois State Historical Society*, 1928, pp. 133, 145; *U. S. Official Register, 1861*, p. 11; *ibid., 1865*, p. 11.

[102] Meany, *History of the State of Washington*, pp. 259–60.

[103] Barrett to Chase, April 9, 1860, Chase Papers, Library of Congress; *The National Cyclopaedia of American Biography*, XIII, 167.

[104] Howells, *Years of My Youth*, pp. 202 ff.

[105] Tarbell, *The Life of Abraham Lincoln*, II, 340; Riddle, *Recollections of War Times, 1860–1865*, pp. 20–24; *U. S. Official Register, 1861*, p. 306.

[106] Sulgrove, "John D. Defrees," *Indiana Magazine of History*, II (1905), 147–50.

[107] B. J. Griswold, *The Pictorial History of Fort Wayne, Indiana*, I, 341.

[108] *Journal of the Illinois State Historical Society*, XVII (1924–25), 343–46.

[109] Bateman and Selby (eds.), *Historical Encyclopedia of Illinois*, I, 592–93.

[110] Arthur C. Cole, *The Era of the Civil War, 1848–1870*, pp. 25, 26, 123, 342.

[111] Springfield *Daily Illinois State Journal*, Jan. 1, 1864; D. L. Phillips to Trumbull, March 20, 1864, Trumbull Papers; Arthur C. Cole, *The Era of the Civil War, 1848–1870*, p. 395.

[112] Franklin W. Scott, *Newspapers and Periodicals of Illinois, 1814–1879*, p. 324; A. C. Cole, *The Era of the Civil War, 1848–1870*, p. 342.

Papal States; [113] Carl Roeser, of the Manitowoc *Wisconsin Demokrat*, clerk in the Treasury Department; [114] Peter L. Foy, of the St. Louis *Missouri Democrat*, postmaster in St. Louis; [115] Henry Boernstein, of the St. Louis *Anzeiger des Westens*, Consul at Bremen; [116] Charles L. Bernays, also of the St. Louis *Anzeiger des Westens*, Consul at Zurich; [117] William F. Switzler, of the Columbia *Missouri Statesman*, Military Secretary of State for the conquered state of Arkansas and later Provost Marshal for the Ninth Congressional District of Missouri; [118] John Teesdale, of the Des Moines *Iowa State Register*, postmaster in Des Moines; [119] Daniel W. Wilder, of the Leavenworth *Conservative*, United States Surveyor General for Kansas and Nebraska; [120] Thomas J. Dryer, of the Portland *Oregonian*, Commissioner to the Hawaiian Islands.[121]

Well could a contemporary observer comment: "Editors seem to be in very great favor with the party in power—a larger number of the fraternity having received appointments at its hands than probably under any previous Administration." [122]

Not all of the newspaper men appointed to jobs by Lincoln lived up to the expectations of the administration. There was the case of John F. McJilton, editor of the Baltimore *Patriot*, who received from Lincoln the post of Surveyor of the Port of Baltimore. Postmaster General Blair, a power in parceling out the

[113] Charles King, "Rufus King: Soldier, Editor and Statesman," *The Wisconsin Magazine of History*, IV (1920–21), 373–81; Lanman, *Biographical Annals of the Civil Government of the United States*, p. 242. King had been appointed in 1861, but he served in the army until 1863, when he went to Rome.

[114] *History of Manitowoc County, Wisconsin*, pp. 98, 99.

[115] Stevens, "Lincoln and Missouri," *The Missouri Historical Review*, X (Jan., 1916), 66; "The Diary of Edward Bates, 1859–1866," ed. by Howard K. Beale, *Annual Report*, American Historical Association, IV (1930), 133 n.

[116] W. E. Smith, *The Francis Preston Blair Family in Politics*, II, 208–9; Hyde and Conard (eds.), *Encyclopedia of the History of St. Louis*, III, 1636.

[117] *Ibid.*, I, 142.

[118] Gentry, "William F. Switzler," *The Missouri Historical Review*, XXIV (Jan., 1930), 161, 168–69.

[119] Gue, *History of Iowa*, IV, 259–60.

[120] Leavenworth *Daily Conservative*, April 20, 1864; *Kansas Historical Collections*, VII (1901–2), 155 n.–56 n.; *The National Cyclopaedia of American Biography*, XI, 191.

[121] Carey, *History of Oregon*, I, 517, 632 n., 640, 645; Horace S. Lyman, *History of Oregon*, IV, 244, 280–81.

[122] Baltimore *Evening Patriot*, March 30, 1861.

Maryland patronage, recommended to Lincoln his removal, explaining:

McJilton was appointed because he had the Baltimore *Patriot*. He has not done us any political service & the office was conferred in consideration of the support which *was expected* from the Baltimore *Patriot*. But Mr. McJilton did not keep faith. He severed his connection immediately with the *Patriot* & never rendered the least assistance to that paper or any other to sustain the Administration. He is a man of no personal influence whatever & no claims of any kind to the position.[123]

Apparently, newspaper men without power to influence public opinion were not wanted.

Before the year 1861 had run its course complaints against Simon Cameron's shameful mismanagement of the War Department and his favoritism and alleged frauds were pouring into Washington almost daily and demands for his removal became more persistent. Many charged him with responsibility for the poor showing of the Union armies. Powerful eastern financial interests insisted that he go. "The Government should know," wrote a member of the New York banking community to Senator Fessenden, "that a feeling of great distrust and dissatisfaction exists . . . with the present Cabinet; it has not the confidence of the moneyied [sic] interests. . . . The *dissatisfaction is with Mr. Cameron*. . . . Public good requires another man in his place." [124] The radicals hated him and resolved to dislodge him.[125] "His presence taints the reputation of the whole Cabinet," wrote William Cullen Bryant, editor of the New York *Evening Post*, "and I think he should be ousted at once." [126] On every hand it was evident that popular discontent over Cameron was weakening Lincoln's administration. In the words of a back-country editor:

Secretary Cameron—It is painfully apparent that there is a growing distrust of the capability of the present Administration to con-

[123] Montgomery Blair to the President, undated (copy), Francis Preston Blair Papers. (In box marked "1864.")

[124] J. G. Butterworth to Fessenden, July 3, 1861, William P. Fessenden Papers.

[125] T. H. Williams, *Lincoln and the Radicals,* pp. 29, 37.

[126] W. C. Bryant to J. M. Forbes in *Letters and Recollections of John Murray Forbes,* ed. by Hughes, I, 243.

duct this war to a successful issue. . . . A great many patriotic men are strongly inclined to the belief that the heads of some of the departments are more interested in fat contracts than in the speedy and successful termination of this war. In a particular manner has Mr. Cameron, Secretary of War, excited this suspicion. . . . As it is, Mr. Lincoln should rise to the dignity of his position, and remove him.[127]

Lincoln was not unaware of the mounting volume of adverse criticism of his Secretary of War. Indeed the President himself had been dissatisfied with Cameron for some time and apparently had not forgotten that the slippery Pennsylvanian had secured his Cabinet post by wirepulling and intrigue, much against Lincoln's better judgment.[128] But Cameron was also aware of the attitude of the country toward him and in the autumn of 1861 endeavored to neutralize his unpopularity by switching from the conservatives to the camp of the radicals. In his right-about-face not only did he authorize the use of Negro soldiers,[129] but, at the secret instigation of Edwin M. Stanton, he inserted in his annual report to Congress a recommendation for the creation of an army of freed slaves. Lincoln was not consulted and the report was hurried to the newspapers unknown to him. As soon as he learned of the proposal to arm the slaves, the nettled President, whose patience with Cameron was now threadbare, ordered the report to be recalled and the section deleted.[130] This occurred on the fourth of December.[131]

[127] Frankfort (Ky.) *Tri-Weekly Commonwealth,* Aug. 26, 1861.

[128] Lincoln's secretary, John G. Nicolay, after a conversation with the President, wrote down on a memorandum: "Cameron utterly ignorant and regardless of the course of things and probable result. Selfish and openly discourteous to the President. Obnoxious to the country. Incapable either of organizing details or conceiving and executing general plans." This is printed in Rhodes, *History of the Civil War,* p. 84.

[129] See Cochrane, *The American Civil War;* New York *Tribune,* Oct. 29, 1861; Washington *National Intelligencer,* Nov. 14, 1861.

[130] According to Gideon Welles, Cameron attempted to justify himself on the ground that there was nothing novel in his report and that his proposal to arm the Negro already had, he supposed, the approval of the President and the Cabinet. During the controversy Chase took it upon himself not only to apologize for Cameron but to defend him. See A. Howard Meneely (ed.), "Three Manuscripts of Gideon Welles," *The American Historical Review,* XXXI, 487. Also "The Diary of Edward Bates, 1859–1866," ed. by Howard K. Beale, *Annual Report,* American Historical Association, IV (1930), 203.

[131] A. B. Ely wrote Senator Sumner, Jan. 14, 1862: "Cameron's report which contained the suppressed part about contrabands was got up by him and put out

A FALL NOT CONTRACTED FOR; CAMERON DISCREDITED

From *Vanity Fair*, IV (Sept. 21, 1861), 133.

With passing weeks the movement for Cameron's dismissal gathered momentum.[132] Lincoln had made up his mind that the unpopular Pennsylvanian must go. Cameron, too clever a politician not to sense the situation, began, half-heartedly, to indicate that he was willing to resign but did not want to leave under fire. Fate played into Lincoln's hands. Cassius M. Clay, minister to Russia, had expressed a desire to return home and enter the Army service. On January 11 (1862) Lincoln sent Cameron two notes. One read: "As you have, more than once, expresed a desire for a change of position, I can now gratify you, consistently with my view of the public interest. I therefore propose nominating you to the Senate, next Monday, as minister to Russia." In the second epistle, more informal and lengthy, Lincoln informed Cameron that "the desire of Mr. Clay to return home and to offer his services to his country in the field enables me now to gratify your wish, and at the same time evince my personal regard for you, and my confidence in your ability, patriotism, and fidelity to public trust." [133] Cameron responded the same day with his resignation from the War portfolio.[134] On January 13 Lincoln nominated him as Minister to Russia.[135] In the opinion of at least one contemporary, Cameron's unwept departure from Lincoln's Cabinet came because he "divided his efforts between Pennsylvania contractors and Massachusetts abolitionists" [136]—these last words being inspired by Cameron's recommendation that the Negroes be armed.

The Senate hesitated about agreeing to Cameron's selection for the St. Petersburg mission and it was only after a bitter fight and by a vote of 28 to 14 that it ratified his appointment to that post.[137] The House of Representatives, however, did not allow

by him not because he cared anything about the slaves, but merely as a tub to the popular whale, so as to turn away inquiry from the corruptions of his department." Ely added: "Thad Stevens said Cameron would add a million to his fortune. I guess he has done it." See Rhodes, *History of the United States from the Compromise of 1850,* III, 576 n.

[132] For Cameron's activities as Secretary of War, consult Meneely, *The War Department, 1861.*

[133] The originals of these two letters are in the Cameron Papers.

[134] *Complete Works of Abraham Lincoln,* VII, 80–82.

[135] *U. S. Senate Executive Journal,* XII (1861–62), 75.

[136] Cincinnati *Daily Commercial,* Jan. 20, 1862.

[137] *The Diary of Orville Hickman Browning, 1850–1864,* ed. by Pease and Randall, I, 524–25. The question of whether Cameron resigned of his own accord or

Cameron's conduct of the War Department to pass unnoticed and in April (1862) that body, by a vote of 79 to 45, adopted the following resolution:

Resolved, That Simon Cameron, late Secretary of War, by investing Alexander Cummings with the control of large sums of the public money, and authority to purchase military supplies, without restriction, without requiring from him any guarantee for the faithful performance of his duties, when the services of competent public officers were available, and by involving the Government in a vast number of contracts with persons not legitimately engaged in the business pertaining to the subject-matter of such contracts, especially in the purchase of arms for future delivery, has adopted a policy highly injurious to the public service, and deserves the censure of the House.[138]

As Cameron's successor Lincoln decided on a Democrat, Edwin M. Stanton, a native of Steubenville, Ohio, who had served as Attorney General in Buchanan's cabinet. Various explanations for Lincoln's action in choosing Stanton for the all-important War Office have been offered. Some insist that for many years prior to his election to the presidency, Lincoln had been impressed by Stanton's ability, energy, and fidelity as a lawyer. Together with Lincoln he had been one of the leading counsels in the noted patent case of *McCormick vs. Manny* [139] and had made a deep impression on the future President by his masterly defense of their client Manny.[140] Others maintain that Lincoln was motivated

---

was removed has been a matter of controversy. Professor A. Howard Meneely, most eminent authority on Cameron, concludes that Cameron was removed. The Russian ambassadorship merely eased the pain of removal. See Meneely, *The War Department, 1861,* pp. 365–70; and also Meneely's sketch of Cameron in *Dictionary of American Biography,* III, 438; New York *Herald,* Jan. 17, 18, 1862.

[138] *Congressional Globe,* 37th Cong., 2d sess., p. 1888.

[139] John McLean, *Reports of Cases . . . in the Circuit Court of the United States for the Seventh Circuit,* VI (1856), 539.

[140] Beveridge, *Abraham Lincoln, 1809–1858,* I, 581. Lincoln's law partner, William H. Herndon, was of the opinion that in appointing Stanton to his Cabinet Lincoln revealed himself as a person of great mental stature. At the time of the McCormick-Manny case (1855), Lincoln was an obscure, illy clad frontier lawyer. Stanton, having little faith in Lincoln's ability and not wanting him in the case, treated him with exceeding discourtesy and in conversation with a third party referred to him as a "damned long armed ape." Lincoln overheard the remark, became discouraged and indignant and left the case. See Hertz, *The Hidden Lincoln,* pp. 153–54.

by Stanton's pro-Unionism. From his days as a Kenyon College undergraduate to the time he entered Lincoln's Cabinet, Stanton adhered quite consistently to the Democratic party. Nevertheless he was outspoken in his disapproval of the institution of slavery, favored the Wilmot Proviso, and opposed the abandonment of Fort Sumter. Though he professed hatred for "Black Republicans" and was unsparing in his criticism of the administration during the early months of Lincoln's presidency, he was on extremely friendly terms with Seward. Indeed, Secretary of the Navy Welles believed firmly that Seward was responsible for the selection of Stanton, and the diary of Attorney General Bates partially supports this contention.[141] Incidentally Secretary of the Treasury Chase, who was to play a prominent part in naming Cameron's successor, was one of the very few who were reluctant to see Cameron leave the War Department.[142]

Still another and more probable explanation of Stanton's selection for the War portfolio lies in the story of his unceasing and oleaginous efforts to secure the post. Oddly enough, though a critic of the administration, Stanton early in 1861 managed to get himself appointed legal adviser to Cameron. Thereafter no course was too tortuous for him to follow in supplanting his chief. Not only did he studiously ingratiate himself with the radicals but with every influential person and group whom he thought he could manipulate in support of his candidacy. His gift for being all things to all men was never more brilliantly demonstrated, and the number of discordant factions and groups he was able to line up in support of his candidacy seems almost unbelievable. The author of *Lincoln and the Radicals* succinctly summarizes Stanton's achievement:

The conservatives in the Cabinet, Seward, Welles, and Blair, pushed Stanton's cause with Lincoln because they thought they were getting an ally to take the place of Cameron, who had deserted to the radicals. For the same reason, moderate Republicans like Senator Doo-

141 Welles to Montgomery Blair, June [no day listed], 1870, Gideon Welles Papers, New York Public Library; "Diary of Edward Bates, 1859–1866," ed. by Howard K. Beale, *Annual Report,* American Historical Association, IV (1930), 226.

142 For Chase's strong attachment to Cameron, see Chase to Cameron (Absolutely Private and Confidential), Jan. 18, 1862, Simon Cameron Papers.

little and the editors of *Harper's Weekly* backed Stanton. The leaders of the Border-State unionists, men who represented slave-holding communities and who would have fought any measures directed against slavery, were delighted that such a doughty foe of abolitionism had replaced the detestable Cameron. They looked to Stanton to save the president from the assaults of the Jacobins. In the same fools' paradise were the Democrats, enraptured at the prospect of a champion in the Cabinet. Stanton had won Bennett and the *Herald* by promising that his policy as secretary would be identical with McClellan's. Loyal Democrats deluged Stanton with congratulatory letters which in a few months would have an ironic and fatuous ring. . . . Finally Stanton had the powerful support of McClellan, who believed the new Secretary to be his truest friend.[143]

Little did McClellan at first realize that at the very time Stanton was posing as his bosom friend he was denouncing him to his enemies, the radicals. With the passage of time not only McClellan but the others who had supported Stanton were to learn, to their chagrin, that the new Secretary of War was indeed wedded to such radicals as Senators Wade, Chandler, Sumner, and Wilson, who everywhere rejoiced that in Stanton they had a War Secretary who would kick out the West Point-trained, pro-slavery generals and who, in other respects, would do their bidding. Well might Chase, who played a major role in lining up support for Stanton among the Republicans, feel assuaged for the loss of Cameron.[144]

Though Stanton's administration of the War Department left much to be desired, he nevertheless brought to it an efficiency and a kind of intregrity unknown under Cameron. Not only was the department pretty completely overhauled and reorganized and its personnel increased, but the work to be done was systematized. Contracts were investigated, those tainted with fraud were revoked, and their perpetrators prosecuted without mercy. Patronage hunters found the pickings considerably less attractive, and the department ceased to be the principal headquarters for spoilsmen. The close relationship between Stanton and the radicals continued to the end of the war, much to the annoyance of Lincoln and

143 T. H. Williams, *Lincoln and the Radicals,* p. 91.
144 On the attitude of radicals toward Stanton, see *ibid.,* pp. 89–90.

others who opposed the radical program. Frequently army commanders, cabinet members, and other officials were the victims of Stanton's unbridled tongue and autocratic decisions.[145]

Following the withdrawal of Cameron from the War Department and the succession of Stanton the press was filled with rumors of additional Cabinet changes.[146] Even before these rumors spread it was common property that the Cabinet, which represented different shades of opinion, was far from harmonious. The two factions into which the official family was split, "conservatives" and "radicals," had no love for each other. Seward, spokesman for the conservatives, was especially disliked by Chase and his fellow radicals both in and out of the Cabinet. Contrary to their wishes, Seward, with Machiavellian skill, had brought Cameron into the Cabinet, much to the disgust of that arch-radical Thaddeus Stevens, himself a candidate, as we have seen, for a Cabinet post. Even more distasteful to the radicals was the role of "prime minister," which, they asserted not without truth, Seward had essayed to play. If Lincoln was the "simple Susan" that Samuel Bowles of the Springfield (Massachusetts) *Republican* thought,[147] then the administration, they reasoned, would be Seward-dominated and -controlled.

It is easy to understand, therefore, why they moved heaven and earth in an effort to compel Lincoln to dismiss the New Yorker. "Seward must be got out of the Cabinet," wrote Joseph Medill of the Chicago *Tribune* to Schuyler Colfax. "He has been President *de facto*, and has kept a sponge saturated with chloroform to Uncle Abe's nose all the while. . . . Smith is a cipher on the right hand of the Seward integer—by himself, nothing but a doughface. Bates is a fossil of the Silurian era—red sandstone, at least—and should never have been quarried out of the rocks in which he was imbedded. . . . Seward, Smith, and Bates

145 E. G. Spaulding to Weed, Feb. 9, 1862, Thurlow Weed Papers, University of Rochester Library; Flower, *Edwin McMasters Stanton*, pp. 118–20, 127–32; Gorham, *Life and Public Services of Edwin M. Stanton*, I, 3–4, 255–67; Shannon, *The Organization and Administration of the Union Army, 1861–1865*, I, 75; Ginsberg, "Corruption and Fraud in Government Contracts During the Civil War," pp. 21–22.

146 Columbus *Daily Ohio State Journal*, Jan. 20, 23, 1862; New York *Herald*, Jan. 15, Feb. 2, 1862, are typical of what other news sheets printed concerning the rumored cabinet shake ups.

147 Merriam, *The Life and Times of Samuel Bowles*, I, 318.

must go out." [148] Seward, in the opinion of one radical journal, was "The Unseen Hand" that had mesmerized the President.[149]

Though some of the radicals, including Senator Fessenden of Maine, despaired of forcing Lincoln to oust Seward, others were still hopeful.[150] General Burnside's disastrous defeat at Fredericksburg seemed to afford a propitious time to put pressure on the discouraged President. Accordingly, three days after the battle, the Republican Senators met in caucus. Senator Morton S. Wilkinson, of Minnesota, opened fire on the Secretary of State; he blamed Seward for all the government's failures and scathingly asserted that "so long as he remained in the Cabinet nothing but defeat and disaster could be expected." [151] Senator James W. Grimes, of Iowa, moved a resolution expressing lack of confidence in Seward, which the conservatives opposed.[152] Finally it was agreed that a committee be appointed to wait upon Lincoln and inform him that the Senate demanded such Cabinet changes as would "give the administration unity and vigor." After conferring with the radically controlled committee in two long sessions Lincoln calmly informed the Senators that Seward had tendered his resignation, but he had refused to accept it. To force the New Yorker out might, Lincoln feared, wreck the administration. Though the radicals continued sporadically to turn their heavy guns on Seward they were never able to dislodge him.[153]

Chase, who was working hand in glove with the radicals to get Seward out, also submitted his resignation at this time. Prior to the Republican caucus he had led the radical spokesmen to believe that Seward was primarily responsible for the lack of Cabinet harmony. When asked by Lincoln in the presence of the members of the Senate committee appointed to wait on the President, and all the members of the Cabinet except Seward, whether he had spread reports damaging to Seward's reputation and to the Cabinet, Chase cringingly and indirectly admitted that he had not told the truth. To save face with the country, he declared

---

[148] Joseph Medill to Schuyler Colfax in Hollister, *Life of Schuyler Colfax,* p. 200.
[149] *Wilkes' Spirit of the Times,* Dec. 6, 1862.
[150] T. H. Williams, *Lincoln and the Radicals,* pp. 207–8.
[151] Quoted in *ibid.,* p. 208.   [152] *Ibid.,* pp. 208–9.
[153] *Ibid.,* pp. 211, 218–19, 315–16; Francis Fessenden, *Life and Public Services of William Pitt Fessenden,* I, 231–51. These pages contain a detailed account of what occurred from the time the Republican caucus was called to the end of the committee's second interview with Lincoln and its aftermath.

that he deemed it advisable to quit the Cabinet, first, because he did not want the public to conclude that he had been instrumental in getting rid of Seward in order to gain control of the Cabinet; and secondly, the hostility of Seward's friends would be so great that his usefulness in Lincoln's official family would be seriously impaired.[154] Whatever the motive back of Chase's action, Lincoln refused to accept the proffered resignation.

While the radicals were scheming to oust Seward, the overworked President was endeavoring to find a way of dispensing with the services of Caleb B. Smith, his Secretary of the Interior. Lincoln had been anxious to get rid of Smith for some time—at least so confided Mrs. Lincoln to Lincoln's friend, Senator Orville H. Browning of Illinois. Browning confided to his diary:

Sunday Decr. 14, 1862: Mrs. Lincoln sent her carriage this morning for me to go to Church with her which I did. The President did not go. After Church she rode with me to Capitol Hill. On our way down she told me the President was anxious to get Secretary Smith out of the Cabinet, and me in his place. That he was anxious to have Mrs. Browning and myself in Washington, and the only thing that would prevent him offering me the place would be the fear of having it said he was giving everything to Illinois, but she thought he would do it— She knew he wished to.[155]

Aside from the honor and patronage enjoyed from his elevated position, Smith had little taste or liking for administering a vast governmental department whose jurisdiction stretched from ocean to ocean.[156] Moreover, he was handicapped, being essentially a jobbing politician and party spellbinder of Indiana. Smith had squeezed himself into the Cabinet by intriguing with Thurlow Weed, Cameron, and Judge David Davis. His friend and successor had this impression of him:

Then there was Mr. Caleb Smith, Secretary of the Interior, whom I succeeded. . . . I knew him well. He was a true orator. He was

---

[154] Consult the long letter, under date of Dec. 20, 1862, sent by Henry Cooke to Jay Cooke and quoted in Oberholtzer, *Jay Cooke, Financier of the Civil War,* I, 224–26.

[155] *The Diary of Orville Hickman Browning, 1850–1864,* ed. by Pease and Randall, I, 595–96.

[156] James G. Blaine was of the opinion that Smith "had no aptitude for so serious a task as the administration of a great department." See Blaine, *Twenty Years of Congress,* I, 285.

a man who, from the rostrum, would talk to you until you would feel the blood tingling through your veins to your finger ends and all the way up your spine. When you meet a man who can do that, argument is at an end; you are carried away by the irresistable power of eloquence.[157]

Smith had high hopes at this time that Lincoln would elevate him to the United States Supreme Court bench, and his friends in Congress worked hard to secure the passage of a measure which would gerrymander the circuits so as to make him eligible for the nation's highest tribunal without interfering with the candidacy of Senator Browning, who aspired to the same high judicial post. [158] But Lincoln finally concluded to appoint neither to the highest Court, much to the disappointment of both.

Upon reflection, however, Smith, much to Lincoln's relief, decided to accept a more modest judgeship. The death in October, 1862, of Judge Elisha M. Huntington had created a vacancy in the United States District Court for Indiana. John P. Usher, fellow Hoosier and close friend of Smith, whom Smith had already rewarded with the post of Assistant Secretary of the Interior, was anxious for the vacant Indiana judgeship. Smith was aware of this fact, but when Usher, absent on a mission to Minnesota, reminded him by wire of an earlier promise to use his influence in Usher's behalf, he responded that he had concluded to resign from the Cabinet in favor of Usher and to take the judgeship himself. Lincoln readily agreed to this arrangement and appointed Smith to the court vacancy and nominated Usher as Secretary of the Interior. Neither Smith nor Usher had any trouble at the hands of the Senate.[159] To the vacant Assistant Secretaryship of the department Usher had Lincoln appoint his

[157] *President Lincoln's Cabinet by Honorable John P. Usher, Secretary of the Interior, January 7, 1863–May 15, 1865,* p. 17.

[158] Under the existing judicial set up Indiana and Illinois were in the same circuit and the appointment of both Smith and Browning to the Supreme Court was therefore impossible. See "The Diary of Edward Bates, 1859–1866," ed. by Howard K. Beale, *Annual Report,* American Historical Association, IV (1930), 228, 244.

[159] *President Lincoln's Cabinet by Honorable John P. Usher. . . .* pp. 6–7; *U. S. Senate Executive Journal,* XIII (1862–64), 10, 21, 22, 28. When Smith died in Indiana in 1864, the statement was made that Usher had desired the judgeship for Indiana when he first came to Washington. See Cincinnati *Daily Gazette,* Jan. 9, 1864.

old friend and Indiana political associate, Judge William T. Otto. The latter had been defeated for state attorney general in 1858; as one of Indiana's delegates at large to the Chicago Convention in 1860 he had served as the Hoosier state's member of the Platform Committee.[160]

These changes, once made, eased Lincoln's mind for the time being. Before his first four years in the presidency were over, however, his official family was to undergo further modification, as we shall see.

[160] Seeds, *History of the Republican Party of Indiana,* I, 28, 31; Zimmerman, "The Origin and Rise of the Republican Party in Indiana From 1854 To 1860," *Indiana Magazine of History,* XIII (Dec., 1917), 365, 382-83, 393; M. M. Gresham, *Life of Walter Quintin Gresham,* I, 75, 77, 110.

Chapter VI

CONTRACTS AND COMMISSIONS

THE IMMENSE PATRONAGE of the national government is subject to much favoritism under almost any administration. Lincoln's was no exception. When armed civil conflict burst suddenly upon an unprepared government in April, 1861, a difficult problem arose in placing the government on a war footing. Vast stores of supplies were required, in addition to those needed for the normal functions of government. It was almost inevitable that promoters, merchants, manufacturers, commission brokers, and inventors should descend on Washington, plying their wares or seeking other favors. But these several categories were outnumbered by the army of office seekers, anxious to feed on the patronage that the military struggle made available in ever-increasing quantity. Lincoln himself seems not to have been averse to turning a little of the spoils into special channels.[1] He was pleased when his friends received contracts "on fair and just claims to the Government and to themselves." [2]

There is little doubt that several of Lincoln's Cabinet members used their positions to award contracts and grant other concessions to their friends and relatives. There were the ubiquitous Blairs, for example, who seemed to be continually giving advice to Lincoln on diverse problems.[3] Postmaster General Blair, wrote Attorney General Bates, "takes special care of himself, his family and special friends." [4] On one occasion Blair introduced a friend to Secretary of War Cameron, with the note: "I wish to introduce Dr. Edward Maynard of the Maynard Rifle. He was at West Point with me & I have always respected him not less for his genius than for his

---

[1] Meneely, *The War Department, 1861,* p. 169.

[2] Lincoln to McClellan, June 10, 1861, in *ibid.,* p. 172.

[3] For a detailed study of the Blairs' political activities, see W. E. Smith, *The Francis Preston Blair Family in Politics.*

[4] "The Diary of Edward Bates, 1859–1866," ed. by Howard K. Beale, *Annual Report,* American Historical Association, IV (1930), 285.

character." [5] In St. Louis, Frank Blair, Jr., was tireless in persuading Major General Frémont, commanding the Department of the West, that contracts for army supplies be awarded to friends of the Blairs. Often collusion entered into these transactions: on one occasion a friend of the younger Frank Blair had supplied such miserable horses that Frémont issued an order that no more Missouri steeds were to be bought.[6] The records of the War Department bear this out. They contain a number of Blair's brief notes to Major McKinstry, Frémont's aide: "Dear Major: If you buy any more horses, I wish you to give Jim Neal a fair chance. He is a personal friend of mine and a sound Union man." Again, "Dear Major: I shall be obliged to you if you can give Mr. Alec Peterson a contract for buying horses. He is a good friend of mine." And to still another officer: "General Meigs: If you want horses in Missouri, I most cordially recommend Mr. Farrar to purchase them for you." It was Farrar, as Professor Allan Nevins points out, who supplied the most defective animals.[7] Indeed, it was the rivalry between Blair's friends and Frémont's friends over army contracts that added fuel to the inflammatory Blair-Frémont feud that disrupted Missouri politics and had its repercussions in national councils during most of the Civil War.[8]

In 1862 Robert H. Pruyn, Minister to Japan—who had received his diplomatic post by the grace of Seward and Thurlow Weed, of whom he was a veteran Albany political lieutenant—was requested by officials of the Japanese government to arrange for the construction in the United States of three vessels of war for the Mikado's navy. Pruyn communicated with Seward, who estimated that the cost for the three ships would be $860,000. The Secretary of State agreed to Pruyn's proposal that Weed and Pruyn's brother-in-law, Charles B. Lansing, be commissioned to undertake the building of the warships.[9] Accordingly the Japanese

[5] Montgomery Blair to Cameron, Jan. 18, 1862, Cameron Papers.

[6] Nevins, *Frémont: Pathmarker of the West,* pp. 497–98.   [7] *Ibid.,* p. 498.

[8] W. E. Smith, *The Francis Preston Blair Family in Politics,* II, 65–67.

[9] Under date of Feb. 9, 1863, the Albany *Daily Knickerbocker* editorialized as follows: "Our minister to Japan, Gen. Robert H. Pruyn, at home or abroad, has always an eye open for the interest of mechanics and laboring men. When a member of the [New York] Legislature, his whole time was devoted to devising plans to furnish employment for the workmen of Albany, and to improve and beautify the city. . . . We see by late proceedings in Congress, that General Pruyn con-

government deposited with Pruyn an advance partial payment of $200,000 with the promise that another $200,000 would be paid on the first of January (1863), another $200,000 on March 1, and the balance on arrival of the ships in Japan. Seward consulted with the Secretary of War and the Secretary of the Navy. Stanton declared that it did not rest with his department to grant or withhold permission to have the ships built in the United States. Welles, for his part, disapproved of an American diplomatic representative being involved in the transaction, since it might commit the United States government to guarantee the contract's faithful execution. Despite Welles's opposition, Seward, apparently with Lincoln's approval, agreed to the construction of the ships, although he forbade the building of certain armaments for the vessels on the ground that such armaments were required by the Army and Navy Departments.[10] A distinguished student of diplomacy has described this action of an American diplomatic representative acting as a commercial agent for the government to which he was accredited as "a highly irregular proceeding." [11] Even more irregular was Seward's acquiescence in the deal and the action of the Secretary of State in allowing the contract to be awarded to his closest friend and political partner, Weed. Secretary Welles maintained later that Pruyn was able to forward to Weed and Lansing a total of $800,000 in gold in payment for the ships, adding:

What return was made—payment and vouchers in currency—I never knew. One vessel was completed in 1865 or '66. Weed & Lansing having the use of the Japanese gold in all that period, without interest.

tinues to interest himself in behalf of our iron workers and ship-builders. The Secretary of State sent a communication to the Senate on Friday, in answer to Mr. Wilkinson's resolution with respect to the Japanese man-of-war transactions. . . . We trust that our Government will not turn this job away from our mechanics."

[10] Robert H. Pruyn, United States Minister Resident in Japan, to Seward, Oct. 29, 1862; Midsuno Idsumi No Kami *et al.* to Pruyn, undated; Seward to Weed, Jan. 17, 1863; Seward to Stanton, Jan. 20, 29, 1863; Seward to Welles, Jan. 20, 24, 1863; Stanton to Seward, Jan. 29, 1863, in "Ships For the Japanese Government," *Senate Executive Document* No. 33, 37th Cong., 3d sess., serial no. 1149, pp. 1–8; Seward to Pruyn, Jan. 29, 1863 (copy), Seward Despatch Book, Vol. II, William H. Seward Papers.

[11] Dennett, *Americans in Eastern Asia,* p. 397.

The whole was managed by the State Depart. . . . It was a long and complicated affair.[12]

By October, 1864, one of the war vessels—a steam corvette named the "Fusijama"—had been completed and it immediately prepared to set sail for Japan. The New York *Times*, Seward-Weed organ, commented that the ship was "strongly built, and twenty of the same kind would be a credit to our navy. . . . The 'Fusijama's' engines performed admirably, and gave universal satisfaction to everyone. . . . She will be a great acquisition to the Japanese Navy." [13] The outbreak of hostilities involving Japan with European Powers prevented the ship's sailing, and she lay in New York harbor. Seward thereupon endeavored to secure Lincoln's approval that she be sold to the Navy Department for $392,000. Lincoln was willing that the "Fusijama" be purchased, but Welles obdurately opposed the transaction, partly on the ground that he would "not consent to be used in swindling operations." Nor would he consent to furnishing a crew for the ship's delivery to Japan. Seward and Weed, who were already arch-enemies of Welles, were thoroughly angry and, in league with Henry J. Raymond, editor of the *Times*, intrigued to have Welles displaced. In this undertaking, however, they made little headway.[14] Finally in September, 1865—after Lincoln's death—the "Fusijama" set sail for Japan.[15] The Japanese officials were by no means satisfied with the corvette. "An unblushing fraud," [16] the transaction has been called. The Japanese found the "Fusijama" to be "very defective and to have cost too much." [17] The result of the official examination of the ship having been announced, the Japanese engineer who participated in the transaction involving the ship's construction committed suicide—"hara

[12] Gideon Welles to Montgomery Blair, June (no day listed), 1870, Gideon Welles Papers, New York Public Library. See also excerpt from Albany *Daily Knickerbocker*, Feb. 9, 1863, in Thurlow Weed Newspaper Scrapbook, Thurlow Weed Papers, Library of Congress.

[13] New York *Times*, Oct. 9, 1864.

[14] *Diary of Gideon Welles*, II, 188–89, 191–92, 561.

[15] New York *Times*, Sept. 4, 5, 1865.

[16] Dickins and Lane-Poole, *Life of Sir Harry Parkes*, II, 63. (Parkes was British minister to Japan.)

[17] New York *Herald*, May 9, 1866.

kiri." [18] Gleefully did Weed's old journalistic foe, James Gordon Bennett, emphasize Weed's role in the proceeding and sarcastically conjectured that the Albany editor-politician might well follow the Japanese engineer's example. In a lengthy article entitled "Anticipated Hari-Kari of Thurlow Weed and Other Japanese Agents," Bennett's New York *Herald* commented:

They are bound in honor to imitate the Japanese engineer who committed suicide so soon as the intelligence of the failure of the vessel was communicated to him. Mr. Weed is particularly in peril, and room No. 11 at the Astor House may be transformed at any moment into a chamber of horrors. . . . Unless he be deprived of all edged tools, even at dinner, we shall not presume to answer for the consequences.[19]

The "Fusijama" alone was completed under the arrangement with Weed and Lansing. Apparently Weed still held some of the money advanced by the Japanese government through Pruyn. Consequently a Japanese mission was sent to the United States in 1867 with instructions to inquire into the affair. To pacify them, the "Stonewall," an iron ram built in France for the Confederates, was transferred to the Japanese government by the United States. Whether Japan was required to pay for it or not is a moot question. The weight of evidence indicates that the Johnson administration, anxious to hush up the matter and improve our relations with Japan, gave it as a gift.[20]

With the outbreak of war and the scouring of the seas by privateers, American shipowners found themselves with a bewildering variety of idle ships on their hands. They accordingly besieged the Navy Department with offers to sell their vessels for regular

---

[18] New York *Herald,* May 9, 1866.   [19] *Ibid.*

[20] The New York *Times* (July 4, 1867) declares: "The amount of money actually paid over to Mr. Pruyn is not definitely known, but it is supposed to have been $600,000 in gold. A settlement was finally effected with him by the [Japanese] Commissioners, under which he paid them $500,000 in currency, and it was with $400,000 of this that the ram *Stonewall* was bought." (The *Times* was a Seward-Weed organ.) Dickins and Lane-Poole, *Life of Sir Harry Parkes,* II, 63, declared that the *"Stonewall Jackson"* [sic] was given to the Japanese as "compensation." The New York *Herald* charged that the United States Government made a "present" of the "Stonewall" to Japan. See New York *Herald,* June 14, 1867, pp. 3, 6. Black also held this opinion, *Young Japan,* II, 199. *War of the Rebellion: Official Records of the Union and Confederate Navies,* Series II, I, 215, gives no price received from the Japanese Government for the "Stonewall."

combat, patrol, or blockade service—vessels that were said to represent "every style of marine architecture from Captain Noah to Captain Cook." [21] The Navy Department was too busy with organization and superintendence of naval operations and other heavy war-time responsibilities to devote itself to the details of purchase. Consequently the department adopted the policy of entrusting the investigation of the seaworthiness of such ships to naval officers, and the purchase of those declared fit to a properly qualified individual, with the explicit understanding that he should devote his whole time, attention, and ability to the work. In no case was he to make any charge against the government for his service and he was to deal always directly and exclusively with the owners of the vessels purchased, thus permitting no brokerage fees, or agents' commissions, between himself and the owners. Finally, his own commission, payable always by the seller, was in no case to exceed the regular mercantile percentage fixed by the Chamber of Commerce of New York and established by the custom of merchants in that city as the rightful and legal rate of remuneration for such services rendered by any person acting between the sellers and purchasers of vessels. [22]

As purchasing agent, Secretary of the Navy Welles designated his brother-in-law, George D. Morgan, [23] who was also a cousin of the governor of New York. The character of Morgan's work was succinctly summarized in after years by Frank M. Bennett, who served in the United States Navy as an assistant engineer:

The progress made in increasing the fleet during the year 1861 was phenomenal. Mr. George D. Morgan of New York was appointed a special agent of the Navy Department with orders to buy every American merchant vessel found at all suitable for war purposes, in the selection of which he was aided by a board of officers of the navy—a constructor, a chief engineer, and an ordnance officer. This board had a small steamer in New York harbor and made a business of boarding and examining every American vessel within reach, a favorable report on any vessel making it obligatory on Mr. Mor-

[21] Paullin, "The Navy Department during the Civil War," *Proceedings of the United States Naval Institute*, XXXIX, 119.

[22] "Report of the Secretary of the Navy, 1861," *Senate Executive Document No. 1*, 37th Cong., 2d sess., serial no. 1119, p. 15.

[23] Sanford J. Ginsberg, "Corruption and Fraud in Government Contracts during the Civil War," p. 67.

gan's part to buy the vessel at the best bargain he could make with the owners. As Mr. Morgan received a commission of two and one-half per cent. on his purchases this obligation to buy was for him a decidedly good thing. From the middle of July until the first of December there were purchased in this manner thirty-six side-wheel steamers aggregating 26,680 tons and costing $2,418,103; forty-three screw-steamers aggregating 20,403 tons and costing $2,215,037, and one hundred and eighteen sailing vessels—ships, barks, and schooners—at a cost of $1,071,898. Sixty of these latter were loaded with stone and sunk for the purpose of closing some of the southern ports; the others, and all of the steamers, were converted into war vessels and put into active service.[24]

Certain peculiar circumstances surrounding Morgan's purchases leaked out, and a Congressional investigation was ordered. Welles kept his brother-in-law advised as to his conduct before the investigating committee.[25] It was disclosed that Morgan, a commission merchant by profession, had never had any experience in shipbuilding or purchasing and relied upon the opinions of three naval officers to tell him the value of each ship examined. In seven weeks Morgan's commissions "from the seller," totaled $51,584. Welles was informed of this fact, "in the hope that the department would correct the practice by which its own agent was amassing a fortune." But nothing was done to stop the practice, and from September 6 to December 1, 1861, Morgan acquired $43,424 more, making in all the sum of $95,008 for his services as agent of the government for a period of four and one-half months.

Undoubtedly the commission which Morgan received was excessive. In this connection testimony revealed that while 2 percent was the normal fee set by the Chamber of Commerce for brokerage, this percentage applied only to purchases below $30,000 in value; in transactions which involved sums above that figure the usual procedure was a special agreement between the seller and the broker as to the size of the commission, in which the commission varied from 0.25 to 1 percent, but seldom rose above the latter figure. Furthermore, the critics were quick to point out that the commission itself was not paid by the seller but ultimately by the

[24] Bennett, *The Steam Navy of the United States*, pp. 214–17.
[25] George D. Morgan to Welles, Dec. 3, 1861; Welles to George D. Morgan (copies), Dec. 30, 31, 1861, Gideon Welles Papers, Library of Congress.

government. Shipowners, in testifying before the committee, admitted that it was common practice to add to the price asked from the government the commission for the agent. On the whole, the vessels purchased through Morgan were in excellent condition.[26] In defending himself against the charges of nepotism and of sanctioning excessive commissions, Welles declared that there "was neither time nor opportunity, nor authority of law to wait and invite proposals for the sale of ships, even if from the nature of the case such a procedure had been possible." [27]

The most flagrant malfeasance was in the War rather than in the Navy Department, for the War Office had at its disposal many fat army contracts. Conditions in this department were made even worse by the fact that the code of political ethics of Secretary of War Simon Cameron made it impossible for him to play the role of crusader in eliminating sharp practices. Indeed, his handling of the financial affairs of the department were scandalous in the extreme. The most glaring favoritism was shown. Some manufacturers could get contracts while others could not. Middlemen abounded and easily obtained lavish contracts, which they sold to manufacturers at a high profit. One gun manufacturer endeavored in vain to secure business from the War Department, but got orders for 200,000 guns from middlemen who, though unable to manufacture the guns, knew how to get contracts. Many contracts went to subcontractors. Either through criminal negligence or criminal collusion on its part, the War Department under Cameron permitted and even encouraged fraud of the grossest character.[28] Moreover, contractors frequently besieged Republican leaders with appeals to intercede for them with Cameron in the award of contracts. A letter to Thurlow Weed is typical of many found in the private papers of influential Republican chieftains of the era:

I have for sale Forty-two thousand (42,000) Guns, consisting of
English Enfield Rifles
Austrian Enfield Rifles

[26] Ginsberg, "Corruption and Fraud in Government Contracts during the Civil War," pp. 67–69.
[27] For Welles's defense of his action, see New York *Herald,* Jan. 17, 1862.
[28] *War of the Rebellion: Official Records of the Union and Confederate Armies,* Series III, II, 191–94; Shannon, *The Organization and Administration of the Union Army, 1861–1865,* I, 55–133.

Prussian Smooth bore muskets
All with bayonets

If you will be kind enough to put me in the way to sell them I should be much obliged to you & glad to compensate you *fully* for your trouble which should be to your entire satisfaction.[29]

Cameron conducted the War Department as if it were a political club house; he used contracts freely to pay off old political debts and to shower additional favors upon his henchmen. General McClellan, who worked in harmony with the Secretary of War, wrote: "Mr. Cameron had not at all interfered with me, but gave me full support. He, so far as I knew, occupied himself solely with contracts and political affairs." [30]

It is beyond the scope of this volume to cite even a small number of the examples of corruption in Cameron's department that were unearthed by a Congressional committee under the chairmanship of Representative Van Wyck, of New York.[31] In September (1861), upon direct orders from Cameron, Quartermaster General Montgomery C. Meigs gave contracts to two Pennsylvanians for 1,000 cavalry horses deliverable at Huntington, Pennsylvania. The price was $117 each at that place. These contractors, acting as middlemen, then bought up available horses to fill the order. It was estimated that the average price paid for each animal did not exceed $75, while a larger number were believed to have cost from $30 to $60; many of these horses would have been high priced at $30. About one-third of the lot were utterly worthless for military purposes.

In May, 1861, a Cameron appointee, John Tucker, was named General Transport Agent and placed in charge of acquiring ships for troop transport for the War Department. Although up to this time Tucker had never had the slightest experience in the building, sale, command, or sailing of a vessel, he and his subagents soon monopolized the field. Subagents quickly appeared in coast ports, chartering and purchasing vessels, each holding that

[29] E. A. Allen to Weed, July 10, 1862, Thurlow Weed Papers, University of Rochester Library.

[30] George B. McClellan, *McClellan's Own Story,* p. 152.

[31] The two-volume report of the Van Wyck Committee numbered over 2,700 pages: "Government Contracts," 37th Cong., 2d sess., *House Reports,* No. 2. See also *War of the Rebellion: Official Records of Union and Confederate Armies,* Series III, II, 190 ff.; Senate Executive Document, 37th Cong., 2d sess.

through him exclusively were sales to be effected in the community. These men took the liberty of reimbursing themselves for their services by a charge of from 2.5 to 5 percent upon the charter or purchase money. One agent in Boston netted $20,000 for one week's work. Tucker himself purchased two ships for $100,000 each, after the engineers had pronounced them unsafe and the Navy had refused to buy them. The construction price of *both* had been $110,000. Subsequently one of these vessels sank on her first voyage with a loss of all stores; the other was so badly damaged she could hardly make port and was condemned for further service.[32]

Perhaps one more illustration of Cameron's crookedness will not be amiss. Alexander Cummings, who, as related elsewhere, was one of Cameron's political lieutenants, had helped to hector Lincoln into appointing the Pennsylvanian to the Cabinet. In April, 1861, Cameron employed Cummings to direct the buying of supplies in New York City. The authority, as granted by Cameron's order, was to be divided between Cummings and Governor Edwin D. Morgan. Shortly afterwards the New York governor delegated his power to his relative and business partner, George D. Morgan, who, as we have just observed, was the brother-in-law of Secretary of the Navy Welles. In this capacity Morgan, in association with Cummings, made purchases up to $250,000 in a thoroughly irresponsible manner.[33] Professor Fred. A. Shannon, the historian of the Union Army, comments on the work of Morgan and Cummings:

A fund of $2,000,000 was left at the disposal of the couple, subject only to nominal oversight by a committee of reputable citizens. A strange era of spending resulted. The sum of $21,000 was expended for *linen pantaloons and straw hats*. The firm of Benedict and Hall received a contract for 75,000 pairs of shoes at $2.20 a pair, which were worth much less. A member of the firm testified that Cummings received no pay from them for the transaction but that the contract was let to them in return for the kindness of an occasional temporary loan of $500 or $1000. Along with other peculiar army supplies

[32] Ginsberg, "Corruption and Fraud in Government Contracts during the Civil War," pp. 24–25, 28–29. Also New York *Herald,* Feb. 1, 1862.
[33] Shannon, *The Organization and Administration of the Union Army, 1861–1865,* I, 61.

purchased by Cummings were large quantities of Scotch ale, London porter, selected herring, and 23 barrels of pickles. Without being bound by oath or bond, Cummings spent $250,000 during the summer of 1861. Even if honest he was thoroughly incompetent; his sole qualification being that he was a friend of Simon Cameron.[34]

In a message to the Senate in January, 1862, Cameron denied that he had ever made "a single contract for any purpose whatever"—whereupon his enemy, Representative Henry L. Dawes, of Massachusetts, produced documents showing that all but 64,000 of the 1,903,800 guns contracted for from August, 1861, to January, 1862, were ordered under Cameron's direction.[35] Dawes declared that Cameron used fat contracts to win political support at meetings "where the hatchet of political animosity was buried in the grave of public confidence and the national credit was crucified between malefactors." [36]

Commissions in the Army—both regular and volunteer—also afforded ample opportunity for patronage. On January 1, 1861, the federal government had a regular Army of barely 16,000 enlisted officers and men, and this number was somewhat decimated following the secession of four additional southern states after the fall of Fort Sumter.[37] Instead of recruiting a large army, the weakened federal government turned to the states for aid. On July 1, 1861, Congress enacted legislation providing for the creation of a volunteer army of 500,000 men. Both this act and a supplementary measure passed three days later expressly stated that not only should the several states raise the men and organize the regiments, but should also provide and commission the field staff and company officers.[38] During the same month, on July 29, Congress authorized the federal government to enlarge the regular Army to 42,000. Such a set up, it can readily be seen, afforded both the President and the governors of the several states an extensive appointive domain. Frequently the state executives appointed

[34] Shannon, *The Organization and Administration of the Union Army, 1861–1865,* I, 61–62.

[35] Ginsberg, "Corruption and Fraud in Government Contracts during the Civil War," p. 45.

[36] *House Reports,* 37th Cong., 2d sess., Vol. I, No. 2; *Congressional Globe,* 37th Cong., 2d sess., pp. 203–4, 298–99, 300–302.

[37] "Report of Provost-Marshal-General," *House Executive Document,* 39th Cong., 1st sess., appendix to "Report of Secretary of War," Part I, p. 102.

[38] *U. S. Statutes at Large,* XII, 268–69, 274.

those who "would produce the most agreeable consequences at the next election-time." [39] In other words, the spoils system prevailed. Nor was it different with the federal executive. Congressmen or Congressional delegations usually gave the President the names of those whom they wished appointed as brigadiers, major generals, and lesser officers.[40] Such a policy could result only in the appointment of many misfits. "The people know," wrote a correspondent to the editor of the New York *Tribune*, "that it takes long to organize an army—longer to discipline it to those qualities which make veterans and insure victories—longer yet to discover the true commanders from among the crowd of egoists, peacocks and place hunters, with which the volunteer system is apt to oppress a great military movement." [41] And the overwhelming weight of evidence indicates that many who had failed to win political office suddenly discovered in themselves, as Professor A. Howard Meneely well says, "talent for military service, for the work of sutler, paymaster, or any other position that promised a pecuniary return and government employment." [42]

Though high Army appointments to pay political debts or mend political fences were frequent, they were not always unfortunate in a military way. Jacob D. Cox, a friend of Chase, for example, was jerked out of the Ohio Senate, without military experience, to be made a brigadier general; and he was one of the best of all Union officers. He served with credit in the Kanawha campaign in West Virginia and afterwards in the Army of the Potomac, commanding the Ninth Army Corps in the battles of South Mountain and Antietam. With the rank of major general of volunteers, he commanded a division and later a corps in the Atlanta campaign.[43] James S. Wadsworth, of New York, another totally inexperienced man, was an equally happy choice. He took part in the battles of Fredericksburg, Chancellorsville, and Gettysburg; commanded a division in the Army and was mortally wounded at the Battle of

[39] Higginson, "Regular and Volunteer Officers," *The Atlantic Monthly*, XIV (Sept., 1864), 354.
[40] Meneely, *The War Department, 1861*, pp. 169, 169 n.
[41] New York *Tribune*, April 29, 1861.
[42] Meneely, *The War Department, 1861*, p. 168.
[43] For the military career of Cox, consult Cox, *Military Reminiscences of the Civil War; Atlanta; The Battle of Franklin, Tennessee;* Schofield, *Forty-Six Years in the Army*, pp. 132 ff.

the Wilderness.[44] Four future presidents, Rutherford B. Hayes, James A. Garfield, Benjamin Harrison, and William McKinley, all originally ignorant of the rudiments of military science, became adequate officers. Yet such men were the exceptions.

In addition to his partiality in awarding contracts, Cameron also remembered his friends and political followers in granting officers' commissions in the Army. Notably was he generous in this respect to many Pennsylvanians, who received military commissions of high rank.[45] Not only was the Military Affairs Committee of the United States Senate startled when it learned of the very large number of officers appointed from the Keystone State, but it was angered when it ascertained that some of these Pennsylvanians were accredited to other states.[46] Such action, said the New York *Herald,* was unfair toward the patriotic citizens from other states, who had repeatedly and in vain sought recognition at the hands of Cameron.[47] One can well understand why legislators from other states were incensed at the small regard shown by Cameron to their constituents and why they rejoiced when Lincoln found a way to get rid of him. Edwin M. Stanton, Cameron's successor, was no novice in the patronage game. The appointment of politicians with little or no military experience did not entirely terminate with his accession to office.

Positions as paymasters in the Army were not uncommon rewards for the party faithful or for their friends. We have already seen how the sons of two Cabinet members—Augustus Seward and Brua Cameron—each received the rank of major, and were stationed at places not too close to the firing line; we have noted, too, that Lincoln's brother-in-law by marriage, Dr. William Wallace, received a similar title and position. But they were not the only ones. The erratic Richard P. L. Baber, of Ohio, an early organizer of the Republican party in the Buckeye State, had aided in publishing the Lincoln-Douglas debates and as delegate to the Chicago Convention had worked to swing the Ohio delegation to Lincoln. Baber's biographer tells us that naturally Mr. Baber

[44] See Pearson, *James S. Wadsworth of Geneseo.*

[45] See the pertinent remarks by John P. Usher regarding Cameron's liberality in giving commissions to his friends, in *President Lincoln's Cabinet, by Honorable John P. Usher, Secretary of the Interior, January 7, 1863–May 15, 1865,* p. 20.

[46] New York *Herald,* Jan. 20, 1862.   [47] *Ibid.*

expected further and more substantial recognition when Mr. Lincoln should come into office. To find a place for him, however, was not easy. The way out was effected in the tender of a paymastership in the Army, which he accepted.[48]

Provost marshals, in turn, were under more or less political pressure. One example will suffice. Under date of August 21, 1863, W. H. De Camp, president of the Nineteenth Ward Republican Association of New York City, sent the following to Captain Fred C. Wagner, Provost Marshal of the Seventh Congressional District:

> The Bearer, Mr. William Jenkins, is a member of the 19th Ward Republican Association and has been for some years.
> If you can furnish him employment in your office you will find him every way capable.[49]

Partisan politics apparently largely governed the appointment of provost marshals during the Lincoln administration. Indeed, incumbents were removed to make way for Republican spoilsmen.[50] Among the conspicuous party men appointed to provost marshalship posts were Nathaniel B. Smithers, organizer of the Republican party of Delaware,[51] and Richard W. Thompson, an Indiana Old Line Whig politician who aided the Lincoln cause in the Hoosier State.[52]

In the highest Army positions there were many unwise political selections. Cassius M. Clay had to be cared for, now that he had vacated the Russian mission which Cameron would fill. Lincoln nominated him to be a major general of volunteers, and the Senate confirmed him several months later.[53] Certainly Clay's limited experience in the Mexican War did not warrant this high rank, and it may be set down as purely a political appointment. And the same was true of that gusty, racy Massachusetts politician,

[48] Taylor, "Richard Plantaganet Llewellyn Baber," *Ohio Archaeological and Historical Quarterly*, XIX (1910), 370–81.

[49] Provost Marshal Papers, Vol. marked "Miscellaneous No. I," New York Historical Society.

[50] Chauncey McKeever to Creswell, Jan. 29, 1864, John A. J. Creswell Papers.

[51] W. T. Smithers, "Memoir of Nathaniel B. Smithers," *Papers of the Historical Society of Delaware*, no. 23 (1899), pp. 24–25.

[52] Roll, "Richard W. Thompson: A Political Conservative in the Fifties," *Indiana Magazine of History*, XXVII (Sept., 1931), 205.

[53] *U. S. Senate Executive Journal*, XII (1861–62), 92, 232.

Benjamin F. Butler, who, prior to the war, had been prominent, and energetically efficient, in organizing the Massachusetts militia. Upon learning that a call had been made upon Massachusetts on April 16, 1861, for troops, Butler immediately wired to United States Senator Henry Wilson, of his state: "A brigade has been ordered, but no brigadier general. See Cameron and have brigadier asked for, and I will see to it that I am detailed." [54] Wilson replied: "Brigadier general has been ordered." [55] Butler, however, was not the senior brigadier from his state, but that fact did not daunt him. He made arrangements with Governor John A. Andrew to have himself appointed to command the Massachusetts troops. [56] In May, 1861, Lincoln boosted Butler to major general of volunteers. [57] It is ironical that Philip H. Sheridan was at the time a mere captain. The civilian politician Butler had been a major general a whole year before Sheridan was elevated to a colonelcy. Sheridan was not the only West Pointer to suffer this kind of embarrassment. The persistence of the War Department in maintaining both a regular and a volunteer army made it extremely difficult for any regular Army officer to be transferred to the volunteers. As a consequence, regular Army lieutenants and captains, though better trained in military affairs, saw untrained civilians with political influence outrank them.

Take, for example, another Massachusetts politician with no military experience, who received high army rank, Nathaniel P. Banks. Former governor of the state, office hunter extraordinary and aspirant for the Republican presidential nomination in 1860, Banks was made a major general. [58]

Ulysses S. Grant, graduate of West Point, who had seen fifteen years' service in the regular Army prior to the outbreak of the war, did not even receive the favor of a reply to his letter tendering his services. [59] In June, 1861, Stanton declared that, with few exceptions, the Army appointments appeared "to be bestowed on

[54] Butler to Gen. Wm. Schouler, July 10, 1870, in *Private and Official Correspondence of Gen. Benjamin F. Butler,* I, 11–13.

[55] *Loc. cit.*   [56] *Ibid.*

[57] *Dictionary of American Biography,* III, 358.

[58] For Banks's opportunistic political career to 1861, see Harrington, "Nathaniel Prentiss Banks: A Study in Anti-Slavery Politics," *The New England Quarterly,* IX (Dec., 1936), 626–54.

[59] U. S. Grant to Col. L. Thomas, Adjutant General, May 24, 1861, in *War of the Rebellion: Official Records of the Union and Confederate Armies,* Series III,

persons whose only claim is their Republicanism—broken-down politicians without experience, ability, or any other merit." [60] There was always present the politicians' distrust of the regular Army man. "Every effort is making to get men from the Regular army into command," wrote one Republican leader in alarm, adding, "Most of the West Pointers are very little account. Most all of them are dissipated and tyrannical; and they hate everybody not of their caste." [61]

The evidence indicates that demands for Army commissions and promotions were most trying on Lincoln. When his old friends, William Butler and Governor Yates, of Illinois, wanted a major generalship in the regular Army for the self-advertising John Pope, the President answered: "I fully appreciate General Pope's splendid achievements, with their invaluable results; but you must know that major-generalships in the regular army are not as plenty as blackberries." [62]

A practice often indulged in by the Lincoln administration, which annoyed and antagonized the governors of the loyal states in their recruiting efforts, was the granting of authorizations to private individuals to raise regiments in their states; in return for this service the administration gave the individual recruiter a high Army commission and command of the troops he succeeded in raising. In particular, Cameron seriously embarrassed his old rival, Governor Andrew G. Curtin, of Pennsylvania, by giving special permission to favorites to enlist regiments in the state. Armed with the authority of the War Department and with all necessary expenses paid, the prospective colonel (strutting about in full military regalia) would locate in Philadelphia, Pittsburgh,

---

I, 234; *Personal Memoirs of U. S. Grant,* I, 239–40; Badeau, *Military History of Ulysses S. Grant, from April, 1861 to April, 1865,* I, 9–10.

60 Meneely, *The War Department, 1861,* p. 171.

61 Gustave Koerner to Trumbull, Jan. 2, 1862, Trumbull Papers. Koerner was the leader of the antislavery German population of the Mississippi Valley. In voicing his opposition to West Pointers he merely echoed the opinion of the Committee on the Conduct of the War, created late in 1861. Its personnel was preponderantly radical, its chairman being Ben Wade. Cf. T. H. Williams, *Lincoln and the Radicals,* pp. 61–76; T. H. Williams, "The Committee on the Conduct of the War," *Journal of the American Military History Institute,* III, 139–56. Williams indicates conclusively that this committee became the spearhead of the radical drive against the Lincoln administration.

62 Lincoln to R. Yates and Wm. Butler (Telegram), April 10, 1862, in *Complete Works of Abraham Lincoln,* VII, 145.

or elsewhere in the state to raise a regiment; and usually made little progress. The life was pleasant, the pay ample, and thus all too many were not in great haste to fill their regiments and get into the field.[63]

One of the first authorizations to raise troops was given by the War Department to William Vandever, Republican Member of Congress from Iowa—this despite the fact that the Iowa governor had previously refused to recognize any independent organizations. Vandever became colonel in command of the Ninth Iowa Volunteer Infantry; the following year Vandever was promoted to brigadier general of volunteers, and in 1865 was brevetted a major general.[64] Similarly two other Iowa regiments were accepted by Cameron over the Iowa governor's head, because, it was said, two friends of Assistant Postmaster General Kasson desired to be colonels.[65]

Another Republican member of Congress and a fiery radical— the magnetic Senator Edward D. Baker, of Oregon—Lincoln's Springfield friend of long standing—was given a commission as colonel by Lincoln personally when he recruited a regiment of Californians and Oregonians. "Unfortunately for himself, the President, and the country," concludes Baker's biographer, the Senator went to war and was killed in action at Ball's Bluff.[66]

Vandever and Baker were only two of the many Members of Congress who, instilled with patriotic ardor and desire for military glory, availed themselves of their political influence to acquire high rank in the Army, either by appointment of Lincoln or by the governors of their respective states. By October, 1861, at least seventeen United States Senators and Representatives had enrolled in the Union Army, almost all of them receiving at least a colonel's commission.[67]

---

[63] Davis, *Pennsylvania Politics, 1860–1863,* pp. 178, 189.

[64] Briggs, "The Enlistment of Iowa Troops during the Civil War," *The Iowa Journal of History and Politics,* XV (July, 1917), 345–46; Ingersoll, *Iowa and the Rebellion,* p. 146; *Biographical Directory of the American Congress, 1774–1927,* pp. 1642–43.

[65] Briggs, "The Enlistment of Iowa Troops during the Civil War," *The Iowa Journal of History and Politics,* XV (July, 1917), 346.

[66] Shutes, "Colonel E. D. Baker," *California Historical Society Quarterly,* XVII (Dec., 1938), 317–18.

[67] The names as listed in the New York *Herald,* of Oct. 20, 1861, were:
Senator Henry Wilson, Massachusetts, McClellan's staff

The ever-mounting number of high-ranking officers, particularly brigadier generals, became a source of concern to certain members of congress. In March, 1862, United States Senator James W. Grimes, of Iowa, anxious to shut the gate against a surplus of applicants for military stars, introduced the motion: "*Resolved*, That, in the opinion of the Senate, no persons should be commissioned as generals of divisions or brigades, except such as shall exhibit superior competency in the command of men, or gallantry in action against the enemy." [68] The resolution was referred to the Committee on Military Affairs.[69] Two weeks later Grimes moved that the committee be discharged from further consideration of the resolution and took the floor in its defense. "At this time," the Iowan charged, "there have been appointed one hundred and eighty brigadier generals in the United States Army—one hundred and seventy-two irregular or volunteer brigadier generals and eight brigadiers in the regular Army." [70] Contending that the cost to the government of brigadier generals alone was $1,000,000 a year, Grimes declared:

Now, sir, I am prepared to say, and I think the facts justify me in saying, that the necessities of the Army and the country do not require one half of this number of brigadier generals. . . . We have to-day brigadiers enough, if they had the command which is supposed to belong to a brigadier, that is, three regiments, to be placed at the head of seven hundred and twenty thousand men. We all know we have not got any such number as that.[71]

Senator James H. Lane, Kansas, Brigadier General
Senator Edward D. Baker, Oregon, Colonel
Hon. Owen Lovejoy, Illinois, Frémont's staff
Hon. John A. McClernand, Illinois, Brigadier General
Hon. John A. Logan, Illinois, Colonel
Hon. Samuel R. Curtis, Illinois, Colonel
Hon. William Vandever, Iowa, Colonel
Hon. J. S. Jackson, Kentucky, Colonel
Hon. James E. Kerrigan, New York, Colonel
Hon. Burt Van Horn, New York, Colonel
Hon. F. P. Blair, Jr., Missouri, Colonel
Hon. John S. Phelps, Missouri, Colonel
Hon. John B. S. Todd, Dacotah [sic], Brigadier General
Hon. John A. Gurley, Ohio, Frémont's staff
Hon. W. A. Richardson, Illinois, Brigadier General
Hon. Philip B. Foulke, Illinois, Colonel.

[68] *Congressional Globe*, 37th Cong., 2d sess., p. 1132.
[69] *Ibid.*   [70] *Ibid.*, p. 1416.   [71] *Ibid.*, p. 1416.

Senator Henry Wilson, of Massachusetts, who was shortly to become attached to General McClellan's staff, took issue with Grimes's statement that the Army was encumbered with too many brigadiers.[72] Senator William P. Fessenden agreed with Grimes and partially exonerated the administration by laying a portion of the responsibility on Members of Congress. "The difficulty," he declared, "is in part with us, and it arises from the fact that we are so ready to lend our names and our influence to certain gentlemen because they belong to our States, who desire to be brigadier generals." [73] The temper of the Senate at this time seems to have been that it did not wish to surrender the privilege of recommending important constituents to high Army places, for it declined to discharge the Committee on Military Affairs from further consideration of Grimes's resolution.[74] The Senate's hostile attitude toward Grimes's resolution lent encouragement to the politicians. And within a week Lincoln sent to the Senate a huge batch of nominations, including those for some fifteen additional brigadier generals.[75]

Not only was Lincoln besieged with requests for military commissions. He was also constantly hounded by those who wanted changes in the Army leadership. Pressure to this end came principally from the radicals and from the radically controlled press. Later dubbed "Jacobins" because of their aggressive, vindictive attitude, the radicals hated slavery and demanded immediate emancipation and, as soon as possible, social and political equality for the Negro. From the first they advocated confiscation of rebel property, the use of colored soldiers, and Republican domination of the South. The program of Lincoln and the moderates was anathema to them. They wanted no pussyfooting. The war, they maintained, should be vigorously prosecuted. Its conduct consequently should not be entrusted to Democrats, conservatives, or even lukewarm Republicans, but to unadulterated radicals.

It is easy, therefore, to understand why the radicals were infuriated when they beheld important Army posts filled by Democrats, every one of whom they suspected of being sympathetic toward slavery and of having treasonable leanings toward the rebellious South. The Army, they declared, was honeycombed

[72] *Congressional Globe,* 37th Cong., 2d sess., p. 1416. [73] *Ibid.*
[74] *Ibid.,* p. 1417. [75] New York *Herald,* April 2, 1862.

McCLELLAN AND THE BRIGADIER GENERAL

From *Vanity Fair,* IV (Aug. 17, 1861), 73.

Member of Congress.—Ah! Major General McClellan, I have a friend here, I wish you to know.—Make a capital Brigadier General—first-rate militia General—splendid politician—carried his county for Old Abe by a big majority. You may have heard of him—General Political Hack.

General McC.—Yes, sir—don't want him, sir, at any price—had enough of that style already.

by "friends of the rebels" and by conservative West Pointers who had neither the spirit nor the military talent necessary for the great task at hand.

In a long letter to Carl Schurz, Lincoln stoutly defended his course:

The plain facts, as they appear to me, are these. The administration came into power, very largely in a minority of the popular vote. Notwithstanding this, it distributed to its party's friends as nearly all the civil patronage as any administration ever did. The war came. The administration could not even start in this, without assistance outside of its party. It was mere nonsense to suppose a minority could put down a majority in rebellion. Mr. Schurz (now Gen. Schurz) was about here then & I do not recollect that he then considered all who were not republicans, were enemies of the government, and that none of them must be appointed to military positions. He will correct me if I am mistaken. It so happened that very few of our friends had a military education or were of the profession of arms. It would have been a question whether the war should be conducted on military knowledge, or on political affinity, only that our own friends (I think Mr. Schurz included) seemed to think that such a question was inadmissible. Accordingly I have scarcely appointed a democrat to a command, who was not urged by many republicans and opposed by none. It was so as to McClellan. He was first brought forward by the Republican Governor of Ohio, & claimed, and contended for at the same time by the Republican Governor of Pennsylvania. I received recommendations from the republican delegations in Congress, and I believe every one of them recommended a majority of democrats. But, after all, many Republicans were appointed; and I mean no disparagement of them when I say I do not see that their superiority of success has been so marked as to throw great suspicion on the good faith of those who are not Republicans.[76]

But the radicals were determined to clean house; before Lincoln's first term had ended not only had they purged the Army of Democrats in high command but had weakened the conservative element in the Cabinet as well.[77]

The radicals first trained their guns on no lesser personage than

[76] Lincoln to Schurz ("Private and Confidential"), Nov. 10, 1862, in *Speeches. Correspondence and Political Papers of Carl Schurz,* ed. by F. Bancroft, I, 212–13.
[77] On the radicals and their program, consult T. H. Williams, *Lincoln and the Radicals,* especially chap. i.

George B. McClellan, who had been called by Lincoln to take command of the demoralized Union Army following McDowell's defeat at the first battle of Manassas. A Democrat and a West Pointer, McClellan for a short time appears to have had the support of the majority of the radicals largely because they believed he was one of them. A series of events, however, culminating in the Union defeat at Ball's Bluff, alienated the radicals, and henceforth McClellan became a target for ruthless attack. All sorts of charges, ranging from incompetence to treason, were leveled against him. Purely fantastic stories were circulated as gospel truth. One tale, for example, asserted that McClellan was the guiding spirit in a plot to involve the United States in war with Great Britain and thus prevent the conquest of the Confederacy. Another even asserted that before every important battle McClellan secretly gave the Confederate generals his plan of battle. Still another, emanating from Senator "Ben" Wade, of Ohio, declared that McClellan had deliberately planned to prolong the war in the interests of the Democratic party and his own political aspirations.[78]

Lincoln was wholly aware of these attacks on his commanding general, but for the time being stood by him. With the accession of the two-faced Stanton to the War Office, the radicals returned to the attack with renewed vigor, for the new Secretary, they believed, would add greatly to their strength. One of their number, Congressman George W. Julian of Indiana, a fiery abolitionist who sincerely believed McClellan to be a traitor, recorded in after years that the radicals were elated when they learned that Stanton fully agreed with them in their estimate of McClellan.[79] Stanton's connection with the radicals was evident from the day he entered Lincoln's Cabinet. After a series of conferences with the Committee on the Conduct of the War in January, 1862, we find him writing Charles A. Dana of the New York *Tribune:* "As soon as I can get the machinery of the office working, the rats cleared out, and the rat-holes stopped, we shall *move. This army* [McClellan's] *has got to fight or run away; and while men are striving nobly in the West, the champagne and oysters on the Potomac must be stopped."* [80]

[78] T. H. Williams, *Lincoln and the Radicals,* pp. 77–79.
[79] Julian, *Political Recollections, 1840 to 1872,* p. 204.
[80] Edwin M. Stanton to Dana, Jan. 24, 1862, Charles A. Dana Papers.

But Stanton and the radicals were not content with letter writing, speeches, and investigations. They went directly to the President and insisted that he do something about what to them was an exceedingly serious situation. Nettled by McClellan's arrogance and concerned over the heavy losses sustained by the Republicans in the fall elections of 1861, Lincoln yielded to radical pressure and public clamor. He first issued orders that McClellan abandon his plans to attack Richmond from the East—orders which the Commander of the Army of the Potomac never executed, for he was able to convince the President that attack from the East was militarily sound. McClellan's failure to attack the Confederates and their withdrawal from Manassas in March, 1862, brought down upon his head a storm of denunciation and the renewed demand that he be removed. This time Lincoln "relieved" McClellan of his position as general in chief, but allowed him to retain his position as Commander of the Army of the Potomac. Then came the famous Peninsula campaign and McClellan's retreat. The radicals were jubilant. They were certain that McClellan was through. Indeed, they had already planned that the bombastic General John Pope, who from the beginning had courted their favor, would be his successor.

Though under terrific pressure to dismiss McClellan, the troubled President did not succumb to hasty action. His confidence in McClellan had been shaken but not destroyed. It was not until July, when McClellan tactlessly penned a letter to Lincoln in which he gave the President advice on how to conduct the political affairs of the government as they related to war, that the pendulum swung definitely against him. Even then Lincoln sought the advice of others, including General Henry W. Halleck. Halleck's victories in the West had enhanced his reputation, and in July Lincoln appointed him General in Chief of the Armies—the position that had once belonged to McClellan. Less than a month later, during which a constant barrage of criticism was leveled at McClellan by Senator Zachariah Chandler, of Michigan, and his fellow radicals, Halleck directed McClellan to transfer his troops to Pope's command.

Unfortunately for McClellan's critics, the much-lauded Pope could no more bag the Confederates than could McClellan. In late August, 1862, and at Manassas—twice previously the scene of Union setbacks—the self-advertising, incompetent Pope suffered defeat at the hands of those two superb Confederate strategists, Lee and Jackson. The radicals worked hard to create the impression that McClellan was responsible for Pope's failure. Their arguments fell on deaf ears as far as Lincoln was concerned, and as he beheld the remnant of Pope's beaten and demoralized army crouching before Washington he resolved to restore McClellan to command.

The opponents of McClellan were furious, the more so when the rumor spread that conservative generals had bullied Lincoln into reappointing McClellan. "It is treason, rank treason, call it by what name you will, which has caused our late disasters," wrote Senator Chandler to his colleague Lyman Trumbull. "Your president is unstable as water if he has as I suspect been bullied by those traitor generals. How long will it be before he will by them be set aside and a military dictatorship set up. . . . For God & country's sake, send someone to stay with the President who will controll [sic] and hold him. I do not despair, but my only hope is in the Lord." [81] Other radicals shared Chandler's pessimistic view.[82]

Meanwhile, McClellan was busy revamping Pope's disorganized army. The task had been scarcely completed before Lee moved north into Maryland in what was feared was the beginning of a Confederate invasion. The only serious obstacle was McClellan's army. The two armies met at Antietam, where a three-day bloody and indecisive battle was fought. Lee, because of smaller numbers and greater proportionate losses, was forced back across the Potomac into Virginia. McClellan failed to hamper this movement, though on every military count he should have done so. His failure on this occasion to attack the retreating Confederates, plus his slowness to carry through an offensive that would end the war, together with the continued insistence of the radicals that all Democratic commanders should go, finally induced Lincoln to act. On November 5, one day after the last of the fall elections, he removed McClellan from command. The radicals rejoiced, but in conservative and Democratic circles Lincoln was accused of playing politics and of planning to rid the Army of every general who was not a Republican.[83]

---

[81] Zachariah Chandler to Trumbull, Sept. 10, 1862, Trumbull Papers.
[82] T. H. Williams, *Lincoln and the Radicals,* p. 180.   [83] *Ibid.,* pp. 181–90.

In radical circles the elimination of McClellan was regarded as certain proof that the President intended at last to purge the Union Armies of Democrats and West Pointers in high command. Only a few days before McClellan's dismissal Lincoln had removed General Don C. Buell, commander of the Department of the Ohio and of the largest army in the West. A Democrat and a West Pointer and a brother-in-law of the Confederate General David E. Twiggs, he was from the first suspected in the minds of the radicals. His friendship with McClellan, the loss of his army's confidence in him, and his slowness to win battles did not help him. William S. Rosecrans, a favorite of the radicals, was named as Buell's successor. With both McClellan and Buell out, the day seemed near at hand when all the Union Armies would be headed by men of the radical Republican stamp. "Be patient a very little while," exclaimed the elated Greeley, "and all the 'augers that won't bore' will be served as Buell has been." [84]

Radical belief that Lincoln had been won to their point of view was severely jolted when, to their consternation, Ambrose Burnside, a Democrat, West Point graduate, and a McClellan protégé, was appointed commander of the Army of the Potomac. Of mediocre ability and wholly unfit for the task assigned him, Burnside in mid-December, 1862, attacked the strongly intrenched Confederates at Fredericksburg, only to have his army reeled back with terrific slaughter. The despairing North was stunned, and a wave of savage criticism was leveled at the Lincoln administration. Indeed, popular dissatisfaction threatened to spell disaster for both the Republican party and the Unionist cause.[85]

Even the radicals were frightened as they strove desperately to bolster public opinion. The real cause for the loss of the battle of Fredericksburg, they asserted, was not Lee's strong position but the incompetency of the McClellan gang—Democrats, West Pointers, traitors all. Burnside saved himself by going over to the radical camp; but W. B. Franklin, one of his corps commanders, who stood high in McClellan's estimation, was relieved of his command by Stanton and sent to an obscure post in the West.[86] Burnside, despite the efforts of the radicals to save him, lost the

[84] New York *Daily Tribune*, Oct. 25, 1862.
[85] T. H. Williams, *Lincoln and the Radicals*, pp. 199–201.   [86] *Ibid.*, p. 228.

confidence of his army and resigned; "Fighting Joe" Hooker, courageous but withal vain and intriguing in character, succeeded him. Hooker, who had studiously sought to please the radicals, was *persona grata* to them.[87]

Meanwhile, the purge of West Point-trained commanders who were Democrats continued in full swing. Fitz John Porter, arrested by Stanton after the second battle of Manassas and brought to trial before a radically dominated court-martial, was found guilty and dismissed.[88] Irwin McDowell, an early favorite of the radicals, was accused of being a convert to McClellanism and underwent humiliating treatment at the hands of Wade and his fellows.[89] Charles P. Stone, who had participated in the battle of Ball's Bluff, was wrongfully accused of treason and his military career ruined.[90] Halleck, though he tried hard to win the favor of the radicals, was never quite able to do so. Though Halleck managed to hold his post to the end of the war, Lincoln was under more or less constant pressure to oust him.[91] Even Meade, who succeeded Hooker after Chancellorsville and triumphed at Gettysburg, did not escape radical onslaughts, and there were insistent demands that he be removed.[92] Grant, a Democrat and a West Pointer, who was villainously attacked by the radicals early in the war, largely escaped later censure by becoming a radical.[93] His colleague in arms, William T. Sherman, however, was the subject of wholly unwarranted abuse. The radicals' attempt to sully his reputation by accusing him of being a traitor, merely because of his honest endeavor to carry out Lincoln's instruction, reveals the extent to which the radicals were willing to go to destroy all those who refused to comply with their wishes.[94]

Lincoln was also under pressure to make a place for the radical favorite, John C. Frémont. Following a bitter quarrel with the Blairs, the temperamental Frémont, contrary to Lincoln's wishes, issued, in late August, 1861, a military proclamation, a portion of which freed the slaves of all persons in Missouri resisting the government. This, coupled with other incidents, was too much for the wearied President and in October, 1861, he issued an order re-

[87] T. H. Williams, *Lincoln and the Radicals,* pp. 266–73.
[88] *Ibid.,* pp. 224–25.   [89] *Ibid.,* pp. 56, 226–28.
[90] *Ibid.,* pp. 47, 94–104.   [91] *Ibid.,* pp. 60, 149, 274, 337.
[92] *Ibid.,* pp. 303–5, 338–41.   [93] *Ibid.,* pp. 334–36.
[94] *Ibid.,* pp. 234, 376–81.

moving Frémont from command of the Western Department. The anger of the radicals at this action knew no bounds. Frémont, they declared, had been a victim of a conspiracy to ruin his influence with the country and to oust him from the Army. Henceforth they never lost sight of an opportunity to restore him to what they believed was his rightful heritage.[95]

Finally, the radicals were almost beside themselves with anger over the treatment accorded the racy Ben Butler, another favorite. Butler was twice removed from command, once by Lincoln and later by Grant. Lincoln's action followed Butler's attempt, while commander of the Gulf Department, to reconstruct Louisiana in accordance with radical principles. Grant acted because the breezy Butler had shouldered his way into the command of an expedition against Fort Fisher in North Carolina, which on account of Butler's bungling ended in dismal failure.[96] Even Nathaniel P. Banks, who was named by Lincoln as Butler's successor in command of the Gulf Department, was not trusted by the radicals. A Democrat converted to conservative Republicanism on the slavery issue, Banks did not see eye to eye with Stanton, Wade, Chandler, and the others. Consequently he was anathema and his handling of the Louisiana situation along nonradical lines enraged them the more. A "flattering stupid general," Wendell Phillips called him, who should be replaced by a Butler or a Frémont.[97]

To his dying day the radicals were a constant thorn in Lincoln's flesh. That he did not yield more quickly to them in the matter of military patronage is a tribute to his greatness.

[95] *Ibid.,* pp. 39–41, 49, 84, 105–6, 274, 277–78.   [96] *Ibid.,* pp. 222, 365–66.
[97] *Ibid.,* pp. 222, 274–77, 341–42; see also New York *Daily Tribune,* Feb. 3, 1863.

Chapter VII

THE JUDICIARY AND THE MARSHALSHIPS

THE DEPARTMENT OF JUSTICE did not escape the heavy hand of the spoils system during the Lincoln administration. Space, the limited scope of this study, and concern to avoid monotonous cataloguing forbid a compilation of all loyal Republicans who found paying jobs under Attorney General Bates's department. The names of several active party men whose political campaign services were recognized will perhaps suffice.

One of Cameron's Pennsylvania managers in his race for the Republican presidential nomination in 1860, Joseph Casey, was appointed a justice of the Court of Claims.[1] Two of Bates's Missouri associates received an appointment as solicitor of the Court of Claims—Charles Gibson, Bates's manager in his contest for the Republican presidential nomination in 1860,[2] and James B. Gardenshire, defeated Republican candidate for governor of Missouri.[3] The Missouri appointments were handled jointly by Bates and the Blairs.[4]

The federal attorneyships in the various districts likewise were given to party men almost without exception. Among them were George F. Talbot, a Bowdoin graduate, active in forming the Maine Republican party and a delegate-at-large to the Chicago Convention, was appointed United States Attorney for the Maine district;[5] the author, Richard Henry Dana, veteran Free-Soiler

[1] Blanchard, *The Progressive Men of the Commonwealth of Pennsylvania*, II, 713–14; Jos. Casey to Cameron, Jan. 28, May 7, 1860, Cameron Papers.

[2] "The Diary of Edward Bates, 1859–1866," ed. by Howard K. Beale, *Annual Report*, American Historical Association, IV (1930), 11 n., 83, 102, 124; Charles Gibson, "Edward Bates," Edward Bates Papers.

[3] McDougal, "A Decade of Missouri Politics, 1860 to 1870: From a Republican Viewpoint," *The Missouri Historical Review*, III (Jan., 1909), 141; Bay, *Reminiscences of the Bench and Bar of Missouri*, p. 318.

[4] Cincinnati *Daily Gazette*, March 22, 1861.

[5] "American Series of Popular Biographies: Maine Edition," pp. 178–80.

and by 1860 a Republican, was, with Sumner's backing, made United States Attorney for the Massachusetts district; [6] George A. Nourse, an early organizer of the Minnesota Republican party, and an outspoken anti-Cameronite, received the post of United States Attorney for the Minnesota district.[7]

The federal marshalships, too, went to loyal Republican organization men. Among the more prominent were Ward H. Lamon, Lincoln's friend and former law partner, member of the Illinois Republican party who had accompanied Lincoln on his journey from Springfield to Washington; Lamon was awarded the post of United States Marshal for the District of Columbia; [8] Washington Bonifant, a leader of the Maryland Republican party and a delegate to the Chicago Convention, was put in as United States Marshal for Maryland; [9] William Rabe, who had withdrawn from the San Francisco postmaster contest, was appointed United States Marshal for the Northern District of California, while Henry D. Barrows, chairman of the Los Angeles County Republican Committee, was made the new United States Marshal for the Southern District of California; [10] for the Northern District of New York State the marshalship went to Edward I. Chase, brother of Secretary of the Treasury Chase.[11]

Of all the appointments to federal marshalships that of Secretary Chase's brother seems to have caused the most friction and in its larger phases was an outstanding illustration of the rivalry between Seward and Chase. Chase had procured for his brother Attorney General Bates's recommendation. Almost foxlike, Seward threw his support for the position to his old political follower Andrew B. Dickinson of Steuben County, New York, described by a contemporary as "illiterate and rough-hewn, but a strong debater." [12] It was a stand-up fight between the two strongest personalities in the Cabinet. Finally Lincoln gave in to Seward

6 Adams, *Richard Henry Dana*, I, 122, 130, 137, 262–76; II, 248–50, 257.

7 "The Genesis of the Republican Party in Minnesota," *Minnesota History Bulletin*, II (Feb., 1917), 26; George A. Nourse to Trumbull, May 13, 1860, Trumbull Papers; *U. S. Official Register, 1861*, p. 193.

8 Lincoln to "Hon. Attorney General," April 6, 1861, in *New Letters and Papers of Lincoln*, ed. by Angle, p. 265; Tilton, "Lincoln and Lamon: Partners and Friends," *Transactions of the Illinois State Historical Society*, 1931, p. 178.

9 Baltimore *Sun*, April 27, 1860; *U. S. Official Register, 1861*, p. 190.

10 San Francisco *Daily Evening Bulletin*, April 17, 23, 1861.

11 Henry B. Stanton, *Random Recollections*, pp. 223–25.   12 *Ibid.*, p. 223.

and appointed Dickinson to the job. "When the news came to Chase, it was a scene for a painter," reminisced an observer. "His eye-brows twitched more nervously than usual, and his breath was short and hot as he spitefully said: 'What a place you New York men have got me into.'" [13] The Secretary of the Treasury was indeed incensed and he lost no time in sending a tart letter to Seward:

Day before yesterday you said to me in reference to the marshalship of the Western [i.e., Northern] district of New York, "Insist on your brother." I replied that the Attorney-General would, as I understood, nominate him, and that Senator Harris [of New York] favored the appointment, as did Representatives Van Horn and Fenton, and that I presumed the other Representatives from Western New York would not object, and that I supposed therefore that the nomination would certainly be made.

To my surprise this morning I learn that another gentleman was brought forward by Mr. King [the other United States Senator from New York] in the conference in your department last night.

I have never favored nor pressed my brother, and never spoke a word in his behalf to the Attorney-General, and never mentioned him until this morning to the President; but I cannot abandon him or consent that the decision of the Attorney-General in his favor shall be rescinded.[14]

This impasse between Seward and Chase over the appointment of the latter's brother under the control of Bates's department was finally broken when Seward received assurances that he could take care of Dickinson by tendering him the appointment of Minister to Nicaragua. Dickinson accepted the diplomatic mission to Nicaragua, and Edward I. Chase received the marshalship. Dickinson, however, derived evident satisfaction in spreading the report in a Washington hotel that it was because of pity for Chase that he agreed to step down from the marshal's position.[15]

[13] Henry B. Stanton, *Random Recollections*, p. 224. For the close relationship between Seward, Thurlow Weed, and Dickinson see Barnes, *Memoir of Thurlow Weed*, p. 326; F. W. Seward, *Seward at Washington as Senator and Secretary of State*, II, 33, 85, 224; New York *Daily Tribune*, Feb. 4, 1861.

[14] Seward to Chase, March 27, 1861, in F. Bancroft, *The Life of William H. Seward*, II, 356 n.–57 n.

[15] Henry B. Stanton, *Random Recollections*, pp. 224–25.

Other considerable tidbits of patronage under the Department of Justice were the positions of Chief Justice of the Supreme Courts of the seven territories—New Mexico, Utah, Washington, Nebraska, Nevada, Colorado, and Dakota. That highest judicial honors in the various territories were eagerly sought after by ambitious Republicans is indicated in the letter written by an Oswego, New York, leader to his friend, Governor Austin Blair, of Michigan, soon after the 1860 elections: "This day I rec'd a communication from the State Republican Committee addressed to the President elect which is highly flattering. As yet I have rec'd no communication that has been other than flattering. I desire the appointment of Chief Justice for Nebraska. . . . *When you have leisure* address a letter to Senator Trumbull in my behalf." [16] This particular Republican did not succeed in acquiring the highest judicial position in Nebraska Territory—it went to William P. Kellogg, a deserving pioneer Illinois Republican, who had been a member of the convention that organized the state party and had been a delegate to the Chicago Convention. [17]

For Chief Justice of Nevada the choice fell to George Turner, who had been active in waging Republican campaigns in his home state of Ohio. [18] Colorado received as its Chief Justice Benjamin F. Hall, a Republican of Seward's city of Auburn, New York, who had read law in Seward's office and who had been active in the campaign to capture the party's presidential nomination for Seward; the hand of the Secretary of State was clearly seen in Hall's appointment. [19] Dakota's Chief Justiceship went to Philemon Bliss, who had served as a Republican Member of Congress from Ohio. [20] Washington Territory was given as its Chief Justice a friend of

[16] N. W. Davis to Blair, Dec. 7, 1860, Austin Blair Papers, Burton Historical Collection.

[17] Sorenson, *The Story of Omaha*, p. 357; J. M. Palmer, *The Bench and Bar of Illinois*, II, 1040.

[18] Mack, *Nevada: A History of the State from the Earliest Times through the Civil War*, p. 222; J. P. Smith, *History of the Republican Party in Ohio*, I, 38.

[19] H. H. Bancroft, *History of Nevada, Colorado, and Wyoming*, p. 413; Storke and Smith, *History of Cayuga County, New York*, pp. 238, 240; "The Diary of Edward Bates, 1859–1866," ed. by Howard K. Beale, *Annual Report*, American Historical Association, IV (1930), 93, 93 n.

[20] *South Dakota Historical Collections*, VI (1912), 314 n.; J. P. Smith, *History of the Republican Party in Ohio*, I, 29, 66; *Biographical Directory of the American Congress, 1774–1927*, II, 711.

Lincoln in the old Illinois days, Christopher C. Hewitt.[21] In the remaining two territories Democratic incumbents were retained— Kirby Benedict in New Mexico,[22] and John F. Kinney in Utah. Benedict and Lincoln were friends of long standing; Kinney, however, was removed in 1863.[23]

Midway in his administration Lincoln was faced with the decision of appointing several Justices to the United States Supreme Court. The Republicans' deep interest in the Supreme Court's personnel dated back at least to the Dred Scott decision of 1857. Seward, then the party's most eminent Senate spokesman, had, in 1858, when the slavery interests were pressing a bill for the admission of Kansas as a slave state, denounced Chief Justice Roger B. Taney for entering an alleged "deal" with President James Buchanan to give a proslavery decision in that celebrated case—a charge wholly unfounded in fact. In the same year Lincoln, in a speech at Springfield, had called attention to what he asserted to be a series of events sponsored by Senator Stephen A. Douglas, former President Franklin Pierce, Chief Justice Taney, and President Buchanan, all leading to the Dred Scott decision and to the fastening of slavery on the territories. Instead of offering proof that the four had connived to this end, Lincoln insinuatingly concluded that "we find it impossible to not *believe* that Stephen and Franklin and Roger and James all understood one another from the beginning. . . ." Indeed, for a decade or more antislavery stump speakers and editors had been hacking away at the prestige of what they deemed a Court dominated by the "Slave Power." The Republicans had become much worried when Mr. Justice Curtis resigned in 1858, leaving Mr. Justice John McLean their sole representative on the nation's highest tribunal. When Buchanan appointed a Maine Democrat, Nathan Clifford, who had been Attorney General under Polk, to fill Curtis's seat, the abusive powers of the Republican press, led by the New York *Tribune*, were turned on full blast. In 1859 when,

---

[21] Bagley, *History of King County, Washington*, I, 584; Hunt and Kaylor, *Washington: West of the Cascades*, III, 568.

[22] Twitchell, "Kirby Benedict," *Old Santa Fe*, I (July, 1913), 50, 83, 85, 90; Usher F. Linder, *Reminiscences of the Early Bench and Bar of Illinois*, pp. 196–205; Twitchell, *Leading Facts of New Mexico History*, II, 393 n.

[23] H. H. Bancroft, *History of Utah*, pp. 462, 604; Gue, *History of Iowa*, IV, 157; "John Fitch Kinney," *Annals of Iowa*, Series III, XVI (Oct., 1927), 145–50.

in a Wisconsin case, *Ableman vs. Booth*, involving the constitutionality of the Fugitive-Slave Law, the Court gave a decision unpopular with the Republicans, the party press again became vituperative.[24] Greeley's *Tribune*, questioning Taney's loyalty, even went so far as to encourage the people of Wisconsin not to submit to the decision.

Before the beginning of the December, 1860, term of the Court, Mr. Justice Peter V. Daniel had died, leaving the Court evenly divided between nothern and southern members. The South was insistent that the new appointee should come from its section. "The Court is the last line of defense which, it seems, is now left us," [25] one southern leader wrote. Finally, in the closing weeks of his administration, Buchanan nominated his Secretary of State, Jeremiah S. Black, a Pennsylvania Democrat, as Daniel's successor. The Republican press was savage in its denunciation. In coalition with the Douglas or anti-Buchanan Democrats, the Republicans in the Senate refused, after battling for sixteen days, to confirm the nomination.[26] Black's biographer, after reviewing the evidence, concludes:

The wound which Black had inflicted on Douglas in the Popular Sovereignty controversy had not healed, and the Douglas Democrats felt no enthusiasm for supporting Buchanan's swordsman in that controversy. But the bitterest opposition came from the Republicans. The radical Republicans were so bitterly hostile to the Supreme Court that they would have opposed the appointment of any Democrat under any conditions. The conservative Republicans were determined that no important appointments of any kind should come out of the Buchanan administration during its closing days, since, if they could block such appointments, the offices would be left for the incoming Republican administration to fill.[27]

And the nation's most widely read Republican journal venomously declared that it would oppose Black, even if he united "the virtues

---

[24] Swisher, *Roger B. Taney*, pp. 511–12, 520–21, 524, 526–31; C. Warren, *The Supreme Court in United States History*, III, 91–92; F. Bancroft, *The Life of William H. Seward*, I, 446–49; Beveridge, *Abraham Lincoln, 1809–1858*, II, 578–81.

[25] Warren, *The Supreme Court in United States History*, III, 80.

[26] *Ibid.*, pp. 85–87; Brigance, *Jeremiah Sullivan Black: A Defender of the Constitution and the Ten Commandments*, pp. 113–16.

[27] *Ibid.*, p. 114.

of a Marshall" with "the learning of a Story," because he was not a Republican! [28]

When Lincoln was inaugurated in March, 1861, it was rumored that he intended to nominate to the Court the moderate and very able Senator John J. Crittenden, veteran statesman of Kentucky, and this was hailed with enthusiasm in nonpartisan circles. Crittenden had supported John Bell, the Constitutional Union candidate for President in 1860. Not only was he an able lawyer but he had been recently one of the most active supporters of an attempt to avert civil war by means of the famous "Crittenden Compromise" in January, 1861. His recognition by the Lincoln administration, one conservative Republican paper declared, would be received with joy all through the border states.[29] Seward, at Lincoln's direction, even requested the outgoing Attorney General, Edwin M. Stanton, to draw up Crittenden's nomination as Associate Justice of the United States Supreme Court. Stanton did so and believed that it would be sent to the Senate for confirmation immediately. But it was not sent, for the more radical Republicans were opposed to it. No "moderate" would have been acceptable to them.[30] As a consequence, Daniel's seat for the time being remained unfilled.

By the summer of 1861 there were two additional vacancies in the highest court. Death had claimed Mr. Justice John McLean, and Mr. Justice John A. Campbell had resigned to travel the road of secession with his native state of Alabama. Lincoln hesitated to fill any of the three places, declaring that he did not desire to give all appointments to the North, thereby making it difficult to do justice to the South when the war should end. "I have been unwilling to throw all the appointments northward," said he in his annual Address to Congress, December 3, 1861, "thus disabling myself from doing justice to the South on the return of peace; although I may remark that to transfer to the

28 New York *Tribune,* Feb. 20, 1861. Stanton wrote to an associate: "Judge Black's nomination for the Supreme Court was not acted upon." See Stanton to P. Deller Lowe, March 4, 1861, Edwin M. Stanton Papers. Technically this was true, for on Feb. 21, 1861, the Senate in a stormy and turbulent session decided not to take up the nomination of judge. Cf. *Harper's Weekly,* March 2, 1861, p. 135.

29 Warren, *The Supreme Court in United States History,* III, 87.

30 Edwin M. Stanton to Buchanan, March 10, 14, 1861, in *The Works of James Buchanan,* ed. by Moore, XI, 163, 169.

North one [Circuit] which has heretofore been in the South would not, with reference to territory and population, be unjust." [31]

The nation, it should be explained, had been divided into nine circuits, in each of which one of the Supreme Court justices, when not sitting in Washington, was required to hold circuit court. But as new states were admitted it had been impossible to make the services of the justices stretch so far, with the result that Wisconsin, Minnesota, Iowa, Kansas, California, and Oregon, as well as Florida and Texas, had never been brought within any of the nine circuits. Congress, therefore, was confronted with the knotty problem of regrouping the nine circuits. Recommendations galore poured in, most of them to the effect that the President should appoint such and such a lawyer to the highest Court, and that the districts should be so arranged that the several Supreme Court aspirants would be geographically available. The first, second, third, and fourth of the existing circuits, embracing the North and Middle Atlantic States, presented no problem, for none of the vacancies were in those circuits. The South was, at the moment, unconcerned as to how Congress might legislate, for no federal judge receiving his appointment from the Washington government would dare to attempt to hold court in most of the seceded territory. The real problem faced by Congress was simply how three circuits were to be carved out of the West, where no possible scheme of grouping could satisfy all the aspiring talent from that region. Perhaps, as never before, Congressmen became geographically minded.[32]

One of the western lawyers pressed most vigorously on Lincoln for a Supreme Court appointment was Noah H. Swayne, of Ohio. Born in Virginia, Swayne had migrated to Ohio in early manhood and had served in the state legislature. He had also held the office of district attorney of Franklin county for nine years and was practicing law in Columbus when his ambition was immediately aroused by the death of Supreme Court Justice John McLean, a fellow Ohioan. McLean had not yet been borne to his last resting place when Swayne began enlisting support for the deceased man's place on the nation's highest bench. McLean died on April 4, 1861,

and on this same day Swayne dispatched the following message
to Secretary of the Treasury Chase:

Intelligence of the death of Judge McLean reached here this morning. My friends will name me to the President as one of those from
whom a selection is to be made to fill the vacancy upon the Bench of
the Supreme Court, thus created. If you can deem it proper to give
me your friendly support you will lay me under a lasting obligation.[33]

Swayne had powerful backing from his fellow Republicans of
Ohio, including Governor William Dennison and the state's two
United States Senators.[34]

Throughout most of 1861 Lincoln delayed filling any of the
three vacancies. By December Governor Dennison, becoming impatient, wrote United States Senator Trumbull of Illinois: "I see
by the papers you are about introducing a Bill to reorganize the
Judicial Circuits of the Sup. Court. I trust you will present nothing to be done that can interfere with the selection of our friend
Mr. Swayne as the successor of Judge McLean." [35] Several days
later the Ohio governor, having heard rumors that a plan was afoot
in Washington to attach Ohio to the same circuit as Kentucky
and that Lincoln was contemplating appointing a Kentuckian to
the Supreme Court, thus disqualifying Swayne, wrote Trumbull
again:

Our friends here [in Columbus] are anxious to have Ohio united with
Ind. & Michigan for a federal Circuit, not only because it may
facilitate the appointment of our friend Mr. Swayne to the Bench,
for which they are very anxious, but from the intimacy of business
intercourse between the people of the states and the long time they
have held this relation with each other. I am satisfied it will be better
for Ohio to have a resident of her state Judge than one from a slave
state, and then he should be a Republican.[36]

It was Senator Wade, however, who appears to have fought
most valiantly for Swayne at the White House. There was good

33 N. H. Swayne to Chase, April 4, 1861, Salmon P. Chase Papers, Library of
Congress.
34 C. Warren, *The Supreme Court in United States History,* III, 100, 100 n.; *Mr
Justice Swayne,* pp. 3–5. This last is an undated pamphlet in the New York Public
Library.
35 William Dennison to Trumbull, Dec. 10, 1861, Trumbull Papers.
36 William Dennison to Trumbull, Dec. 16, 1861, *ibid.*

reason why Wade should exert himself, for at this very time Swayne in Columbus was working hard for Wade in the Senator's uphill fight for reëlection to the United States Senate.[37] That each kept in close touch with the other is evident from their correspondence. Under date of January 10, 1862, for example, Swayne wrote Wade as follows:

Yours of the 7th inst. is before me. Governor Dennison and Mr. Wolcott—Geiger and Judge Willson—and some others will be in Washington by the middle of next week. . . . Gov. Dennison is still quite confident that the Kentucky gentleman [Crittenden] referred to in your letter will not be seriously in the way. Among his reasons for so thinking are the following:

The President has always from the first frankly said that he must appoint Mr. Browning.

He has never in any conversation with any of my friends named the gentleman referred [to].

He has said repeatedly that if the Circuit were divided & Ohio disjoined from Illinois that he would appoint me. He has never made any other condition.

At the instance of a friend of mine—he put into his message— the suggestion that the Ohio Circuit should be divided. Secty Smith [of the Interior Department] has always said that I had no one to fear but B[rowning] & Co. Mr. L[incoln] has said within a fortnight that Gov. C[hase] was not & would not be in the least in my way. Wolcott says that when he was in Washington the last time *two persons* as likely to know the President's sentiments as any one in the City told him that the President desired to appoint me & would do so provided he could appoint Mr. B[rowning] & myself both.

He has to two of my friends used stronger language as to his judgment of my qualifications. . . . He can appoint the Kentucky gentleman—if he desire to place him on the bench for the far South in Circuit. . . .

It would not be treating the loyal & Republican state in which we live well to appoint the Judge of our Circuit from Kentucky

It would increase the number of Southern men—already too large —upon the bench of the Supreme Court.

The gentleman referred to is not and never was a Republican. I understand Mr. L. refused to appoint him in the place of Campbell or Daniel. I can hardly think that *under the circumstances* he will

[37] R. F. Paine to Wade, Jan. 10, 1862, Benjamin F. Wade Papers.

appoint him in place of McLean, & impose him on Ohio against her wishes.

The Gov. [Dennison] mentions other reasons with which I will not trouble you. He will see & consult with you in a few days. After my conversation with him & Wolcott today the matter wears a more favorable aspect to my mind. I have written you this fully that you may be in possession of the views entertained here & of the reasons of them. Gov. C [Chase] told G. [Geiger] just before he left Washington that he would support me. Sec. S. [Smith] told me the last time I saw him that every member of the Cabinet was for me except C. and that he thought C. could be if he should conclude not to be a candidate himself

You will of course regard all this as confidential.[38]

To this Swayne added a postscript to the effect that he had shown Wade's letter to Geiger and that Dennison had wired for leave for Geiger to visit Washington and that he would undoubtedly join Wade in a few days. From this document it is evident that Swayne feared only Lincoln's old associate, United States Senator Orville H. Browning, of Illinois, and Crittenden.[39]

There is some evidence—of an inconclusive nature—that the influence of Swayne's relative and law partner, Richard P. L. Baber, aided Wade, Dennison, and Swayne's lesser friends in persuading Lincoln to appoint Swayne to the High Bench. Baber had journeyed from Columbus to Springfield in 1859 to induce Lincoln to have the Lincoln-Douglas debates collected and published and had further succeeded in having the then little-known Lincoln make a speech in Ohio in September of that year; at the Chicago Convention in 1860 Baber, a delegate, had worked to swing portions of the Buckeye State delegation to the Rail Splitter—for all of which Lincoln had appointed him a paymaster in the Army in 1861. There are indications that Baber had induced Swayne to aid in financing publication of the famed debates between Lincoln and Douglas, which were such a potent factor in making Lincoln more than an Illinois personality.[40]

[38] Noah H. Swayne to Wade, Jan. 10, 1862, *ibid.*

[39] Though he had voted for the Crittenden resolution defining the purposes of the war, Wade was in reality much opposed to both the resolution and its author. See Riddle, *Life of Benjamin F. Wade,* p. 290.

[40] Taylor, "Richard Plantaganet Llewellyn Baber," *Ohio Archaeological and Historical Publications,* XIX (1910), 370–73.

The continued efforts of Wade, Dennison, and others in support of Swayne were crowned with success, for on January 21, 1862, Lincoln nominated him for Associate Justice of the United States Supreme Court to fill the vacancy occasioned by the death of McLean.[41] There seems to be no basis for the persistent tradition that Lincoln confused Swayne's name with that of Joseph R. Swan, Swayne's more brilliant fellow lawyer, also of Columbus, and really meant to appoint Swan to the Court.[42]

Swayne hastened to Washington to wear the robe sacred to all lawyers—but hastened back to Columbus in late February to aid Wade in his long-drawn-out battle for the Senatorship. Wade's lieutenants, led by Robert F. Paine, United States Attorney for the Northern District of Ohio, were fighting hard for their leader against Columbus Delano, who aspired to Wade's Senate seat.[43] The appreciative Swayne entered the thick of the fray. Wrote one Ohio paper: "Hon. Judge Swayne, recently returned from Washington, also states that Secretary [of War] Stanton asserts that the defeat of Mr. Wade would be 'a public calamity.' " [44] And one of Wade's managers at Columbus reported to the Senator the progress of the Senatorial struggle:

Hon. N. H. Swayne got home this morning. I was glad to see him on your account for he is greatly interested in your success and will *work*. He is already doing what he can and his high position and acquaintance give him influence. . . . Your opponents are working boldly. . . . The arrival of Judge Swayne is much in our favor for he is very zealous and enters into the work with heart. He has just gone to the "Fact" office to see what he can do to enlist it for you. The sheet is entirely mercenary and can be perhaps controled [sic]. . . . Swayne will see Tod . . . [and] will talk to him definitely.[45]

Wade won and Swayne was among those who were elated over his victory.

[41] R. F. Paine to Wade, Jan. 22, 1862, Wade Papers; *U. S. Senate Executive Journal*, XII (1861–62), 94, 98.

[42] Statement of Alonzo H. Tuttle in his sketch of Swayne in *Dictionary of American Biography*, XVIII, 240.

[43] R. F. Paine to Wade, Feb. 15, 1862, Wade Papers. "The great obstacle in the way of Senator Wade's immediate election [reëlection] is the false & foolish report here industrially and persistently circulated that Mr. Wade is violently hostile to the measures of the [Lincoln] Administration."

[44] Cincinnati *Daily Commercial*, Feb. 21, 1862.

[45] J. H. Geiger to Wade, Feb. 20, 1862, Wade Papers.

Another of the many contenders for a seat on the Supreme Court was Samuel F. Miller, of Iowa. Born in Kentucky and reared in the tradition of Henry Clay, Miller had in 1850 removed to Keokuk, Iowa, where he mixed law with Whig politics. Later he became active in the Republican party, supporting Lincoln for President in 1860. In 1859 he had unsuccessfully contested with Governor Kirkwood for the party's gubernatorial nomination.[46] Miller's friends worked like beavers in his behalf. At length one of them, First Assistant Postmaster General John A. Kasson, an Iowa Republican leader, was summoned by Lincoln:

When, at his request, I called upon President Lincoln to ascertain the cause of the delay in his [Miller's] nomination, I found that his reputation as a lawyer had not then even extended so far as Springfield, Illinois, for the President asked me if he was the same man who had some years before made a frontier race for Congress from the southern district of Iowa, and had trouble about the Mormon vote. Correcting Mr. Lincoln's misapprehension on this point, I proceeded to give the President a sketch of Mr. Miller's career and characteristics.[47]

Apparently Lincoln had reference to Daniel F. Miller, former Congressman from an Iowa district.[48]

Miller also had the backing of Iowa's two United States Senators, James Harlan and James W. Grimes.[49] Governor Kirkwood also lent his voice in support, for he desired to remove from the state a dangerous and powerful political rival.[50] In fact, Kirkwood joined Senator Harlan and two or three Members of Congress from Iowa in personally presenting Miller's cause to Lincoln. The President, taking pen and paper in hand, is quoted as having queried: "What is the office and whom do you wish to be placed in it?" Harlan replied that they desired Miller to be appointed to the Supreme Court. "Well, well," commented Lincoln, replacing his pen and pushing back his paper, "that is a very important position, and I will have to give it serious consideration. I had supposed

[46] Fairman, *Mr. Justice Miller and the Supreme Court, 1862–1900,* chap. i, pp. 18 ff., 28, 34; Gregory, *Samuel Freeman Miller,* pp. 2–14.

[47] John A. Kasson to Charles Aldrich, Nov. 10, 1893, in Strong, "Justice Samuel Freeman Miller," *Annals of Iowa,* Series III, I (Jan., 1894), 252.

[48] New York *Daily Tribune,* July 18, 1862.

[49] Brigham, *James Harlan,* pp. 176–77, 365.

[50] Gregory, *Samuel Freeman Miller,* p. 8.

you wanted me to make some one a Brigadier-General for you." [51]

Finally, on July 16, 1862, Lincoln nominated Miller to fill one of the two Supreme Court vacancies and the Senate gave its approval.[52] In the last analysis Miller, the first member of the High Bench to come from the regions west of the Mississippi, owed his appointment largely to the efforts of Senators Harlan and Grimes.[53] So obscure was Miller nationally that leading Republican journals continued to confuse him, as did Lincoln, with Daniel F. Miller. "Mr. Miller's name is printed *Samuel* in the dispatches," said Greeley's New York *Tribune*, "but we presume it is Daniel F. Miller, the first Whig Member of Congress ever chosen from Iowa." [54] At least two other widely circulated Republican organs were no better informed.[55] Harlan himself acknowledged that it was "a unique appointment. He [Miller] had never before held any office, local, state, or national; and had not been in the active practice as a lawyer over twelve years." [56] Harlan knew him to be a strong Republican and in coöperation with Grimes drew up and circulated in both Houses of Congress a petition asking for Miller's appointment to the bench.[57] Lincoln could not well ignore the Harlan-Grimes request.

With the selection of Miller there remained only one vacancy on the High Bench. This was in the Eighth Circuit, which was made up of Michigan, Wisconsin, and Illinois.[58] But who was to be appointed? The bar of Illinois was urging Lincoln to select Judge Thomas Drummond, of the United States District Court of Illinois; that of Michigan was pressing the name of William A. Howard; that of Wisconsin was backing one of its United States Senators, the conservative James R. Doolittle.[59] Lincoln himself was toying with the idea of choosing his old friend, United States

[51] Charles N. Gregory, "Samuel Freeman Miller: Associate Justice of the Supreme Court of the United States," *Yale Law Journal*, XVII (April, 1908), 426.

[52] *U. S. Senate Executive Journal*, XII (1861–62), 416–417.

[53] "I think he was indebted to me," wrote Harlan, "more than to any one man living, for this great distinction. He frequently said to his intimate friends that if it had not been for me, he never would have been appointed." Brigham, *James Harlan*, p. 176.

[54] New York *Tribune*, July 18, 1862.

[55] Cincinnati *Daily Gazette*, July 22, 1862; Springfield *Daily Illinois State Journal*, July 24, 1862.

[56] Brigham, *James Harlan*, p. 176.   [57] *Ibid.*, pp. 176–77, 365.

[58] Springfield *Daily Illinois State Journal*, July 24, 1862.

[59] C. Warren, *The Supreme Court in United States History*, III, 101–2.

Senator Orville H. Browning, of Illinois.[60] Then there was Lincoln's staunch compatriot, Judge David Davis, of the Eighth Judicial Circuit of Illinois, who, at Chicago in 1860, had been so instrumental in capturing the Republican presidential nomination for Lincoln and about whom much has already been narrated.

After months of meticulous and devoted service to make Lincoln President, Davis had good reason to believe that he would be rewarded with a lucrative federal office; when his friend Ward H. Lamon, Lincoln's former law partner, whom he appointed United States Marshal for the District of Columbia, suggested to Lincoln that Davis be chosen as Commissioner of Patents, the President instantly declined to consider it. After a month in Washington, where he exerted influence in securing federal jobs for others, Davis had returned to his home in Bloomington, Illinois, to the "small business of holding Courts on $1,000 a year." In May, 1861, his friend, Secretary of War Cameron, whom he had aided so vigorously in securing a Cabinet place, appointed Davis to the Board of Visitors to the United States Military Academy at West Point—an honorary gesture which by no means satisfied him. "Knowing nothing of military matters, could I be of any service?" he asked, "Mere loafing and looking wise and pretending knowledge about things of which I am ignorant is not to my taste." [61]

Apparently Cameron realized this fact and soon appointed him to serve as chairman of a committee to investigate the reputedly bad military administration of General Frémont in the Department of the West and particularly in Missouri. This inquisitorial work, which unearthed almost unheard of extravagance and corruption, engaged him for several months. Meanwhile, Davis's friends were urging Lincoln and Lincoln's advisers to appoint him to the Highest Bench.

Probably the most indefatigable worker in Davis's cause was Leonard Swett. In April, 1861, this closest of Davis's friends wrote Lamon concerning Davis's ambitions for the Supreme Court: "Also tell Lincoln that Judge Davis will be an applicant. . . . See

[60] Leonard Swett to W. H. Herndon, Aug. 29, 1887, in Hertz, *The Hidden Lincoln*, pp. 338–39.

[61] Pratt, "David Davis, 1815–1886," *Transactions of the Illinois State Historical Society*, 1930, p. 169.

'without fail' Cameron, Caleb B. Smith and Gov. Seward." [62] Apparently Swett remembered well his and Davis's coöperation with Seward and Thurlow Weed in bringing Cameron and Smith into the Cabinet during those stirring days of wire pulling between Lincoln's election and inauguration.

Davis, for his part, was pessimistic about realizing his ambition; he knew only too well that he had made enemies within Illinois and outside the state, particularly among the radical or Chase elements of the Republican party, because of the part played by him in securing the appointment of Cameron and Smith to the Cabinet. To Lamon he wrote dejectedly in April, 1861: "I have neither hope or [sic] expectation that Lincoln would appoint me Supreme Judge. If he even had any notion of doing it, he would be pressed & would give way. Trumbull & Chase would never let him do it." [63]

Torn between Browning and Davis and hard pressed by the radicals, Lincoln moved slowly in filling the vacancy. Undiscouraged, Davis's friends continued to put pressure on the President and his close associates in Davis's behalf. Even before Swayne's appointment, a Bloomington friend of Davis, Lawrence Weldon, wrote to Lamon: "I see Judge McLean has departed this life. The question is, who shall succeed to the ermine so worthily worn by him. . . . Why should not David Davis . . . especially when he was so instrumental in giving position to him who now holds the matter in the hollow of his hand?" [64] Weldon added the request: "Dear Hill [Lamon's nickname], if justice and gratitude are to be respected, Lincoln can do nothing less than to tender the position to Judge Davis. . . . I want you to suggest it to Lincoln." [65]

Meanwhile Swett, in Bloomington, was becoming decidedly alarmed at reports that Lincoln, pushed by influential Senators, was leaning toward Browning. After consulting with Davis, he decided to pack his carpetbag for Washington and to see Lincoln in person.[66] Swett, later describing his interview with Lincoln

[62] Leonard Swett to Ward H. Lamon, April 7, 1861, in Pratt, "David Davis, 1815–1886," p. 93.

[63] David Davis to Ward H. Lamon, April 14, 1861, in *ibid.*, p. 94.

[64] Lawrence Weldon to Ward H. Lamon, April 16, 1861, in Pratt, "David Davis, 1815–1886," *Transactions of the Illinois State Historical Society*, 1930, p. 170.

[65] *Ibid.*

[66] Leonard Swett to W. H. Herndon, Aug. 29, 1887, in Hertz, *The Hidden Lincoln*, pp. 338–39.

at the White House, alleged that he told the President: "If Judge Davis with his tact and force had not lived, and all other things had been as they were, I believe you would not be sitting now where you are sitting. . . . It is the common law of mankind that one raised into prominence is expected to recognize the force that lifts him. . . . Here is Judge Davis, whom you know to be in every respect qualified for this position, and you ought in justice to yourself give him this place." [67] In the belief that Missouri would be grouped with Illinois in the same judicial circuit under the pending bill in Congress, Swett enlisted the support of Missouri interests. His letter to Judge Samuel Treat, of the United States District Court at St. Louis, and an influential War Democrat, is informing:

Bloomington Jan 31 1862

Hon Samuel Treat
St Louis Mo

Dear Sir

I take the liberty of addressing you a note in behalf of our mutual friend Hon David Davis. As one of his friends, I am desirous that the President should appoint him Judge of the U S Supreme Court for the new district. I have been giving the matter some attention, and am quite positive the choice, in the mind of the President, lies between Judge Davis & Hon. O. H. Browning.

It seems to me that the legal men of the district should be consulted, and I have no doubt the President would pay great regard to their opinions.

The Convention [state constitutional convention of 1862] now in session at Springfield, in this State, have very generally, irrespective of party, recommended Judge Davis. . . .

If you think proper to move in this matter, & will get such a recommendation, I should think it a great favor; or if you prefer it, I will come there & do what I can myself.

I would be glad to hear from you upon this subject.

Yours Truly,
Leonard Swett [68]

On the above letter is an endorsement in Judge Treat's handwriting: "He came here, and with the cooperation of friends, the

[67] Leonard Swett to W. H. Herndon, Aug. 29, 1887, in Hertz, *The Hidden Lincoln*, p. 339.

[68] This letter is printed in Fairman, *Mr. Justice Miller and the Supreme Court, 1862–1900*, pp. 54–55.

DAVID DAVIS

desire and recommendation of the Mo. Bar was had, also large recommendations from Ills. . . . President Lincoln asked us to get up and forward the recommendations." [69]

The pressure on Lincoln to appoint Davis to the Court was terrific. Hawkins Taylor, who had been an Iowa delegate to the convention that nominated Lincoln and who had witnessed the behind-the-scenes maneuvers that resulted in Lincoln's selection as Republican standard bearer and who finally received his reward when Lincoln appointed him Post Office Inspector for Kansas, threw himself into the fight with unrelenting energy. In July, 1862, Taylor wrote Lincoln frankly:

. . . . I will say that in my honest opinion, with every opportunity of knowing, that but for the *extraordinary* effort of Judge Davis, you would not have received the nomination at the Chicago Convention. I can say to you that I consider your nomination providential. . . . Viewing the case in the light that I do, I feel that it is due to yourself as well as to Judge Davis that you should tender him the appointment of Supreme Judge. [70]

Finally Lincoln yielded. Browning was dropped from consideration. On December 1, 1862, Lincoln named David Davis Associate Justice of the United States Supreme Court and a week later the Senate confirmed the appointment. Davis resigned his office of Judge of the Eighth Circuit of Illinois and took his seat on the most elevated of American tribunals during the same month. [71] Probably no one worked so valiantly and vigorously to achieve this result as did Leonard Swett. [72]

Lincoln had opportunity to fill still a fourth seat in the United States Supreme Court. This opportunity came because it was deemed expedient to have a tenth Justice and considered imperative that a majority of the Court should be unquestionably loyal. The question of the loyalty of the Court assumed serious propor-

[69] *Ibid.*

[70] Hawkins Taylor to Lincoln, July 12, 1862, in Pratt, "David Davis, 1815–1886," *Transactions of the Illinois State Historical Society*, 1930, p. 171 n.

[71] Dent, "David Davis—A Sketch," *The American Law Review*, LIII (1919), 545; *U. S. Senate Executive Journal*, XIII (1862–64), 1, 7.

[72] Lincoln's former law partner and friend, William H. Herndon, wrote Henry C. Whitney in Aug., 1887: "Davis, at Bloomington, told me, by inference at least, that Lincoln didn't give him the judgeship of his own accord, but that some one else got it for him, etc." See Hertz, *The Hidden Lincoln*, p. 202. Perhaps the "some one else" was Leonard Swett.

tions when, in 1863, the issue of the legality of the Union blockade of the southern ports came before the Supreme Court.[73] "Contemplate, my dear sir," wrote Richard Henry Dana, one of the counsel of the United States in this litigation, to Charles Francis Adams, "the possibility of a Supreme Court deciding that this blockade is illegal!" The five-to-four decision of the Court, upholding the legality of the blockade, was handed down in March (1863) and came as a relief to the friends of the Union. But the closeness of the vote in the Supreme Court illustrated that in future the conduct of the war against the Confederacy might be inadvertently sabotaged by judges who were more deeply devoted to the South or to their conceptions of the law than to the immediate needs of the government. Sentiment demanded that the personnel of the Court be so changed as to obviate any possible danger from this particular quarter. Accordingly, early in March, 1863, Congress passed an act reorganizing the judicial circuit on the Pacific Coast and providing for the *tenth* Justice of the United States Supreme Court.[74]

The choice of the Republican Senators and Representatives in Congress from California was Stephen J. Field, chief justice of the California supreme court. Field, born in New England, brother of David Dudley Field, the eminent New York lawyer, of Cyrus W. Field, proponent of the Atlantic cable, and of Henry M. Field, the noted clergyman, had gone to California in 1849. He entered Democratic politics, serving in the California legislature, and in 1857 was elected to the state supreme court. Upon the outbreak of the war, Field, as a Buchanan Democrat, instantly aligned himself with the pro-Union party, which had helped to keep California in the Union.[75]

One of the staunchest supporters of Stephen J. Field for the Court appointment was Governor Leland Stanford, then a power in the Republican party of California. Field had been interested in some of the old Mexican land grants, genuine or otherwise, in California, and it was largely through the influence of the promoters of these claims, as well as the influence of Stanford and his associate railroad promoters, that Field was elected to the Cali-

---

[73] The Prize Cases, 67 U. S. 635.
[74] Swisher, *Stephen J. Field: Craftsman of the Law,* pp. 113–16.
[75] Swisher's *Field* is the best work ever done on the subject.

fornia supreme court, becoming its chief justice in 1859. Governor Stanford personally urged Lincoln to appoint Field to the nation's highest Court.[76]

Influence on Lincoln came from another source—from Field's brother, David Dudley Field, who had played a major part in the organization of the Republican party in New York and had supported Lincoln for the Republican presidential nomination at the Chicago Convention in 1860.[77] While the nomination was pending, wrote Henry M. Field:

Mr. John A. C. Gray, a well known citizen of New York, and an old friend of Mr. Lincoln, went to speak to him about it. He found the President agreed entirely on the fitness of Judge Field, and had but one question to ask: "Does David want his brother to have it?" "Yes," said Mr. Gray. "Then he shall have it," was the instant reply, and the nomination was sent in that afternoon, and confirmed by the Senate unanimously.[78]

An examination of the secret proceedings of the United States Senate indicates that Lincoln sent in Field's name for nomination as Associate Justice of the United States Supreme Court on March 6 (1863) and that the appointment was confirmed four days later.[79]

In the space of slightly more than one year—from January, 1862, to March, 1863—Lincoln had appointed four justices to the nation's highest court—Swayne, Miller, Davis, and Field. Before his career was cut short by tragic assassination he was to make still another Supreme Court appointment—that of Secretary of the Treasury Chase to be Chief Justice. The withdrawal of Chase from the Cabinet and his elevation to the bench—a long and complex story—is intimately connected with the presidential election of 1864 and will be treated in that connection in later pages.

[76] G. Myers, *History of the Supreme Court of the United States*, pp. 501–2, 502 n.
[77] Swisher, *Stephen J. Field: Craftsman of the Law*, p. 116.
[78] Henry M. Field, *The Life of David Dudley Field*, p. 196 n.
[79] *U. S. Senate Executive Journal*, XIII (1862–64), 223, 275.

Chapter VIII

PATRONAGE AND THE SLAVE STATES

THE DISTRIBUTION of federal jobs in the "loyal" border-slave states and in those parts of the Confederacy dominated by the Union armies occupied much of Lincoln's attention throughout the war.

Like the nation as a whole, Kentucky, Missouri, Maryland, and Delaware, although slave states, were divided against themselves— "half slave and half free." Their populations ranged all the way from uncompromising secessionists to equally uncompromising abolitionists. Most of the inhabitants of the four states probably belonged to that intermediate group which had sympathies with both the North and the South. As such, they dreaded disunion and hoped that their respective states might escape participation in the war. An ever-increasing number in these border-slave states were staunch Unionists. This faction Lincoln cultivated—partly by the use of the patronage. In the interim between his election and inauguration Lincoln emphatically indicated to John A. Gilmer, of Kentucky, that he did not intend to inflict on the people of the slave states federal officeholders who because of Republican sympathies would be obnoxious. Writing Gilmer under date of December 15, 1860, Lincoln said:

As to the use of patronage in the slave States, where there are few or no Republicans, I do not expect to inquire for the politics of the appointee, or whether he does or not own slaves. I intend in that matter to accommodate the people in the several localities, if they themselves will allow me to accommodate them. In one word, I never have been, am not now, and probably never shall be in a mood of harassing the people either North or South.[1]

Most of the slave states, convinced that the election of a "Black Republican" President constituted a threat to their institutions

---

[1] Lincoln to John A. Gilmer (Strictly confidential), Dec. 15, 1860, in *Complete Works of Abraham Lincoln*, VI, 80–81.

and way of life, did not share Lincoln's contention that he did not intend to harass them. When Lincoln entered the White House in March, 1861, he found several slave states out of the Union and several others preparing to follow along the road of secession.[2] In his First Inaugural Address the newly inducted President declared that he would use his powers to retain control of federal government properties and to this extent only would he exercise his appointing power. Lincoln declared, in part:

The power confided to me will be used to hold, occupy, and possess the property and places belonging to the Government and to collect the duties and imposts; but beyond what may be necessary for these objects, there will be no invasion, no using of force against or among the people anywhere. Where hostility to the United States in any ulterior locality shall be so great and universal as to prevent competent resident citizens from holding the Federal offices, there will be no attempt to force obnoxious strangers among the people for that object. While the strict legal right may exist in the Government to enforce the exercise of these offices, the attempt to do so would be so irritating and so nearly impracticable withal that I deem it better to forego for the time the uses of such offices.[3]

On assuming office Lincoln immediately cultivated the Unionist element in the border-slave states. The appointment of Green Adams, of eastern Kentucky, to a position in the Treasury Department was viewed by the press as "the commencement of a wise and conservative policy in reference to the distribution of the patronage of the Administration in the border-slave states. Mr. Lincoln will not appoint all Republicans to the offices at his disposition in any of these states. There are, in fact, but few influential Republicans in any of them, with, possibly, the exception of Missouri and Maryland. He will, therefore, throw himself upon the counsels of the Union men."[4] Green Adams, who served four years, became one of Lincoln's closest advisers on the Kentucky situation.[5] In late March, 1861, before the firing on Fort Sumter and

2 John Bach McMaster, *A History of the People of the United States during Lincoln's Administration*, p. 3.

3 Richardson (comp.), *Messages and Papers of the Presidents, 1789–1897*, VI, 7–8.

4 Philadelphia *Press*, March 21, 1861. For Adams's appointment as Sixth Auditor of the Treasury Department, see Connelly and Coulter, *History of Kentucky*, II, 1206.

5 "In answer to your inquiries of this morning, I have to say I am very anxious to have the special force in Kentucky raised and armed. But the changed conduct

the start of hostilities with the Confederacy, Lincoln consulted on patronage with Union-minded political leaders from the border states.[6] Lincoln's policy in these states, when evolved, consisted of awarding patronage not only to the handful of Republican leaders but also to non-Republican Unionists, many of whom were slave owners. In deep disgust one ardent Republican leader assailed the President's "silly desire to conciliate *loyal slaveholders*." [7] But Lincoln's paramount purpose was to build up a strong Unionist party in the border-slave regions, and to this end he selected the federal officers, both civil and military.

Lincoln devoted much attention to his native state of Kentucky, which he considered the most vital of the loyal border-slave states. "I think to lose Kentucky," Lincoln confided in September, 1861, to his old Illinois friend, United States Senator Orville H. Browning, "is nearly the same as to lose the whole game. Kentucky gone, we cannot hold Missouri, nor, as I think, Maryland." [8] Kentucky was torn between two loyalties: to the South by origin and sentiment, a partial slave economy, marriage, and other social ties; to the North by love for the Union and desire to promote closer economic relations.[9]

An examination of Lincoln's principal appointments for Kentucky indicates that he selected men whose loyalty to the Union was above all question. Cassius M. Clay, principal Republican leader in the Blue Grass State, he persuaded to go to St. Petersburg as United States Minister, and it was well that that impetuous firebrand was removed from the delicate state of Kentucky poli-

---

toward me of some of her members of Congress and ominous misgivings as to what the governor and legislature of Kentucky intend doing, admonish me to consider whether any additional arms I may send are not to be turned against the government." Lincoln to Green Adams, Jan. 7, 1863, in *Complete Works of Abraham Lincoln*, VIII, 175.

[6] Baltimore *Evening Patriot*, March 18, 30, 1861. "A delegation of Union men from the Border States have waited upon the President to urge the propriety and importance of considering the Union element of the South in the distribution of appointments. This presentation of the case was not necessary in order to set Mr. Lincoln right upon the point in question, for he already fully understood the importance of the policy suggested, and has followed it so far as opportunity has occurred. . . ."

[7] Dr. P. A. Allaire to Trumbull, Dec. 10, 1861, Trumbull Papers.

[8] Lincoln to O. H. Browning (Private and confidential), Sept. 22, 1861, in *Complete Works of Abraham Lincoln*, VI, 360.

[9] Coulter, *The Civil War and Readjustment in Kentucky*, p. 17.

tics. As United States District Attorney for Kentucky Lincoln named James Harlan (not to be confused with United States Senator James Harlan, of Iowa). Harlan, an Old Line Whig, had served in Congress and as state attorney general, but with the approach of civil war, he, like most of the other leading Kentucky Whigs, became a staunch Union man, opposing secession. In March, 1861, Harlan had taken an active part in preventing passage by the Kentucky legislature of a resolution which was avowedly the initial step toward secession. In May of the same year, in combination with other Unionists, he formulated and executed plans for arming the Unionists in Kentucky, notably by distributing the so-called "Lincoln Guns" to those opposed to Confederate sympathizers.[10] "It was no doubt in recognition of his services in opposing secession as well as in recognition of his legal abilities," writes Professor Robert S. Cotterill, "that Lincoln appointed him [Harlan] district attorney of Kentucky." [11]

Harlan died in 1863, and for his successor as United States District Attorney for Kentucky Lincoln decided on Thomas E. Bramlette.[12] A native Kentuckian and like Harlan a staunch Whig Unionist, Bramlette had served as a state judge and, with the approach of civil war, came out unreservedly for the preservation of the Union. Consequently, he exhibited little patience with the strange "neutrality" policy set forth by Kentucky in 1861. In July of that year, at a time when the state was attempting to maintain her neutral position, Bramlette accepted from the Lincoln administration a commission in the Union Army and boldly set about raising the Third Kentucky Infantry, which he commanded as colonel—all in violation of the state's tacit agreement with the federal government. In 1862 Bramlette resigned from the Army and when, early in 1863, Lincoln offered him the federal district attorneyship to succeed the deceased Harlan, he accepted. In his new position Bramlette set about enforcing the war-time laws enacted by Kentucky against Confederates and secessionist sym-

---

[10] A. H. Harlan, *History and Genealogy of the Harlan Family*, p. 275; Speed, *The Union Cause in Kentucky, 1860–1865*, pp. 74, 99–115; Stevenson, "General Nelson, Kentucky, and Lincoln Guns," *The Magazine of American History*, X (Aug., 1883), 114–39.

[11] *Dictionary of American Biography*, VIII, 267.

[12] *United States Senate Executive Journal*, XIII (1862–64), 157, 199.

pathizers. He soon relinquished his federal office, however, to become governor of the state.[13]

For Bramlette's successor as United States District Attorney Lincoln appointed Joshua Tevis. A resident of Louisville and former member of the state legislature, Tevis was an ardent Union man and had served as colonel of the Tenth Kentucky Cavalry.[14] When Judge Thomas B. Munroe, of the United States District Court for Kentucky, resigned, Lincoln chose as his successor an uncompromising Unionist, Bland Ballard.[15]

Other key federal positions in Kentucky went to men who could be entrusted to combat those of Confederate leanings. The federal marshalship of Kentucky was vital for the Lincoln administration in its efforts to stamp out secessionist influences, inasmuch as it devolved upon the United States Marshal to take into custody those accused of being sympathetic with the Confederacy.[16] As United States Marshal for Kentucky Lincoln appointed a strong foe of secession, Alexander H. Sneed.[17] For the Louisville postmastership, the most lucrative in Kentucky, the President chose Dr. John J. Speed, of the Union-loving Speed family.[18] Shortly before his assassination Lincoln appointed another Speed, James Speed, of Louisville, as Attorney General in his Cabinet.[19] Charles S. Todd, veteran Whig leader who had been Minister to Russia under President Tyler, was appointed Assessor of Internal Revenue for the First Kentucky District.[20] To another Kentucky Unionist, Joseph Holt, an erstwhile Democrat and Postmaster General in Buchanan's Cabinet, Lincoln gave the post of Judge Advocate General of the Army.[21]

[13] See E. Merton Coulter's sketch of Bramlette in *Dictionary of American Biography*, II, 595.

[14] Speed, *The Union Cause in Kentucky, 1860–1865*, pp. 78–79, *U. S. Senate Executive Journal*, XIII (1862–64), 368, 384; *U. S. Official Register, 1863*, p. 269.

[15] Speed, *The Union Cause in Kentucky, 1860–1865*, p. 80; *U. S. Senate Executive Journal*, XII (1861–62), 15, 96.

[16] Frankfort (Ky.) *Tri-Weekly Commonwealth*, Oct. 18, 1861.

[17] *U. S. Official Register, 1861*, p. 192; Frankfort (Ky.) *Tri-Weekly Commonwealth*, Aug. 21, 1861.

[18] Speed, *Records and Memorials of the Speed Family*, pp. 76–77; *U. S. Official Register, 1861*, p. 252.

[19] See p. 310.

[20] Speed, *The Union Cause in Kentucky, 1860–1865*, p. 74; *U. S. Senate Executive Journal*, XIII (1862–64), 15.

[21] Holt was the first incumbent of this office. It was created by Congress for the

At least three diplomatic appointments were given by Lincoln to loyal Kentuckians: Cassius M. Clay, as already noted, became United States Minister to Russia; Allan A. Burton was made Minister Resident to Colombia;[22] and Thomas H. Clay, son of the venerated Henry Clay, was rewarded with the post of Minister Resident to Nicaragua.[23]

Most of the federal appointments in Kentucky went to non-Republicans, for there was only a skeleton Republican party in the state, almost all of the opposition to the secession wing of the Democratic party being in the Constitutional Union party, which was composed of conservative Unionists, Old Line Whigs, and erstwhile Know-Nothings.[24] It was upon the Whig-tainted Constitutional Unionists that Lincoln bestowed most of the patronage at his disposal. With the exception of Cassius M. Clay, the only other out-and-out Republican leader of Kentucky who received an important position from Lincoln seems to have been George D. Blakey, appointed Collector of Internal Revenue for the First Kentucky District.[25] Blakey had been Clay's coworker in organizing the militant but numerically small Republican party in the Blue Grass State.[26]

In addition to giving jobs to those who were upholding the Union cause in his native state, Lincoln appears to have awarded government advertising and printing to editors who were supporting his policies. His bounty to George D. Prentice, editor of the widely circulated Louisville *Journal*, is illustrative. Official records indicate that sums of $482 and $335 were paid to Prentice by the State Department alone for printing in the *Journal*.[27] Prentice, it will

purpose of receiving, revising, and recording the proceedings of all courts martial, courts of inquiry, and military commissions. See Mary B. Allen's sketch of Holt in *Dictionary of American Biography*, IX, 181–82.

22 Speed, *The Union Cause in Kentucky, 1860–1865*, p. 79; *U. S. Official Register, 1861*, p. 10.

23 Speed, *The Union Cause in Kentucky, 1860–1865*, p. 76; *U. S. Senate Executive Journal*, XIII (1862–64), 25, 88.

24 John Bell carried Kentucky in the presidential election of 1860 on the Constitutional Union ticket, Lincoln polling only 1,364 votes in the state. See Coulter, *The Civil War and Readjustment in Kentucky*, p. 24.

25 *U. S. Senate Executive Journal*, XIII (1862–64), 15.

26 Cassius M. Clay to Cephas Brainerd, May 7, 1860, in "The 1860 Presidential Campaign," *The Moorsfield Antiquarian*, I (Aug., 1937), 105.

27 *U. S. Official Register, 1863*, pp. 15, 16.

be observed, had taken a vigorous stand against secession in the columns of his paper.[28]

Much of the patronage which Lincoln gave to Kentucky was in the form of military commissions. They went to staunch Union men, of course. In April, 1861, the secessionist-minded Governor Beriah Magoffin had refused Lincoln's call for four regiments of troops from Kentucky to aid in subduing the seceded slave states. Without hesitation Magoffin had replied to the President defiantly: "I say, emphatically, Kentucky will furnish no troops for the wicked purpose of subduing her sister Southern States"—and the state, almost as a unit, applauded.[29] State Senator Lovell H. Rousseau, emissary of the Unionists of Kentucky, was appointed a colonel by Lincoln and was authorized to raise twenty companies of men for the Union cause.[30] Soon Lincoln made Rousseau a brigadier general of volunteers [31] and later promoted him to major general.[32] Rousseau was described as a portly, piratically mustached man, who "loved Bourbon whisky, blunt speech, and the Constitution." [33] Lincoln also gave Rousseau a voice in the distribution of federal jobs to Kentuckians.[34]

By June, 1862, Kentucky, practically free of any control by the Confederacy, was largely at the mercy of the Union Army. As military commander of the Kentucky Division of the Department of the Ohio Lincoln decided on Jeremiah T. Boyle, who established his headquarters at Louisville. A native Kentuckian and lawyer of Danville and a slaveholder, Boyle had been a Whig. Upon the outbreak of the war he determined his attitude toward secession more by his political affiliations than by his economic interests, becoming one of the most active Union men in the state. In late 1861 his zeal in recruiting for the Union Army gained for him a commission as brigadier general of volunteers. Boyle remained in command in Kentucky until January, 1864. His conduct as military

[28] Perrin, The Pioneer Press of Kentucky, pp. 72–73, 81–82.
[29] Coulter, The Civil War and Readjustment in Kentucky, p. 38.
[30] Schuckers, The Life and Public Services of Salmon Portland Chase, p. 419.
[31] U. S. Senate Executive Journal, XII (1861–62), 58.
[32] Ibid., XIII (1862–64), 59, 261.
[33] Lloyd Lewis, Sherman: Fighting Prophet, p. 183.
[34] Lincoln to Secretary of the Navy Gideon Welles, June 17, 1861, in Uncollected Letters of Abraham Lincoln, comp. by Tracy, p. 186.

commander has long been the subject of acrimonious controversy. Every shred of available evidence indicates that he was not very efficient against the Confederates. Morgan raided Kentucky almost at will, guerillas ravaged far and wide, and Louisville, Boyle's headquarters, was saved only by the dilatoriness of the Confederate leader, Bragg. In fact, Boyle was finally removed because of his military ineptitude. Against noncombatants he made a better showing, but his arbitrary and perhaps necessary acts in arresting persons suspected of Confederate sympathy, of using troops to control elections, and of dominating the judiciary made enemies of many people who had hitherto been neutral. One major result of his policy was the forced resignation of the pro-Confederate Governor Magoffin.[35]

Boyle was succeeded in command of the Kentucky department in 1864 by Brigadier General Jacob Ammen. Although a native of Virginia, Ammen had Kentucky connections, having taught mathematics in Transylvania College. Ammen was absent on military duty much of the time, and his command was handled by a native Kentuckian, Brigadier General Stephen G. Burbridge. When Burbridge proved himself unpopular, Lincoln decided to appoint as his successor in command in Kentucky his old Illinois political associate, John M. Palmer, who was born in the Blue Grass State. Palmer was emphatic that all important military and civil offices at the President's disposal should go to Republicans. Even so in his military appointments in Kentucky Lincoln seems to have endeavored to select men who had some connection with the state.[36]

Lincoln's patronage problems in Kentucky seem almost inconsequential, especially when compared with those in that other pivotal border-slave state, Missouri. To Lincoln, Missouri proved a virtual nightmare—a discordant medley of Blairs, General Frémonts, emancipationists, militant antislavery Germans, proslavery protagonists, contract seekers, office hunters, and other heteroge-

---

[35] Manning, "Reconstruction in Kentucky," pp. 1–4, 8. Also sketch of Boyle by Professor R. S. Cotterill in *Dictionary of American Biography*, II, 532.

[36] Manning, "Reconstruction in Kentucky," pp. 16–17, 20, 29. See sketches of Ammen and Burbridge in *Dictionary of American Biography*, I, 259; III, 270. For Palmer see *Personal Recollections of John M. Palmer*, pp. 224–26.

neous groups. Valiantly did Lincoln struggle to bring order out
of chaos in his efforts to sustain his administration and keep Missouri within the Union.

In distributing the federal offices for Missouri during the first
months of his administration Lincoln was guided by the wishes of
the Blairs and Attorney General Bates.[37] Controlling many of
the Republican and Unionist forces in Missouri was Francis P.
("Frank") Blair, Jr., brother of Postmaster General Montgomery
Blair. Thus, for example, to the loyal Blair-Bates leader, Peter L.
Foy, editor of the moderate Republican *Missouri Democrat*, went
the post office in St. Louis.[38] Lincoln himself referred to the St.
Louis postmastership as "the best office in my gift within Missouri." [39] It was fortunate that Lincoln favored this group with
government patronage, for Frank Blair and Bates's brother-in-
law, Governor Hamilton R. Gamble, were political warriors of the
first magnitude in the struggle to keep Missouri from seceding.[40]
By August, 1861, it was evident that the state would remain in
the Union; spectacular events of the spring and summer had cul-
minated in the political elimination and military defeat of the Confederate sympathizers.[41]

Although Lincoln's concern over Missouri's loyalty to the Union
was ended, conditions within the state gave rise to a new crop of
worries. They centered chiefly about the personalities of Frank
Blair and General John C. Frémont and the issue of emancipation, supplemented by the rivalry engendered over the distribution
of federal offices and the award of army contracts—all of which
divided Missouri Unionists into two main factions, the "conservatives" and the "radicals." The feud between these factions, which
tormented Lincoln until his death and shook the whole Northwest,
originated primarily in the struggle between Blair and Frémont.

[37] W. E. Smith, *The Francis Preston Blair Family in Politics,* II, 2.

[38] "The Diary of Edward Bates, 1859–1866," ed. by Howard K. Beale, *Annual
Report,* American Historical Association, IV (1930), 133 n.; Peter L. Foy to Montgomery Blair, Sept. 17, 1861 (*Private*), Francis Preston Blair Papers.

[39] Hertz, *Abraham Lincoln: A New Portrait,* II, 891.

[40] For the work of Frank Blair and Gamble in the Union cause during 1861, see
W. E. Smith, *The Francis Preston Blair Family in Politics,* II, 19 ff.; and also
Potter, "Hamilton R. Gamble, Missouri's War Governor," *The Missouri Historical
Review,* XXXV (Oct., 1940), 25–40.

[41] Barclay, "The Liberal Republican Movement in Missouri," *The Missouri Historical Review,* XX (Oct., 1925), 4.

For several years the Blair and the Frémont families had been
intimate friends; indeed, it was the powerful Blair clan that had
persuaded Lincoln to appoint Frémont as Commander of the Department of the West, with the rank of major general and headquarters at St. Louis. But temperamentally Frank Blair and Frémont clashed. Both were ambitious, hot-tempered, and tenacious,
and there soon ensued between the two a many-sided battle for control of the state. Frank Blair regarded Missouri as his own particular domain, and the independent attitude of the erratic, impetuous, visionary Frémont annoyed him excessively. It especially
disturbed the Blairs to witness the efforts of Frémont to win the
support of the powerful German element in St. Louis. Frémont,
they feared, intended to build a political machine of his own and
to challenge the Blair supremacy. Frémont's insistence on awarding army contracts to his California friends [42] rather than to deserving Blair supporters lent color to the Blair suspicions.

To make matters worse, Frank Blair came to the conclusion that
Frémont was stupid and lacking in military talent and that he was
administering his command inefficiently, extravagantly, and perhaps downright dishonestly. Frémont, in turn, fervently hoped
that Frank Blair would accept an army post in the East and
thereby ease himself out of the Missouri picture. But Blair had
no such intention, and the elder Blair, believing that his son was
on the high road to the presidency, continued to insist by letters
and telegrams that Frémont coöperate with him. The situation
was not improved by Frank Blair's reports to Washington of what
he deemed to be Frémont's shortcomings or by Mrs. Frémont's
tenacious efforts in her husband's behalf.

In the thick of the battle Lincoln dispatched Postmaster General Montgomery Blair (elder brother of Frank) and his brother-
in-law, Quartermaster General Meigs, to St. Louis to make a thorough inquiry and at the same time to give Frémont friendly advice
and admonition. Inevitably enough, the Postmaster General, after
talking with his embittered brother, returned to Washington with
a report to Lincoln that recommended Frémont's removal as Commander of the Department of the West. This highly unfavorable

---

[42] "California vultures," the Blairs called them—see Nevins, *Frémont: Pathmarker of the West*, p. 509.

report, coupled with Mrs. Frémont's display of temper in an exchange of words with the President, deepened Lincoln's feeling that Frémont had been an unfortunate choice to command the Union forces in the West.

The bitterness between the two opposing families reached new heights when Frémont, at his wife's instigation, had Frank Blair (who was Frémont's military subordinate) arrested for insubordination. Upon his release from custody Blair filed formal charges against Frémont which were laid before Lincoln. Included in the list were neglect of duty, disobedience of orders, conduct unbecoming an officer, extravagance and waste, and despotic and tyrannical conduct. It was evident, as never before, that Missouri had become too small to hold both Frank Blair and Frémont.

Possibly Frémont might have retained Lincoln's confidence had he not antagonized the President by issuing without Lincoln's consent a proclamation [43] which, among other things, proclaimed martial law in Missouri and provided for the confiscation of property and liberation of slaves owned by those taking up arms against the United States. Lincoln, determined to keep the Unionist element of the slave regions friendly to his administration, rebuked Frémont: "I think there is great danger that the closing paragraph, in relation to the confiscation of property and the liberating slaves of traitorous owners, will alarm our Southern Union friends and turn them against us." [44] Lincoln, to the utter disgust of the radicals, directed Frémont to modify the order.

Meanwhile, the Blairs kept insisting that Frémont go. Lincoln in deciding what action to take could not forget that Montgomery Blair was in his Cabinet; that the Blairs were the most powerful personal force in the border states, for Montgomery Blair and his father, Francis P. Blair, Sr., were powers in Maryland no less than was Frank in Missouri. Irrespective, therefore, of how much of the right was on Frémont's side, Lincoln felt that there was no other course than to remove him from his command, and in October, 1861, an order to this effect was issued. [45]

---

[43] This proclamation was issued Aug. 30, 1861. See Laughlin, "Missouri Politics during the Civil War," *The Missouri Historical Review*, XXIV (1929–30), 87–93.

[44] Lincoln to Frémont, Sept. 2, 1861, in *Complete Works of Abraham Lincoln*, VI, 350.

[45] Nevins, *Frémont: Pathmarker of the West*, pp. 507–9, 509 n., 510–49. See also New York *Herald*, Sept. 18, 1861. Professor William E. Smith, biographer of the

The removal of Frémont aroused a tremendous storm of protest throughout the country. The colorful explorer and soldier had for many years captured the imagination of the westerners. Moreover, he was the idol of the radicals.[46] When he took his leave of St. Louis, a great mass meeting of Germans was held in his honor, and this was followed by similar demonstrations of affection in other parts of the West. His journey from Missouri to New York took on the color of a triumphal procession. In the eastern metropolis he was lauded by Senator Sumner and other prominent radicals before a great meeting in Cooper Union.[47] Charges were freely heard from antislavery men that Lincoln, under influence of the Blairs, had removed Frémont because of his proposed proclamation liberating the slaves of disloyal masters. Unquestionably Frémont had raised the emancipation issue in both Missouri and the nation.

The immediate result of Frémont's proclamation and of his removal was to split the Missouri Unionists, as we have noted, into two camps: conservatives ("Claybanks") and radicals ("Charcoals"). Blair apparently headed the conservatives, who, with some notable exceptions ("Chocolates"), favored gradual, compensated emancipation of the Negro, while Blair's own cousin, B. Gratz Brown, editor of the St. Louis *Missouri Democrat*, led the radicals, who stood for immediate emancipation. The overwhelming majority of Germans, endeared to Frémont and strongly antislavery, repudiated Blair and aligned themselves with the radicals.[48] The radicals' discontent with the conservatives was not confined solely to the issues of Frémont and emancipation. The radicals believed that their rivals were receiving too much of the federal patronage, for the President was giving much of his support to the provisional government headed by Governor Gamble, Attorney General Bates's brother-in-law and a conservative.[49] In July, 1862, the

Blairs, writes of the feud between Frank Blair and Frémont: "St. Louis was not large enough to hold the two men." See W. E. Smith, *The Francis Preston Blair Family in Politics*, II, 67.

[46] T. H. Williams, *Lincoln and the Radicals*, pp. 48–50, 105–6, 277–78.

[47] Nevins, *Frémont*, II, 625.

[48] Laughlin, "Missouri Politics during the Civil War," *The Missouri Historical Review*, XXIV (1929–30), 87–93; Arden R. Smith to Montgomery Blair, Oct. 22, 1861, Francis Preston Blair Papers.

[49] Barclay, "The Liberal Republican Movement in Missouri," *The Missouri Historical Review*, XX (Oct., 1925), 5, 7.

Democrat, now the chief radical organ in St. Louis, complained in no uncertain terms:

No More Republicans Appointed: It is said that Gov. Gamble has determined not to appoint any more Republicans to office in the military, or civil service of this State, or the United States, so far as those appointments come through him. After what the Governor has already done to depose and proscribe Republicans, this announcement will astonish nobody; and our Republican President should undoubtedly take special pains to appoint to all the Federal offices from this State the pets and partisans of Gov. Gamble. This will give our intensely patriotic Governor all the rope he wants.[50]

Blair, who had lost his following among the Germans, sought to win them back by having Lincoln give military promotions to high-ranking German officers in the Union Army. For example, there was Brigadier General Franz Sigel. "He ought to be made Major General," wrote Gustave Koerner to a Republican leader. "The soldiers have confidence in him. . . . The President who has so much displeased the Germans by Frémont's removal ought not to hesitate a moment about it." [51] Blair induced Lincoln not only to appoint Sigel a major general, but likewise to make another German leader, Peter J. Osterhaus, a brigadier general.[52] These appointments seem not to have pacified the Germans. In June, 1862, Blair announced his candidacy for Congress from the First (St. Louis) Missouri District, and the *Democrat*, aided by the two German organs, the *Westliche Post* and the *Anzeiger des Westens*, began an editorial bombardment against him.[53]

To wean the Germans away from the radicals, Blair enlisted the services of Henry Boernstein. Boernstein, a native of Hamburg, Germany, and trained at the University of Lemberg, had come to the United States in 1848, settling in St. Louis, where he became owner of the *Anzeiger des Westens*. In 1861 Blair had secured for him from Lincoln the post of United States consul in Bremen. When Postmaster General Montgomery Blair and Henry T. Blow accompanied the President to Yorktown in 1862, they agreed that

[50] St. Louis *Daily Missouri Democrat*, July 28, 1862.
[51] Gustave Koerner to Trumbull, Jan. 2, 1862, Trumbull Papers.
[52] Laughlin, "Missouri Politics during the Civil War," *The Missouri Historical Review*, XXIV (1929-30), 100.
[53] St. Louis *Daily Missouri Democrat*, June 23, 26, July 9, 1862.

Boernstein should be persuaded to return from his duties in Bremen and devote his time to influencing his fellow Germans in Missouri to support Lincoln and the Blair interest in the state against the radical tide. Blow, then a Blair ally, wrote Boernstein that if he returned to the United States and "went heartily into the reconciliation of this [German] element, so that it could be seen that his influence & exertions were beneficial to the Govt., that he could rely on such *sympathy* in return, as would secure to him as high a position as he had ever desired." [54]

Boernstein accepted the offer, left Bremen, and returned to St. Louis, where he resumed control of the *Anzeiger*, changing its editorial policy to one upholding Blair in the latter's fight for Congress.[55] Fierce editorial warfare broke out in the summer of 1862 between the *Anzeiger* and the radical German organ, the St. Louis *Westliche Post*.[56] To assist Boernstein in editing the *Anzeiger* Frank Blair insisted on the appointment of another German-American leader, Charles L. Bernays, to a position which would pay him a salary and could be run by a clerk so that Bernays might do work for the *Anzeiger*. Accordingly Lincoln appointed Bernays to a paymastership in the Army, a sinecure.[57] Boernstein's efforts by means of the *Anzeiger* to stem the rush of German votes into the radical ranks apparently were satisfactory, for we find Frank Blair writing to his brother: "Boernstein has acted most nobly and done glorious service since his return. I have no doubt that he has accomplished more to reconcile the Germans to the Administration than any other man of that race is capable of doing in so short a time." [58]

Federal patronage was used in another manner to bolster the conservative cause in Missouri and Frank Blair's campaign for election to Congress: A new organ, the *Union*, was started, with Postmaster Peter L. Foy of St. Louis as editor. Foy, appointed by Lincoln through the influence of the Blairs and Attorney General Bates, had formerly been editor of the *Democrat* but had severed

54 Henry T. Blow to Francis P. Blair, Jr., July 30, 1862, Francis Preston Blair Papers; W. E. Smith, *The Francis Preston Blair Family in Politics*, II, 208–9.

55 St. Louis *Daily Missouri Democrat*, July 12, 26, 1862.

56 *Ibid.*, July 31, Aug. 6, 1862.

57 W. E. Smith, *The Francis Preston Blair Family in Politics*, II, 210.

58 Francis P. Blair, Jr. to Montgomery Blair, Aug. 1, 1862, Francis Preston Blair Papers.

his connection with that organ because of its radical course and enmity toward the Blairs.[59] The radicals were angered that the *Union* should receive the support of the Lincoln administration, one radical organ referring to it as "this contemptible office-hunter's affair, which is edited in the Post Office by Mr. Foy and some of his clerks." [60] This journal complained further: "The people pay the salaries for the benefit of the public in general, but with this money of the people a paper is now edited for the benefit of a single politician! At last we see the real character of Mr. Blair." [61]

Despite efforts of the radicals to defeat him, Blair was elected to Congress. The election left in its train an atmosphere super-charged with bitterness, and radicals and conservatives drew farther apart. The newspaper organs were especially vindictive. The continued circulation of the *Union* was most obnoxious to the radicals because in their opinion it lived on "Administration pap" and its editor held the post office.[62] The *Democrat* intimated through its columns that Lincoln would do well to remove Frank Blair's brother, the Postmaster General, from his Cabinet.[63] Lincoln ignored the suggestion at this time.

More fuel was added to the fires of dissension between the two main Missouri Unionist groups when in January, 1863, the legislature of that state took up the task of selecting a representative to the United States Senate. One of the leading candidates for the long term was none other than B. Gratz Brown. Convinced that the federal officeholders within the state were operating against his election, Brown during the course of the balloting wired Lincoln: "Does the administration desire my defeat, if not, why are its appointees working to that end?" [64] Lincoln sought to disabuse Brown's fears, and tactfully answered:

Hon. B. Gratz Brown, Jefferson City, Missouri: Yours of today just received. The administration takes no part between its friends in Missouri, of whom I, at least, consider you one; and I have never

[59] Peter L. Foy to Montgomery Blair (Private), Sept. 17, 1861, Francis Preston Blair Papers.
[60] St. Louis *Daily Missouri Democrat*, July 29, 1862.
[61] *Ibid.*   [62] *Ibid.*, Nov. 10, 1862.   [63] *Ibid.*, Nov. 14, 1862.
[64] Laughlin, "Missouri Politics during the Civil War," *The Missouri Historical Review*, XXIV (1929–30), 102.

before had an intimation that appointees were interfering, or were inclined to interfere.[65]

In view of the activity of the Blair-controlled federal office-holders some critics are inclined to question whether this statement was entirely accurate. But the President was usually the diplomat.

With passing weeks the Missouri situation became no better; complaints and protests continued to roll into the White House. His patience exhausted, Lincoln wrote a Missouri leader, Henry T. Blow: "It is very painful to me that you in Missouri cannot or will not settle your factional quarrels among yourselves. I have been tormented with it beyond endurance for months by both sides. . . . Neither side pays the least respect to my appeals to your reason. I am now compelled to take hold of the case." [66] Lincoln "took hold" by removing Brigadier General Samuel R. Curtis, a favorite of the radicals, as commander of the Department of Missouri. His reason for his action he explained at length in a communication to Curtis's successor, John M. Schofield:

Having relieved General Curtis and assigned you to the command of the Department of the Missouri, I think it may be of some advantage for me to state to you why I did it. I did not relieve General Curtis because of any full conviction that he had done wrong by commission or omission. I did it because of a conviction in my mind that the Union men of Missouri, constituting, when united, a vast majority of the whole people, have entered into a pestilent factional quarrel among themselves—General Curtis, perhaps not by choice, being the head of one faction and Governor Gamble that of the other. After months of labor to reconcile the difficulty, it seemed to grow worse and worse, until I felt it my duty to break it up somehow; and as I could not remove Governor Gamble, I had to remove General Curtis.[67]

And, in a letter penned shortly afterward to General Curtis, Lincoln stated that his removal was not in any way a censure or an endorsement of the charges made against him by others. Rather it was "almost a matter of personal self-defense to somehow break

[65] Lincoln to B. Gratz Brown, Jan. 7, 1863, in *Complete Works of Abraham Lincoln,* VIII, 176.
[66] Lincoln to H. T. Blow, May 15, 1863, in *ibid.,* VIII, 276.
[67] Lincoln to John M. Schofield, May 27, 1863, in *ibid.,* VIII, pp. 282–83.

up the state of things in Missouri." [68] Despite this apparent frankness on the part of Lincoln, one is tempted to ask whether in view of the power of the Blairs he would have removed Governor Gamble, even had he had the authority. Certainly the weight of evidence would indicate that Curtis was removed to pacify the conservatives whom he had offended. [69]

Schofield proved a disrupting force in Missouri, for he seems to have favored the conservatives too strongly to satisfy the radicals. The quarrel between the two groups over emancipation and patronage became more intense. A climax was reached when in September, 1863, the radicals formed a committee of seventy, headed by Charles D. Drake, to journey to Washington and urge on Lincoln their considered demands. After presenting a long list of accumulated grievances and reviewing at length the origin and development of the antagonism between the Gamble administration and the radical Union men, Drake demanded, among other things, an end to the "intolerable pro-slavery oppression" of the Blair machine and the removal of Schofield in favor of General Benjamin F. Butler as commander of the Union force in Missouri. Lincoln promptly and judicially refused either to relieve Schofield of his command or to interfere with the state government. [70]

Protests continued to pour in. The appointment of Schofield

[68] Lincoln to Samuel R. Curtis, June 8, 1863, in *ibid.,* VIII, 294–95.

[69] See Gallaher, "Samuel Ryan Curtis," *The Iowa Journal of History and Politics,* XXV (July, 1927), 351–52.

[70] Laughlin, "Missouri Politics during the Civil War," *The Missouri Historical Review,* XXIV (1929–30), 111–12; Barclay, "The Liberal Republican Movement in Missouri," *The Missouri Historical Review,* XX (Oct., 1925), 7–8; "Diary of Edward Bates, 1859–1866," ed. by Howard K. Beale, *Annual Report,* American Historical Association, IV (1930), 308; Hay, *Lincoln and the Civil War in the Diaries and Letters of John Hay,* ed. by Dennett, pp. 95–97; James S. Rollins to Montgomery Blair, Sept. 12, 1863, Francis Preston Blair Papers. That the Missouri radicals were not highly regarded is evident from an examination of the Diaries of Edward Bates and John Hay. Under date of May 30, 1863, Bates made this entry: "The appointment of Gen. Schofield to succeed Gen. Curtis has produced great excitement among the Jacobins in Mo. [Missouri] and among their radical sympathisers and supporters at the North . . . It was the only course that could save Mo. from Social War and utter anarchy . . . The Radicals seem to have come to the conclusion that Mr. Lincoln's plan of emancipation was all wrong, too slow and cost too much money and that the best way to abolitionize Mo. was by violence and fraud . . . Those devilish designs, I trust, will all be frustrated by the appointment of Schofield, and the expected harmony between him and Gamble." Governor Gamble was Bates's brother-in-law, and Bates and his Missouri friends had long sought the removal of Curtis.

became more embarrassing. Finally in December (1863) the President wrote a lengthy letter to Secretary of War Stanton, treating the situation:

I believe Gen. Schofield must be relieved from command of the Department of Missouri, otherwise a question of veracity, in relation to his declarations as to his interfering, or not, with the Missouri Legislature, will be made with him, which will create an additional amount of trouble, not to be overcome by even a correct decision of the question— The question itself must be avoided. Now for the mode—Senator Henderson, his friend, thinks he can be induced to ask to be relieved, if he shall understand he will be generously treated; and, on this latter point, Gratz Brown will help his nomination, as a Major General, through the Senate. In no other way can he be confirmed; and upon his rejection alone, it would be difficult for me to sustain him as Commander of the Department. Besides, his being relieved from command of the Department, and at the same time confirmed as a Major General, will be the means of Henderson and Brown leading off together as friends, and will go far to heal the Missouri difficulty.

Another point. I find it is scarcely less than indispensable for me to do something for Gen. Rosecrans; and I find Henderson and Brown will agree to him for the command of their Department.[71]

Lincoln ended his letter to Stanton with the words:

In a purely military point of view it may be that none of these things is indispensable, or perhaps, advantageous; but in another aspect, scarcely less important, they would give great relief, which, at the worst, I think they could not injure the military service much. I therefore shall be greatly obliged if yourself and Gen. Halleck can give me your hearty co-operation, in making the arrangement. Perhaps the first thing would be to send Gen. Schofield's nomination to me— Let me hear from you before you take any actual step in the matter.[72]

Try as he might, Lincoln was unable to heal the Missouri breach. The *Missouri Democrat*, chief radical organ, continued to bait the conservatives and the Lincoln administration. "Can you not through Gratz Brown control the *Mo. Democrat*," United States

[71] Lincoln to the Secretary of War (Photostat), Dec. 18, 1863, Lincoln Letters; Photostats.
[72] *Ibid.*

Marshal David L. Phillips, of the Southern District of Illinois, appealed to Senator Trumbull in March, 1864. "It is doing infinite mischief. We, in Illinois, must make war on it unless its tone is modified. Its course will cost us thousands of votes. The disorganizing tendency of the paper is what is objectionable. Our Germans in Illinois are true to our party as yet. Its [the *Democrat's*] great effort now is to put them in a position where they cannot vote for Mr. Lincoln if he is nominated." [73] Both the radicals and the conservatives sent a "Missouri" delegation to the Union National Convention at Baltimore which renominated Lincoln for the presidency in June, 1864. The radicals were recognized as the regular Missouri delegation—and voted for General Grant, not Lincoln, as their preference for President.

The patronage quarrel between the two factions never was healed during Lincoln's lifetime, and early in 1865, only two months before Booth's bullet struck down the President, Postmaster Peter L. Foy, of St. Louis, was writing to an associate: "You know, I suppose, that the Radicals are straining every nerve to turn me out of the post office. I am, of course, the most conspicuous Blair man in office . . . the one who is most obnoxious to the Radicals and my overthrow would be a great triumph to them." [74] The failure of Lincoln to alter the character of his Missouri appointments was generally regarded by the radicals as conclusive evidence of the malign influence of Blair, Bates, and other conservative leaders.

Another pivotal "border-slave" state where the Blairs played a conspicuous role and which gave Lincoln almost as much trouble as Missouri was Maryland.

Because of its proximity to the national capital, Maryland, the administration felt, had to be prevented from seceding. In addition to using military force to quell secessionists, Lincoln filled the federal offices in the state with Union men, as he had in Kentucky and Missouri. In Maryland, Lincoln was confronted with the same problem as in Kentucky, namely, a skeleton Republican party, largely the instrument of the Blair family. The bulk of the opposition to the secessionist-minded Democratic party was en-

[73] D. L. Phillips to Trumbull, March 23, 1864, Trumbull Papers.
[74] P. L. Foy to Rollins, Feb. 7, 1865, in Barclay, "The Liberal Republican Movement in Missouri," *The Missouri Historical Review*, XX (Oct., 1925), 34 n.

rolled in the Constitutional Union party of John Bell.[75] By the
time Lincoln took up his duties at the White House in March, 1861,
the Unionist element in Maryland was divided into two distinct
factions—the Republicans, controlled by Postmaster General
Montgomery Blair and his father, Francis P. Blair, Sr.; and
the Constitutional Unionists, led by Congressman Henry Winter
Davis, who, chameleonlike, had been in quick succession Whig,
Know-Nothing, and Constitutional Unionist. During the presidential campaign of 1860, the Blairs and their Republican following had supported Lincoln, while Davis and his Constitutional
Unionists had given their votes to John Bell.

The rivalry between Montgomery Blair and Davis grew more
bitter following Lincoln's election and the arrival of the time for
the division of the spoils. Both were positive and stubborn, but,
of the two, Blair was more conciliatory. Both had Cabinet aspirations. The influence of the Blair family was powerful, but Davis
had the backing of the astute Thurlow Weed. When the President
chose Blair instead of Davis as the Maryland member of his departmental family, the latter did not disguise his bitterness, and
the resulting breach between him and Lincoln was never healed.
The Davisites now asserted themselves as the true Unionists of
Maryland, and henceforth prolonged and violent warfare between
Blair and Henry Winter Davis for political control of the state
ensued. The federal patronage and the President's favor were
to be the deciding factors in the feud.[76]

The Davis-led Constitutional Unionists, supporting as they did
John Bell for President in 1860, were fearful lest Lincoln give
to the handful of Blair-dominated Maryland Republicans all of
the federal offices in the state. Accordingly, when Lincoln in the
days preceding the firing on Fort Sumter was making up the slate
of Maryland appointments, the Constitutional Union organ, the
Baltimore *Clipper*, sent out a guarded appeal to the new President

[75] Lincoln polled only 2,294 votes in Maryland in his campaign for President in
1860, while John Bell, the Constitutional Union candidate, received 41,760. Breckinridge, the "southern" Democratic presidential candidate, carried the state's electoral
vote, with 42,482. Douglas, the "northern" Democratic candidate, polled 5,966. See
The Tribune Almanac, 1861, p. 49.

[76] W. E. Smith, *The Francis Preston Blair Family in Politics*, I, 487–89, 501–2,
513–15; Steiner, *Life of Henry Winter Davis*, p. 189; M. P. Andrews, *Tercentenary
History of Maryland*, I, 788–89, 820; W. L. Marshall to Montgomery Blair, May 27,
1860, Francis Preston Blair Papers.

for recognition, in a lengthy editorial entitled *Republicanism in Maryland:*

Republicanism, *eo nomine*, in Maryland, is a simple farce. In the last Presidential campaign, there were certain persons who believed that the Chicago nominee would be elected. They did not care whether they contributed to his success or not. They conceived the idea that if they proclaimed themselves Republicans, they would be entitled to the Federal offices in the State. They attempted to organize a Republican party. . . . They were aware that their running a Lincoln ticket here would result in giving the electoral vote of the State to the candidates of the secession Democracy, yet they persevered and effected this result. *They* wantonly and knowingly gave the State to Breckinridge, only to place themselves in the line of promotion and appointment to the Federal offices. They cared not how much they contributed to the secession movement. . . . Now they are swarming in Washington like flies about a molasses barrel. . . . The appointment of any one of these would invoke more indignation against the administration, and go farther to drive Maryland into the vortex of secession, than anything that could possibly be done. . . . It is in the power of the administration to confirm Maryland in her loyalty to the Government, or to drive her Union men to desperation and place them in a miserable and impotent minority. We cannot doubt the result. There is surely too much wisdom in the administration to commit an error in this respect.[77]

Apparently Lincoln was much too wise to be cajoled by this unsolicited advice. On the other hand, he realized that it would not be the part of wisdom to give the Maryland Republican party of the Blairs a monopoly of the federal appointments in the state. Hopefully, therefore, he suggested that the two rivals, Henry Winter Davis and Postmaster General Blair, together arrange a slate.[78] Of the highest positions, some went to Constitutional Unionists and some to Republicans. For Collector of Customs of the Port of Baltimore, Lincoln agreed to Henry W. Hoffman, a Constitutional Unionist and a supporter of Davis.[79] For Post-

[77] Baltimore *Clipper*, April 13, 1861.
[78] Attorney-General Bates wrote to Blair: "I understood at the time, that the Maryland appointments were made chiefly on arrangement made by you & Mr. Davis." See Bates to Montgomery Blair, May 4, 1861, Francis Preston Blair Papers.
[79] W. H. Purnell to Montgomery Blair, Feb. 3, 1864, Francis Preston Blair Papers; Scharf, *History of Western Maryland*, II, 1400; *Biographical Directory of the American Congress*, p. 1105.

master of Baltimore William H. Purnell, also a Constitutional Unionist, was chosen. For Naval Officer of the Baltimore Custom House Lincoln approved the selection of Francis S. Corkran, a Republican associate of Blair and delegate to the Chicago Convention of 1860.[80] For Navy Agent the choice agreed upon was William P. Ewing, who had also aided the Blairs in forming the Republican organization; he had served as alternate to the Chicago Convention.[81] Still another pro-Blair Republican, Judge William L. Marshall,[82] received a worthy appointment—the position of Surveyor of the Port of Baltimore. Constitutional Union men, on the other hand, filled three jobs as Appraisers in the Baltimore Custom House. And a pro-Blair Republican, Washington Bonifant, became United States Marshal for Maryland.[83] The slate filled, it was given to the public through the columns of a Maryland journal:

Collector—Henry W. Hoffman (Union)
Postmaster—William H. Purnell (Union)
Naval Officer—Francis S. Corkran (Republican)
Navy Agent—Wm. Pinkney Ewing (Republican)
Surveyor—Judge Marshall (Republican)
Appraisers—Messrs. Fred'k Schley, Montague and Meredith (Union)
U. S. Marshal—[Washington] Bonifant (Republican) [84]

Similarly, in the two foreign appointments awarded to Maryland Lincoln treated both Unionist factions equally: a Davis follower, James R. Partridge, was made Minister Resident to Honduras,[85]

---

[80] Baltimore *Sun*, April 27, 1860. Corkran, a Quaker, wrote to Blair later: "I owe to thee and thy worthy father all I owe to mortal man for not only my present position but political standing." See. F. S. Corkran to Montgomery Blair, Dec. 23, 1863, Francis Preston Blair Papers.

[81] Baltimore *Sun*, April 27, 1860.

[82] *Ibid.;* W. L. Marshall to Montgomery Blair, May 5, 27, 1860, Francis Preston Blair Papers.

[83] Baltimore *Sun*, April 27, 1860; Edward Bates to Montgomery Blair, May 4, 1861, Francis Preston Blair Papers.

[84] Baltimore *Clipper*, April 16, 1861. The Baltimore *Sun*, April 16, 1861, mentioned eleven main federal appointments for Maryland and commented: "Of the whole number but five have acted openly with the Republican party. The others were prominent members of the late 'American' organization."

[85] *The National Cyclopaedia of American Biography*, VII, 519; Steiner, *Life of Henry Winter Davis*, p. 194; Baltimore *Sun*, April 24, 25, 1861.

while a Blair lieutenant, George E. Wiss, became consul in Rotterdam.[86]

Despite his effort to treat both factions impartially, peace did not reign long for Lincoln in Maryland. When Naval Officer Corkran, a Blairite, did not immediately appoint a certain Constitutional Unionist, French S. Evans, as Deputy Naval Officer, Lincoln rebuked Corkran:

I am quite sure you are not aware how much I am disobliged by the refusal to give Mr. F. S. Evans a place in the Custom-House. I had no thought that the men to whom I gave the higher offices would be so ready to disoblige me. I still wish you would give Mr. Evans the place of Deputy Naval Officer.[87]

Lincoln also referred the matter to Secretary of the Treasury Chase: "I have been greatly—I may say grievously—disappointed and disobliged by Mr. Corkran's refusal to make Mr. Evans deputy naval officer, as I requested him to do." [88]

But it was Davis and Postmaster General Blair themselves who precipitated much of the friction. Maryland was not large enough to hold both. The state was hardly over the dangers of secession when the old Davis-Blair feud broke out again, if, indeed, it had ever abated.

Soon after the attack on Fort Sumter, Henry Winter Davis became a frequent visitor at the White House, where he became increasingly intimate with Lincoln, largely, it would seem, by virtue of Davis's close association with Governor Thomas H. Hicks. Hicks had been the only chief executive of a border-slave state to respond affirmatively in April, 1861, to the President's call for volunteers.[89] Apparently Davis persuaded Lincoln to place more Maryland patronage under his control, on the plea that he needed aid in his campaign for Congress,[90] and in this Blair finally reluctantly acquiesced. Davis ran for Congress from a Baltimore district on a platform of "unconditional maintenance of the Union" and was defeated.[91]

[86] Baltimore *Sun*, April 27, 1860; *U. S. Official Register, 1861*, p. 5..
[87] *New Letters and Papers of Lincoln*, ed. by Angle, pp. 271–72.
[88] *Ibid.*, p. 272.
[89] Baltimore *Sun*, April 24, 25, 1861. For Davis's association with Hicks, see W. L. Marshall to Blair, May 30, 1860, Francis Preston Blair Papers.
[90] New York *Herald*, June 21, 1861.
[91] Steiner, *Life of Henry Winter Davis*, p. 194; Baltimore *Clipper*, June 14, 1861.

The Davis-Blair rivalry for political control of the state was further complicated and intensified by the action of Secretary of the Treasury Chase. Blair wanted one John F. McJilton removed from a Treasury job in Baltimore and his own man put in. Chase refused to agree and began coöperating with Davis.[92] What occurred and the manner in which Davis secured more patronage for his faction is perhaps best related in Blair's letter of complaint to Lincoln:

I am struggling earnestly to make a party in the State of Maryland for the Administration on the basis of your Messages. Mr. Chase opposed the appointment of the names I submitted to you for the State & the bulk of them were finally given to Mr. Winter Davis's friends with my consent because I could not get those I preferred. Davis did not keep faith with me as to the management of the matter & instead of allowing the smaller offices to go to new & unobnoxious men as I would have done he gave them to the most obnoxious plugs in Baltimore to a considerable extent. They were to get [him] the nomination for Congress. It secured that & also his defeat before the people. I have found him impracticable & selfish & not likely to be of much service in the organization for this reason.[93]

Blair's intention to form a party in Maryland on the basis of Lincoln's "Messages" was in reference to the question of Negro emancipation. The election of Augustus W. Bradford as governor in November, 1861, by the Unionists definitely ended the threats of secession; the Unionists were henceforth to fight among themselves over the policy of emancipation. About this question revolved Maryland politics for the next several years.

Lincoln's Proclamation of September 22, 1862, advocating "compensated" emancipation, stirred anew the struggle between the Maryland factions. The Blair faction approved, but not so Davis and his followers. The Blair party—the "conservatives"—became known as the Conditional Union party favoring a gradual compensated policy of emancipation; in its ranks were Postmaster Purnell and Mayor Swann, of Baltimore. The Davis party—the "radicals"—favored "immediate" emancipation; in its ranks,

[92] Montgomery Blair to the President, undated (copy), Francis Preston Blair Papers. (In box marked "1864.")
[93] Ibid.

aside from Davis, were Collector Henry W. Hoffman and Congressman John A. J. Creswell.[94] Davis and Blair, paradoxically enough, had by 1863 shifted positions since the beginning of the war, insofar as the terms "radical" and "conservative" were applicable to them on the Negro question. Blair, who in 1860 had been interested in the slavery question and had supported Lincoln for President, was henceforth regarded as a "conservative" because he opposed immediate emancipation of the slave and advocated compensation for the slaveholder. As Secretary of Navy Welles expressed it:

The Blairs were all early emancipationists though southern men. Frank took the bull by the horns in Missouri and Montgomery & his father here [in Washington] and in Maryland. They broke the ice—they fought the battle for ten years at least before those who now claim to be stronger emancipationists than the Blairs. Winter Davis was a Know Nothing and opposing Blair only a short time ago. But Davis now claims to go farther than Blair. . . .[95]

Intertwined with the emancipation issue in engendering bad blood between the Davis and the Blair factions was the jealousy aroused among the Blairites because Lincoln permitted Secretary of War Stanton and Secretary of the Treasury Chase to award much of the patronage of their respective departments to Davis and his radicals; both Stanton and Chase were radicals on the emancipation issue and personal enemies of Postmaster General Blair and Secretary of the Navy Welles. The Provost Marshals assigned to Maryland by the War Department owed their jobs to the Davis group; and Davis, having subsequently succeeded in having himself elected to Congress again, paid more than one visit to Lincoln in the interest of his Provost Marshal friends.[96] Chase, for his part, saw to it that the Baltimore Custom House, under jurisdiction of the Treasury Department, used its power to sustain the Davis faction, rather than the Blair group.[97]

[94] H. Winter Davis to Creswell, Dec. 20, 1863, March 15, 1865, John A. J. Creswell Papers; *A Biographical Sketch of Hon. A. Leo Knott, with a Relation of Some Political Transactions in Maryland, 1861–1867*, pp. 37 ff.; W. S. Myers. *The Maryland Constitution of 1864*, pp. 8–9, 12–15.

[95] Welles to his son, Feb. 24, 1864, Gideon Welles Papers, Library of Congress. See also H. Winter Davis to Wade, June 21, 1864, Benjamin F. Wade Papers.

[96] George M. Russum to Creswell, Feb. 26, 1864; John Frazier, Jr., to Creswell, Nov. 20, 28, 1863, Creswell Papers.

[97] W. E. Smith, *The Francis Preston Blair Family in Politics*, II, 255.

MONTGOMERY BLAIR

HENRY WINTER DAVIS

Probably the most outstanding single incident in disrupting further the relations between the followers of Davis and Blair concerned the post of Collector of Internal Revenue for the Second Maryland District. Naval Officer Francis S. Corkran had deserted the Blair fold to align himself with the Davis faction, becoming a radical emancipationist. In connivance with Chase, Corkran had succeeded in having a pro-Blair officeholder, Collector James L. Ridgely, removed and his own friend, Joseph J. Stewart, appointed in his place by Lincoln. Blair was furious. The fight assumed formidable proportions, and committee after committee from both Davis and Blair factions waited on the President, seeking justice. Blair endeavored to persuade Lincoln to remove Stewart and reappoint Ridgely.[98] In anger Blair wrote to Corkran, quoting Lincoln as saying to him (Blair):

My friend Corkran has got me into a scrape. He got me to sign a paper appointing a friend of his to office and removing Mr. Ridgely, a friend of Col. Webster's [Blair's follower], a fast friend of the administration then in the field fighting the enemies of his country. I do not wish to remove Mr. Stewart for he has been a faithful officer but I am satisfied I have done injustice to Mr. Ridgely. I have been looking around for something for Mr. Stewart, but as yet nothing has turned up. Time flies and Mr. Ridgely's friends are sore, can you not induce Mr. Stewart to resign? [99]

In the showdown with Lincoln, Secretary Chase defended the appointment of Stewart.[100] Lincoln allowed the appointment to stand, and the Senate confirmed Stewart.[101] This was only one instance of the manner in which the Secretary of the Treasury, a radical emancipationist and contender for the presidency to succeed Lincoln, coöperated with the Davis or the radical faction in patronage matters, much to Blair's disgust. Between Stanton and Chase, life for the conservative Postmaster General became miserable. Dejectedly he wrote a Maryland lieutenant:

98 F. S. Corkran to Chase, Dec. 21, 1863, April 21, 1864; Jos. J. Stewart to Chase, Feb. 3, 1864, Salmon P. Chase Papers, Library of Congress; *U. S. Senate Executive Journal*, XIII (1862–64), 15, 387.

99 Statement of Montgomery Blair to Corkran, as quoted in Jos. J. Stewart to Chase, Feb. 3, 1864, *ibid.*

100 F. S. Corkran to Chase, April 21, 1864, *ibid.*

101 *U. S. Senate Executive Journal*, XIII (1862–64), 498.

The Provost Marshals & their Deputies aided by the Custom House employees carry the primary elections in parts of the county [of Baltimore] easily—nobody but themselves attending. Mr. Stanton's advisers for Md. are known to be Judge Bond & Mr. Henry Winter Davis, who are equally confided in. . . . Also the protegees of the late Secy of the Treasury [Chase]; so that we have the Purse & the Sword of the Nation against us in Md. in our efforts to sustain the President.[102]

If Blair and his followers were critical of the President for permitting most of the Maryland federal jobs to go to the radicals, the latter were no less impatient with him for giving any consideration to the Blairs and their schemes for "gradual" or compensated emancipation. They resented particularly the action of Lincoln in permitting Blair to use the Post Office patronage to fight them —Purnell, postmaster of Baltimore, operated for Blair, while Hoffman, Collector of the Port, was a Davis man, or radical emancipationist.[103] One Baltimore radical leader complained to Judge Bond, a Davis lieutenant:

I would suggest that President Lincoln certainly ought to know that Blairism is a mere myth in this State. Please impress this upon his attention if necessary. There are, as we all know, but two political parties in this State, viz: the Unconditional emancipationist, and the so-called States Rights [Democratic] party. Conditional emancipation or apprenticeships, meet with but little favor anywhere in Maryland. The masses are either in favor of retaining negro slavery as it now is, or for its immediate, unconditional abolishment.

Neither Mr. Blair or [sic] the P. O. Department of this State have legitimately anything to do with the Custom Office of this Port. . . . Please draw heavily upon the President. We must be sustained, or go to the wall.[104]

Lincoln did not live to see the end of the Davis-Blair feud. Ultimately it led to Blair's downfall, and in the chaotic days following Lee's surrender at Appomattox this rivalry between the state's two most influential Unionists was to be a force in producing the debacle of Reconstruction.

[102] Montgomery Blair to Edward L. Thomas (copy, "Confidential"), July 14, 1864, Francis Preston Blair Papers.
[103] W. H. Purnell to Montgomery Blair, Feb. 3, 1864, ibid.
[104] R. H. Jackson to Judge Bond, April 18, 1864, Creswell Papers.

Extending from Maryland was Delaware, another border-slave state. As in Maryland, Unionist groups from Delaware were early on the scene in Washington, besieging Lincoln with assurances of their loyalty and requests for federal offices. Indeed, the President had no sooner been inaugurated than the Delaware office seekers joined the motley array of patronage hunters that descended on the White House. Let the correspondent of a Dover newspaper tell the story:

Delawareans At the Court of St. Abe: We understand that quite a number of Delawareans are now in Washington, (and Dover furnishes her full quota), waiting at the kitchen door for the morsel that is to reward them for voting for "Old Abe." Would-be Consuls, Marshals, Inspectors and Lighthouse-Keepers are quite plenty.[105]

Substantially the same political situation confronted Lincoln in Delaware as in Maryland: Delaware had been carried in the election of 1860 by John C. Breckinridge, the "southern" Democratic presidential candidate, and Lincoln had shared the state's anti-Democratic vote with the Constitutional Union candidate, John Bell.[106] The two most influential anti-Democratic leaders were Nathaniel B. Smithers and George P. Fisher. Smithers had organized the state Republican party and had been a delegate to the Chicago Convention which had nominated Lincoln. Fisher, on the other hand, was a Constitutional Unionist and, as such, had just been elected to Congress.[107] Fisher was determined that his faction should be given its share of federal offices for Delaware and consulted with Lincoln to that end. "Hon. Geo. P. Fisher, our new Representative in Congress," wrote one Delaware contemporary following Lincoln's inauguration, "is making earnest appeals to the President and his Cabinet so to distribute the patronage in this State 'as to recognize all the elements of opposition to the Disunionists in the late Presidential Campaign.' " [108] It was to Fisher that Lincoln awarded the distribution of most of the Delaware

[105] Dover *Delawarean*, March 16, 1861.

[106] The popular vote of Delaware in 1860 was: Lincoln, 3,815; Bell, 3,864; Breckinridge, 7,337; Douglas, 1,023. See *The Tribune Almanac, 1861*, p. 49.

[107] W. T. Smithers, "Memoir of Nathaniel B. Smithers," *Papers of the Historical Society of Delaware*, No. 23 (1899), pp. 24–25.

[108] Dover *Delawarean*, March 16, 1861.

offices.[109] Fisher's position as Member of Congress made him the favorite over Smithers to dispense the presidential bounty in the state. One Delaware observer was fully aware of this fact:

But how is it that Mr. Fisher has got the inside track of Mr. Smithers, who had all the electioneering to do for Mr. Lincoln, while Mr. Fisher had his hands full to repel the "foul aspersion" that he was a Republican. We expected of course that Mr. S. would be consulted, but unfortunately for him he has no vote to sustain the administration in Congress and all his powder, so far, appears to have been wasted.[110]

Lincoln did care for Smithers in 1862 by appointing him Provost Marshal for Delaware.[111] Moreover, one of Smithers' family, Enoch J. Smithers, received from the President a consulship in Turkey.[112] Smithers had his chance for higher honors. In the election of 1862 Fisher lost his seat in Congress to his Democratic opponent, William Temple; whereupon Lincoln appointed Fisher a Judge of the Supreme Court of the District of Columbia. At the next election Smithers, in turn, contested with Temple for the seat in Congress and won.[113] Of the foreign appointments, Delaware seems to have received only one, aside from that given to the younger Smithers: Dr. John S. Prettyman, editor of the strongly Unionist paper, the Milford (Delaware) *Peninsular News and Advertiser*, was given the post of consul in Glasgow, Scotland.[114]

Besides the nonseceding slave states of Kentucky, Missouri, Maryland, and Delaware—which Lincoln kept loyal partly by use of the patronage—there were other slaveholding regions which demanded Lincoln's attention, notably those southern states which

[109] Charles B. Lore writes: "President Lincoln conceived a warm feeling and had a high regard for Mr. Fisher. He made him a confident and his almoner of Presidential favors in Delaware." See Lore, "The Life and Character of George P. Fisher," *Papers of the Historical Society of Delaware*, No. 36 (1902), pp. 10–11.

[110] Dover *Delawarean*, March 16, 1861.

[111] Milford (Del.) *Peninsular News and Advertiser*, Sept. 19, 1862.

[112] *Ibid.*, Jan. 31, 1862.

[113] Lore, "The Life and Character of George P. Fisher," *Papers of the Historical Society of Delaware*, No. 36 (1902), pp. 10–11; W. T. Smithers, "Memoir of Nathaniel B. Smithers," *Papers of the Historical Society of Delaware*, No. 23 (1899), pp. 25–26; *Biographical Directory of the American Congress, 1774–1927*, pp. 968, 1555.

[114] Wilmington *Delaware State Journal and Statesman*, Aug. 16, 1861; Milford (Del.) *Peninsular News and Advertiser*, Sept. 20, 1861; Nov. 28, 1862.

had seceded and had been partially conquered by the force of Union arms. Lincoln's policy toward these "recovered" states was based upon the belief that there existed within each a loyal element which might be made the nucleus of a civil government owing allegiance to the centralized authority at Washington. Lincoln felt, therefore, that all federal appointments in these "recovered" states should be made with a view to their restoration and return to the Union. On the basis of this formula, conservative Union men—usually residents of the respective states—were given the federal positions of authority. In this way, Lincoln believed, could best be accomplished the reinstatement of the Union-conquered members of the Confederacy to their former places in the Union. Tennessee was the first of the "erring sisters" to which this policy was applied.

While eastern Tennessee was still in the Confederacy's grip, the central and western parts of the state were wrested from the Confederates by Grant's successful operations. In late February, 1862, Grant had proclaimed martial law in West Tennessee. As military governor of Tennessee, Lincoln appointed Andrew Johnson. Destined to be Lincoln's successor in the White House, Johnson was at the time a member of the United States Senate from Tennessee. Previously he had taken courageous ground against secessionist threats in his state. "You are hereby appointed," read Johnson's commission, "military governor of the state of Tennessee, with authority to exercise and perform" the duties of such office, "including the power to establish all necessary offices and tribunals and suspend the writ of habeas corpus during the pleasure of the president, or until the loyal inhabitants of that state shall organize a civil government in conformity with the Constitution of the United States."

Johnson's task was an extremely difficult one and to better enable him to function smoothly with military and nonmilitary officialdom Lincoln made him a brigadier general. Johnson established himself at Nashville, the Union Army furnishing the persuasive power of his administration. Johnson selected four staunch Unionists for his chief aides—Edward H. East for secretary of state, Joseph S. Fowler for comptroller, Horace Maynard for attorney general, and Edmund Cooper as private secretary and confidential agent. Johnson extended military supervision over the press, even suppressing the Nashville *Daily Times* and the Nashville *Banner* and imprisoning the latter journal's editor. Moreover, a vehement Kentucky Unionist, S. C. Mercer, was encouraged by Johnson to start a Lincoln administration newspaper, the *Daily Union*. This sheet had the support of the federal government in every way. Johnson's administration in Tennessee proved highly successful from the viewpoint of the Union and Lincoln.[115]

North Carolina was another partially "recovered" state that engaged Lincoln's concern. No sooner had federal troops gained a foothold in the Old North State than the President made efforts to gather together, under a new state government, such of the people as favored the Union cause. Lincoln's appointive power and his presidential position as Commander in Chief of the Armed Forces were utilized when, in May 1862, he appointed a native North Carolinian, Edward Stanly, as military governor of North Carolina. On Stanly the President bestowed the rank of brigadier general as he had done in the case of the military governor of Tennessee. Stanly's duties were similar to those of Johnson. He was to perform all the duties of governor and to appoint officers, institute courts, and suspend the writ of *habeas corpus* during the pleasure of the President or until a civil government should be organized. So far as devotion to the Union was concerned, Stanly was a most suitable choice, for throughout his political career in the state and in Congress he had fought all disunionist influences. In line with Lincoln's policy of using his military powers to aid in creating civil governments in the recovered seceded states, Secretary of War Stanton instructed General Burnside to coöperate with Stanly, who established his headquarters at New Bern. Unfortunately, Stanly failed to establish a loyal state government, largely because of interference from abolitionist elements, his own uncontrolled temper, and the fact that Unionist sentiment in North Carolina had not yet fully crystallized. In 1863 Stanly submitted his resignation to Lincoln. The President's appointment of Stanly as military governor represented a premature attempt to tear North Carolina from the Confederacy.[116]

[115] C. R. Hall, *Andrew Johnson, Military Governor of Tennessee*, pp. 18–19, 32–33, 42–43. See also *U. S. Official Register, 1863*, p. 15.
[116] Hamilton, *Reconstruction in North Carolina*, pp. 5, 81, 87–95.

In still another seceded state, Arkansas, Lincoln attempted to create a loyal state government. As early as July, 1862, with part of Arkansas under Union Army control, the President felt that the time had arrived for definite assistance to the state's loyal people. Accordingly he appointed a Missouri Unionist, John S. Phelps, as military governor. The War Department assured Phelps of its coöperation and support and instructed the raffish Benjamin F. Butler, then in command of the Department of the Gulf, to detail an adequate military force for the special purpose of serving under Phelps's direction. The exigencies of the situation were such, however, as to permit scant scope for the exercise of civil functions, and Phelps confined his activity to organizing the Second Arkansas Cavalry. Disappointed by Phelps's lack of accomplishment, Lincoln revoked his commission within a year; the continuance of the military governorship of Arkansas, the President declared, was no longer advisable. The following year, however, Lincoln was induced to renew his efforts. "I am, and have been, thoroughly convinced," wrote Major General Hurlburt from Memphis, "that Arkansas can, by vote of its people, be brought into the Union without slavery by simply encouraging and sustaining the 'Unconditional Union' men of that state, and by so directing military operations as to give them the opportunity of action. . . ." Lincoln acted favorably upon General Hurlburt's suggestion, but it was not until 1864, and then after some confusion, that a loyal state regime was established.[117]

Louisiana was probably the most pivotal member of the Confederacy to which Lincoln gave his attention in efforts at reconstruction. By May, 1862, strategic and commercially desirable New Orleans was under the control of General Ben Butler's Union forces. The following month Lincoln appointed George F. Shepley as military governor of Louisiana. In the portion of the state controlled by the Union Armies there sprang up "a certain group of men eager to push on the work of reorganization, either for the plums of office, or, on the part of the old slaveholders, for the sake of saving a portion of their slaves, or for the sake of casting off

[117] Staples, *Reconstruction in Arkansas, 1862–1874*, pp. 9–10; Reynolds, "Presidential Reconstruction in Arkansas," *Publications of the Arkansas Historical Association*, I (1906), 354, 356–57.

martial law." [118] Governor Shepley, acting with Lincoln's permission, ordered an election for two Congressmen from the New Orleans district. Lincoln cautioned, however, that "to send a parcel of Northern men here as representatives, elected, as would be understood (and perhaps really so), at the point of the bayonet, would be disgusting and outrageous." [119] The election resulted in the choice of B. F. Flanders and Michael Hahn as Representatives in Congress from the First and Second Louisiana Districts, respectively. Both were permitted to take their seats, but as the Thirty-seventh Congress expired in March, 1863, neither of them had opportunity to serve. [120]

One incident connected with the election in the First District, in which Flanders defeated one J. E. Bouligny, illustrated Lincoln's reluctance to give federal jobs to any who did not enjoy the confidence of the Union people in their constituencies. Previous to the election, Bouligny had visited Washington in quest of a job, and Lincoln had been impressed by him. "Might not Mr. Bouligny," Lincoln wrote to Secretary of the Treasury Chase, "be appointed surveyor of the port of New Orleans? If there be no objections, please send nomination." [121] Just what action was taken in finding a place for Bouligny cannot be determined, for Bouligny returned to New Orleans to run for Congress against Flanders, who defeated him. [122] Bouligny now renewed his request to Lincoln for a position. The President's reply is illuminating:

I did not certainly know the object of your call yesterday, but I had a strong impression in regard to it. When our national troubles began, you and I were not personally acquainted, but all I heard of you placed you in my estimation foremost among Louisianians as a friend of the Union. I intended to find you a position, and I did not conceal my inclination to do so. When, last autumn, you bore a letter from me to some parties at New Orleans, you seemed to expect, and consequently I did expect, you would return here as a member of one or the other branch of Congress. But you were not so re-

[118] Ella Lonn, *Reconstruction in Louisiana After 1868*, p. 1.
[119] Ficklen, *History of Reconstruction in Louisiana through 1868*, p. 41.
[120] *Ibid.*, p. 42.
[121] Lincoln to Chase, July 14, 1862, in *Complete Works of Abraham Lincoln*, VII, 278.
[122] "Diary and Correspondence of Salmon P. Chase," *Annual Report*, American Historical Association, II (1902), 335, 336.

turned, and this negative evidence, with other of like character, brings me to think that the Union people there for some reason prefer others for the places here. Add to this that the head of the department here [Chase?] in which finding a place for you was contemplated, is not satisfied for the appointment to be made, and it presents, as you see, an embarrassing case for me. My personal feelings for Mr. Bouligny are not less kind than heretofore.[123]

The most remunerative federal appointment in Louisiana was that of Collector of Customs of the Port of New Orleans. Lincoln awarded this post to George S. Denison.[124] A favorite of Secretary Chase, Denison gave as one of his aims: "To appoint to office such men and of such political opinions, that the Government (through its officials) can present here a strong nucleus for a Republican party." [125]

Denison gave strong support to those groups endeavoring to construct a free-state government. To Major General Nathaniel P. Banks, who, as we have observed, had succeeded Butler as commander of the Department of the Gulf with headquarters at New Orleans, Lincoln wrote: "I am much gratified to know that Mr. Dennison [sic], the Collector at New Orleans, and who bears you this, understands your views and will give you his full and zealous cooperation. It is my wish and purpose that all others holding authority from me shall do the like; and, to spare me writing, I will thank you to make this known to them." [126]

General Banks, acting on Lincoln's authority, set February 22, 1864, as the date for an election for governor and other state officers. Two parties sprang into existence, one nominating the conservative Unionist, Michael Hahn, the other B. F. Flanders, a radical. The weight of the Lincoln administration was thrown to Hahn, and Collector Denison took a prominent part in the election. Hahn won, and became Louisiana's first "free-state" governor. On March 4, 1864, Hahn was inaugurated, and ten days

[123] Lincoln to J. E. Bouligny, April 14, 1863, in *Complete Works of Abraham Lincoln*, VIII, 246–47.

[124] *U. S. Senate Executive Journal*, XIII (1862–64), 139, 199.

[125] George S. Denison to Chase, June 28, 1862, in "Diary and Correspondence of Salmon P. Chase," *Annual Report*, American Historical Association, II (1902), 308.

[126] Lincoln to Gen. N. P. Banks, Jan. 13, 1864, in *Complete Works of Abraham Lincoln*, IX, 282–83.

later Lincoln invested in him the powers hitherto exercised by
Shepley.[127] Soon afterwards, Louisiana drew up a new state
constitution, and Lincoln made known to his federal officeholders
that he expected their support in having it ratified. The President's instructions to General Banks ran as follows:

I have just seen the new Constitution adopted by the Convention of
Louisiana & I am anxious that it shall be ratified by the people. I
will thank you to let the civil officers in Louisiana, holding appointment under me, know that this is my wish, & to let me know at once
who of them openly declares for the Constitution, & who of them, if
any, decline to so declare.[128]

Among the conspicuous civil appointments made by Lincoln
for the state was that of the strong foe of secession, Edward H.
Durell, to be Judge of the United States District Court for Eastern Louisiana. Durell was recommended for this particular job
by General Banks and also had the backing of several Louisiana
Unionists. Among them was John Parker, who, in a letter to
Trumbull, averred that no better appointment could have been
made.[129]

In a class by itself was Virginia. Nature had divided the state
into eastern and western segments that were markedly different.
Geographically the eastern region belonged to the Atlantic sea-
board. Soil and climate had made it almost exclusively agricul-
tural. The western counties that lay behind the long parallel ridges
of the Alleghenies belonged to the Mississippi Valley. Mountain-
ous in character and a region of small independent farms and
rich mineral deposits, its natural outlets to market were South,
West and North—with Cincinnati, Chicago, Pittsburgh, and
Baltimore rather than with Richmond or Norfolk.

Institutions and traditions as well as geography divided the

[127] George S. Denison to Chase, Feb. 5, 1864 (Private), Salmon P. Chase Papers,
Library of Congress; Ficklen, *History of Reconstruction in Louisiana through
1868*, pp. 52, 55, 57–60, 62–63; Lincoln to Michael Hahn, March 15, 1864, in *Complete Works of Abraham Lincoln*, X, 42–43; Philadelphia *North American and
United States Gazette*, March 4, 1864.

[128] Lincoln to General Banks, Aug. 9, 1864 (copy), Salmon P. Chase Papers,
Library of Congress.

[129] "Hon. Edward Henry Durell," *The Granite Monthly*, April, 1888, pp. 118–21;
The National Cyclopaedia of American Biography, XIII, 121; N. P. Banks to
Trumbull, Feb. 4, 1864; John Parker to Trumbull, Feb. 6, 1864, Trumbull Papers.

two regions. The people of the western counties—a mixture of English, Germans, and Scotch-Irish—had come largely from Pennsylvania, Maryland, and New Jersey. The leveling tendencies of the frontier had molded their tastes and their outlook on life. Usually of English origin, the eastern Virginians, "wellborn" and basking in ancestral memories, were essentially aristocratic. And eastern aristocrats and western democrats could not seem to fashion themselves into fellowship with each other. The schism in Virginia was aggravated by an unfair system of representation which discriminated in favor of the Tidewater and the Piedmont.[130] The western counties were also grieved at the Richmond government for neglecting to provide adequate internal improvements.[131]

The question of slavery drove another wedge between the Virginia sections. Slavery thrived in eastern Virginia. The western counties had no great stake in preserving slavery if it meant dissolution of the Union. Out of almost 500,000 slaves in Virginia in 1860, it was estimated that less than 13,000 were owned by the counties that subsequently became the state of West Virginia.[132]

The center of early Republican party activity in Virginia was in and around Wheeling. In 1853 Wheeling had become connected with the Atlantic seacoast by means of the Baltimore and Ohio Railroad, linking western Virginia with Baltimore, thus further alienating northwestern Virginia from Richmond.[133] Moreover, Wheeling was only a stone's throw from Ohio. The backbone of the Wheeling Republican movement was the Ohio-born Archibald W. Campbell, editor and owner of the Wheeling *Daily Intelligencer*, probably the strongest journalistic advocate of Republicanism south of the Ohio.[134] Associated with Campbell in spreading the gospel of Republicanism in this region was Alfred Caldwell,

[130] See especially Ambler, "The Cleavage between Eastern and Western Virginia," *The American Historical Review*, XV (July, 1910), 762–80.

[131] Boughter, "Internal Improvements in Northwestern Virginia," pp. 171–72, 250, 264, 275, 284, 286.

[132] W. P. Willey, *An Inside View of the Formation of the State of West Virginia*, pp. 10–11.

[133] Boughter, "Internal Improvements in Northwestern Virginia," pp. 266–67, 280–81; Reizenstein, *The Economic History of the Baltimore and Ohio Railroad, 1827–1853*, pp. 62–63, 71, 77 n.–78 n.

[134] Ambler, *West Virginia: Stories and Biographies*, pp. 237–38; Cranmer, *History of Wheeling City and Ohio County, West Virginia*, p. 178.

an antislavery member of the Virginia legislature.[135] On May 2, 1860, the Virginia Republicans, under the leadership of Campbell and Caldwell, had met in state convention and selected delegates "from Virginia" to represent the state in the Republican National Convention at Chicago.[136] Of the twenty-three Virginia delegates, eleven were from Wheeling, indicating that Republican strength in the state was centered primarily in the western counties.[137] Of the twenty-three Virginia votes cast at Chicago, Lincoln received fourteen.[138]

Upon entering the White House in 1861 Lincoln did not forget his convention supporters from Virginia. He appointed Campbell postmaster in Wheeling [139] and sent Caldwell to Honolulu as United States consul to the Hawaiian Islands.[140] At least three other Virginia delegates to the Chicago Convention were remembered by Lincoln: Thomas Hornbrook was given the post of Surveyor of Customs at Wheeling, Edward M. Norton became United States Marshal for the Western District of Virginia, and John C. Underwood was appointed Fifth Auditor of the Treasury.[141] Subsequently (1863), Lincoln made Underwood Judge of the United States District Court for the Eastern District of Virginia.[142]

Lincoln's appointment of Campbell as postmaster in Wheeling proved an especially fortunate choice. He became the most potent force of all original Virginia Republicans in keeping the western region of his state loyal to the Union. In fact, a distinguished authority on West Virginia declares that Campbell's ability in this respect "approached genius." [143] Around him and his Wheel-

---

[135] Miller and Maxwell, *West Virginia and Its People,* II, 12–13.

[136] Monteiro, "The Presidential Election of 1860 in Virginia," *Richmond College Historical Papers,* I (June, 1916), 245; Detroit *Daily Tribune,* May 3, 4, 1860.

[137] Halstead, *Caucuses of 1860: A History of the National Political Conventions of the Current Presidential Campaign,* p. 126.

[138] *Ibid.,* pp. 146–48.

[139] *United States Executive Journal,* XI (1858–61), 321, 337.

[140] *Ibid.,* XII (1861–62), 28, 97.

[141] *Ibid.,* XI (1858–61), 386, 474, 481, 492, 497, 538; Halstead, *op. cit.,* p. 126.

[142] Lanman, *Biographical Annals of the Civil Government of the United States,* p. 436. It was in the Eastern District of Virginia that Jefferson Davis was indicted for treason. Judge Underwood refused to release him on bail.

[143] Ambler, *Francis H. Pierpont: Union War Governor of Virginia and Father of West Virginia,* p. 54.

ing *Intelligencer* rallied opponents of secession in western Virginia and adjacent counties in Ohio. Civil and military officials leaned heavily on him, and his unwearied pen was most effective in spreading Unionist arguments and in combating the force of the Confederate government at Richmond.[144]

With the secession of the states of the lower South, Virginia faced the problem of its future course. Eastern Virginia with its institution of slavery had a common interest with its seceded sister commonwealths. Western Virginia, on the other hand, regarded secession as largely the work of "hot-heads." The average inhabitant west of the mountains cared little about the Negro other than to be rid of him. Despite protests from the western counties, Governor Letcher, of Virginia, thought it incumbent upon him to call an extra session of the legislature, which met at Richmond on January 7, 1861, during the interim between Lincoln's election and inauguration. The fear of the western Virginians that the legislature would authorize a convention which might fall under the influence of secession-minded leadership and thus "drag" Virginia out of the Union was fully justified. A convention was authorized and on April 17, following the firing on Fort Sumter and Lincoln's call for volunteers to suppress the rebellion, it adopted an ordinance of secession by a vote of 88 to 55. This ordinance was to be valid only if ratified by the people of the state at their regular spring elections in May. As things turned out, this referendum was in many respects entirely farcical.[145]

At least three of those who voted against the ordinance of secession at Richmond received Lincoln appointments. They were John S. Burdett, Edmund Pendleton, and John J. Jackson.[146] Burdett and Pendleton were given commissions in the Army.[147] Jackson was chosen by Lincoln as Judge of the United States District

[144] Willey, *An Inside View of the Formation of the State of West Virginia,* pp. 202–3.

[145] Ambler, *A History of West Virginia,* pp. 295–309. For a more detailed account, see Shanks, *The Secession Movement in Virginia, 1847–1861,* chaps. vii–xi. Of the 47 delegates from what is now West Virginia in the Secession convention, 32 voted against secession, 11 for it, and 4 did not vote.

[146] The list of members of the Virginia convention who voted against the ordinance of secession is printed in full in G. D. Hall, *The Rending of Virginia,* pp. 540–41.

[147] *U. S. Senate Executive Journal,* XII (1861–62), 4, 45, 109.

Court for the Western District of Virginia.[148] Jackson had been the spokesman for the delegates who had voted against the ordinance of secession—the same group, who, meeting clandestinely in a Richmond hotel bedroom, decided to keep Virginia or as much of her as possible loyal to the Union, even though it meant dismemberment of the state.[149]

West of the mountains the returning delegates from Richmond were greeted with enthusiasm. Less than a month elapsed before they with others of like sympathies met at Wheeling to consider what action should be taken against the secessionists. At this gathering—the "First Wheeling Convention"—the ordinance of secession was denounced and arrangements made for another meeting to consider the "reorganization of the Virginia government on a Unionist basis."

At the "Second Wheeling Convention," which assembled June 11, 1861, Lincoln's Surveyor of Customs at Wheeling, the energetic Thomas Hornbrook, served as Sergeant at Arms.[150] John S. Burdett, recipient, as already noted, of an Army commission from Lincoln, was a delegate. So, too, was Joseph A. J. Lightburn, whom the President made a brigadier general of volunteers.[151] John Hawkshurst, within a year to receive from Lincoln the post of tax commissioner to collect "direct taxes" in the insurrectionary regions of Virginia, was also a delegate.[152]

The "Second Wheeling Convention" sat from June 11 to June 25, and its work was most historic. It adopted an ordinance providing for the reorganization of the Virginia government on a loyal basis, thus making it possible for Unionists in the western part of the Old Dominion to maintain a dual allegiance in matters governmental and to plan for the dismemberment of their commonwealth in a legal manner. The convention elected Francis H.

---

[148] *The National Cyclopaedia of American Biography*, XI, 521; *U. S. Senate Executive Journal*, XI (1858–61), 481, 538.

[149] Ambler, *A History of West Virginia*, pp. 312–13.

[150] G. D. Hall, *The Rending of Virginia*, pp. 301–2; *Journal of the Convention Assembled at Wheeling, on the 11th of June, 1861*, p. 6. The list of delegates is printed in this journal, a photostatic copy of which is in the New York Public Library. At Hornbrook's invitation the convention on the third day of its sessions moved to the United States Custom House.

[151] E. C. Smith, *A History of Lewis County, West Virginia*, pp. 291, 296; *U. S. Senate Executive Journal*, XII (1861–62), 364, 365; *ibid.*, XIII (1862–64), 311, 312.

[152] *Ibid.*, XII (1861–62), 405.

Pierpont governor. The selection of Pierpont was a fortunate one, for he was indefatigable in stamping out Secessionist influences and keeping western Virginia in the Union. The Lincoln administration lost no time in letting it be known that Pierpont and his anti-Secessionist followers had the backing of Washington.[153] In a special message to Congress on July 4, 1861 Lincoln declared:

The people of Virginia have . . . allowed this giant insurrection to make its nest within her borders ; and this government has no choice left but to deal with it where it finds it. And it has the less regret as the loyal citizens have, in due form, claimed its protection. Those loyal citizens this government is bound to recognize and protect, as being Virginia.[154]

In the distribution of the civil offices in those parts of Virginia under Unionist control, Lincoln often consulted Pierpont. On one occasion at least, Pierpont was apparently nettled by certain presidential appointments for, under date of October 16, 1862, we find Lincoln writing him as follows:

Your despatch of today received. I am very sorry to have offended you. I appointed the collector as I thought, on your written recommendation, and the assessor also with your testimony of worthiness, although I know you preferred a different man. I will examine tomorrow whether I am mistaken in this.[155]

In his next letter to Pierpont the following week, Lincoln makes amends:

Your letter of the 17th just received. When you come to Washington, I shall be pleased to show you the record upon which we acted. Nevertheless answer this, distinctly saying you wish Ross and Richter, or any other two you do really want and they shall be appointed.[156]

Meanwhile, the more radical Union men of northwestern Virginia—Pierpont among them—had succeeded in formally detaching their region from the rest of the Old Dominion and setting up the state of "West Virginia." A bill admitting the new common-

[153] Ambler, *Francis H. Pierpont,* pp. 102–4.
[154] *Complete Works of Abraham Lincoln,* VI, 307.
[155] Lincoln to Pierpont, Oct. 16, 1862, in Tarbell, *The Life of Abraham Lincoln,* II, 352.
[156] *Ibid.*

wealth into the Union passed Congress on December 10, 1862. Although in doubt at first as to what action he should take, Lincoln finally signed the measure, and West Virginia became our thirty-fifth state.[157] Lincoln's explanation of his decision is illuminating:

But is the admission into the Union of West Virginia expedient? This, in my general view, is more a matter for Congress, than for the Executive. Still I do not evade it. More than on anything else, it depends on whether the admission or rejection of the new State would, under all the circumstances, tend the more strongly to the restoration of the national authority throughout the Union. That which helps most in this direction is the most expedient at this time. Doubtless those in remaining Virginia would return to the Union, so to speak, less reluctantly without the division of the old State than with it; but I think we could not save as much in this quarter by rejecting the new State, as we should lose by it in West Virginia. We can scarcely dispense with the aid of West Virginia in this struggle; much less can we afford to have her against us, in Congress and in the field. Her brave and good men regard her admission into the Union as a matter of life and death. They have been true to the Union under very severe trials. We have so acted as to justify their hopes, and we cannot fully retain their confidence and coöperation if we seem to break faith with them. In fact, they could not do so much for us, if they would. Again, the admission of the new State turns that much slave soil free, and thus is a certain and irrevocable encroachment upon the cause of the rebellion. The division of a State is dreaded as a precedent. But a measure made expedient by a war is no precedent for times of peace. It is said that the admission of West Virginia is secession, and tolerated only because it is our secession. Well, if we call it by that name, there is still difference enough between secession against the Constitution and secession in favor of the Constitution. I believe the admission of West Virginia into the Union is expedient.[158]

Later Lincoln told Governor Pierpont that a despatch from Postmaster Archibald W. Campbell, of Wheeling, caused him to sign the West Virginia statehood bill.[159]

[157] Ambler, *A History of West Virginia*, pp. 323–30.

[158] "President's Opinion on the Admission of West Virginia into the Union, December 31, 1862," printed in *Complete Works of Abraham Lincoln*, VIII, 159–60.

[159] Wheeling *Intelligencer*, Feb. 4, 1899, in Ambler, *A History of West Virginia*, p. 333 n.

Lincoln's interest in West Virginia did not cause him to overlook developments in the eastern section of the Old Dominion, most of which was under Confederate control. Here he was quick to give patronage to any group fostering loyalist sentiment. His recognition of Joseph E. Segar was a case in point. Segar had been elected as a "Unionist" member of Congress from certain Eastern Shore counties which the Union army had brought under its control.[160] Shortly after we find Lincoln issuing these instructions to George S. Boutwell, Commissioner of Internal Revenue:

Sir: It was by mere oversight that the Eastern Shore counties of Virginia, and some other counties of Hon. Mr. Segar's District, were not classed as loyal in the proclamation of July. I intend to set this right the first convenient opportunity. Meantime, consult with Mr. Segar, and act with his District, in regard to the Revenue, as with a loyal District.[161]

Lincoln's concern for Virginia was also evident in a note to Postmaster General Blair:

The bearer of this, Mr. C. T. Hemptow, is a Virginian who wishes to get, for his son, a small place in your Dept. I think Virginia should be heard, in such cases.[162]

Pierpont, who, as we have seen, collaborated with other Unionists in establishing the state of West Virginia, had in the meantime become governor of the "restored" state of Virginia—in other words, of the few Virginia counties outside of West Virginia which were in federal hands. Because of circumstances he made Alexandria, a short distance from Washington, his capital. Here under the military protection of the Lincoln administration he remained until the fall of the Confederate government, when he moved to Richmond and became in fact the governor of Virginia.[163]

---

[160] *Biographical Directory of the American Congress, 1774–1927*, II, 1506.

[161] Lincoln to the Commissioner of Internal Revenue, Nov. 24, 1862, Emanuel Hertz Photostats, Library of Congress. This letter is also printed in *Uncollected Letters of Abraham Lincoln*, ed. by G. A. Tracy, p. 218.

[162] Lincoln to the Postmaster General, March 13, 1861, in Tarbell, *The Life of Abraham Lincoln*, II, 340.

[163] See Thomas P. Abernethy's sketch of Pierpont in *Dictionary of American Biography*, XIV, 584–85. Had Lincoln lived, it is reasonable to assume that he would have used the patronage as a means of restoring the seceded states to their old legal status in the Union.

Chapter IX

FEDERAL OFFICEHOLDERS AND THE RENOMINATION OF LINCOLN

As the grim military conflict wore on, Lincoln became more than ever concerned with bolstering his administration for the paramount object of preserving the Union. A vital part of his policy was still a desire for harmonious relations with Congress—and by 1864 there was in both the Senate and the House of Representatives an atmosphere of insurgency and revolt. Constituents of some members demanded peace, others clamored for a more vigorous prosecution of the war. Almost all of the patronage had long since been distributed, but Lincoln continued to consult with senators and representatives before filling vacancies caused by death or resignation. His letter to the two Iowa senators was typical of many which he sent at this time: "Messrs. Grimes & Harlan: Would your friend Sanders be Surveyor General of Nevada?" [1] Or one of his Cabinet members would request some prominent Republican to see Lincoln at once concerning some job. For example we find Chase writing United States Senator Trumbull, of Illinois: "The President would like to see you in relation to an appointment of assessor for the 12th District of Illinois." [2]

In his policy of securing Congressional support for his administration by feeding members of his party the fruits of patronage —a practice followed by every President of the United States before and since—Lincoln became exasperated at times, particularly when Republican members from the same state could not agree on an applicant. "I did not doubt yesterday that you desired to see me about the appointment of assessor in Kansas," he wrote to United States Senator Samuel C. Pomeroy, of Kansas, who was at odds with his colleague, Senator James H. Lane. "I wish you

[1] Lincoln to James W. Grimes and James Harlan (undated), in *New Letters and Papers of Lincoln,* comp. by Angle, p. 375.
[2] S. P. Chase to Trumbull, Feb. 6, 1864, Trumbull Papers.

and Lane would make a sincere effort to get out of the mood you
are in. It does neither of you any good. It gives you the means of
tormenting the life out of me, and nothing else." [3]

The feud between Pomeroy and Lane centered, in the last analysis, around the question of Lincoln's renomination for a second
term. While Lane was satisfied with Lincoln, Pomeroy was not. As
a matter of fact, long before the end of Lincoln's first term the
radicals and other dissident groups within the President's party
were casting about for a candidate to succeed him. As early as 1863
Greeley thought that General Rosecrans was the man, but the
failure of his Tennessee campaign quickly removed him from consideration.[4] Pomeroy's candidate was Secretary of the Treasury
Chase. On February 20, 1864, there appeared in a Washington
newspaper a copy of a circular worded "strictly private," which
bore Pomeroy's signature. A manifesto for Chase, the "Pomeroy
Circular" declared that as long as no effort was made to forestall
the political action of the people, it had been well for friends of
the government to do all possible in crushing the rebellion. But now
that "party machinery and official influence" were being employed
to perpetuate the administration, "friends of the Union and of
freedom" would have to assert themselves. The circular then went
on to say that Lincoln's reëlection was an impossibility and, even
were it possible, it was undesirable because of the President's tendency toward "compromise and temporary expediency." Moreover,
the patronage had been so extended and abused as to render the
one-term principle essential to the preservation of republican institutions. The circular demanded a more vigorous prosecution of
the war and asserted that Salmon P. Chase was the man for the
task.[5]

At the beginning of the Civil War both Seward and Chase—

[3] Lincoln to S. C. Pomeroy, May 12, 1864, in *Complete Works of Abraham Lincoln*, X, 98. On the Lane-Pomeroy feud, consult Schofield, *Forty-Six Years in the
Army*, especially chaps. v, vi.

[4] T. H. Williams, *Lincoln and the Radicals*, p. 306.

[5] For the "Pomeroy Circular," see Wilson, "The Original Chase Organization
Meeting and *The Next Presidential Election*," *The Mississippi Valley Historical
Review*, XXIII (1936), 64–76; Dudley, "The Election of 1864," *The Mississippi
Valley Historical Review*, XVIII (1932), 502. The Wilson article treats fully the
scurrilous attack made upon Lincoln by the Chase managers in the pamphlet
The Next Presidential Election. Also consult D. V. Smith, *Chase and Civil War
Politics*, pp. 116–17.

each of whom had been governor, United States senator, prominent in party councils, and a leading presidential aspirant—became convinced that the presidential job was too big for Lincoln, who had hitherto filled no higher office than that of congressman from Illinois. The Secretary of State had even written the President an outline of what the domestic and foreign policies should be and intimated that he, as premier, was the man to carry them out. By means of tactful language and gentle firmness, Lincoln overruled Seward, and the chief Cabinet officer, absorbed in the arduous duties of his department, and apparently realizing that officially he could climb no higher and that coöperation with the President was the part of wisdom, finally accepted his subordinate position. Not so Chase. In the Secretary of the Treasury defeat for the presidential nomination in 1860 produced an entirely different effect. He believed himself entitled to more influence and destined for a higher role.[6] This was very evident in the Victor Smith case: Chase had been instrumental in having Smith, editor of the strongly pro-Chase newspaper, the Cincinnati *Commercial*, appointed special Treasury agent and Collector of Customs at Puget Sound. Smith had fallen under suspicion of dishonesty and lost the confidence of the people of Washington Territory.[7] Lincoln, after sharp words with Chase over the matter, removed Smith during Chase's absence. Chase was sulky despite the fact that Lincoln, knowing Smith to be a friend of Chase, expressed willingness to try to find another place for him. "Governor Chase's feelings were hurt by my action in his absence," [8] wrote Lincoln. Chase, despite his own personal integrity, retained his confidence in Smith.[9] Possibly Chase's irritable attitude on this as on other occasions was caused by his daily realization that another whom he

[6] In assuring Senator H. B. Anthony, of Rhode Island, that he would recommend two appointments to the President, Chase wrote: "I do not care to assume the responsibility of decision in such a case unless I know my decision is to be regarded as final; and I have had already experience enough to teach me that it does not prevail even against what seem to me bad reasons for appointments not the best." See "Some Unpublished Letters of Salmon P. Chase," ed. by Young, p. 46.

[7] H. H. Bancroft, *History of Washington, Idaho, and Montana*, pp. 219–23.

[8] Tarbell, *The Life of Abraham Lincoln*, II, 364; *Compete Works of Abraham Lincoln*, VIII, 270, 272.

[9] For Chase's assurance to Smith of his confidence, see "Some Unpublished Letters of Salmon P. Chase," ed. by Young, pp. 74–75.

regarded as well-meaning and good-hearted, but limited in talent, held the glittering prize that had eluded him.

Letters reaching Chase from all parts of the North after 1861, informing him that he was indispensable, did not help him to forget his ambition of 1860, even had he tried to do so. If it were the consensus of opinion that he was the only man competent to handle the crisis why should he therefore not hope to accomplish in 1864 what he had failed to do some years earlier?

It was in this political atmosphere that the question of emancipation of the negro slaves came to the fore and caught the popular fancy. Chase became an ardent emancipationist, for freedom for all Negroes was close to his heart and it also provided him with an issue. Radical antislavery men of the Horace Greeley stamp, impatient with Lincoln's conservative course, began to turn to Chase for leadership. Sensing the situation, the Secretary of the Treasury became a strong antislavery contributor to the press. Announcement of Lincoln's Proclamation of Emancipation in September, 1862, took much of the wind out of his sails, but he was not discouraged. In Lincoln's conduct of the war he found a new live issue. He cultivated the friendship of all those who were critical of the President's military policies and by early 1863 had become the rallying point of most of the anti-Lincolnites within the Republican-Union party. Also in the patronage of the Treasury Department he saw opportunity to build up support for his presidential candidacy. He used the offices of his department to win support from Senator John Conness, of California, to his standard.[10] In the appointment of "Special Treasury Agents," made necessary by the conduct of the war, Chase was careful to pick those who were sympathetic to his candidacy—many of them from Ohio.[11] Wrote the collector of the conquered port of New Orleans: "We are forming a Chase Club here and meet for organization next Monday. . . . I believe we can control the election of delegates to the National Convention." [12] In October, 1863, Attorney General

[10] D. V. Smith, *Chase and Civil War Politics*, pp. 31–53, 89–90, 99.

[11] W. W. Davis, *The Civil War and Reconstruction in Florida*, pp. 349–51, 353, 371 n., 411; George S. Denison to Chase (Private), Feb. 19, 1864, Chase Papers, Library of Congress; R. J. Howard to Montgomery Blair, Sept. 24, 1864, Francis Preston Blair Papers.

[12] George S. Denison to Chase (Private), March 5, 1864, Chase Papers, Library of Congress.

Bates confided to his diary: "I'm afraid Mr. Chase's head is turned by his eagerness in pursuit of the presidency. For a long time back he has been filling all the offices in his own vast patronage, with extreme partisans, and contrives also to fill many vacancies, properly belonging to other departments." [13] And Secretary of the Navy Welles had a like impression: "I think there are indications that Chase intends to press his pretensions as a candidate, and much of the Treasury machinery and the special agencies have that end in view." [14]

That Chase's boom might endanger Lincoln's renomination and reëlection was apparent to many. For the opposition to Lincoln by the opening of 1864 was formidable. The losses, the agonies, the desolations of war, the nation's resources dedicated to destruction of life and property—all these were beginning to injure the spirit, endurance, and resolve of the northern people.[15] And this fact played directly into the hands of the radicals and other heterogeneous groups who wanted Lincoln out of the White House. Despite the President's hold upon the affections of the rank and file, many spokesmen for those who did not like him openly indicated their opposition. "The feeling for Mr. Lincoln's reelection *seems* to be general," wrote Senator Trumbull, "but much of it I discover is only on the surface. You would be surprised in talking with public men we meet here [Washington], to find how few when you come to get at their real sentiments are for Mr. Lincoln's reelection. There is a distrust & fear that he is too undecided & inefficient ever to put down the rebellion. You need not be surprised if a reaction sets in before the nomination in favor of some man supposed to possess more energy & less inclination to trust our brave boys in the hands, & under the leadership of Generals who have no heart in the war." [16] Trumbull's attitude was not unrepresentative. Well might Henry J. Raymond, who was soon to become Republican National Chairman and manager of the President's campaign for reëlection, declare:

Nearly all the original Abolitionists and many of the more decidedly anti-slavery members of the Republican party were dissatisfied, that

---

[13] "The Diary of Edward Bates, 1859–1866," ed. by Howard K. Beale, *Annual Report,* American Historical Association, IV (1930), 310.

[14] *Diary of Gideon Welles,* I, 525.

[15] Raymond, *The Life and Public Services of Abraham Lincoln,* p. 548.

[16] Lyman Trumbull to H. G. Pike, Feb. 6, 1864, Trumbull Papers.

Mr. Lincoln had not more rapidly and more sweepingly enforced their extreme opinions. Many distinguished public men resented his rejection of their advice, and many more had been alienated by his inability to recognize their claims to office.[17]

Lincoln was fully aware of the movement against him; he knew that his enemies were rallying about Chase. He said nothing, however, about the Pomeroy Circular; nor did he make any move toward removing any of Chase's Treasury agents who were promoting Chase's candidacy. But there were those who had benefited from Lincoln's patronage who would not let the Chase activity pass unnoticed. For instance, John W. Forney, publisher of a powerful chain of Republican newspapers, and Secretary of the United States Senate through Lincoln's influence, assailed Chase in the columns of his Philadelphia *Press:*

If Mr. Chase sanctions the unjust attacks upon the gentleman under whom he holds place, it will require little talent at figures to prove that the enormous catalogue of offices (almost a Blue Book in itself) attached to the Treasury Department is crowded with the personal adherents of the distinguished Secretary.[18]

Neither the pamphlet entitled *The Next Presidential Election* nor the "Pomeroy Circular" met with the reception hoped for by their authors. In fact, both aroused hostility and condemnation. Embarrassed and somewhat humiliated, Chase protested to Lincoln that the "Circular" had been issued without his knowledge and offered to resign. To his friends the Treasury head wrote that he had finally, very reluctantly, consented to allow his name to be used for the presidency. For Lincoln his ambitious Cabinet officer presented a dilemma. For the President to intimate that Chase should resign his post would be an admission that he feared the talented Ohioan as a rival; moreover, the nation might interpret such a course as notice that Lincoln had cast his lot with the conservatives, and thus further alienate the radical antislavery wing of the party. Any such split would not only endanger the Unionist cause but jeopardize Lincoln's own reëlection. On the other hand, if he retained Chase he would place his administration in the uniquely embarrassing position of having one of its chief officers striking at it

17 Raymond, *The Life and Public Services of Abraham Lincoln,* p. 548.
18 Philadelphia *Press,* clipped in Columbus *Daily Ohio State Journal,* March 4, 1864.

from within. Shrewdly Lincoln refrained from accepting Chase's resignation. Instead, he endured what must have been a galling situation and awaited developments as the state Republican-Unionist conventions met to decide on their presidential preferencs.[19]

Despite the awkwardness of the situation, Lincoln must have been confident, for like all Presidents he had in his possession a mighty weapon which he could wield against any rival contender—namely, the patronage. "President Lincoln" commented a midwestern Daily, "can now so wield the patronage as to secure his election for a second term." [20] More than a month before the publication of the "Pomeroy Circular" his supporters, even if not himself, had started his campaign for renomination and reëlection. Many who aided in launching the fight were his officeholders, and those who had formerly received jobs or favors from him, or hoped to receive them.

It was little New Hampshire, where Chase was born, which led off with a Lincoln endorsement for renomination. The Granite State Republicans met in convention in Concord on January 7, 1864, to renominate Governor Joseph A. Gilmore. The convention was called to order by N. G. Ordway, chairman of the state central committee and Sergeant at Arms of the United States House of Representatives. Among the active working delegates was Thomas L. Tullock, then holding the office of Navy Agent at Portsmouth, by appointment of Lincoln. Tullock was a member of the important Committee on Resolutions.[21] Another member of this committee was William E. Chandler of Concord, a Harvard graduate, then state legislator but subsequently to be appointed by Lincoln as Solicitor and Judge Advocate General of the Navy Department.[22] Chandler it was who moved a lengthy resolution ending with the words: "We, therefore, declare Abraham Lincoln to be the people's choice for reelection to the Presidency in 1864" [23]—

[19] D. V. Smith, *Chase and Civil War Politics*, pp. 119–20; Hart, *Salmon Portland Chase*, p. 312.

[20] Indianapolis *Daily State Sentinel*, March 11, 1864.

[21] For Tullock, see Manchester (N.H.) *Daily Mirror and American*, May 31, 1864; also *U. S. Official Register, 1863*, p. 227.

[22] For Chandler, see G. V. Fox to Chandler, Feb. 23, 1865, William E. Chandler Papers; *Biographical Directory of the American Congress, 1774–1927*, p. 801; *U. S. Senate Executive Journal*, XIV, Part I (1864–66), 252, 266.

[23] Portsmouth (N.H.) *Journal of Literature and Politics*, Jan. 9, 1864.

an action that brought the delegates to their feet with thunderous applause. In the regular resolutions, drafted by Tullock and Chandler and adopted by the convention, was one pledging Lincoln support and another which gave a thrust at Chase.[24] The latter resolution complimented Chase, but hinted that he was not alert enough at detecting corruption in the expenditures of public monies. This left-handed compliment to the Treasury head read in part:

Resolved, . . . Having the fullest confidence in the integrity and financial ability of Hon. Salmon P. Chase, the Secretary of the Treasury, we call upon him, and all other officers of the Government in any way responsible for public expenditures, to establish and enforce a rigid system of accountability, and promptly to detect, expose and punish all corruption and fraud upon the Government. . . .[25]

Outside of New Hampshire this resolution received much publicity. The New York *World,* an anti-Lincoln sheet, was confident that it was "concocted" in Washington.[26] The Albany *Evening Journal*—edited by George Dawson, postmaster of Albany, and Thurlow Weed, who as Seward's political partner controlled much New York federal patronage—gave the New Hampshire resolution huge space. It "deserves to be written in letters of gold," this Seward-Weed organ declared. "The people will demand that those who have the administration of the National affairs on their hands, shall not only practice economy but promptly 'expose and punish all corruption and fraud' on the part of the officials, whether high or low." [27]

The Republicans and Union men of Pennsylvania followed the example of New Hampshire in endorsing Lincoln. In this they had the services of Simon Cameron. The former Secretary of War had given up his post at St. Petersburg and was back in Harrisburg and Washington working for richer rewards. On January 9 one of the President's secretaries, John Hay, recorded: "Cameron has written to the President that the entire Union force of the Pa. Legislature, House and Senate, have subscribed a request that the

[24] *Ibid.*   [25] *Ibid.*
[26] New York *World,* Jan. 13, 1864.
[27] Albany *Evening Journal,* Jan. 11, 1864.

President will allow himself to be reelected, and that they intend visiting Washington to present it. He says 'I have kept my promise.' " [28] Less than a week later a letter signed by every Union member of the Pennsylvania legislature requested Lincoln to stand for renomination and reëlection.[29]

At this time—during the first months of 1864—Thurlow Weed seems to have been one of the powers behind the scenes in promoting Lincoln's pre-convention campaign for renomination, and it was probably no accident that the Albany *Evening Journal* became highly critical of Chase. One anti-Weed New York City newspaper noted that the Albany editor-politician was a frequent visitor at the White House, adding:

Mr. Weed, however, was so successful with the President, securing the promise of certain official patronage in the New York Custom House and otherwise, that he rolled up his sleeves and went to work making his combinations. He enlisted Cameron and Forney, of Pennsylvania, and other manipulating and trading politicians in that section, as well as those in other Northern States. In due time came the New Hampshire Convention, where Mr. Fogg, of the National Committee of 1860 [and whom Lincoln appointed Minister to Switzerland], figured, and, through postmasters, provost marshals and other government officials getting elected to the Convention, the endorsement of Lincoln for another term was obtained. Then came the resolution of the Pennsylvania Legislature, which Cameron pocketed and took in person to Washington, claiming it as his special work, and in due time that of two or three other legislative bodies —where this trio, Weed, Cameron, and Forney, could operate upon the wire-pulling politicians.[30]

The Connecticut Republicans were next in expressing their wish that Lincoln continue for another term. In this state the federal patronage was a source of strength in procuring an instructed delegation for Lincoln in the forthcoming National Convention.

For long there had raged a feud over federal patronage among Connecticut Republicans—between the "state" faction led by Mark Howard, Calvin Day, and Governor Buckingham, having

[28] Hay, *Lincoln and the Civil War in the Diaries and Letters of John Hay*, ed. by Dennett, pp. 152–53.
[29] The full text is printed in Philadelphia *Daily News*, Jan. 15, 1864.
[30] New York *Herald*, May 24, 1864.

THURLOW WEED

radical views and inclined to be sympathetic toward Chase; and the "Congressional" faction led by United States Senator James Dixon, James F. Babcock, Collector of the Port of New Haven, and Nehemiah D. Sperry, postmaster in New Haven. Notwithstanding the efforts of Secretary of the Navy Welles to preserve party harmony within his native state, the split had opened wider when, in 1862, Dixon, in a secret session of the United States Senate, opposed Howard for Collector of the Hartford District.[31] In conformity with the practice of Senatorial courtesy, Lincoln distributed the lion's share of the Connecticut jobs in line with Senator Dixon's wishes, much to the fury of Howard's group.

The death of the Unites States Marshal for Connecticut in early December, 1863, provoked another fight over a successor; and the Howardites were in open rebellion when Lincoln tendered the vacant marshalship to Dixon's man, Henry Hammond, instead of to their candidate. The Howardites were particularly strong in the "Union Leagues," while the Dixonites' strength lay in the party organization by virtue of the Senator's control over federal appointments.[32] Howard, in his intense opposition to Dixon and as a slap at the President, began to communicate with Chase. From the correspondence it seems clear that he had plans to throw the support of the Union League to the Secretary of the Treasury.[33] In a letter to Chase denouncing Dixon, Howard wrote in December, 1863: "As you will have learned from Judge Barrett & others, probably, the spirit of our Grand Council was fully in harmony with yours. . . . Upon my motion, the Council adjourned to meet at some place and at ('about') some time (not after) as the Republican National Convention."[34] Just a month later Howard protested to Secretary Welles that he had "never passed one word with Mr. Chase in any form as to the Presidency," and explained:

31 *Diary of Gideon Welles,* I, 78, 81, 81 n., 235, 239; M. Howard to Welles, Nov. 20, 1863, Gideon Welles Papers, Library of Congress.

32 New Haven *Morning Journal and Courier,* Dec. 17, 1863, Jan. 20, 1864; M. Howard to Welles, Nov. 20, Dec. 2, 22, 1863; Calvin Day to Welles, Dec. 2, 22, 1863; Moses Pierce to Welles, Oct. 4, 1864, Welles Papers, Library of Congress.

33 Under date of Nov. 20, 1863, Howard wrote Welles that "Federal office holders" were "malignantly intent upon breaking down an institution [Union League] devoted solely to the support of the Gov't, and the loyal sentiment of the country." M. Howard to Welles, Nov. 20, 1863. Welles Papers, Library of Congress.

34 M. Howard to Chase, Dec. 19, 1863, Chase Papers, Library of Congress

While we are friendly to the President—in fact his *truest* friends—
the thinking and honest men of our State believe it best not to mix
up the Presidential with our State contest,—for local reasons, which
if explained would be satisfactory to the President, if he could understand them: Among these is the unpopularity of some of the
Federal appointments, and the dread of their continuance. . . .
What we ask of the President is that he have faith in us, and treat
us fairly. But if he allows himself to be the victim of Dixon's sympathetic deception, why of course he forces us into a position in
relation to himself that we would not choose to occupy. . . . Now
we desire that you will come to a frank understanding with the
President in our behalf *at once*, that we may know whether we are
to be treated by him as friends or enemies. And whether our radicalism is to bar us from his sympathy.[35]

Another letter from Howard to Welles told of his faction's reason
for opposing the idea of bringing up the question of Lincoln's
renomination in the state convention, set for February 17:

It would appear that Dixon has played the courtier enough to get
complete control of the Prest. and that he (D.) is to have all the
power necessary to crush the "radical" men and sentiments of his
State. And if this be our relation to Mr. Lincoln, there seems no
other alternative for us than an attitude of open hostility to him,
or to entirely surrender to the semi-disloyal, temporizing, tricky and
plundering influence of our state. None of us desire to occupy such
an attitude to the Pres't., but fidelity to the country, to our political and moral convictions and common self-respect would seem to
demand our opposition. And as our State Convention is soon to
assemble, this will soon become a practical question. Dixon, thinking
he has got possession of the Prest., is pressing upon his instruments
to have the State Convention nominate him and thus force us to
swallow our self-respect or to assume an attitude of opposition, that
will strengthen him still further at the White House.

We desire to keep the Presidential matter in abeyance, and in the
meantime to effect a better understanding with the Prest, if possible.

Dixon has no doubt impressed him with the idea that we are com-
bining for Chase.[36]

Howard's strategy to hold up the presidential question until
overtures came from Lincoln was doomed to failure. Senator

[35] M. Howard to Welles, Jan. 19, 1863, Welles Papers, Library of Congress.
[36] M. Howard to Welles, Jan. 16, 1864, *ibid.*

Dixon's officeholders controlled completely the state convention that met at Hartford on February 17.[37] Governor Buckingham was renominated, but Collector Babcock of New Haven, a Dixon follower, took over control of the presidential question. Babcock moved that delegates at large to the National Convention be appointed by the Congressional districts in convention. This was in contrast to the old custom of having each Congressional district choose them between the time of adjournment and the National Convention. Babcock's motion prevailed, and a full slate of delegates at large was selected to the National Convention, with the request that they give Lincoln their "united support" for renomination. It was a clear victory for the Dixon forces and incidentally for Lincoln, assuring him of the Connecticut delegation.[38] In disgust did Calvin Day, a Howard ally who attended the state convention, write:

Our convention was large and on the subject of President & Governor was perfectly unanimous, on the surface at least. I have never seen such an exhibition of office holders in any convention before. From Hammond [United States Marshal] down to Cleveland. I do not know of any office holder except Bolles & Rockwell that were not present & *very active*. All the arrangements made for officering the meeting & appointing of delegates had been made by them & they generally carried them out. . . . The [Dixon] ring did not dare to trust their plans in full convention & so divided the state in Congressional districts to make the appointment of *delegates at large*. We shall make the best fight we can but our best men & true were thoroughly disgusted with the distribution of government patronage.[39]

Five days following the Connecticut State Convention, the Republicans of both Maryland and Iowa held their state conclaves and instructed their delegates to the National Convention to support Lincoln.

On February 22, Washington's birthday, the very same day that the Republicans of these two widely separated states were taking this action, the National Committee which had been formed at the Republican National Convention at Chicago in 1860—it

37 James G. Bolles to Welles, Feb. 18, 1864, *ibid*.
38 Hartford *Daily Courant*, Feb. 18, 1864.
39 Calvin Day to Welles, Feb. 18, 1864, Welles Papers, Library of Congress.

was now called the "Union National Committee"—met at the
Washington home of its chairman, Edwin D. Morgan, United
States Senator from New York. The committee decided on Balti-
more as the site and June 7 as the time for the "Union" National
Convention. Seventeen members were present:

Messrs. Edwin D. Morgan, of New York, President; Lawrence
Brainerd, of Vermont; John Z. Goodrich, of Massachusetts; Thomas
G. Turner, of Rhode Island; Gideon Welles, of Connecticut; Denning Duer, of New Jersey; Edward McPherson, of Pennsylvania;
Nathaniel B. Smithers, of Delaware; James F. Wagner, of Maryland; Thomas Spooner, of Ohio; Henry S. Lane, of Indiana; Ebenezer Peck, of Illinois; H. M. Hoxie, of Iowa; William D. Washburn,
of Minnesota; Cornelius Cole, of California; O. H. Irish, of Nebraska; Joseph Gerhardt, of the District of Columbia.[40]

To Secretary of the Navy Welles, Connecticut member of the
National Committee, it appeared that "four fifths" of those at
this momentous gathering at Senator Morgan's home were for
the reëlection of Lincoln.[41] And why not? Aside from their love for
the Union and their awareness that Lincoln was backed by the
masses, almost every one of the seventeen present was either a
Republican Member of Congress who had received patronage for
their followers from Lincoln or else was a federal officeholder by
appointment of Lincoln: Edwin D. Morgan, chairman and the
New York member, was United States Senator from his state, in
addition to having in 1862 received a commission as major general
of volunteers in his capacity as governor of New York.[42] Lawrence
Brainerd, Vermont member, and a man of strong antislavery
convictions, held no federal position at this time; he was a former
United States Senator, engaged in business in his home commonwealth.[43] John Z. Goodrich, Massachusetts member, was at the
time Collector of Customs of the Port of Boston.[44] Thomas G.

[40] New York *Times*, Feb. 23, 1864; New York *Herald*, Feb. 23, 1864. Greeley
wanted the convention postponed to late summer, in the hope that in the meantime enthusiasm for Lincoln would have cooled and that a candidate more agreeable to the radicals could then be named. See New York *Tribune*, Jan. 14, 1864.

[41] *Diary of Gideon Welles*, I, 529–30.

[42] *U. S. Senate Executive Journal*, XII (1861–62), 56, 241.

[43] *Biographical Directory of the American Congress, 1774–1927*, p. 729.

[44] Case, *The Goodrich Family in America*, p. 173; *U. S. Official Register, 1863*,
p. 62; *Biographical Directory of the American Congress, 1774–1927*, p. 1022.

Turner, Rhode Island member, held the job of Assessor of Internal Revenue for the First Rhode Island District.[45] Gideon Welles, Connecticut member, was, of course, in Lincoln's Cabinet. Denning Duer, New Jersey member, was not on the public pay roll so far as can be learned, but had a voice in determining the distribution of federal offices, even in New York.[46] Edward McPherson, Pennsylvania member, had only two months before resigned as Deputy Commissioner of Internal Revenue to become Clerk of the United States House of Representatives.[47] Nathaniel B. Smithers, Delaware member, was then Congressman from his state, while in 1862 Lincoln had given him the post of Provost Marshal for Delaware ;[48] besides, a relative of Smithers received a consulship in Turkey.[49] James F. Wagner, Maryland member, was at the time holding a position in the Baltimore Custom House.[50] Thomas Spooner, Ohio member, was Collector of Internal Revenue for the Cincinnati District.[51] Henry S. Lane, Indiana member, was United States Senator from his state.[52] Ebenezer Peck, Illinois member, was an old friend of Lincoln and, from 1863 to 1865, Judge of the United States Court of Claims, by appointment of Lincoln.[53] Herbert M. Hoxie, Iowa member, was United States Marshal for Iowa.[54] William D. Washburn, Minnesota member, was United States Surveyor General for the Minnesota District.[55] Cornelius Cole, California member, was then sitting in Congress from his state.[56]

[45] U. S. Senate Executive Journal, XIII (1862–64), 12, 112; U. S. Official Register, 1863, p. 37.

[46] Denning Duer to Welles, June 28, Aug. 29, 1864, Welles Papers, Library of Congress.

[47] Biographical Directory of the American Congress, 1774–1927, p. 1277.

[48] W. T. Smithers, "Memoir of Nathaniel B. Smithers," Papers of the Historical Society of Delaware, No. 23 (1899), pp. 25–26; Milford (Del.) Peninsular News and Advertiser, Sept. 19, 1862.

[49] Milford (Del.) Peninsular News and Advertiser, Jan. 31, 1862; U. S. Senate Executive Journal, XII (1861–62), 3, 96.

[50] U. S. Official Register, 1863, p. 87.

[51] U. S. Senate Executive Journal, XIII (1862–64), 15, 112; U. S. Official Register, 1863, p. 39.

[52] Biographical Directory of the American Congress, 1774–1927, p. 1201.

[53] U. S. Senate Executive Journal, XIII (1862–64), 224, 275; U. S. Official Register, 1863, p. 265; ibid., 1865, p. 298.

[54] Annals of Iowa, Series III, IX (1909–10), 434; U. S. Official Register, 1863, p. 269.

[55] Folwell, A History of Minnesota, III, 84; Washburn, Genealogical Notes of the Washburn Family, p. 74; U. S. Official Register, 1863, p. 102.

[56] Memoirs of Cornelius Cole, pp. 174 ff.

Orsamus H. Irish, member from Nebraska Territory (a veteran office seeker since 1861),[57] was then Superintendent of Indian Affairs for the Territory of Utah.[58] Efforts to locate data concerning Joseph Gerhardt, District of Columbia member, have proved unavailing.

Four days after the meeting at Morgan's home the Union members of the Ohio legislature, sitting in Columbus, unanimously endorsed Lincoln for renomination.[59] Apparently this endorsement was put through with the aid of federal officeholders in the Buckeye State, W. H. West, law partner of Assessor James Walker, being especially active.[60] Such action by the Union legislators at Columbus was a terrific shock to Chase and his followers, since Ohio was his home state. It placed Chase in an embarrassing position, for only a few weeks before he had replied to one of his Ohio supporters, State Senator James C. Hall, regarding the use of his name for the presidency, that he was willing to run:

Of course, under these circumstances, I desire the support of Ohio. If, however, it should be the pleasure of a majority of our friends in Ohio to indicate a preference for another, I should accept their action with that cheerful acquiescence which is due from me to the friends who have trusted and honored me beyond any claim or merit of mine.[61]

Whatever Chase's feelings and thoughts may have been following the action of the Union members of the legislature of his home state in endorsing Lincoln, he deemed it wise to make the graceful gesture of withdrawing publicly from the presidential race. Consequently on March 5 and upon the advice of Greeley and James A. Garfield,[62] he dispatched the following letter to Senator Hall: ". . . . The recent action of the Union members of our Legislature indicates such a preference [for another]. It becomes my

---

[57] O. H. Irish to Welles, April 2, 1861, Welles Papers, Library of Congress.

[58] *U. S. Senate Executive Journal*, XIII (1862–64), 324, 393.

[59] Columbus *Daily Ohio State Journal*, Feb. 27, 1864.

[60] Wm. Lawrence to Chase (Private), June 14, 1864, Salmon P. Chase Papers, Library of Congress.

[61] Chase to James C. Hall, Jan. 18, 1864, in the Columbus *Daily Ohio State Journal*, March 11, 1864.

[62] Horace Greeley to Salmon P. Chase, March 2, 1864, in Bartlett, *John C. Frémont and the Republican Party*, p. 92; T. C. Smith, *The Life and Letters of James Abram Garfield*, I, 376.

duty, therefore, and I count it more a privilege than a duty, to ask that no further consideration be given to my name." [63]

But apparently Chase did not intend to have his withdrawal from the presidential race taken too seriously by his workers. It was freely charged by his critics and political enemies that his retirement from the contest was only a "ruse"; that it was the intention of the Chase men to reënter him at a more opportune time.[64] James Gordon Bennett, editor of the New York *Herald*, asserted that the latest Chase move was a feint, a trick of some sort, and cautioned his readers to remember that "the Salmon is a queer fish; very shy and very wary, often appearing to avoid the bait just before gulping it down." [65] "It proves that only the *present* prospects of Mr. Lincoln are too good to be openly resisted, at least, by men within the party," [66] observed Attorney General Bates. And so it seemed. The contest between the Lincoln men and the Chase men for delegates to the National Convention continued in all of the pivotal states.

Of the 516 convention votes destined to be cast at Baltimore, 264, a clear majority, would come from the seven largest states: New York, 66; Pennsylvania, 52; Ohio, 42; Illinois, 32; Indiana, 26; Massachusetts, 24; and Kentucky, 22.[67] To what extent was federal patronage used to secure pro-Lincoln delegations from these states to the Baltimore Convention?

All-important was New York, with the largest bloc of convention and electoral votes. The feud between the Chase or "radical" faction and the Seward-Weed or "conservative" faction in the Empire State became more intense because of quarrels over the use of federal patronage and the policy to be pursued toward the prosecution of the war and the emancipation of the Negro.[68] Collector Barney of the Port of New York, appointed by Lincoln to his very influential position through Chase's instrumentality,

[63] Chase to James C. Hall, March 5, 1864, in the Columbus *Daily Ohio State Journal*, March 11, 1864.

[64] Indianapolis *Daily State Sentinel*, April 15, 1864.

[65] D. V. Smith, *Chase and Civil War Politics*, pp. 128–29; New York *Herald*, March 11, 1864.

[66] "The Diary of Edward Bates, 1859–1866," ed. by Howard K. Beale, *Annual Report*, American Historical Association, IV (1930), 345.

[67] For these figures, see C. W. Johnson, *The First Three Republican National Conventions . . . 1856, 1860, and 1864*, p. 234.

[68] New York *Herald*, April 17, June 26, 1862.

had used the Custom House patronage to elect a pro-Chase man, George Opdyke, as mayor of New York City, much to the disgust of the Seward-Weed faction. The latter group became more incensed when, in 1862, the Chase followers used the Custom House patronage to nominate an anti-Weed Republican, James S. Wadsworth, for governor of New York.[69] "Delighted this morning by news of Gen. Wadsworth's nomination for Governor of New York on the first ballot," [70] commented Chase in Washington. The Seward-Weed Republicans were furious, and, while the evidence is not conclusive, it indicates that they "knifed" Wadsworth at the polls and assured the election of Horatio Seymour, the Democratic gubernatorial candidate.[71]

Meanwhile, Horace Greeley, ingenious editor of the widely circulated New York *Tribune*, not yet having full satisfaction against Seward and Weed and impatient at what he deemed Lincoln's slow prosecution of the war, quite logically fell, as already noted, into the orbit of the Chase faction. To him, therefore, Chase turned to aid his interests in New York, courting the *Tribune* editor's favor by telling him that one or two remunerative Treasury clerkships were vacant and would be filled upon his recommendation.[72] Greeley, for his part, informed Chase of his desire to see him elected President, writing the Treasury head late in 1863: "I know no man in our country who is in my view better qualified for President than yourself, nor one whom I should more cordially support. . . . If in 1864 I could *make* a President (not merely a candidate) you would be my first choice." [73] In combating the Seward-Weed influence in the Empire State, Chase also had the aid of David Dudley Field and James A. Briggs. He intended to reward Field with the position of Assistant Secretary of the Treasury as soon as Congress should create the office. Briggs already was Deputy Collector of the Port of New York.[74]

[69] Barnes, *Memoir of Thurlow Weed,* pp. 322, 424–25; Rufus F. Andrews to Chase (Confidential), Dec. 15, 1863, Salmon P. Chase Papers, Library of Congress.
[70] *Diary and Correspondence of Salmon P. Chase,* p. 94.
[71] William Alexander to Montgomery Blair (Private), July 18, 1863, Francis Preston Blair Papers; Pearson, *James S. Wadsworth of Geneseo,* p. 165.
[72] D. V. Smith, *Chase and Civil War Politics,* p. 53.
[73] Greeley to Chase ("Private"), Sept. 29, 1863, Chase Papers, Historical Society of Pennsylvania.
[74] D. V. Smith, *Chase and Civil War Politics,* pp. 78–79.

Notwithstanding his clever maneuvers, Chase's efforts to attract to his cause New York delegates to the National Convention of 1864 came to naught. For Thurlow Weed, beneficiary of much patronage from Lincoln and a loyal supporter of the administration, scotched any attempt by the Chase forces to control the New York State Union convention by the use of Custom House patronage. Unfortunately for Chase and his New York adherents, Collector Barney had not lived up to expectations. Among other things he had appointed as one of his secretaries a young man named A. N. Palmer—who under the clever tutelage of Weed soon was hand in glove with members of the Seward-Weed faction.[75] "Our friends all know," wrote one Chase follower to the Secretary of the Treasury, "that Mr. Barney is a failure as an officer, and as a politician. The fact that he has been managed by Palmer, and that Palmer has been a tool of Weed's is notorious." [76] Chase, determined to get rid of Barney, consulted Greeley as to whether Daniel S. Dickinson, an anti-Weed Republican, would be acceptable as Barney's successor. The *Tribune* editor replied that "no other living man would be so acceptable," adding that the New York Custom House had it in its power to select the state delegation to the National Convention.[77] Lincoln, however, did not remove Barney, and, when the year 1864 opened, it was evident that the Seward-Weed faction had wrested control of the Custom House from the Chase forces.

In February (1864) while the Chase men were still fuming over the impotence of Collector Barney in aiding their cause, Weed and Abram Wakeman, the latter then holding the job of postmaster of New York City by Lincoln's appointment, stealthily engineered a Lincoln endorsement through the state Republican central committee. Not all of the members were present at the meeting, among those absent being the friends of Chase. The latter protested the endorsement of the President, but it was too late. The circulars were already in the mails! [78]

[75] New York *Herald,* Jan. 9, 1864; D. V. Smith, *Chase and Civil War Politics,* p. 79.
[76] J. F. Bailey to Chase, Jan. 13, 1864, Chase Papers, Library of Congress.
[77] Greeley to Chase, Feb. 10, 1864, Chase Papers, Historical Society of Pennsylvania.
[78] D. V. Smith, *Chase and Civil War Politics,* pp. 109–10.

Not until May 25, at Syracuse, did the Republicans of New York state assemble in convention to select delegates to the Baltimore Convention. Weed was early on the scene, as was his partner and co-editor of the Albany *Evening Journal*, Postmaster George Dawson, of Albany.[79] The composition of the delegates that made up the Syracuse gathering was characterized by a Democratic newspaper of Albany, the *Atlas and Argus*, as follows:

A glance at the list of delegates to the Republican state convention will satisfy anyone that the people have had nothing to do with their selection, and that they represent only the great army of office-holders in our state. From every county comes the internal revenue collector, the assessor, the sub-collectors, the provost marshal or his deputy, and the city and village postmasters. It was a happy thought that called for three delegates from each district; for in no other way could the ambition of the more prominent of these place men have been gratified. Their task will be an easy one. Self-appointed as many of them are—without a constituency, and careless of the public weal or woe, so long as they may stand well with the powers at Washington—it only remains for them to pass the stereotype resolutions of "loyalty" to the administration, interspersed with bitter denunciations of the Democracy, and then to choose a delegation to Baltimore that will faithfully represent their fealty to power and its corruptions, and their abandonment of principle. It will be a motley gathering, in whose doings the people will take no interest other than as mere lookers-on.[80]

The *Atlas and Argus* proved to be a good prophet, for the convention at Syracuse passed its "stereotype" resolution by acclamation amidst cheers. It approved the Lincoln administration and expressed its "preference for his renomination for the office of President of the United States." [81] The convention also selected delegates at large, delegates, and alternates to represent New York State at the Baltimore Convention. The list included such appointees of Lincoln as Rufus F. Andrews, Richard Busteed, Abram Wakeman, Sheridan Shook, and Thomas Hillhouse.[82] Andrews was Surveyor of Customs of the Port of New York.[83] Busteed, of Irish extraction and former Democratic corporation counsel of

---

[79] New York *Herald*, May 25, 1864.
[80] Albany *Atlas and Argus*, clipped in New York *World*, May 27, 1864.
[81] New York *Herald*, May 26, 1864.
[82] *Ibid.*   [83] *U. S. Official Register, 1863*, p. 81.

New York City, was a Brigadier General of Volunteers and later Judge of the United States District Court for Alabama—although military activities prevented his taking his seat on the bench immediately.[84] Wakeman was postmaster in New York City;[85] Shook, Collector of Internal Revenue for the Thirty-second District of New York;[86] and Hillhouse, Assistant Adjutant General, with the rank of major.[87] Thus was the Empire State, with its huge bloc of 66 convention votes, assured to Lincoln.

Second only to New York in voting strength was Pennsylvania, with 52. In this state also the convention which selected delegates to Baltimore seems to have been controlled by men holding public office under Lincoln.

The Republicans of the Keystone State met in state convention at Harrisburg on April 28, 1864. Ever directing operations behind the scenes was Simon Cameron.[88] But it was George Bergner, editor of the pro-Cameron organ, the Harrisburg *Telegraph*, and holding the job of postmaster of Harrisburg, who actively directed strategy at the convention. Bergner it was who nominated the man unanimously elected temporary chairman of the convention; Bergner it was who successfully moved that a committee of one from each Senatorial district be appointed by the Senatorial delegates to nominate permanent officers; Bergner it was who offered the resolution that provided the manner in which four delegates at large to the Baltimore Convention were to be selected; and Bergner it was who moved that the delegates be instructed to vote as a unit for Lincoln's renomination at Baltimore. A committee on resolutions of seven members was appointed—and Bergner was one of the seven. To top it off, Bergner offered a resolution opposing all efforts to postpone the Baltimore Convention. Greeley and the other Chase men, as we have observed, as well as other anti-

[84] *U. S. Senate Executive Journal*, XIII (1862–64), 325, 384; Owen, *History of Alabama and Dictionary of Alabama Biography*, III, 272; Fleming, *Civil War and Reconstruction in Alabama*, pp. 394, 744; *The United States vs. Richard Busteed*, pp. 2–3. (The latter pamphlet in the New York Public Library.)

[85] *U. S. Senate Executive Journal*, XII (1861–62), 148, 172; *U. S. Official Register, 1863*, p. 517.

[86] *U. S. Senate Executive Journal*, XIII (1862–64), 13, 112; *U. S. Official Register, 1863*, p. 38.

[87] *U. S. Senate Executive Journal*, XII (1861–62), 69, 154.

[88] Hay, *Lincoln and the Civil War in the Diaries and Letters of John Hay*, ed. by Dennett, p. 177.

Lincoln groups were attempting to postpone the National Convention until September. Of the four delegates at large selected to represent Pennsylvania at Baltimore—Simon Cameron, Alexander K. McClure, Morrow B. Lowry, and W. W. Ketcham [89]—three had received of the bounty of Lincoln. Cameron, of course, had received the Secretaryship of War and later the mission to St. Petersburg. McClure had been appointed Assistant Adjutant General by the President.[90] Ketcham had earlier received from Lincoln a federal judgeship in Nebraska Territory.[91] Morton McMichael, editor of the Philadelphia *North American* and beneficiary of much advertising patronage from the Lincoln administration, was selected as a delegate to Baltimore.[92] After the convention adjourned Cameron was able to send good news to the White House, the President's private secretary John Hay making this notation: "April 28, 1864. . . . A despatch just rec'd from Cameron stating that the Harrisburg [convention] had elected Lincoln delegates to Baltimore properly instructed." [93]

Subsequently in district conventions regular delegates were chosen to represent the Keystone State at Baltimore, to supplement the four delegates at large. An unusually large percentage of Lincoln's appointees appear among them, including, besides Bergner, Cornelius A. Walborn, postmaster in Philadelphia; H. Jones Brooke, commissary of subsistance with the rank of major; James H. Campbell, recently chosen as minister to Sweden; Levi Kauffman, Collector of Internal Revenue for the Fifteenth Pennsylvania District; Edward Scull, Collector of Internal Revenue for the Sixteenth Pennsylvania District; Edward G. Fahnstock, paymaster in the Army; and Henry Johnson, storekeeper in the medical department of the Army.[94] Under the circumstances the Chase men must have known that the huge Pennsylvania delegation was certain to vote for Lincoln's renomination.

[89] Proceedings of this convention printed in Philadelphia *North American and United States Gazette,* April 29, 1864.

[90] *U. S. Senate Executive Journal,* XIII (1862–64), 61, 199.

[91] *Ibid.,* pp. 277, 282.

[92] Philadelphia *North American and United States Gazette,* April 29, 1864.

[93] Hay, *Lincoln and the Civil War in the Diaries and Letters of John Hay,* ed. by Dennett, p. 177.

[94] C. W. Johnson, *The First Three Republican National Conventions . . . 1856, 1860 and 1864,* pp. 250–51; *U. S. Official Register, 1863,* pp. 38, 602; *U. S. Senate Executive Journal,* XIII (1862–64), 14, 34, 112, 147, 375, 415, 507, 550.

Next to Pennsylvania and third largest of the states in convention votes was Ohio, with 42.

Those who held high positions under Lincoln were determined that the Chase movement must be halted in the Secretary's home state. In March, 1864, Postmaster General Montgomery Blair, loyal to Lincoln, and hating Chase intensely, wrote a confidential letter to Edwin Cowles, postmaster of Cleveland and editor of the Cleveland *Leader*. In this communication the Postmaster General enclosed a copy of an anti-Chase speech by his brother, Frank Blair, in Congress on February 27, with the request that Cowles print it in the *Leader*.[95] In this speech Blair had made a virulent attack upon the Treasury Department's trade regulations for occupied areas in the South, charging inefficiency and corruption and asking for a Congressional inquiry.[96] At almost the same time another Lincoln appointee to an important place was utilizing his office to combat the Chase movement in the latter's home state. He was Robert F. Paine, United States Attorney for the Northern District of Ohio, who engineered a Grand Jury attack on Richard C. Parsons, one of the most active Chase workers in the Buckeye State.[97]

The Republicans of Ohio met in state convention in Columbus on May 25 (1864). The convention was called to order by William Dennison, former governor of the state and four months later to join Lincoln's Cabinet as Postmaster General.

One of the dominating figures at the Ohio convention and ranking second to Dennison was John A. Bingham.[98] Having failed of reëlection to Congress, Bingham had been cared for by Lincoln in the form of an appointment as Judge Advocate, with the rank of major, for the Department of the Susquehanna.[99] The Ohio conclave selected four delegates at large to the Baltimore Convention, leaving the regular delegates to be selected by district conven-

[95] R. C. Parsons to Chase, March 7, 1864 (Confidential), Chase Papers, Library of Congress.

[96] *Congressional Globe*, 38th Cong., 1 sess., *Appendix*, pp. 46–51; W. E. Smith, *The Francis Preston Blair Family in Politics*, II, 256–60.

[97] R. C. Parsons to Chase, March 7, 1864 (Confidential), Chase Papers, Library of Congress.

[98] Cincinnati *Daily Commercial*, May 27, 1864.

[99] For Bingham, see Philadelphia *Inquirer*, Jan. 14, 1864; *U. S. Senate Executive Journal*, XIII (1862–64), 360, 370. Also Thomas D. McCormick's sketch of Bingham in *Dictionary of American Biography*, II, 277.

tions. Lincoln was endorsed for another term in the White House in the following resolution:

Resolved, That the loyal instinct of the people of Ohio, in demanding the re-election of Abraham Lincoln to the Presidency, illustrates the highest wisdom; and that, in obedience to it, this Convention cordially recommends to the Union National Convention his renomination.[100]

Chase had to be content with the following:

Resolved, That with just pride we proclaim the fact, that in the Cabinet and in the councils of the nation the ability, fidelity and patriotism of Ohio has been manifested.[101]

The Chase men were furious over the refusal of the Lincolnites to recognize Chase by name in the resolutions adopted. Charged the pro-Chase Cincinnati *Commercial:*

The Union State Convention for 1864 has passed into history. . . . If any disturbing element existed, the adroit management of experienced politicians, who shaped its course, and marked out its line of action, effectually suppressed it. . . .

But the men and women of that day will wonder that a convention of the loyal men of Ohio met and adjourned without recognizing in some marked manner the services to his country of Ohio's most distinguished citizen, the Honorable Salmon P. Chase. What had Mr. Chase done, they will ask, that the people of his own State should fail to make mention, by resolution or otherwise, of his name? We may as well put the facts on record for the benefit of posterity.

Upon the appointment of the Committee on Resolutions, it was moved and carried that all resolutions should be submitted to the committee, without debate and acted upon by them. When the committee was in session, and while the resolutions were yet in embryo, M. P. Gaddis, of the second District, offered the following for consideration:

"*Resolved,* That Ohio regards, with proud approval, her distinguished citizen, Salmon P. Chase, who, during the most gigantic civil war ever known, has so controlled and directed the finances of the nation, as to supply the necessities of the contest, sustain the credit of the Government and preserve a healthful condition of the currency and business of the people."

[100] Cincinnati *Daily Gazette,* May 26, 1864.   [101] *Ibid.*

Mr. Gaddis supported the resolution in an earnest speech. C. K. Watson from the Ninth District opposed it, as did the Hon. John A. Bingham of the Sixteenth District. . . . Mr. E. Archibald, of the Fifteenth District, opposed it. . . .

The fact is, that there is a shoal of office-seekers hereabouts [in Columbus] today, who are watching for the crumbs from the master's table. . . . There are aspirants for Congress, who expect Administration favor, and who will solicit Executive patronage for those actively supporting their claims, and they dare not so much as wag their tongues without first soliciting leave to do so. There be [sic] fellows here, and they were on that committee [on Resolutions], who will tag at the White House with unwearying importunity for consulships, postmasterships, and Heaven only knows what, whose refusal to vote for this complimentary resolution to Mr. Chase was based on grounds of the lowest self-interest.[102]

Among the Ohio delegates selected who had received or were to receive jobs or Army commissions of a noncombatant nature from Lincoln were William Dennison, E. P. Fyffe, Chambers Baird, and John A. Hunter.[103] Dennison, as noted, was soon to receive from Lincoln a Cabinet post—that of Postmaster General.[104] Fyffe became a colonel in the reserve corps;[105] Baird and Hunter each received an appointment as paymaster in the Army.[106]

Illinois with 32 votes ranked fourth largest at the National Convention.

Much of the spade work for the Republican or "Union" state convention in Lincoln's home state seems to have been done by Ebenezer Peck,[107] whom Lincoln had appointed Judge of the United States Court of Claims. In Illinois, David L. Phillips, United States Marshal for the Southern District of Illinois with headquarters at Springfield, had taken the lead in issuing the "call" for the convention to meet at Springfield on May 25. Notifying Senator Lyman Trumbull of this fact he observed: "All goes well. The Union Leagues may cause us some little trouble . . .

[102] Cincinnati *Daily Commercial*, May 27, 1864.
[103] C. W. Johnson, *The First Three Republican National Conventions . . . 1856, 1860 and 1864*, pp. 251-52.
[104] See p. 277.
[105] *U. S. Senate Executive Journal*, XIII (1862-64), 604, 637.
[106] *U. S. Senate Executive Journal*, XIII (1862-64), 76, 147, 375, 415.
[107] Hay, *Lincoln and the Civil War in the Diaries and Letters of John Hay*, ed. by Dennett, p. 145.

but nothing serious. . . ."[108] The convention met on the appointed day in the Illinois state capital and adopted resolutions praising the Lincoln administration. One resolution adopted resolved that "our delegates to Baltimore are hereby instructed to use all honorable means to secure his renomination, and to vote as a unit upon all questions which may arise in that Convention . . . ."[109] Burton C. Cook was selected as a delegate at large and chairman of the delegation.[110] Cook had a voice in distributing the federal patronage in Illinois.[111] Among the other delegates chosen to represent the state at Baltimore were John H. Bryant and Wilson Shaffer.[112] Bryant held the position of Collector of Internal Revenue for the Fifth Illinois District.[113] Shaffer had received from Lincoln a commission as colonel of volunteers.[114] It was apparent that Lincoln would go into the Baltimore Convention with the solid support of his home state.

Another north central state, Indiana, ranked next to its neighbor Illinois in the number of convention delegates. It had 26 votes.

Indiana Republicans—they were now called "Unionists"—were to hold their state convention at Indianapolis on February 23, 1864, for the purpose of renominating Governor Oliver P. Morton and selecting delegates to Baltimore. One of Chase's field agents in the Hoosier State reported from Indianapolis to the Secretary of the Treasury on February 5:

I hold a commission from you, as Assistant Special Agent of the Treasury Department, and assigned to duty in the Cairo district. . . .

Many of Mr. Lincoln's appointees are working with great industry to have him nominated at the coming State Convention, and it is reported several agents have been out here for that purpose. Gov. Morton and many other politicians are opposing any such action by the State Convention as being premature, and impolitic.[115]

[108] D. L. Phillips to Trumbull, March 20, 23, 1864, Trumbull Papers.
[109] Springfield *Daily Illinois State Journal,* May 26, 1864.
[110] *Ibid.*   [111] B. C. Cook to Trumbull, Feb. 13, 1864, Trumbull Papers.
[112] Springfield *Daily Illinois State Journal,* May 26, 1864.
[113] *U. S. Senate Executive Journal,* XIII (1862–64), 17, 113; *U. S. Official Register, 1863,* p. 40.
[114] *U. S. Senate Executive Journal,* XII (1861–62), 423, 433.
[115] B. F. Tuttle to Chase, Feb. 5, 1864, Chase Papers, Library of Congress.

Governor Morton—who despite Lincoln's generosity to him in federal appointments was at odds with the President—opposed the injection of national issues into the state convention on the ground that it would jeopardize the state ticket.[116] But the Lincoln office-holders were determined that a Lincoln endorsement should be forthcoming. John D. Defrees, former editor of the Indianapolis *Journal* and then Superintendent of Public Printing by appointment of Lincoln, writing from Washington to his friend Richard W. Thompson, who had been made a Provost Marshal for Indiana and who was also a Lincoln appointee, insisted: "The right sort of resolution must be adopted." [117] And Secretary of the Interior John P. Usher, also a Hoosier, wrote Thompson to the same effect.[118] Throughout Indiana other federal officeholders—"serving their country at prices ranging from $3,500 to $600 per annum," charged the chief Democratic organ in Indiana [119]—were operating for Lincoln in the county conventions which were selecting delegates to the state convention in Indianapolis.[120]

On February 23 the state convention met in Indianapolis. Superintendent of Public Printing Defrees journeyed all the way from Washington to work among the delegates.[121] Provost Marshal Thompson was also active in the plan to secure an endorsement of Lincoln for renomination.[122] Only five of the eleven district conventions had instructed their delegates with regard to the presidency and each of these had directed that no indorsement of a presidential candidate should be made. Immediately after the selection of a temporary president and secretary and before there was opportunity to proceed with the selection of a permanent organization, Lincoln's friend, Cyrus M. Allen, stepped quickly to the platform and introduced two resolutions to be considered

116 D. V. Smith, *Chase and Civil War Politics*, p. 111.

117 John D. Defrees to R. W. Thompson, Feb. 2, 1864, in Harbison, "Indiana Republicans and the Re-Election of President Lincoln," *Indiana Magazine of History*, XXXIV (March, 1938), 52 n.

118 *Ibid.*   119 Indianapolis *Daily State Sentinel*, Feb. 18, 1864.   120 *Ibid.*

121 The Democratic newspaper, the Indianapolis *Daily State Sentinel*, May 28, 1864, charged that Defrees was one of those who was "sent out as agents to control Conventions and Legislatures in the interests of Mr. Lincoln," declaring that Defrees was one "office-holder" who operated "at Indianapolis, on the 23d February last."

122 Harbison, "Indiana Republicans and the Re-Election of President Lincoln," *Indiana Magazine of History*, XXXIV (March, 1938), 53.

as one. The first was an endorsement of President Lincoln and the war and the second renominated Governor Morton. Allen had scarcely finished before pandemonium burst forth.

In the meantime and while Allen was still speaking, Alexander Metzger, a Chase man, had made his way to the platform and handed a paper to the presiding officer, who, noting its contents, held it in his hand. It was a counter resolution, drawn by the Germans of Indiana, to frustrate any effort that might be made to instruct the delegates to the Baltimore Convention. The Metzger resolution was ruled out of order, the Allen proposal put to a vote and declared adopted, though, so far as is known, the nays were not called for. The majority of the delegates, instructed to vote for Morton, could not have voted against the resolution endorsing Lincoln for a second presidential term without violating their instructions. The pro-Chase men were taken so suddenly by surprise that they were helpless to do anything to stem the Lincoln machine, thus permitting the convention, not even yet regularly organized, to bind the Hoosier State for Lincoln.[123] The report of one Chase worker to the Secretary of the Treasury indicates that the Chase men at the Indianapolis Convention were caught napping:

The late efforts made by the appointees and agents sent here by Mr. Lincoln succeeded yesterday in convention, by getting the within Resolutions unanimously adopted. But not in a very creditable manner. The delegates from several of the Districts were opposed to giving any expression whatever, for the next candidate for the Presidency. The friends of Mr. Lincoln, after using every means to have his name presented fairly before the convention, found the opposition was too great, consequently they resorted to the following plan. Before a *temporary* organization was hardly made, one Cyrus Allen who desires the favor of Mr. Lincoln, and who is a *personal,* as well as *political* enemy of Gov. Morton, presented the resolution in order to get it through, on the popularity of the Gov., which proved a success. The resolution could not have passed the convention without an overwhelming opposition but for the *enthusiasm* for, and *popularity* of Morton. The course they pursued was altogether without the knowledge, consent, or approval of the Gov.[124]

[123] D. V. Smith, *Chase and Civil War Politics,* pp. 120–22.
[124] B. F. Tuttle to Chase, Feb. 24, 1864, Chase Papers.

Among the delegates or alternates chosen to represent Indiana at Baltimore were James L. Yater, William M. Dunn, and Silas Colgrove.[125] Lincoln had given to Yater the position of Collector of Internal Revenue for the Fourth Indiana District.[126] Dunn had received the noncombatant military post of Judge Advocate, with the rank of major.[127] Lincoln nominated Colgrove for brigadier general of volunteers, but the Senate refused to confirm him.[128]

Ranking closely after Indiana in the number of convention votes was Massachusetts, with 24. The Massachusetts state Republican convention met in Boston on May 19, 1864, for the purpose of choosing delegates to the Baltimore Convention. Wendell Phillips, radical antislavery reformer, severe critic of the Lincoln administration, and with little taste for the ways of the practical politician, proved a thorn in the side of the Lincolnites. A resolution presented by G. M. Brooks, of Haverhill, that the assembled body cannot "knowingly vote for any man as delegate to the Baltimore convention who will not vote for Abraham Lincoln as candidate for the presidency" particularly roused his ire. For nearly an hour Phillips held the floor against this resolution. When the Lincoln-dominated committee on resolutions reported the platform, the last resolution of which declared that Lincoln's achievements entitled him to continued support, Phillips returned to the attack and moved that it be recommitted, with instructions to retain the reference to his (Lincoln's) past services and to strike out the recommendation for his reëlection. This motion was rejected by a large majority.[129] With evident desire to punish the Confederate "rebels" and to prevent the federal officeholders in the conquered parts of the seceded states from aiding Lincoln in his quest for renomination, Phillips then offered the following resolution: "*Resolved*, that in the opinion of this convention neither Tennessee, Mississippi, Arkansas, Louisiana, Florida, North or South Carolina, is in such condition as to be entitled to a repre-

125 C. W. Johnson, *The First Three Republican National Conventions . . . 1856, 1860 and 1864*, p. 252.

126 *U. S. Official Register, 1863*, p. 40; *U. S. Senate Executive Journal*, XIII (1862–64), 16, 113.

127 *U. S. Senate Executive Journal*, XIII (1862–64), 278, 309.

128 *Ibid.*, pp. 391, 392.   129 Worcester *Daily Spy*, May 20, 1864.

sentation in the convention at Baltimore." [130] In supporting this resolution Phillips charged that movements were afoot to secure representation at the Baltimore Convention from states which were in no condition to have a voice in the selection of a presidential candidate. John Z. Goodrich, Collector of Customs of the Port of Boston, a staunch defender of Lincoln, quickly met the challenge by stating that under the terms of the call for the National Convention, no state could be represented at Baltimore which had no representation in Congress. Thereupon the Phillips motion was rejected. All of the recommendations of the committee on resolutions were adopted, including the endorsement of Lincoln.[131]

The delegates and alternates finally chosen to represent Massachusetts in Baltimore included several federal employees holding office by grace of Lincoln. Among them (all originally appointed by the President) were William Whiting, George S. Boutwell, Charles F. Swift, Charles R. Train, and George O. Brastow.[132] At the time Whiting was Solicitor of the War Department; [133] Boutwell, United States Commissioner of Internal Revenue; [134] Swift, Collector of Customs of the Barnstable District; [135] Train, Assistant Adjutant General with the rank of captain; [136] and Brastow, paymaster in the Army.[137]

Tied for seventh place in the size of the convention vote were the two border states, Kentucky and Missouri, each with 22. The Kentucky Unionists met in state convention in Louisville on May 25. They, too, selected a delegation to the Baltimore Convention that included men who had received federal appointments from Lincoln, among them George D. Blakey, William C. Goodloe, and Green Clay Smith.[138] Blakey had received from Lincoln the Collectorship of Internal Revenue of the First Kentucky District; [139] Goodloe, an assistant adjutant generalship with the rank of captain; [140] and Smith, a brigadier generalship of volunteers.[141]

[130] Worcester *Daily Spy*, May 20, 1864.   [131] *Ibid.*
[132] *Ibid.*, June 2, 1864.   [133] *U. S. Official Register, 1863*, p. 126.
[134] *U. S. Senate Executive Journal*, XII (1861–62), 401, 403.
[135] *Ibid.*, pp. 89, 154; *U. S. Official Register, 1863*, p. 65.
[136] *U. S. Senate Executive Journal*, XIII (1862–64), 384, 550.
[137] *Ibid.*, pp. 67, 145.
[138] Frankfort (Kentucky) *Tri-Weekly Commonwealth*, May 27, 1864.
[139] *U. S. Senate Executive Journal*, XIII (1862–64), 15, 112.
[140] *Ibid.*, pp. 357, 439.   [141] *Ibid.*, XII (1861–62), 338, 340.

Moreover, another Kentucky delegate selected to go to Baltimore on the pro-Lincoln delegation was the conservative James Speed,[142] subsequently to be taken into the Cabinet by Lincoln as Attorney General.[143]

Lincoln was unable to secure control of the Missouri delegation, its votes going to General Grant.[144] The votes of the delegations from the seven most populous states, however, were sufficient to renominate him for a second term. To these should be added small Connecticut, the first state to select its delegates, and in whose state convention federal officeholders were active in picking a pro-Lincoln delegation. Even in some southern states—states held largely by Confederates and technically in insurrection and without representation in Congress—conventions were held, as Wendell Phillips had foreseen, in which Lincoln's appointees participated and in which delegations to Baltimore favorable to Lincoln's renomination were selected. Such, for example, were Louisiana and Florida.

Governor Michael Hahn, elected first free-state governor of Louisiana by aid of Lincoln's patronage, threw his influence and the support of his organ, the New Orleans *True Delta*, to Lincoln. "Hahn's paper, the 'True Delta,' is out for Lincoln, as I supposed it would be," [145] wrote one federal officeholder in New Orleans. It was on May 16, 1864, in the Louisiana metropolis that a "Lincoln Convention" was held to select delegates to the Baltimore Convention. Cuthbert Bullitt, Acting Collector of the Port of New Orleans, was chairman. The convention declared for Lincoln's renomination and reëlection and selected fourteen delegates. At least four of the principal delegates had received appointments from Lincoln: Bullitt was Acting Collector; B. Rush Plumly was also in the Customs service; Max Bonzano was Direct Tax Commissioner for Louisiana; and Edward H. Durell was Judge of the United States District Court for the Eastern District of

142 Frankfort (Kentucky) *Tri-Weekly Commonwealth*, May 27, 1864.
143 Springer, "James Speed, the Attorney General, 1864–1866," *The Filson Club History Quarterly*, XI (1937), 169.
144 Barclay, "The Liberal Republican Movement in Missouri," *The Missouri Historical Review*, XX (Oct., 1925), 9.
145 George S. Dennison (Collector of Customs of the Port of New Orleans) to Chase (Private), March 5, 1864, Chase Papers, Library of Congress.

Louisiana.[146] The delegation left for Baltimore solidly for Lincoln,[147] and Lincoln's secretary, John Hay, greeting them as they passed through Washington, made the notation: "June 5 [1864]. . . . Cuthbert Bullitt is here with Louisiana in his trousers pocket." [148]

John Hay, perhaps more than any other person, paved the way for Florida to send pro-Lincoln delegates to Baltimore.

In 1862 the Unionist forces had gained a foothold on the east coast of seceded Florida, and Lincoln had appointed three direct tax commissioners in October of that year, among whom was Lyman D. Stickney. In September, 1863, Stickney had visited Washington, and it was reported in the press that he had come to petition the President, in the name of Florida's loyal citizens, to send a large military force into the state to rescue it from Confederate rule. To what extent Stickney influenced Lincoln to attempt the political reorganization of Florida is problematical; however, it is not without significance that Lincoln manifested a keen interest in Florida from the time of Stickney's visit.[149] Lincoln's critics almost immediately asserted, and not without some truth, that his southern political program was designed primarily to obtain votes for himself in the nominating convention and the ensuing national election.[150] That the President sincerely desired to bring Florida back into its old place in the Union is unquestionable, but it seems equally true that he was not averse to having the state represented in the Baltimore Convention. Unknown to Secretary of War Stanton and Secretary of the Navy Welles,

[146] New Orleans *Times,* May 17, 1864. For Bullitt: *U. S. Official Register, 1863,* p. 95. For Plumly: "Diary and Correspondence of Salmon P. Chase," *Annual Report,* American Historical Association, II (1902); *U. S. Official Register, 1861,* p. 62. For Bonzano: *U. S. Senate Executive Journal,* XIII (1862–64), 558, 636. For Durell: "Hon. Edward Henry Durell," *The Granite Monthly,* April, 1888, p. 119; *The National Cyclopaedia of American Biography,* XIII, 121; *U. S. Official Register, 1863,* p. 268.

[147] George S. Dennison to Chase (Private), May 31, 1864, Chase Papers, Library of Congress.

[148] Hay, *Lincoln and the Civil War in the Diaries and Letters of John Hay,* ed. by Dennett, p. 185. For a criticism of the practice of sending Louisiana delegates to Baltimore when only a small percentage of the people of the state could express their views, see Cincinnati *Daily Gazette,* May 24, 1864.

[149] W. W. Davis, *The Civil War and Reconstruction in Florida,* pp. 272-73. For Stickney, see *U. S. Senate Executive Journal,* XII (1861–62), 405.

[150] W. W. Davis, *The Civil War and Reconstruction in Florida,* p. 273.

he sent a military expedition to the state. Moreover, he sent John Hay to Florida, presumably to aid in reconstructing a "loyal" state government.[151] "The President's private Secretary, Mr. John Hay," wrote Tax Commissioner Stickney, "has arrived, commissioned by the President to proceed at once to enroll Florida votes." [152] James Gordon Bennett, still critical of Lincoln, charged in his New York *Herald:*

It is rumored that the expedition was intended simply for the purpose of securing the election of three Lincoln delegates to the National Convention, and of John Hay to Congress. The cost of the operation to the government is estimated at about one million of dollars.[153]

Hay's efforts to reconstruct Florida proved futile. What his specific work was, is still a mystery. Hay's biographer concludes: "It is quite probable that, if the conditions in Florida had turned out to be as the President had expected, there would have been Florida delegates at Baltimore, and that they would have been instructed for Lincoln." [154] As a matter of fact Florida did send six pro-Lincoln delegates to Baltimore. Two of these were federal officeholders appointed by Lincoln—John S. Sammis, a Direct Tax Commissioner, and Philip Fraser, Judge of the United States District Court for the Northern District of Florida.[155]

As the date for the Baltimore Convention approached, the scene shifted to Washington. Many delegates on their way to Baltimore in late May and early June lingered in the national capital to prepare the way for Lincoln's renomination. From Washington one critic of the administration wrote home: "But sad as is the picture, who will have the hardihood to speak the truth in reference to the unprincipled wire-working now going on here, by the officeholders, for the purpose of securing the election of the President

[151] *Ibid.,* pp. 274–76; Tyler Dennett, *John Hay: From Poetry to Politics,* pp. 43–44. For the political motives of the military expedition, see Jones (Major General, C.S.A.), "The Battle of Olustee, or Ocean Pond, Florida," in Johnson and Buel (eds.), *Battles and Leaders of the Civil War,* IV, 76.

[152] L. D. Stickney to Chase (Private), Jan. 26, 1864, Chase Papers, Library of Congress.

[153] New York *Herald,* Feb. 23, 1864.

[154] Dennett, *John Hay,* pp. 42–43.

[155] W. W. Davis, *The Civil War and Reconstruction in Florida,* pp. 272 n., 295, 295 n.; *U. S. Senate Executive Journal,* XII (1861–62), 355, 405.

for a second term?" [156] And one Chase man, downcast at the now totally deflated Chase boom, wrote dejectedly to the Secretary of the Treasury: "I am further convinced that the Baltimore Convention has been packed in favor of Mr. Lincoln and that he has used the power and patronage of his office." [157]

On June 7 (1864) the Union National Convention assembled in Baltimore. One of Lincoln's private secretaries, John G. Nicolay, was on the ground to give advice to the delegates.[158] The renomination of his chief was, of course, a foregone conclusion, but apparently there was rivalry among the delegates as to who should place Lincoln in nomination. Wrote one observer:

The struggle between several of the delegates to be recognized as the mover of the nomination of Lincoln was ridiculous in the extreme. Charges were made that others were trying to cheat others out of the motion. The whole affair looked like a struggle of delegates to obtain capital upon which they could lay claim upon Old Abe for a fat office.[159]

The only state delegation which did not vote unanimously for Lincoln's renomination was that of Missouri. The Frémonts, Butlers, and Chases had been outdistanced.[160]

A lively contest ensued for the vice-presidential nomination between Vice President Hannibal Hamlin, Governor Andrew Johnson, of Tennessee, Daniel S. Dickinson, of New York, and others. Johnson, an erstwhile Democrat, was finally chosen as Lincoln's running mate to bolster the claims of the Republicans that the organization to which they belonged was a Union party. Well might Secretary of the Navy Welles comment: "Except the nomination of Vice-President, the whole proceedings were a matter of course." [161] Welles might have added that federal officeholders under Lincoln had aided materially in effecting such a result.

[156] Indianapolis *Daily State Sentinel*, May 28, 1864.
[157] A. B. Mullett to Chase, May 16, 1864, Chase Papers, Library of Congress.
[158] Carr, *My Day and Generation*, pp. 140–43; John G. Nicolay to John Hay, June 5, 1864, in *Complete Works of Abraham Lincoln*, X, 114.
[159] New York *Herald*, June 9, 1864.
[160] Thomas S. Barclay, "The Liberal Republican Movement in Missouri," *The Missouri Historical Review*, XX (Oct., 1925), 9.
[161] *Diary of Gideon Welles*, II, 47.

Chapter X

PATRONAGE AND THE ELECTION
OF 1864

LINCOLN was renominated. The Chase boom had collapsed entirely, largely because of the deft management of adroit Lincoln officeholders. The Baltimore Convention adjourned *sine die* on June 8, 1864. The delegates departed for home to put into motion the machinery for Lincoln's reëlection. En route many stopped off at Washington to pay homage to the President.

On June 9 returning delegates took virtual possession of Washington, swarming about hotels and forming processions to the White House, where, from eleven in the morning until late at night, Lincoln was busily engaged in receiving their felicitations. Delegation after delegation was presented to him, sometimes singly, sometimes *en masse*.[1] "It seemed that every man who was in the Convention," wrote one observer as he watched the continual arrivals and departures from the Executive Mansion, "was anxious to convey the idea that he was particularly instrumental in procuring the nomination at Baltimore, and especially glad that Lincoln was nominated." [2] This same critical eyewitness continued:

Everybody had something pleasant to say, and Mr. Lincoln endeavored to say something pleasant to everybody, so that everybody should go home entirely satisfied that such an impression had been made on the President-that-is-to-be, that at least a first class mission, if not the vacant seat in the Cabinet, under the sixth resolution of the platform, had been secured.[3]

The next day witnessed a repetition of the scenes of the previous day. Again Lincoln was continuously occupied in giving audiences.[4] "Numbers of delegates," ran the news from Washington, "are still anxiously awaiting their turn to present themselves be-

[1] New York *Herald*, June 10, 1864. [2] *Ibid.*
[3] *Ibid.* [4] New York *Herald*, June 11, 1864.

fore the throne and claim a share of the benefits expected to be
derived from the work done at Baltimore." [5] Some, of course, had
already been rewarded with patronage favors. Among these were
several members of the new Union National Committee chosen at
Baltimore to carry on until 1868, notably Nehemiah D. Sperry,
of Connecticut; Cuthbert Bullitt, of Louisiana; John D. Defrees,
of Indiana; Erasmus D. Shattuck, of Oregon; Archibald W.
Campbell, of West Virginia; William H. H. Waters, of Nebraska
Territory; and William H. Wallace, of Idaho Territory.[6] Sperry
was postmaster in New Haven; [7] Bullitt was Acting Collector of
Customs of the Port of New Orleans; [8] Defrees was Superintendent
of Public Printing; [9] Shattuck had been United States Attorney
for Oregon; [10] Campbell was postmaster in Wheeling; [11] Waters
was Receiver of Public Moneys for the sale of lands for the
Nebraska District; [12] and Wallace was governor of Idaho Territory.[13]

For chairman of the Union National Committee, the Baltimore
Convention selected Henry J. Raymond, New York member and
editor of the New York *Times*.[14] Raymond's selection was a distinct victory for the conservative or Seward-Weed forces over the
radical or pro-Chase faction among the Empire State Republicans. Raymond's *Times* was the New York City mouthpiece of the
Weed interest and as such opposed the radical anti-Lincoln organs,
Greeley's New York *Tribune* and William Cullen Bryant's New
York *Evening Post*.[15] Hardly had the Baltimore Convention ad-

[5] New York *Herald*, June 11, 1864.
[6] New York *Times*, June 9, 1864; New York *Herald*, June 9, 1864.
[7] Atwater, *History of the City of New Haven to the Present Time*, pp. 381–82;
Biographical Directory of the American Congress, 1774–1927, pp. 1554–55; *U. S.
Official Register, 1863*, p. 315.
[8] "Diary and Correspondence of Salmon P. Chase," *Annual Report*, American
Historical Association, II (1902), 382; *U. S. Official Register, 1863*, p. 95.
[9] *Ibid.*, p. 124.
[10] *U. S. Senate Executive Journal*, XII (1861–62), 113, 154; *ibid.*, XIII (1862–64),
2, 11.
[11] *U. S. Official Register, 1863*, p. 673.
[12] *U. S. Senate Executive Journal*, XIII (1862–64), 368, 390; *U. S. Official Register, 1863*, p. 101.
[13] Lanman, *Biographical Annals of the Civil Government of the United States*,
p. 447; *U. S. Official Register, 1863*, p. 14.
[14] New York *Times*, June 9, 1864.
[15] Brummer, *Political History of New York State during the Period of the Civil
War*, pp. 17–19; Fahrney, *Horace Greeley and the Tribune in the Civil War*,
chaps. i–vi.

journed than a lively press battle opened between Weed and his opponents.

Fundamentally this battle was merely part of that larger struggle between the radicals and conservatives which so frequently threatened to split the Republican party and which was always a nightmare to Lincoln. For months prior to the Baltimore Convention, the radicals, as we have seen, had hoped that in some way Lincoln might be sidetracked and a candidate more to their liking nominated. In this they were doomed to disappointment. The Chase movement, so pleasing to them and so promising at first, ultimately bogged down and finally became so hopeless that both Chase and his radical followers knew that it was futile to continue in the race.[16] Nor did the presidential "boomlets" launched for Ben Butler and John C. Frémont make much headway. True, a combination of radical Germans from St. Louis and abolitionists from New England, who were backing Frémont, succeeded in calling a convention to meet in Cleveland in late May. This convention, attended by delegates representing every shade of opposition to the Lincoln administration, nominated the Pathfinder for the presidency and adopted a platform uncompromisingly radical.[17]

Strange as it may seem, the Frémont candidacy failed to win expected support. Many radical leaders were apathetic; they feared that at best it was a political venture which might divide the Republicans and thus pave the way for a Democratic victory. Such an eventuality would, in their opinion, be catastrophic. In view of the strong popular feeling for Lincoln, they knew that Frémont had no chance of endorsement at Baltimore, packed as it was with federal officeholders. It would be far better, they reasoned, to accept a nomination they could not prevent, though it be more galling to them than to support the Frémont ticket. Moreover, though Lincoln be nominated there was still hope that his Cabinet might be cleansed of conservatives. Consequently Frémont as a presidential candidate was forgotten for the time being, and at the Baltimore Convention the radicals devoted their attention primarily to the platform. The sixth resolution of this document read as follows: ". . . we deem it essential to the general welfare that harmony should prevail in our National Councils,

[16] T. H. Williams, *Lincoln and the Radicals*, p. 312.
[17] *Ibid.*, p. 314; Nevins, *Frémont: The West's Greatest Adventurer*, II, 658–59.

and we regard as worthy of public confidence and official trust those only who cordially endorse the principles proclaimed in these resolutions, and which should characterize the administration of the government." The principles alluded to were emancipation, the use of Negro soldiers, and the vigorous, unrelenting prosecution of the war.[18]

The immediate occasion for Weed's declaration of war was an editorial appearing in the pro-Chase radical New York *Evening Post*, insinuating that the sixth resolution adopted at Baltimore was aimed at Weed's partner and protégé, Secretary of State Seward. The Convention, the editorial insisted, had to all intents and purposes advised Lincoln to sever his relationship with Weed, Cameron and Company, and to rid himself for all time of Seward and Postmaster General Blair. Weed in his Albany *Evening Journal* stoutly defended Seward, and the *Post* countered by assailing Weed as the father of the lobby at Albany. Weed, striking back, accused one of the *Post's* proprietors, Henderson, of corruption in the office of naval agent. Soon after Lincoln removed Henderson.

Not content, Weed then trained his editorial guns upon another of Chase's friends, former Mayor George Opdyke, accusing the latter of making "more money by secret partnerships in army cloth, blankets, clothing and gun contracts than any fifty sharpers." Thoroughly aroused, Weed next fired a broadside at Greeley's *Tribune*, accusing its associates and correspondents of making money out of government contracts and also of supplying the Confederates through the New York Custom House—a thrust at Chase's friends, Collector Barney and Surveyor of the Port Rufus F. Andrews. He also charged Greeley himself with being financially interested in cotton speculations. Greeley lost no time in publishing a curious editorial card in which he made a sweeping denial:

I, Horace Greeley, do solemnly declare . . . that I have been a partner in *no* contract, job, or undertaking of any sort, with, to, or for the Government of this State, or of the United States, since Abraham Lincoln became President; and that, except by the publication of advertisements in the *Tribune* at the usual and regular prices charged to advertisers generally, I have made no dollar of money

18 C. W. Johnson, *The First Three Republican National Conventions . . . 1856, 1860 and 1864*, p. 226; New York *Independent*, June 20, 1864.

out of either or any Government, whether by job, contract, commission or otherwise.[19]

This statement merely added fuel to the fire and a whole series of charges, denials, and countercharges were exchanged between Weed and his enemies, many of the latter being the personal and political friends of Chase. Raymond joined in the attack on Greeley. The Weed faction in New York, with which Raymond was affiliated, claimed to be the especial friends of Lincoln, and this was substantially correct. Nevertheless, Lincoln endeavored to conciliate the two factions in the Empire State. But it was impossible. Warfare broke out again in the closing days of June, when Chase insisted on the appointment of his man to succeed John J. Cisco as Assistant Treasurer at New York.[20]

In naming Cisco's successor, Lincoln desired someone unobjectionable to the pro-Weed faction and therefore consulted United States Senator Edwin D. Morgan, who for eight years had served as chairman of the Republican National Committee. This was also in keeping with Lincoln's policy of consulting with Republican members of the United States Senate on major appointments for their respective states. Chase insisted that the Assistant Treasurership go to Maunsell B. Field. Morgan protested, and suggested Richard M. Blatchford, Dudley S. Gregory, or Thomas Hillhouse. Lincoln submitted these three names to Chase.[21] "It will really oblige me," the President wrote Chase, "if you will make choice among these three, or any other man that Senators Morgan and Harris will be satisfied with, and send me a nomination for him." [22] This brief note was followed on the same day (June 28, 1864) by a long letter in which Lincoln indicated the annoyance to which patronage subjects any American President.

. . . As the proverb goes, no man knows so well where the shoe pinches as he who wears it. I do not think Mr. Field a very proper man for the place, but I would trust your judgment and forego this were the greater difficulty out of the way. Much as I personally like

[19] New York *Tribune,* June 25, 1864.
[20] Brummer, *Political History of New York State during the Period of the Civil War,* pp. 384–92.
[21] Lincoln to Chase, June 28, 1864, in *Complete Works of Abraham Lincoln,* X, 137–38.
[22] *Ibid.,* p. 138.

Mr. Barney [Collector of Customs of the Port of New York], it has been a great burden to me to retain him in his place when nearly all our friends in New York were directly or indirectly urging his removal. Then the appointment of Judge Hogeboom [a Chase follower] to be general appraiser brought me to, and has ever since kept me at, the verge of open revolt. Now the appointment of Mr. Field would precipitate me in it unless Senator Morgan and those feeling as he does, could be brought to concur in it. Strained as I always am at this point, I do not think I can make this appointment in the direction of still greater strain.[23]

Chase had relieved the tension temporarily by inducing Cisco to withdraw his resignation, but after receiving the President's second letter, cleverly intimating that Field's appointment might necessitate the removal of Barney from the lucrative New York Collectorship, he promptly tendered his resignation. That Chase felt it was a choice between Seward and himself is clear from his letter to Jay Cooke under date of July 1, part of which follows:

When I found that upon the question of Mr. Cisco's successor I was not to be left free from all other considerations except simple fidelity to the general cause and fitness for the place, but was expected to take into consideration questions of local politics, I felt myself constrained to make it a turning point. I had been so much embarrassed and injured by the standing of one of the members of the cabinet that I could not feel at all safe unless that office was in hands on which I could personally depend. The President differed with me and I tendered my resignation, and he thought it best to accept it. I could not remain and feel that my department was really under my own control or that I had any real ability to serve the country in it. The President did not see the matter as I did.[24]

If Lincoln was surprised, Chase must have been more so after reading Lincoln's reply. "Your resignation of the office of Secretary of the Treasury sent me yesterday is accepted," the President's brief note to Chase read. "Of all I have said in commendation of your ability and fidelity I have nothing to unsay; and yet you and I have reached a point of mutual embarrassment in our official relations which it seems cannot be overcome or longer sus-

[23] Lincoln to Chase (Private), June 28, 1864, in *ibid.*, pp. 138–39.
[24] Chase to Jay Cooke, July 1, 1864, in Oberholtzer, *Jay Cooke, Financier of the Civil War*, I, 421.

tained consistently with the public service." [25] It is doubtful if
Chase had intended to resign. The correspondence preserved does
not indicate a strong desire on his part to leave the Cabinet.[26] In
all probability he meant his letter of resignation to the President
to be, as on previous occasions, the beginning of a correspondence
which would finally terminate in a soothing letter from Lincoln with
concessions.

Lincoln's acceptance of Chase's resignation rekindled the anger
of the radicals. They could find no words strong enough to con-
demn Seward and Weed, who, they asserted, had long schemed to
force Chase out. Nor did they spare Blair, who, on more than one
occasion, had directed savage thrusts at the Treasury head. Chase's
departure from the Cabinet was to them added evidence of Lincoln's weakness and of his deplorable willingness to yield to Seward.[27]

Chase's resignation was most pleasing to the Seward-Weed
forces. "Heaven be praised for this gleam of sunshine," [28] Weed
exclaimed in the Albany *Evening Journal*. And in the same vein
the Albany editor-politician subsequently wrote:

The despotism from which I felt . . . a sense of relief, is well understood at Washington. Mr. Chase, in the exercise of the vast patronage of his department, was a despot. . . . The organization of the
New York Custom House is a living, burning disgrace. Mr. Chase
had evidence of infamous practices but refused to act. . . . He has
known for three years that gross custom house dishonesty exists at
Oswego. But he gave "no sign." . . . There are other and grave
reasons for rejoicing that Mr. Chase is out of the Cabinet. He ab-

[25] Lincoln to Chase, June 30, 1864, in *Complete Works of Abraham Lincoln*, X,
140–41. Also E. D. Webster to Weed, June 30, 1864, Weed Papers, Library of
Congress.
[26] For instance, Chase wrote his friend Cameron: "My feelings of going out of
office are of a mixed sort—regret that I leave great work half over—satisfaction in
relief from cares & manifold annoyances. Sometimes one of these feelings predom-
inates—sometimes the other." See Chase to Cameron, July 11, 1864, Cameron Papers,
Library of Congress. See also Chase to Nettie Chase, July 5, 1864, Chase Papers,
Library of Congress.
[27] See Schuckers, *The Life and Public Services of Salmon Portland Chase*, pp.
505–9; M. B. Field, *Memories of Many Men and of Some Women*, pp. 296 ff.; H. C.
Fahnestock to Jay Cooke, June 30, 1864, in Oberholtzer, *Jay Cooke*, I, 420–21; New
York *Herald*, June 30, 1864.
[28] Albany *Evening Journal*, June 30, 1864, in Brummer, *Political History of New
York State during the Period of the Civil War*, p. 393.

olitionized that Cabinet; and if our government should be overthrown and our Union severed he, as the chief of a class to which Sumner, Greeley, Phillips, *etc., etc.,* belong, will be responsible for the calamity.[29]

As Chase's successor to head the Treasury Department Lincoln decided on former Governor David Tod, of Ohio. Opposition developed at once, for Tod was reputed to be without financial experience and, even worse, was said to be a "Blairish Republican." [30] A struggle loomed in the Senate, but before it could take action in confirming or rejecting him Tod telegraphed his refusal. Finally Lincoln chose United States Senator William Pitt Fessenden, of Maine, as his new Secretary of the Treasury. Fessenden, Chairman of the Senate Finance Committee, had a keen knowledge of the government's fiscal policies, but felt more at home in the Senate than in an executive position. It was with reluctance, therefore, that he resigned his Senate seat and joined Lincoln's official family.[31]

One consideration that prompted Lincoln to invite Fessenden into the Cabinet was said to have been his desire to create a Senate vacancy from Maine for Vice President Hamlin, with whose disappointment over his defeat for renomination at Baltimore the President sympathized.[32] On appointing Fessenden to head the Treasury, Lincoln penned the following:

Executive Mansion, Washington, July 4, 1864.

I have today said to Hon. W. P. Fessenden, on his assuming the office of Secretary of the Treasury, that I will keep no person in office in his department, against his express will, so long as I choose to continue him; and he has said to me, that in filling vacancies he will strive to give his willing consent to my wishes in cases when I

[29] Brummer, *Political History of New York State during the Period of the Civil War,* p. 393.

[30] H. C. Fahnestock to Jay Cooke, June 30, 1864, in Oberholtzer, *Jay Cooke,* I, 420.

[31] Francis Fessenden, *Life and Public Services of William Pitt Fessenden,* I, 294–95, 315–16; "Diary of Edward Bates, 1859–1866," ed. by Howard K. Beale, *Annual Report,* American Historical Association, IV (1930), p. 381; M. B. Field, *Memories of Many Men and of Some Women,* 298–99; J. P. Smith, *History of the Republican Party in Ohio,* I, 44.

[32] Samuel Wilkinson to Greeley, Nov. 29 (1864), Horace Greeley Papers, New York Public Library.

may let him know that I have such wishes. It is, and will be, my sincere desire, not only to advance the public interest by giving him complete control of the department, but also to make his position agreeable to him.

In Cabinet my view is that in questions affecting the whole country there should be full and frequent consultations, and that nothing should be done particularly affecting any department without consultation with the head of that department.[33]

Some Republican leaders urged Fessenden to remove Chase's special Treasury subordinates who had aided the Chase boom. But the new Secretary of the Treasury wisely allowed the personnel of his department to remain as it was, lest wholesale removals cause a wider schism in the party during the critical campaign.[34]

Chase was not the only member of Lincoln's original Cabinet whose fall was occasioned by the exigencies of the presidential campaign of 1864. Postmaster General Montgomery Blair, who, unlike Chase, prided himself on his conservatism, was also virtually forced out. The circumstances leading to his resignation not only illumine the factional character of the Republican party, but indicate the terrific pressure to which Lincoln was subjected during the summer months of 1864.

In retrospect it is apparent that, aside from his officeholders' maneuvers, Lincoln's nomination at Baltimore was possible partly because of his popularity with the rank and file of his party and partly because the anti-Lincoln factions could not agree on a candidate sufficiently strong to defeat the President for the nomination. Even after the Convention had adjourned, an undertone of hostility to Lincoln prevailed and it was openly rumored that plans were afoot to force him to withdraw and to nominate another.[35] "Many, many have not yet made up their minds to go for him, and what is still worse, to go for his Sewards and Blairs," recorded Count Gurowski. "It is . . . probable that a new Republican convention may be called, and a new nomination made." [36]

[33] Hertz, *Abraham Lincoln: A New Portrait*, II, 935–36.
[34] See the New York *Herald*, Sept. 29, Oct. 8, 1864; Salter, *The Life of James W. Grimes*, p. 265.
[35] Chandler, *Memoir of Governor Andrew*, pp. 111–14; *Diary of Adam Gurowski*, pp. 69, 91, 258; T. H. Williams, *Lincoln and the Radicals*, p. 316.
[36] *Diary of Adam Gurowski*, pp. 251–52.

Gurowski made this entry in his diary on June 9. By July popular discontent with the Lincoln administration was assuming alarming proportions: The resignation of Chase; the mounting price of gold, with the evident lack of national credit; the failure to recruit the army by volunteers, making necessary Lincoln's call for half a million men by draft; the open Copperhead rebellion in Ohio led by Clement Vallandigham; and the rabid attacks printed in the New York *World* combined to swell the opposition to flood tide.[37]

To make matters worse, the radicals and Lincoln clashed over the issue of reconstruction. Distrusting the President's program, the radicals formulated a plan of their own for the readmission of the disloyal states. This plan was embodied in the famous Wade-Davis bill, which squarely challenged Lincoln by taking entire control of reconstruction out of the hands of the President and placing it under the jurisdiction of Congress. Lincoln met the challenge by pocket-vetoing the measure and issuing a proclamation in which he tersely set forth the reasons for his action.[38]

Enraged to the point of fury, the more extreme radicals now determined to destroy Lincoln politically by forcing him to withdraw from the head of the ticket.[39] The moment for such a move seemed opportune. Outwardly at least the military prospects were far from promising; Grant, in his march on Richmond, had been slowed up and his army had suffered terrific toll. The Treasury was empty and the country was war-weary. Rumors that Lincoln was about to make peace by recognizing the Confederacy gained credence in two unofficial peace moves—one of which centered around the eccentric Greeley and the other around J. R. Gilmore, Greeley's friend, and Colonel Jaquess, a former Methodist College president.[40]

While these peace feelers—both fiascos—were still fresh in the

[37] Dudley, "The Election of 1864," *The Mississippi Valley Historical Review*, XVIII (March, 1932), 510.

[38] *Complete Works of Abraham Lincoln*, IX, 120–41; *Congressional Globe*, 38th Cong., 1st sess., pp. 3448–49; Richardson (comp.), *Messages and Papers of the Presidents, 1789–1897*, VI, 222–23.

[39] T. H. Williams, *Lincoln and the Radicals*, pp. 321–25.

[40] Kirkland, *The Peacemakers of 1864*, pp. 68, 73, 76, 96; J. R. Gilmore, *Personal Recollections of Abraham Lincoln and the Conflict*, II, 664–66; *Complete Works of Abraham Lincoln*, IX, 186–92; T. H. Williams, *Lincoln and the Radicals*, pp. 322–23.

public mind the radicals, guided by Wade and Chandler, struck what they hoped would be the fatal blow. It took the form of the Wade-Davis Manifesto—probably the most scathing attack ever made upon Lincoln within his own party.[41] Not only was Lincoln's reconstruction policy denounced, but he was portrayed as a would-be dictator. His proclamation, explaining the pocket-veto of the Wade-Davis bill, was labeled as "a studied outrage on the legislative authority of the people." It was high time that the President understood "that our support is of a cause and not of a man," that the authority of Congress is paramount and must be respected; that the whole body of the Union men of Congress will not submit to be impeached by him of rash and unconstitutional legislation; and if he wishes our support he must confine himself to his executive duties—to obey and to execute, not make the laws to suppress by arms armed rebellion, and leave political reorganization to Congress. "If the supporters of the government fail to insist on this they become responsible for the usurpations which they fail to rebuke. . . . Let them consider the remedy for these usurpations, and, having found it, fearlessly execute it."

The reaction to the manifesto was a varied one. The elated radicals were certain that a revulsion of popular feeling against Lincoln would so weaken him that he would be forced to withdraw. The conservatives were filled with dismay and apprehension. Even Henry J. Raymond, Republican National Chairman and editor of the New York *Times*, the President's leading newspaper champion, was most pessimistic about Lincoln's chances.[42] And on August 23 Lincoln himself wrote this memorandum, requesting each of his Cabinet members to sign it:

This morning, as for some days past, it seems exceedingly probable that this administration will not be reëlected. Then it will be my duty to so cooperate with the President-elect as to save the Union between the election and the inauguration; as he will have secured

[41] New York *Tribune*, Aug. 5, 1864; Hosmer, *Outcome of the Civil War, 1863–1865*, pp. 139–41; E. G. Scott, *Reconstruction during the Civil War*, pp. 412–25; Sandburg, *Abraham Lincoln: The War Years*, III, 135–36.

[42] H. J. Raymond to Cameron, Aug. 19, 21, 1864, Cameron Papers, Library of Congress. See also H. H. Elliott to Welles, Aug. 31, 1864, Welles Papers, Library of Congress. The sagacious politician Thurlow Weed told the President in mid-August that his reëlection was an impossibility.

his election on such ground that he cannot possibly save it afterward.[43]

The Democrats were jubilant, for they felt that the manifesto had driven such a deep wedge into their opponents that all hope of unity had been destroyed. But Wade, Henry Winter Davis, Chandler, and the other Jacobins soon realized that the manifesto had not borne the desired results. It failed both to detach the masses from Lincoln and to win hearty press approval even among some of the radicals. "We have read with pain the manifesto of Messrs. Wade and Winter Davis," ran an editorial in *Harper's Weekly*, "not because of its envenomed hostility to the President, but because of its ill-tempered spirit, which proves conclusively the unfitness of either of the gentlemen for grave counselors in time of national peril. . . . To charge him with extraordinary and dangerous assumptions of power, is childish. . . . It is simply impossible to make the American people believe that the President is a wily despot, or a political gambler." [44] Both the New York *Evening Post* and the New York *Tribune* were lukewarm in their approval,[45] while the Chicago *Tribune* as well as other radical western papers were bitter in condemnation of Wade and Davis.[46] As for the conservative Republican press, no words could be found strong enough to denounce both the manifesto and its authors.[47]

The attitude of the country toward the manifesto lifted the spirits of the Lincolnites. Before the month of August had run its course the New York *Herald* predicted that in due time all the bolters would be back in Lincoln's camp:

Whatever they say now, we venture to predict that Wade and his tail; and Wendell Phillips and his tail; and Weed, Barney, Chase and their tails; and Winter Davis, Raymond, Opdyke and Forney who have no tails; will all make tracks for Old Abe's plantation, and will soon be found crowing and blowing, and vowing and writhing, and swearing and stumping . . . declaring that he and he alone, is

[43] Memorandum, Aug. 23, 1864, printed in *Complete Works of Abraham Lincoln*, X, 203–4. The original is in possession of the Manuscript Division of the Library of Congress.

[44] *Harper's Weekly*, Aug., 1864.

[45] New York *Evening Post*, Aug. 8, 1864; New York *Tribune*, Aug. 5, 1864.

[46] Chicago *Tribune*, Aug. 11, 1864; T. H. Williams, *Lincoln and the Radicals*, p. 326.

[47] *Ibid.*, pp. 325 ff.

the hope of the nation, the bugaboo of Jeff Davis, the first of Conservatives, the best of Abolitionists, the purest of patriots, the most gullible of mankind, the easiest President to manage, and the person especially predestined and foreordained by Providence to carry on the war, free the niggers, and give all the faithful a fair share of the spoils.[48]

This statement proved to be prophetic. The task of rallying all factions of the Republican party to the Lincoln standard was greatly eased by the nomination of General McClellan by the Democrats for the presidency and by the clever work of none other than that radical spokesman, Senator Zachariah Chandler, of Michigan.

Though diametrically opposed to Lincoln in matters of major policy, Chandler's personal relations with the President were reasonably pleasant, largely, in all probability, because Lincoln allowed him to control "a generous share of the federal patronage" in his state.[49] Moreover, the Michigan Senator was a wise enough politician to realize that a divided Republican party would undoubtedly mean the election of McClellan on a peace platform drafted by the hated Copperhead, Vallandigham. Bad as were Lincoln and Seward, they were to be preferred a thousand times over to weaklings and traitors.[50] Consequently, he quickly made up his mind to restore harmony within the Republican ranks for the duration of the campaign at least. Chandler's plan of procedure involved the withdrawal of Frémont from the presidential race and the retirement from the Cabinet of Postmaster General Montgomery Blair.

Radical dislike of the Blairs was genuine and of long standing. Postmaster General Blair, the radicals asserted not without truth, had used his Cabinet office—just as his brother Frank has used his seat in Congress—to oppose the Chase boom.[51] Unquestionably, too, the radicals resented the Blair influence over Lincoln:

48 New York *Herald*, Aug. 24, 1864.

49 Harbison, "Zachariah Chandler's Part in the Reëlection of Abraham Lincoln," *The Mississippi Valley Historical Review*, XXII (Sept., 1935), 269.

50 This feeling appears to have been widely prevalent among the radicals. For instance, we find Alphonso Taft writing Senator Benjamin F. Wade, of Ohio: "Bad as Lincoln's associates are, McClellan's are worse." See Alphonso Taft to Wade, Sept. 8, 1864, Benjamin F. Wade Papers, Library of Congress.

51 D. V. Smith, *Chase and Civil War Politics*, pp. 74, 133–39; Harbison, "Indiana Republicans and the Re-Election of President Lincoln," *Indiana Magazine of History*, XXXIV (March, 1938), 56. In Sept., 1863, for example, Frank Blair in a

As for Postmaster General Blair, and Major General Blair, and the old man of all, Lieutenant General Blair, in assuming to take into their own especial charge and keeping Old Abe, his administration, the war, the negro question, the division of the spoils, the State of Missouri, the State of Maryland, and the Presidential succession in the bargain, they were cutting it entirely too fat, and they have, or very soon will have, their reward. They have domineered it over Old Abe to his heart's content, until he has become afraid of them. . . .[52]

Efforts on the part of the radicals to induce Lincoln to oust the Postmaster General gathered momentum during the first half of 1864. Finally, the militant radical Congressman Thaddeus Stevens, of Pennsylvania, went to Lincoln in person and urged the President to get rid of Blair. That Lincoln refused to accede to the request is evident in his written reply to the Pennsylvania Congressman:

Mr. Stevens, I am very sorry to be compelled to deny your request to make such a promise. If I were even myself inclined to make it, I have no right to do so. What right have I to promise you to remove Mr. Blair, and not make a similar promise to any other gentleman of influence to remove any other member of my cabinet whom he does not happen to like? The Republican party wisely or unwisely has made me their nominee for President, without asking any such pledge at my hands. Is it proper that you should demand it, representing only a portion of that great party? Has it come to this, that the voters of this country are asked to elect a man to be President—to be Executive—to administer the Government, and yet that this man is to have no will or discretion of his own? Am I to be the mere puppet of power? To have my constitutional advisers selected beforehand, to be told I must do this, or leave that undone? It would be degrading to my manhood to consent to any such bargain—I was about to say it is equally degrading to your manhood to ask it.

I confess that I desire to be reelected. God knows I do not want the labor and responsibility of the office for another four years. But I have the common pride of humanity to wish my past four years' administration endorsed; and besides I honestly believe that I can

public letter to Lincoln denounced Chase as a political Judas. See W. E. Smith, *The Francis Preston Blair Family in Politics,* II, 165–67.

[52] New York *Herald,* June 12, 1864.

better serve the nation in its need and peril than any new man could possibly do. I want to finish this job of putting down the rebellion, and restoring peace and prosperity to the country. But I would have the courage to refuse the office rather than to accept on such disgraceful terms as really not to be President after I am elected.[53]

The above letter from Lincoln to Stevens was in sharp contrast to his note to the Pennsylvania Congressman, dated August 10, 1864, regarding the removal of a lesser federal officeholder:

If Hon. Thaddeus Stevens will say in writing, on this paper, that he wishes this man discharged, I will discharge him.

Aug. 10, 1864.   Abraham Lincoln.[54]

Quite as antagonistic toward Montgomery Blair as Thaddeus Stevens was General Frémont, for the Postmaster General's brother, Frank Blair, had been the spearhead in the successful effort to induce Lincoln to depose Frémont as military commander of the Department of the West back in 1861, when Missouri became too small to hold both the Pathfinder and Frank Blair. At that time, it will be recalled, the Postmaster General and his brother-in-law, Quartermaster General Meigs, had been sent to St. Louis by Lincoln to investigate Frémont's allegedly inefficient, incompetent and extravagant military administration and had returned to Washington with a report highly unfavorable to Frémont. Soon after the President had removed Frémont from his command. It was not difficult, therefore, to account for the bad blood existing between Frémont and the Blairs.[55] The two sponsors of the radical or Congressional plan of reconstruction, Wade and Davis, were also avowed enemies of Montgomery Blair—particularly Davis, who for several years had struggled with Blair over federal patronage and political control in Maryland and who had been deeply disappointed in his aspirations for a Cabinet seat when Lincoln appointed Blair instead of himself as Postmaster General.

Such was the situation with which Chandler had to contend.

[53] Reply of Lincoln to Thaddeus Stevens, undated, in Hertz, *Abraham Lincoln: A New Portrait*, II, 947.

[54] *Ibid.*, p. 938.

[55] Cf. Nevins, *Frémont: Pathmarker of the West*, chap. xxx, "Frémont *vs.* Blair and Lincoln."

As his initial step Chandler journeyed to Ashtabula, Ohio, and saw Senator Wade. The latter agreed to withdraw his opposition to Lincoln's reëlection if the President would remove Montgomery Blair from the Cabinet. On his return East, Chandler obtained similar assurances from other radical leaders on condition that Blair be ousted. At the White House Chandler extracted from Lincoln a promise to remove Blair if Frémont would withdraw from the race. Whatever his feelings in this matter may have been, Lincoln apparently saw his chances of reëlection jeopardized and the Union further imperiled if the radicals were not appeased. Chandler then visited Henry Winter Davis in Baltimore and secured Davis's concurrence in supporting Lincoln if his traditional archrival, Blair, was driven out of the Cabinet. Finally, Chandler went to New York, where, after strenuous argument, he finally persuaded Frémont to withdraw from the presidential race.

The long-accepted thesis that Frémont was induced to withdraw from the race only after being assured of Blair's removal from the Cabinet and the promise of either restoration to high Army command or to a place in Lincoln's official family is no longer tenable. While the evidence to the contrary is not entirely conclusive, it is sufficient to indicate that Frémont, to his credit, refused to be a party to any bargain. He withdrew, he said, out of "consideration for the Republican party" and for what it stood. "In respect to Mr. Lincoln," he declared, ". . . I consider that his administration has been politically, militarily, and financially a failure, and that its continuance is a cause of regret for the country." He withdrew not because he approved Lincoln's policies, he continued, but because the Democrats proposed to restore the Union with slavery. As between Lincoln and McClellan, he regarded the former as the lesser of two evils.[56] Frémont's letter of withdrawal was published on September 22. On the next day, the twenty-third, Lincoln requested Blair to send in his resignation:

[56] This account is based on: Harbison, "Zachariah Chandler's Part in the Reëlection of Abraham Lincoln," *The Mississippi Valley Historical Review,* XXII (Sept., 1935), 267–76; Letter of Charles Moore in "Zachariah Chandler in Lincoln's Second Campaign," *The Century Magazine,* XXVIII, New Series (July, 1895), pp. 476–77; Buell, "Zachariah Chandler," *Magazine of Western History,* IV (1886), 437–38; Wilson, "New Light on the Lincoln-Blair-Frémont 'Bargain' of 1864," *The American Historical Review,* XLII (Oct., 1936), 71–78. On the question of whether Frémont was a party to a bargain, consult especially Nevins, *Frémont: Pathmarker of the West,* pp. 578–81.

Executive Mansion,
Washington, September 23, 1864.

Hon. Montgomery Blair.

My Dear Sir:—You have generously said to me, more than once, that whenever your resignation could be a relief to me, it was at my disposal. The time has come. You very well know that this proceeds from no dissatisfaction of mine with you personally or officially. Your uniform kindness has been unsurpassed by that of any other friend, and while it is true that the war does not so greatly add to the difficulties of your department as to those of some others, it is yet much to say, as I most truly can, that in the three years and a half during which you have administered the General Post-Office, I remember no single complaint against you in connection therewith.

Yours, as ever,
A. Lincoln.[57]

Blair immediately complied by sending Lincoln a letter of resignation.[58]

Blair's downfall was the occasion for wild rejoicing on the part of the radicals. The elated Chandler was almost inundated with congratulations. "When I saw it announced in the papers that he [Blair] was to leave," wrote Wade, "I knew it was brought about by your labor. I also noticed in my last Tribune that you had done what would entitle you to the gratitude of the nation. I don't see how you effected it, except it was by working on Old Abe's fears, for I know him well enough to know that he would not have done it because all his political friends desired it; he was governed by a fear that Blair's continuing might affect his reelection. . . . But he has gone and I thank God for it, I only wish Seward was with him. It *is* a great victory and you may well be proud of it." [59] Chandler himself celebrated by getting drunk.[60]

As Blair's successor to head the Post Office Department Lincoln selected former Governor William Dennison, of Ohio.[61] Dennison

[57] Lincoln to Montgomery Blair, Sept. 23, 1864, in Raymond, *The Life and Public Services of Abraham Lincoln,* p. 602.

[58] Reply of Blair to Lincoln, *ibid.*

[59] Harbison, "Zachariah Chandler's Part in the Reëlection of Abraham Lincoln," *The Mississippi Valley Historical Review,* XXII (Sept., 1935), 275.

[60] J. K. Herbert to Butler (Confidential), Sept. 26, 1864, in *Private and Official Correspondence of Gen. Benjamin F. Butler during the Period of the Civil War,* V, 168.

[61] Reid, *Ohio in the War,* pp. 1017–19.

was a loyal Lincoln man. Not only did he preside over the Ohio state Union convention held at Columbus in May (1864), which selected a pro-Lincoln delegation to the Baltimore convention from the Buckeye State,[62] but he likewise served as Permanent Chairman of the Baltimore Convention which renominated Lincoln the following June.[63] One of his main supporters in persuading Lincoln to appoint Dennison Postmaster General was United States Supreme Court Justice Noah H. Swayne.[64] Swayne, as we have already noted, had been aided in his appointment to the nation's highest court by Dennison's efforts. At the time of selection as Postmaster General, Dennison was on the stump for Lincoln in southeastern Ohio—"preaching the gospel to the heathen," [65] as Mrs. Dennison expressed it.

In addition to Chase and Montgomery Blair, another important head fell during the President's campaign for reëlection—that of Hiram Barney, Collector of Customs of the Port of New York.

Much of the opposition to Barney revolved about the belief of the Seward-Weed faction of New York Republicans that he was too favorable to the Chase interest, even though Barney had been a deep source of disappointment to the Chase men by his failure to utilize the Custom House patronage to further Chase's presidential boom. Weed had succeeded in controlling A. N. Palmer, confidential secretary to Barney, and, in the opinion of many persons, the Collector *de facto*, and thus exerted much control over the Custom House employees. But suddenly in January (1864) Weed saw his grip slipping when Palmer was arrested, charged with malfeasance in office.[66] Immediately Weed and his lieutenants started agitating for removal of Barney as collector; in the lobby of the state legislature they solicited signatures to petitions asking the removal of Barney and the appointment of Postmaster Abram Wakeman, of New York City, as collector.[67] "When he [Weed] found that

[62] Columbus *Daily Ohio State Journal*, May 26, 1864.

[63] New York *Daily Tribune*, June 8, 1864.

[64] N. H. Swayne to Montgomery Blair, Sept. 26, 1864, Francis Preston Blair Papers.

[65] *Ibid.* (Swayne was quoting Mrs. Dennison.)

[66] Palmer was charged with collusion with parties engaged in contraband trade with the Confederate states and of abusing his position in the Collector's office to further that trade. See New York *Herald*, Jan. 9, 1864.

[67] New York *Herald*, Jan. 9, 1864; George Opdyke to Chase, Jan. 15, 1864; R. Campbell to Chase, Jan. 19, 1864, Chase Papers, Library of Congress.

Palmer could not be saved, seeing that his own ascendancy in the C. H. [Custom House] was at an end, he turned upon Barney and the Wakeman movement is the result," [68] explained one New York Republican in a letter to Chase.

The whole situation was trying to Lincoln.[69] "I have felt considerable anxiety concerning the Custom House at New York," the President informed Chase. "Mr. Barney has suffered no abatement of my confidence in his honor and integrity; and yet I am convinced that he has ceased to be master of his position." [70] This was in January. In the midst of the campaign and with Chase, Barney's erstwhile champion, out of the Cabinet, the Seward-Weed forces renewed their drive to force Barney out and to persuade Lincoln to appoint Wakeman or Simeon Draper in his stead. In this connection the following communication of Charles S. Bartles, a Custom House employee, to United States Senator Trumbull is illuminating:

I have some important news to communicate to you. It is generally understood here . . . that Mr. Barney is to resign—and that either Mr. Simeon Draper, or Postmaster Wakeman is to be his successor. . . .

The Collector has had a great deal of opposition to encounter from those who should have been his most earnest supporters. Time and again during the present year have his Republican enemies gone to Washington, and told Mr. Lincoln that he was opposed to the election of the Baltimore nominees—an assertion I know to be *untrue*. And it now seems that these men have succeeded in inducing the President to give credence to their stories, and promise the appointment of either Mr. Wakeman or Mr. Draper. Both of these gentlemen are personal and political friends of Secretary Seward.[71]

Apparently Lincoln was impressed by the hazard of retaining so weak a leader as Barney in charge of the huge patronage-dispensing New York Custom House in the midst of his campaign for reëlection. Moreover, the President was now dependent largely on the Seward-Weed influence in carrying New York State. Lin-

[68] J. F. Bailey to Chase, Jan. 13, 1864, Chase Papers, Library of Congress.

[69] Lincoln to Chase, Jan. 11, 1864, in *Complete Works of Abraham Lincoln*, IX, 281.

[70] Lincoln to Chase, Feb. 12, 1864, in *ibid.*, X, 6.

[71] Charles S. Bartles to Trumbull (Personal), Sept. 1, 1864, Trumbull Papers. For the activity of Seward and Weed, see New York *World*, July 2, 1864.

coln, therefore, happily accepted Barney's resignation as collector
and appointed Simeon Draper as his successor.

Draper, friend and ally of Seward and Weed, had for long been
combating the Chase movement in New York and had been a pro-
Lincoln delegate to the Baltimore Convention.[72] Lincoln's opponents were quick to emphasize his possible motives in replacing
Barney with Draper. An anti-Lincoln New York journal commented: "Mr. Barney's . . . incompetency to distribute the patronage of the Custom-House and use the services of its officials to
aid the re-election of Mr. Lincoln were deemed a sufficient reason
for his removal. Mr. Barney's resignation was therefore procured,
and Mr. Simeon Draper, an abler politician, now reigns in his
stead." [73]

Lincoln lost no time in utilizing the Custom House. On the day
following the accession of the new Collector, the President instructed Draper to aid the New Jersey leader, former Governor
W. A. Newell.[74] Utmost excitement prevailed among Custom
House employees, who feared that their official heads were by no
means safe under the new regime.[75] There were, indeed, some removals of deputy collectors, weighers, inspectors, and debenture
officers immediately upon the appointment of Draper.[76] These few
dismissals seem to have been sufficient to bring all into line. "It is
remarkable to note," one New York reporter observed, "the change
which has taken place in the political sentiments of some of these
gentlemen within the last forty-eight hours—in fact, an anti-
Lincoln man could not be found in any of the departments yesterday." [77]

In the same month (September, 1864) Lincoln removed Surveyor of the Port Rufus F. Andrews, a pro-Chase man, and
appointed Postmaster Wakeman as his successor. Another Weed
lieutenant, James Kelly, was given the New York postmastership.[78] "Thus this important patronage, which Weed and his fol-

---

[72] Barnes, *Memoir of Thurlow Weed,* p. 251; S. Draper to Cameron, Feb. 20, 1864,
Cameron Papers; New York *Herald,* May 26, 1864.

[73] New York *World,* Sept. 9, 1864.

[74] Lincoln to Simeon Draper, Sept. 8, 1864, in Hertz, *Abraham Lincoln: A New
Portrait,* II, 943–44.

[75] New York *Herald,* Sept. 7, 1864.   [76] *Ibid.*   [77] *Ibid.*

[78] Brummer, *Political History of New York State during the Period of the Civil
War,* pp. 394–95.

lowers so long coveted," writes one New York historian, "was at last captured from his adversaries." [79] The appointment of Draper as collector, Wakeman as surveyor, and Kelly as postmaster of New York City indicated that Lincoln fully realized that the Seward-Weed faction of Republicans must be awarded more recognition if the Empire State was to be made secure for Lincoln in November.

There were other resignations from the federal service during the presidential contest of 1864—resignations consistent with a more vigorous campaign for Lincoln's reëlection. The President, now that Chase was out, let it be known that he would brook no treachery from those holding appointments under him. This was apparent in the case of Charles Gibson, whom Lincoln had in 1861 appointed Solicitor of the United States Court of Claims.[80] Gibson, finding it inconsistent with his principles to support Lincoln for reëlection, sent in his letter of resignation to Lincoln through James C. Welling, the clerk of the Court of Claims. Lincoln's tart reply to Gibson was communicated to Welling through one of his secretaries, John Hay. Hay's letter to Welling follows:

Executive Mansion,
Washington, July 25, 1864.

J. C. WELLING, ESQ. :—
According to the request contained in your note, I have placed Mr. Gibson's letter of resignation in the hands of the President. He has read the letter, and says he accepts the resignation, as he will be glad to do with any other, which may be tendered, as this is, for the purpose of taking an attitude of hostility against him.

He says he was not aware that he was so much indebted to Mr. Gibson for having accepted the office at first, not remembering that he ever pressed him to do so, or that he gave it otherwise than as usual, upon a request made on behalf of Mr. Gibson.

He thanks Mr. Gibson for his acknowledgment that he has been treated with personal kindness and consideration, and he says he knows of but two small drawbacks upon Mr. Gibson's right to still receive such treatment, one of which is that he could never learn of

---

[79] *Ibid.*, p. 395.
[80] "The Diary of Edward Bates, 1859–1866," ed. by Howard K. Beale, *Annual Report*, American Historical Association, IV (1930), 11 n.

his giving much attention to the duties of his office, and the other is this studied attempt of Mr. Gibson's to stab him.

I am, very truly,

Your obedient servant,

JOHN HAY.[81]

When Hay informed Welling that Lincoln would be glad to accept the resignation of any other officeholder who resigned for the purpose of embarrassing him, he undoubtedly expressed Lincoln's views accurately. Lincoln was also not averse to depriving of a voice in the federal patronage those members of Congress who had manifested hostility to his reëlection. This was evident in the case of Senator Pomeroy, of Kansas, one of the chief instigators of the ill-starred pro-Chase "Pomeroy Circular."[82] On one occasion John Hay noted in writing: "*May 14, 1864*. . . . Pomeroy has recently asked an audience of the President for the purpose of getting some offices. He is getting starved out during the last few months of dignified hostility and evidently wants to come down. He did not get any."[83]

If Lincoln "starved out" his enemies in Congress, he was careful to stand staunchly by his friends among the national legislators. During the campaign he became provoked if a federal officeholder attempted to use the patronage of his position to defeat for reelection an administration Member of Congress. This was apparent when he rebuked the postmaster at Philadelphia, Cornelius Walborn, who endeavored to induce his subordinates to defeat Representative William D. Kelley for renomination. Lincoln summoned Walborn to the White House.[84] Of the interview with him Lincoln made the following notation:

What I said to Postmaster of Philadelphia, June 20, 1864:

Complaint is made to me that you are using your official power to defeat Judge Kelley's renomination to Congress.

I am well satisfied with Judge Kelley as a member of Congress, and

[81] John Hay to J. C. Welling, July 25, 1864, in Raymond, *The Life and Public Services of Abraham Lincoln*, p. 564.

[82] Hay, *Lincoln and the Civil War in the Diaries and Letters of John Hay*, ed. by Dennett, p. 181 n.

[83] *Ibid.*, p. 181.

[84] Lincoln to C. A. Walborn (telegram), June 18, 1864, in *Complete Works of Abraham Lincoln*, X, 131.

I do not know that the man who might supplant him would be as satisfactory; but the correct principle, I think, is that all our friends should have absolute freedom of choice among our friends. My wish, therefore, is that you will do just as you think fit with your own suffrage in the case, and not constrain any of your subordinates to do other than he thinks fit with his.

This is precisely the rule I inculcated and adhered to on my part when a certain other nomination now recently made was being canvassed for.[85]

Apparently Postmaster Walborn was not guided too rigidly by Lincoln's directions, for soon Lincoln communicated to one of his Philadelphia supporters: "I am now told that, of the two or three hundred employees in the [Philadelphia] Post-office, not one of them is openly for Judge Kelley. This, if true, is not accidental."[86] Lincoln requested further: "Please tell the postmaster he must find a way to relieve me from the suspicion that he is not keeping his promise to me in good faith."[87] At this very time an identical case occurred in Chicago, whose postmaster, John L. Scripps, was persuading his subordinates to go against the renomination of Representative Isaac N. Arnold, an administration supporter. Lincoln, upon hearing that Scripps was using the patronage of the Chicago Post Office to combat Arnold, forwarded to Scripps the same instructions that he had given to Walborn.[88]

Still another instance in which Lincoln directed one of his appointees to cease opposing the reëlection of a Congressional administration supporter during the campaign of 1864 occurred when Representative George W. Julian, of Indiana, complained to him that his reëlection was endangered by the activities of Commissioner of Patents David P. Holloway, also a Hoosier. Holloway, editor of a Republican newspaper in Julian's Congressional district in Indiana, refused to recognize Julian as the regular party candidate for reëlection to Congress and kept the name of Julian's defeated competitor for the Republican nomination standing in his newspaper. Julian, incensed, went to Lincoln and asked that

[85] "Memorandum of an Interview with the Postmaster of Philadelphia," June 20, 1864, in *ibid.*, pp. 132–33.
[86] Lincoln to Morton McMichael (Private), Aug. 5, 1864, in *ibid.*, p. 182.
[87] *Ibid.*
[88] Lincoln to John L. Scripps, July 4, 20, 1864, in *ibid.*, pp. 141–42, 168.

Holloway be removed from the office of Commissioner of Patents.[89]
"Your nomination," Lincoln replied, according to Julian, "is as
binding on Republicans as mine, and you can rest assured that
Mr. Holloway shall support you, openly and unconditionally, or
lose his head." [90] Julian added that Lincoln called in Holloway and
directed that he refrain from opposing Julian. Reminisced Julian:
"It was perfectly evident that the business would now be attended
to, and in a few days my name was duly announced, and the work
of party insubordination ceased." [91]

In line with his policy of supporting for renomination and re-
election administration Republican Members of Congress during
the campaign of 1864, Lincoln staunchly backed Roscoe Conkling, who had served in Congress previously from the Utica, New
York, district. Wrote one commentator during the campaign:

It seems that Mr. Lincoln is determined to have a Congress elected
in his personal interest, and has been using his power and patronage
unsparingly to that end. Among others whom he had set his heart
upon having in the next House of Representatives is Mr. Roscoe
Conkling of this state, who was defeated in the convass two years
since by a small majority. Mr. Ward Hunt is Mr. Lincoln's special
agent in this matter, and he wrote his master it was essential that
two delegates to the nominating convention, Messrs. Kellogg and
Barber, should be secured for Conkling. . . .[92]

This statement was not without foundation, for Lincoln in a letter to Hunt had made it clear that he desired Conkling's nomination:

Executive Mansion,
Washington, Aug. 16, 1864.

HON. WARD HUNT.

MY DEAR SIR: Yours of the 9th inst. was duly received, and submitted
to Secretary Seward. He makes a response, which I herewith enclose
to you. I add for myself that I am for the regular nominee in all
cases, and that no one could be more satisfactory to me as the nominee in that district than Mr. Conkling. I do not mean to say there

---

[89] Statement of George W. Julian in Rice (ed.), *Reminiscences of Abraham Lincoln by Distinguished Men of His Time*, pp. 51–52.
[90] *Ibid.*, p. 52.   [91] *Ibid.*
[92] New York *World*, Sept. 29, 1864.

are not others as good as he in the district, but I think I know him to be at least good enough.

Yours truly,
A. LINCOLN.[93]

The press of the day reported that the above letter from Lincoln "was read at the convention. It secured Conkling's nomination." [94] The anti-Lincolnites were furious.[95] Conkling reciprocated Lincoln's support in his behalf. He declined an invitation to join in a movement to supersede Lincoln as the Republican presidential candidate. Moreover, six days after his nomination the Utica aspirant for Congress spoke for Lincoln's reëlection in Oneida county—denouncing the Confederacy, advocating a continuance of the war, and emphasizing that the nation's life and free institutions depended on the reëlection of Lincoln.[96]

Lincoln was not averse to offering a well paying position to an influential molder of public opinion if by so doing he could attract him to his support. His appointment of so many newspaper men to federal offices at the beginning of his administration indicated that he recognized the power of the press.[97] James Gordon Bennett, editor of the New York *Herald*, was still on the rampage against the administration during the critical summer of 1864.[98] It so happened that in the Pierce administration Bennett had sought in vain the post of Minister to France.[99] Now, in late September (1864), United States Senator James Harlan, of Iowa, close friend of Lincoln and head of the Republican Executive Congressional Committee which coöperated in the fight to reëlect

---

[93] Lincoln to Ward Hunt, Aug. 16, 1864, in A. R. Conkling, *The Life and Letters of Roscoe Conkling*, p. 199. This letter was also printed in New York *World*, Sept. 29, 1864.

[94] New York *World*, Sept. 29, 1863.

[95] *Ibid.* "This is certainly the most extraordinary step ever taken by a President of the United States. The use of patronage to carry a measure through Congress has been often suspected, but there is no case upon record where the direct action of the President himself is known to have induced unwilling members to support an administration measure. But here is an instance of where a President and his Secretary of State openly interfere in the action of a county convention to force a nominee of their own into the canvass. To insure a henchman in the House they corrupt the very fountains of political power. . . ."

[96] A. R. Conkling, *The Life and Letters of Roscoe Conkling*, pp. 200–203.

[97] See pp. 118–29.   [98] New York *Herald*, July 8, 9, 16, Aug. 18, Sept. 3, 1864.

[99] Nichols, *The Democratic Machine, 1850–1854*, p. 210.

Lincoln, suggested to the President's secretary, John Hay, and perhaps to Lincoln himself, that Bennett be given a foreign mission.[100] There is abundant evidence that during the campaign Lincoln, without even consulting his Cabinet, proffered the French mission to the *Herald* editor.[101] Moreover, there is another story— not entirely authenticated—that Lincoln, in order to secure Horace Greeley's support, offered the eccentric but able New York *Tribune* editor the Postmaster Generalship.[102]

The soldier vote was important too. Soon after General McClellan's nomination as the Democratic standard bearer, his principal New York backer penned the following: "The conviction now seems to be almost universal that no one but McClellan can control any large portion of the army vote in the field and at home: that he alone can prevent the use of the army by Mr. Lincoln." [103] The President's popularity with the troops of the Union Army was generally high. Nevertheless, minor federal officeholders under the administration were used to propagandize the Army, with the view of returning Lincoln to the White House for another term. This work consisted largely of distributing party documents to the soldiers. Nearly a million documents were distributed among the men in the field under the supervision of one particular officeholder.[104]

In the distribution of campaign documents among both the soldiers and the general public the "Union" (Republican) National Committee utilized the services of government employees. One Democratic critic in Washington complained:

[100] Hay, *Lincoln and the Civil War in the Letters and Diaries of John Hay,* ed. by Dennett, p. 215.

[101] Thurlow Weed to John Bigelow, April 26, 1865, in Bigelow, *Retrospections of an Active Life,* II, 520, 520 n.; McClure, *Abraham Lincoln and Men of War-Times,* pp. 80–82; New York *World,* March 17, 1865. Though Bennett declined the proffer, he was much flattered by it and became one of Lincoln's most appreciative friends and hearty supporters.

[102] Seitz, *Horce Greeley, Founder of the New York Tribune,* pp. 266–70; "Lincoln's Faith in Greeley," *The Magazine of History,* XL, No. 1 (1930), 4–8. The supporting evidence rests largely upon the account of D. S. Alexander, printed in the Aug. 3, 1921, issue of the Lyons, New York, *Republican* and is quoted at length by Seitz. The fact that the Sept. 6, 1864, issue of Greeley's *Tribune* did contain the editorial referred to by Alexander lends support to the story.

[103] Samuel M. L. Mitchell to Marble, Aug. 21, 1864, Manton Marble Papers. (Marble was editor of the Democratic New York *World.*)

[104] George T. Brown to Trumbull, Oct. 30, Nov. 5, 1864, Trumbull Papers.

The National Republican Committee have taken full possession of all the Capitol buildings, and the committee rooms of the Senate and House of Representatives are filled with clerks, busy in mailing Lincoln documents all over the loyal States.

One hundred of these clerks there employed, I am assured, have been detailed from the government department, and continue to draw their salaries while engaged in re-electing Abraham Lincoln. They neglect the business of the country, for which only they ought to be paid.

In addition to the clerks being taken from the departments for the purpose of assisting in the re-election of Lincoln, I have it from undoubted authority that arrangements have been made to send home all the clerks, at the rate of one-half cent a mile.

The Post Office Department, of course, is attending to the lion's share of this work. Eighty bags of mail matter, all containing Lincoln documents, are daily sent to Sherman's army.[105]

Lincoln, true to the then-accepted custom of presidential candidates, did not take the stump for his reëlection. However, on several occasions he addressed callers at the White House or spoke a few words to soldiers in the field, referring to the desirability of a Republican-Union victory in November, if the Union were to prevail. To troops of an Ohio regiment on their way home to vote in the October state election he said:

Soldiers:—I suppose you are going home to see your families and friends. For the services you have done in this great struggle in which we are engaged, I present you sincere thanks for myself and the country.

I almost always feel inclined, when I say any thing to soldiers, to impress upon them, in a few brief remarks, the importance of success in this contest. It is not merely for the day, but for all time to come, that we should perpetuate for our children's children that great and free government which we have enjoyed all our lives. I beg you to remember this, not merely for my sake, but for yours. I happen, temporarily, to occupy this big White House. I am a living witness that any of your children may look to come here as my father's child has. It is in order that each of you may have, through this free government which we have enjoyed, an open field and a fair chance for

[105] Indianapolis *Daily State Sentinel,* Oct. 12, 1864. On this point see also New York *World,* Sept. 23, 1864.

your industry, enterprise, and intelligence; that you may all have equal privileges in the race of life, with all its desirable human aspirations—it is for this that the struggle should be maintained, that we may not lose our birthrights, not only for one, but for two or three years, if necessary. The nation is worth fighting for to secure such an inestimable jewel.[106]

Lincoln did not attempt to manage the countless technical details of his campaign. To one he wrote: "Well, I cannot run the political machine; I have enough on my hands without *that*. It is the *people's* business—the election is in their hands." [107] The task of inducing the people to vote for Lincoln in November was entrusted to Henry J. Raymond, editor of the New York *Times*, who, in his official capacity as chairman of the Union National Committee, became Lincoln's campaign manager.

Early in the contest Raymond let it be known—indeed, he took it for granted—that those holding federal government positions under the Lincoln administration would be required to contribute to the campaign.[108] Already, in March, at least three Cabinet officers, Secretary of State Seward, Secretary of the Interior Usher, and Postmaster General Blair, had each contributed $500 to the party chest.[109] Accordingly, Raymond directed the collection of a campaign fund by assessing federal government employees in all departments. When in some cases officeholders refused to pay or obstructed the collection, Raymond requested and even insisted upon their removal. Pressure was brought upon Lincoln, who seems to have had full knowledge of this expedient and at least did nothing that served to discourage it.[110] Generally

[106] Hertz, *Abraham Lincoln: A New Portrait*, II, 941.   [107] *Loc. cit.*

[108] In July Raymond wrote Simon Cameron, who was conducting the campaign in Pennsylvania: "Does your State Committee expect to make *exclusive* assessments upon Federal office-holders within the state for purposes of the canvass, or is our Committee to go over the same ground?" See H. J. Raymond to Cameron, July 17, 1864, Cameron Papers.

[109] *Diary of Gideon Welles,* I, 534. "Judge Edmunds and Senator Lane called on me on Monday morning for funds. Showed me two papers, one with Seward's name for $500. On another was Blair's and Secretary Usher, each for $500, with some other names for like amount. Told them I disapproved of these levies on men in office, but would take the subject into consideration; I was not, however, prepared to act. Something should, perhaps, be contributed by men when great principles are involved, but these large individual subscriptions are not in all respects right or proper. Much of the money is wasted or absorbed by the electioneers."

[110] Cole, "Lincoln and the Presidential Election of 1864," *Transactions of the Illinois State Historical Society,* 1917, p. 134.

officeholders contributed in good spirit as part of their political responsibility, although at least one—Captain Melancthon Smith, Provost Marshal of the Second Illinois Congressional District— protested against payment of $67.40 assessment levied against him.[111]

The Post Office and the Custom House in New York City provided a convenient source of money for Raymond.[112] In late September a circular went out from the Union National Committee to all employees in the Custom House, assessing each "an average three per cent of their yearly pay" for campaign purposes.[113] The following was said to be a duplicate copy of the notice received by each of the Custom House personnel:

> Custom House,
> New York, September 30.
>
> *Sir:* The undersigned, having been authorized for the purpose, are prepared to receive the assessment made by the Union committees, and will be found at the basement room formerly occupied by the United States measurers, from 9 a.m. to 3 o'clock p.m., this day, and to-morrow.
>
> JOHN MARALIOUS.
> RICHARD WYNKOOP.[114]

From outside New York came a ready response to the appeal of the Union National Committee. W. C. Flagg, Collector of Internal Revenue for the Twelfth Illinois District, forwarded $50 to Chicago to be invested in documents.[115] William N. Grover, United States Attorney for the Eastern District of Missouri, sent a $200 contribution directly to the White House, and Lincoln's secretary, John Hay, forwarded part of the amount to Raymond with the following letter:

> *Executive Mansion*
> *Washington*, October 17, 1864
>
> *Confidential*
> MY DEAR MR. RAYMOND:
> My friend Mr. Wm N. Grover Esq. of St. Louis, U. S. District

---

111 Springfield *Illinois State Register,* Sept. 24, 1864, in *ibid.,* p. 134 n.

112 "Raymond walks into the Post Office and Custom House and collects his bills like one having authority." See New York *Herald,* Oct. 16, 1864.

113 New York *World,* Oct. 4, 1864.   114 *Ibid.*

115 W. C. Flagg to Trumbull, June 24, 1864, Trumbull Papers.

Attorney for East*n* Dist. of Missouri was recently taxed, among others, by Senator Lane's Western Committee, for $200.00. Mr. Grover, not recognizing the right of this Committee to make such assessments, refused to honor the draft, but sent to me the sum asked for in two different checks of $100.00 each, the first of which I gave to Senator Harlan here, and the second I enclose to you. He prefers to make his contributions thus voluntarily and to give them this destination, rather than the one demanded by the Western Branch Committee.

Please acknowledge receipt and oblige

Yours truly
JOHN HAY.[116]

There is some evidence that Raymond did not confine his fundraising appeal to federal officeholders. He seems to have turned also to those who had received government contracts for war supplies. In the opposition press of October, 1864, there appeared the following copy of a circular letter sent out and said to have been signed by Raymond himself.

Rooms of the National Union Executive
Committee, Astor House,
September 15.

(Private)

Dear Sir: Your name, with others, has been handed to me as having been employed by the government in furnishing supplies to the medical department of the army during the past year. I take it for granted you appreciate the necessity of sustaining the government in its contest with the rebellion, and of electing the Union candidates in November, the only mode of carrying the war to a successful close, and of restoring a peace which shall also restore the Union.

I trust you will have anticipated the application now made for a contribution to the fund which we need for organizing and carrying on the presidential canvass. The amount of this contribution I of course leave to yourself. Please remit whatever you feel inclined to give in a check, payable to my order as treasurer of the national

[116] John Hay to Henry J. Raymond (Confidential), on stationery of the "Executive Mansion, Washington," Oct. 17, 1864, George Jones Photostats. Jones was Raymond's business partner. These photostats are in possession of Dr. Francis Brown, of the New York *Times,* who is now preparing a biography of Raymond. Dr. Brown graciously allowed the present authors to examine this material.

executive committee. I respectfully ask your immediate attention to this matter, as the need of funds is pressing and the time for using them is short.

[signed] H. J. RAYMOND,
Chairman.[117]

A month before Raymond had written Simon Cameron: "We are not in funds at present—but hope to have enough for useful purposes in time." [118]

The proprietors of Phelps, Dodge, and Company, a New York firm dealing in metals, contributed at least $3,000 to Lincoln's campaign for reëlection, as revealed by this letter:

Phelps, Dodge & Co.
Nos. 19 & 21 Cliff St.

New York, Oct. 12, 1864

MY DEAR SIR

I enclose check for $3000—from members of our firm who sympathize most heartily with the good cause in which your Committee is working.

We shall be glad to do more if necessary.

Very respectfully & truly yours etc.
W. E. DODGE Junr [119]

H. J. RAYMOND
Chairman.

The Dodge family, loyal to Lincoln, personally received favors from the administration: William E. Dodge, Sr., who had retired from active business, was given the Republican-Union nomination for Congress from the Eighth Congressional District in New York City. One of his sons in the Army, Charles C. Dodge, was promoted to the rank of brigadier general.[120]

In Pennsylvania Raymond evidently had an able ally in Simon Cameron, so far as the raising of funds went. Less than a month following election day, M. Hall Stanton, of Anspach and Stanton,

---

117 New York *World,* Oct. 4, 1864.
118 H. J. Raymond to Cameron, Aug. 19, 1864, Cameron Papers.
119 A photostate of this letter is in the George Jones Photostats previously referred to, in possession of Dr. Francis Brown, of the New York *Times.*
120 Martyn, *William E. Dodge: The Christian Merchant,* pp. 191, 195, 209.

a Philadelphia firm soliciting Cameron's aid in securing government contracts, wrote:

After my interview with *you* at the Girard House, we handed over to your Ex. Committee an additional seven hundred and fifty dollars. Also when—by authority of the Secy. of War Mr. M. Campbell in company with Mr. Winthrop of Cincinnati called upon us to collect money for the National Ex. Committee, we give [sic] him five hundred dollars—making our election expenses nearly fifty-seven Hundred dollars. I only mention these facts to show that we should have —when we do not, some consideration in national matters, but let this pass.

My object of writing you is this, you stated at the interview alluded to above that you would be willing to try and do something for us in way of contracts. . . .[121]

Another fund-raising agency—and one apparently working in close coöperation with the Union National Committee—was the "Union Executive Congressional Committee," composed of three Republican members of the United States Senate and three Republican members of the House of Representatives.[122] As its secretary this committee had the services of D. N. Cooley, whom Lincoln had appointed to the post of Direct Tax Commissioner for the conquered regions of South Carolina.[123] The Union Executive Congressional Committee took it upon itself to assess postmasters for electioneering funds, the levy ranging from $2 to $150, depending upon the size of the particular post office held.[124] Accordingly, copies of the following summons went out to postmasters throughout the North, under the "frank" of Senator James Harlan, of Iowa, whom Lincoln appointed to his Cabinet after the election:

Presidential Campaign of 1864—Union Executive Congressional Committee.

Hon. E. D. Morgan of New York;
Hon. James Harlan of Iowa;
Hon. L. M. Morrill of Maine; (Senate).

[121] M. Hall Stanton to Cameron (Private), Nov. 30, 1864, Cameron Papers.
[122] Indianapolis *Daily State Sentinel*, Sept. 20, 1864.
[123] *Ibid.;* Boston *Daily Advertiser,* Feb. 27, March 2, 1864; *U. S. Senate Executive Journal,* XIII (1862–64), 419, 431.
[124] Indianapolis *Daily State Sentinel,* Sept. 20, 1864.

Hon. E. B. Washburne of Illinois;
Hon. R. B. Van Valkenburg of New York;
Hon. J. A. Garfield of Ohio; (House of Representatives).

E. D. Morgan, Chairman;
Jas. Harlan, Treasurer;
D. N. Cooley, Secretary.

Dear Sir: To defray, in part, the necessary expenses of conducting this important campaign, in printing and distributing speeches and documents, the Committee, presuming you will esteem it a privilege to do something in aid of a work so vital to our country, have assessed you five dollars which, to save the trouble and expense of drawing upon you for, you will please remit on receipt of this to Hon. James Harlan, Treasurer, or to the Secretary. The Committee would be pleased to hear from you, with suggestions as to the canvass in your locality.[125]

The Democratic press roundly denounced the Union Executive Congressional Committee's action in sending copies of the above circular to the postmasters. One New York Democratic daily commented bitterly, perhaps enviously:

The Democrats will enter the coming canvass under the great disadvantage of having to contend against the greatest patronage and the greatest money-power ever wielded in a presidential election. An administration in power has always money in hand as well as swarms of well-drilled office-holders to conduct the canvass; but the Lincolnites will control a thousand dollars where former administrations could not raise ten. By the above circular it will be seen that they are determined to bleed the office-holders to the utmost and are intent upon getting the few as well as the many dollars.[126]

That the Lincoln administration could command one thousand dollars to former administrations' ten was probably a gross exaggeration—a partisan charge made against the Republicans in the heat of a campaign. Nevertheless, that large sums were collected to finance Lincoln's campaign for reëlection and to assure Republican success is indicated by the sums of money which Chairman Raymond sent into various states. From Utica, New York, Roscoe Conkling, running for Congress, wrote Raymond in mid-September: "I am exceedingly indebted for your offer of assist-

125 *Ibid.*   126 New York *World,* Aug. 25, 1864.

ance. Of course we want all the help we can get, & the Democrats as well as their allies have & use money here very largely. We should be very glad of anything we may properly have of sinews of war." [127]

From Augusta, Maine, James G. Blaine, similarly campaigning for Congress and anxious to keep his state in the Republican-Union column, acknowledged receipt of funds in a letter to Raymond: "Very greatly obliged for your prompt response to our wants in Maine. . . . Your draft for $2500 was very timely—and the additional $1000 which I have just drawn for will 'put us through' in good shape." [128] And in late October, from New Hampshire, there came to Raymond the following receipt:

Union Republican State Committee, Concord, N. H.,
October 31, 1864.

Received of H. J. Raymond, Chairman Union National Committee, *Five Thousand Dollars* for campaign expenditures in New Hampshire; to be by us transmitted to T. L. Tullock, Treasurer of the N. H. Committee; the above being in addition to $5000. delivered to John B. Clarke; $4000. of which has been by him paid to said Tullock.

WILLIAM E. CHANDLER
Chairman
B. F. PRESCOTT
Secretary [129]

Lincoln appointed William E. Chandler to a position in the Navy Department following the election. Thomas L. Tullock already held a naval agent's position by Lincoln's appointment.[130]

The total amount of money expended to return Lincoln to the White House and to aid the election of Republican-Unionists in Congressional and local contests is impossible of determination. It was an exceptionally large amount, if the expenditures in pivotal Pennsylvania alone are to be taken as a barometer. One Democratic worker, given perhaps to exaggeration, reported to the New York *World's* editor, Manton Marble:

[127] Roscoe Conkling to Henry J. Raymond, Sept. 15, 1864, George Jones Photostats.
[128] James G. Blaine to H. J. Raymond, Sept. 10, 1864, George Jones Photostats.
[129] There is a photostate of this document in George Jones Photostats.
[130] *U. S. Official Register, 1863,* p. 227.

I am informed on authority which I consider entirely reliable, that the Republican managers in Phila have on hand a fund of *one million dollars!* Simonds, a fortunate contractor and builder of wagons for Gov*t* has given $50,000. An officer has been detailed both at Phila and New York to ascertain from the Quarter Masters in each of these places, the names of those who have been favored with Gov*t* patronage, for the purpose of levying assessments upon them.[131]

Two days later another Democratic worker, Henry M. Phillips, questioned the accuracy of the above staggering amounts, writing Marble from Philadelphia: "The Republicans are raising a very large sum of money here but it will be nothing like the 'million' mentioned, tho' probably more than half that amount. Contractors and office-holders are required to subscribe and even laborers in the Public employment are assessed." [132] Any attempt to calculate the money expended in any election is, at best, a historically hazardous undertaking which rarely, if ever, produces fruitful results. That the sums raised and spent by both Republican-Unionists and Democrats were far from small seems conclusive, to judge by the foregoing evidence.[133]

Little doubt of the outcome of the contest between Lincoln and McClellan remained after the Republican-Union victories in Pennsylvania, Indiana, and Ohio, which held their state elections in October. Sherman's march to the sea and other victories of the Union Armies in the field, plus the soldiers' vote, were powerful arguments to convince the northern electorate that Lincoln should be returned to the nation's highest office for another term.[134] It should be noted that the Republican-Union officers made special appeals to the men in the field—at least in Pennsylvania and In-

[131] Samuel North to Marble, Sept. 28, 1864, Manton Marble Papers.

[132] Henry M. Phillips to Marble, Sept. 30, 1864, *ibid.*

[133] In 1908 Representative William Sulzer, Democrat of New York, in a speech in Congress, estimated that in 1864 the Republican National Committee spent $125,000 and the Democratic National Committee $50,000. This was in contrast to 1860, when the Republican National Committee spent $100,000 and the Democrats $50,000. Sulzer did not mention the source of his information. His figures are often quoted, but they are probably of little historical value. See *Congressional Record,* 60th Cong., 1st sess., pp. 6470–71.

[134] Brillhart, "The Election of 1864 in Western Pennsylvania," *Western Pennsylvania Historical Magazine,* VIII (1925), 26–36. Harbison, "Indiana Republicans and the Re-Election of President Lincoln," *Indiana Magazine of History,* XXXIV (March, 1938), 49 ff.; Yager, "The Presidential Campaign of 1864 in Ohio," *Ohio Archaeological and Historical Quarterly,* XXXIV (1925), 582.

diana. In some instances promotions in the Army were contingent upon correct party allegiance; provost marshals in the Keystone State were busy lining up support for the Republican-Union ticket; and quartermasters in the Hoosier State attended "all Republican meetings," according to Secretary of War Stanton.[135]

With Lincoln's reëlection in November reasonably assured as a result of the verdicts in the three "October states," interest in the remainder of the campaign centered in New York, with the largest electoral vote. Here, too, federal officeholders contributed money and time to steer their state into the Lincoln column.

Thurlow Weed, in charge of the New York campaign, seems to have had a share in the work of assessing officeholders. This is indicated by the following letter which Weed received from one particular federal employee:

Paying my assessment for the election, I found a youth lately introduced into my bureau who is no great honor, and yet was assessed for a salary above $1,000 pr. ann.—I called several times to tell you, but failed to hit the time.—I was slow to enter on the present office —but am thankful that I did—and will be grateful for an opportunity, by diligence and fidelity, to occupy a higher situation.[136]

Federal officials in New York were most active for Lincoln throughout the campaign. A monster Lincoln-Johnson ratification meeting was held in New York City in June, the week following the Baltimore Convention. The United States Attorney for the Southern District of New York, E. Delafield Smith, was the leading spirit of the meeting. Horace Maynard, holding a federal position under Andrew Johnson, military governor of Tennessee, also spoke at this rally.[137] Smith proved to be very useful during the campaign, speaking at meetings and working to harmonize discordant groups within the local Republican-Union organization.[138]

Another important appointee of Lincoln who gave time and energy to the contest was Abram Wakeman, recently selected as

[135] Dennett, "Lincoln and the Campaign of 1864," *Abraham Lincoln Association Papers,* 1935, pp. 53–55; Joseph J. Lewis to Cameron, Sept. 17, 1864; E. P. Thompson to Cameron, Oct. 14, 1864, Cameron Papers.

[136] Henry Dana Ward to Weed, Oct. 11, 1864, Weed Papers, Library of Congress.

[137] New York *Herald,* June 16, 1864.

[138] New York *Evening Post,* Oct. 7, 22, 1864.

Surveyor of the Port of New York.[139] Still another ardent worker in the Lincoln cause was Richard Busteed, who had been appointed United States District Judge for Alabama, but who could not assume his duties because his district was under Confederate control. He remained on the government pay roll the while, filling in his time stumping New York State for Lincoln.[140] On September 27 at Cooper Institute the New York Lincolnites held their largest meeting. An anti-administration mouthpiece critically scrutinized those at the rally and reported:

Lincoln Ratification Meeting: Gathering of Office-Holders, Office-Seekers. . . . At Cooper Institute. . . . The custom-house and other administration officials were out almost *en masse*, and formed no inconsiderable part of the audience. . . . At the meeting inside the hall, William Curtis Noyes presided, and the officers were, almost without exception, either recent or present office-holders, or candidates struggling for a taste of the shoddy pap-spoon. It would fill a column to mention the names of all, but the following list is a specimen of the whole:

James Kelly, postmaster; Sheridan Shook, collector of internal revenue; Thomas Robinson and John Pitch, custom-house attaches; Chas. T. Polhemus, of street commissioners office, placed there by ex-Mayor Opdyke; A. J. Dittenhoffer, Republican Presidential elector; Henry Richard, Chas. Kassman, Geo. Manchot, C. F. E. Lueder, custom-house attaches; Peter Cook, a perpetual candidate for the Assembly on the Republican ticket of the Tenth and Twelfth districts; Andreas Willman, occasional Republican candidate for the Senate from the Fifth district, lately defeated for state prison inspector, and now in the custom-house; Samuel J. Glassy, counsel to the collector; Thomas Little, Republican supervisor, whose term will soon expire; Simeon Draper, collector of the port; Edmund Remack, custom-house attache; Geo. F. Steinbrenner, assessor of internal revenue; John D. Ottiwell, Republican alderman; W*m* Allen Butler, of Flora McFlimsey and custom house pickings; E. Delafield Smith, United States district attorney; Jas. R. Whiting, reported can-

[139] *Ibid.*, Oct. 22, 1864.
[140] *Ibid.*, Sept. 10, 1864; Brooklyn *Daily Eagle*, Oct. 12, 1864. "Modest Dick Busteed is running about from State to State canvassing for Mr. Lincoln, and at the same time abusing in the foulist terms in all probability a majority of the people to-day. This noisy fellow draws $5,000 a year from the Treasury of the United States as Deputy Judge of the State of Alabama. It is perhaps asking the 'Second Washington [Lincoln]' too much to pay his own electioneering expenses."

didate for mayor; Rufus F. Andrews, late surveyor of the port. . . .
The meeting was addressed by Hon. Henry Denning, of Connecticut,
military governor of New Orleans under Gen. Butler, and others. . . .[141]

Mention has been made of the dismissal of some anti-Lincoln
employees in the New York Custom House in September. During
October, in the midst of the campaign, there were likewise dismissals in the Brooklyn Navy Yard. Out of fifty-three workmen in
the ironclad shop of the yard, fifty-one were summarily dismissed
because, the Democrats charged, they made known their intention
to vote for McClellan.[142] The *Daily Union,* Brooklyn Republican
organ, did not deny the accusation, but gave its own explanation:
"Some [men] had to be discharged, and as a matter of course it
was desirable that none but loyal men should receive the preference
of retention. The only questions asked were, whether they were
loyal men or not, and whether they were Union men or Democrats,
which amounted to just the same thing." [143]

Lincoln did not have the clear-cut victory over McClellan in
New York that he had in other states, carrying it over his opponent
by a scant 7,000 votes. Public weariness with the war and its ac-
companying high prices and other burdens, hostility to the draft,
dissatisfaction with the administration's policies, and the popularity of McClellan all contributed to swell the vote for the General.
The Union victories in the field, the desire in some quarters not to
change administrations in war time, Lincoln's popularity in some
circles, and the efficient organization led by Thurlow Weed and
Raymond turned the scale in Lincoln's favor.[144] With such a per-
ilously close majority for Lincoln in the Empire State, it was
fortunate, from his own viewpoint, that he catered to the Weed
faction by the removal from office of such Chase sympathizers as
Collector Barney and Surveyor Andrews and replaced them with
Weed's followers. In the words of Dr. Sidney D. Brummer, historian of Civil War New York: "Thurlow Weed had now routed

---

[141] New York *World,* Sept. 28, 1864.

[142] Brooklyn *Daily Eagle,* Oct. 14, 1864; New York *World,* Oct. 17, 1864.

[143] Brooklyn *Daily Union,* Oct. 15, 1864.

[144] Brummer, *Political History of New York State during the Period of the Civil War,* pp. 439–41.

JEFF DAVIS'S NOVEMBER NIGHTMARE

From *Frank Leslie's Illustrated Newspaper*, XIX (Dec. 3, 1864), 176.

his adversaries from the federal patronage and worked heartily for Lincoln." [145]

Other states followed New York into the Lincoln column in the November election. The military victories of Generals Sherman and Sheridan, the naval triumph of Admiral Farragut, and popular trust in Lincoln were probably the main arguments that induced the American electorate to continue him at the helm for another four years. Certainly the triumph of Union arms on land and sea made Lincoln's vote more impressive. [146]

Lincoln's success in 1864 guaranteed that the war would be prolonged until the South conceded defeat. At the same time it helped to discourage the Confederacy sufficiently to shorten the conflict. Moreover, the election returns impressed foreign powers with the strength of the government at Washington.

Reëlection saved the name of Abraham Lincoln from the stigma that would have accompanied defeat. The memories of McClellan, Chase, and Frémont, on the other hand, correspondingly suffered. The presidential election of 1864 stands out conspicuously as one of the most decisive in American annals. [147] And, as in elections before and since, patronage played its part. On this point, John Hay's biographer has written a fitting conclusion:

It cannot be denied that as the campaign of 1864 wore on, the party organizers and leaders yielded to the temptation to make use of power and position already held to bring pressure to bear on recalcitrant voters. Patronage was withheld and contracts were awarded as might affect the November poll in the interests of Republican victory. Even promotions in the army appear to have been in some instances contingent upon correct party allegiance. [148]

[145] *Ibid.*, p. 440.
[146] See, for example: Yager, "The Presidential Campaign of 1864 in Ohio," *Ohio Archaeological and Historical Quarterly*, XXXIV (1925), 565–66, 583–86.
[147] Dudley, "The Election of 1864," *The Mississippi Valley Historical Review*, XVIII (March, 1932), 518.
[148] Dennett, "Lincoln and the Campaign of 1864," *Abraham Lincoln Association Papers*, 1935, p. 53.

Chapter XI

THE LAST MONTHS: FINISHED AND UNFINISHED BUSINESS

CAN'T YOU AND OTHERS start a public sentiment in favor of making no changes in offices except for good and sufficient cause? It seems as though the bare thought of going through again what I did the first year here, would *crush* me." [1]

Thus spoke Lincoln to Senator John B. Clark, of New Hampshire, following his reëlection to the presidency in 1864. And on another occasion he is reported to have said: "I have made up my mind to make very few changes in the offices in my gift for my second term. I think now that I will not remove a single man except for delinquency. To remove a man is very easy, but when I go to fill his place, there are *twenty* applicants, and of these I must make *nineteen* enemies." [2]

Whether these were Lincoln's words or not, they undoubtedly expressed his desire not to make wholesale changes in his second administration. A week following the election, Lincoln's secretary, John Hay, and the President discussed appointments. Hay intimated that his Chief should use his power to punish those who, in the recent campaign, had been disloyal to him and the party. Lincoln was unresponsive to this hint, Hay recorded at the time, adding: "It seems utterly impossible for the President to conceive of the possibility of any good resulting from a rigorous and exemplary course of punishing political dereliction. His favorite expression is, 'I am in favor of short statutes of limitations in politics.' " [3] Despite Lincoln's attitude, the feeling that the Confederacy was about to collapse and that the twice-elected War President would reshuffle his administration in favor of the radi-

---

[1] Carpenter, *Six Months at the White House with Abraham Lincoln*, p. 276.
[2] *Ibid.*
[3] Dennett, "Lincoln and the Campaign of 1864," *Abraham Lincoln Association Papers*, 1935, p. 57.

cals inspired a rush of job seekers only less numerous and vigorous than in the spring and summer of 1861.

Hardly had the November election returns been counted in the fall of 1864 when the real rush for jobs began. Republican members of the Senate and of the House of Representatives were besieged by appeals from constituents, requesting that Lincoln be consulted regarding their or their friends' claims to office and favors. "We think him deserving and worthy of some appointment of honor & profit at the hands of the Administration, and ask for him your assistance to procure such a position" [4]—this letter to a Republican United States Senator was typical of the innumerable communications sent to Members of Congress. Cabinet officers were similarly annoyed. Secretary of the Treasury Fessenden, for example, complained that he was exceedingly plagued by applications for Treasury appointments, founded only on statements by clerks and others that there were vacancies to be filled, and even designating those vacancies. [5] Numerous positions, including several federal judgeships, had been allowed to remain unfilled during the course of the campaign, and for these the keenest kind of competition among the party faithful now ensued. [6]

As in 1861, Lincoln himself was not left unmolested. From the time of his reëlection to the eve of his assassination Washington was filled with seekers of federal jobs who literally lay in wait for him. One witness of his second inauguration in March, 1865, sent word home from Washington: "Many persons are here from a distance, looking after their private interests, and seeking influence to assist them in the procurement of high as well as low positions. They do not seem to be mindful of the fact that there are to be no wholesale removals from place." [7]

Throughout the month of March, 1865, the rush for office continued unabated, and fear was expressed that the President would fall a victim to the remorseless tormentors as had Presidents Harrison and Taylor, whose health was said to have become impaired by the constant pressure of job seekers. [8] During April,

[4] Peeples and Ridgway to Trumbull, Feb. 2, 1865, Trumbull Papers.
[5] Philadelphia *Public Ledger*, Nov. 23, 1864.
[6] New York *Herald*, Nov. 6, 1864.
[7] *Ibid.*, March 6, 1865.   [8] *Ibid.*, March 22, 1865.

the month of Lincoln's assassination, the federal capital was still filled with spoilsmen who maneuvered to secure the President's ear regarding appointments for themselves or their supporters.[9]

The demands on the Lincoln administration for positions in the New York Custom House were particularly heavy. Collector Simeon Draper, to relieve himself of the importunities of those who would replace the incumbents in the Custom House, had inserted in a New York Republican organ the following notice:

Interesting To Office-Seekers

A large number of applications to the Collector for situations in the Custom-House are made daily; and much time is consumed in hearing the claimants. The Collector considers it essential to the interests of the service that the public should know, and office-seekers particularly observe, that as all applications are regularly numbered and filed for examination hereafter, there is as a rule no necessity for the personal interviews which the candidates and their friends almost invariably seek.

Every man in the Custom-House is to be invited to renew the papers on which his appointment was originally made, or to procure other documents. The papers are to be filed, like so many new applications.[10]

Although Lincoln had decided that no wholesale changes should occur, there were certain patronage obligations that he felt had to be taken care of. Among these was the nephew of his old friend, Robert C. Schenck, of Ohio. It is not surprising, therefore, that he should pen the following to the Secretary of the Treasury:

The office of Collector of Internal Revenue for the Fifth Collection District of California is vacant by the resignation of Charles Maltby. I would like to oblige General Schenck by the appointment of his nephew, William C. S. Smith, long a resident of the District, to fill the vacancy. I am satisfied that he is competent, and of good character, and that his appointment will be satisfactory in the District and State. Unless you know some valid objection, send me an appointment for him.[11]

[9] New York *Herald*, April 1, 2, 3, 1865.
[10] New York *Evening Post*, Nov. 18, 1864.
[11] Lincoln to the Secretary of the Treasury, April 13, 1865, in Hertz, *Abraham Lincoln: A New Portrait*, II, 966.

The Secretary of the Treasury did not have opportunity to reply to this order, dated April 13, 1865. For the President was felled by Booth's bullet on the night of the following day.

Nevertheless, between his reëlection to the presidency in November, 1864, and his assassination the following April, Lincoln managed to pay some political debts with federal offices—appointing officials who had shown their loyalty to him in the recent campaign or in the course of his four years in the White House. The New Jersey Republican leader Horace N. Congar, editor of the Newark *Daily Mercury*, whom Lincoln had appointed consul at Hong Kong in 1861, was back from the Orient in impaired health. Lincoln cared for him by tendering him the position of United States Commissioner of Immigration.[12] Robert S. Rantoul, of Massachusetts, who had been active in the Republican campaigns of 1856 and 1860 and who had been passed over for the postmastership of Salem in 1861, was appointed in January, 1865, Collector of Customs for Salem and Beverly.[13] Horace Rublee, chairman of the Republican State Committee of Wisconsin and a Lincoln supporter, who had not been rewarded during Lincoln's first term, was made consul at Funchal, Madeira, in February, 1865.[14] George Bergner, postmaster in Harrisburg, who, as we have noted, performed yeoman service in helping to send a pro-Lincoln delegation from Pennsylvania to the Baltimore Convention, fared well, for his commission as postmaster in the Pennsylvania capital city was renewed in March, 1865.[15] Similarly, Richard W. Thompson, Provost Marshal for Indiana, who had been instrumental in sending an instructed Lincoln delegation from the Hoosier State to the Baltimore Convention, received from Lincoln the post of Collector of Internal Revenue for the Seventh Indiana District.[16]

[12] Shaw, *History of Essex and Hudson Counties, New Jersey,* I, 283; *U. S. Official Register, 1865,* p. 2.

[13] Rantoul, *Personal Recollections,* pp. 28–29; Eliot, "Robert Samuel Rantoul," "Essex Institute Historical Collections," LVIII (1922), 267; *U. S. Senate Executive Journal,* XIV, Part I (1864–66), 17, 83.

[14] Willard G. Bleyer's sketch of Rublee in *Dictionary of American Biography,* XVI, 213; *U. S. Senate Executive Journal,* XIV, Part I (1864–66), 191, 220.

[15] *U. S. Senate Executive Journal,* XIV, Part I (1864–66), 281, 296.

[16] *U. S. Senate Executive Journal,* XIV, Part I (1864–66), 274, 297.

In the newly created Judicial District for Eastern New York there were three principal offices to be filled. Lively competition ensued among contenders for the judgeship in this district. Among these was William E. Robinson, well known among New York politicians as "Richelieu." Robinson had the backing of leading New England and many New York political spokesmen. Republican National Chairman Henry J. Raymond, however, won the coveted bench for his candidate, Charles L. Benedict of Brooklyn.[17] For this same district Lincoln selected Benjamin D. Silliman for United States Attorney and Anthony F. Campbell for United States Marshal.[18] Silliman had been a staunch Republican party man.[19] Benedict and Campbell had been delegates from New York to the Baltimore Convention.[20]

At least a score of party leaders who had served as delegates or alternates to the Baltimore Convention were appointed by Lincoln to high Army posts or to federal jobs in the period between his reëlection and death.[21]

Intense rivalry flared among contenders for diplomatic missions. The most coveted post was that at Paris, left vacant in December (1864) by the death of Minister William L. Dayton. "There will be no trouble in obtaining a competent man for minister to France," wrote one Washington observer, a few weeks following Dayton's death. "Up to to-day the President has received applications in favor of fifty different gentlemen." [22] At this time Gustave Koerner, who had recently been Minister to Spain, wrote Senator Trumbull: "I thank you very much for the trouble you have taken in my behalf. The truth is I think that the President has pledged himself already as regards every mission of importance." [23]

Koerner might have had reference to Lincoln's tender of the

[17] New York *Herald*, Feb. 28, March 3, 1865; [Benedict], *Proceedings of Meetings of Members of the Bar Held January 9 and 16, 1901, to Do Honor to the Memory of Honorable Charles L. Benedict . . .* , p. 8.

[18] *U. S. Senate Executive Journal*, XIV, Part I (1864–66), 222, 266.

[19] *The National Cyclopaedia of American Biography*, VI, 54–55.

[20] C. W. Johnson, *The First Three Republican National Conventions . . . 1856, 1860 and 1864*, p. 249.

[21] For these appointments, consult *Appendix*, pp. 337–38.

[22] New York *World*, Dec. 24, 1864.

[23] Gustave Koerner to Trumbull, Dec. 21, 1864, Trumbull Papers.

French mission to James Gordon Bennett, editor of the New York *Herald*—an offer made by the President while the important campaign of 1864 was in progress. On February 20 (1865) Lincoln made good his promise to Bennett in this message: "I propose, at some convenient and not distant day, to nominate you to the United States Senate as Minister to France." [24] The *Herald* editor declined the proffer for some reason never revealed. [25]

Upon Bennett's declination, Lincoln cast about for one who could fill the French mission adequately. It was a most important post, considering the strained relations with France engendered by Emperor Napoleon's support of Maximilian's dynasty in Mexico. It was currently rumored that the President offered the post to Rev. Dr. John McClintock, a Methodist Episcopal clergyman and pastor of St. Paul's Church in New York City. McClintock had formerly been pastor of the American Chapel in Paris and might have made a competent envoy. McClintock, however, promptly declined the invitation, giving as his reason poor health. [26] Finally Lincoln gave the place to John Bigelow, then Consul General at Paris. [27] Bigelow, a former part owner of the Republican New York *Evening Post*, proved a fortunate choice.

In Bigelow's vacated place, the Paris consulate, Lincoln placed his private secretary, John G. Nicolay. [28] For secretary of legation under Bigelow the President named his other confidential secretary, John Hay. Hay, poet, raconteur, epicure, and later Secretary of State under William McKinley and Theodore Roosevelt, disliked routine and was especially pleased with his appointment; [29] moreover, four years' intimate association with political Washington had been too repulsive to his sensitive soul. "It is a

24 Lincoln to Bennett, Feb. 20, 1865, in Seitz, *The James Gordon Bennetts: Father and Son,* p. 193.

25 For further evidence that Lincoln offered the French mission to Bennett in the winter of 1864–65, see Pierce, *Memoir and Letters of Charles Sumner,* IV, 255; Bigelow, *Retrospections of an Active Life,* II, 520 n.; *Diary of Gideon Welles,* II, 258; New York *World,* March 17, 1865.

26 New York *World,* March 2, 1865.

27 Bigelow, *Retrospections of an Active Life,* II, 423.

28 *U. S. Senate Executive Journal,* XIV, Part I (1864–66), 294, 298.

29 Dennett, *John Hay: From Poetry To Politics,* p. 57.

pleasant and honorable way of leaving my present post, which I should have left in any event very soon," Hay wrote to his brother. "I am thoroughly sick of certain aspects of life here, which you will understand without my putting them on paper. . . . I very much fear that all my friends will disapprove this step of mine, but if they knew all that induced me to it they would coincide." [30]

During the months preceding his death one of Lincoln's vexing problems was what to do with Vice President Hannibal Hamlin, who had failed to be renominated at Baltimore and whose term would expire on March 4, 1865. Bad blood had long existed between Hamlin and his rival in Maine politics, Secretary of the Treasury William Pitt Fessenden. Many political wiseacres believed that the President had persuaded Fessenden to leave his seat in the United States Senate and accept the Treasury portfolio partly to make room in the upper chamber of Congress for Hamlin.[31] Hamlin had taken the stump for Lincoln and Johnson in the West during the campaign, after receiving what he considered assurances from his Maine political friends that Fessenden would remain in the Treasury and that he, Hamlin, would be elected to the Senate by the Maine legislature.[32] Fessenden had other ideas. He wanted to return to his seat in the Senate and prepared to resign the Secretaryship of the Treasury. Fessenden's son later defended his father in these words: "Mr. Fessenden, however, desired to return to the Senate, and had accepted the office of Secretary of the Treasury upon the understanding with the President that he would give up the office as soon as the safety of the public finances would justify it. Mr. Hamlin, not being informed as to Mr. Fessenden's intentions and wishes, became a candidate for the senatorial vacancy." [33]

Immediately after election Fessenden, from his office in Washington, started his campaign for return to the Senate, writing on November 18 to his chief lieutenant in Maine, Israel Washburn, Jr., Collector of Internal Revenue at Portland: "I think him

[30] John Hay to Charles Hay, March 31, 1865, in Thayer, *The Life and Letters of John Hay*, I, 218–19.

[31] See p. 268.

[32] C. E. Hamlin, *The Life and Times of Hannibal Hamlin*, pp. 490–95.

[33] F. Fessenden, *Life and Public Services of William Pitt Fessenden*, II, 1–2.

[Hamlin] a very ordinary affair, at best, and that he should not have the place any how." [34] A Washington correspondent wrote home: "Mr. Fessenden . . . turned the whole patronage, power and machinery of his [Treasury] department into the effort to secure his own return to the Senate and the defeat of Mr. Hamlin. In this work it is averred he found a willing tool in his Collector of Internal Revenue at Portland, Israel Washburn, Jr. who in turn is looking with covetous eyes upon the other seat in the Senate now occupied by Senator Morrill." [35] When the legislature met at Augusta furious warfare broke out between the Hamlin and Fessenden forces, with Fessenden winning the Senate seat.[36]

In December (1864) Hamlin returned to Washington with the assembling of Congress. Lincoln still felt that he had to find something for him, but what? Hamlin's son maintained that Lincoln offered the Secretaryship of the Treasury to his father, but that Fessenden "threatened war if he should appoint Mr. Hamlin to the Cabinet." [37] The younger Hamlin contended that Lincoln feelingly informed his father: "You have not been treated right. It is too bad, too bad. But what can I do? I am tied hands and feet." [38] And Thurlow Weed declared that when he suggested to Lincoln that the retiring Vice President be appointed Secretary of the Treasury, the President dismissed the proposal with the words: "Hamlin has the Senate on the brain, and nothing more or less will cure him." [39]

Several days after the inauguration of Lincoln and Johnson, Hamlin, still unplaced, left Washington for his home. A notice in a leading journal carried this announcement: *Mr. Hamlin Going Home Disgusted:* Ex-Vice President Hamlin departed for his home in Maine this morning, thoroughly disgusted with everything and almost everybody in public life, excepting the President. He complains that almost every one with whom he has had anything to do has played him false." [40]

According to Congressman Samuel Hooper, of Massachusetts, Lincoln finally managed to care for the disappointed former Vice

[34] Fessenden to I. Washburn, Jr., Nov. 18, 1864, William P. Fessenden Papers.
[35] New York *Herald,* March 10, 1865.   [36] Hatch, *Maine: A History,* II, 465–66.
[37] C. E. Hamlin, *The Life and Times of Hannibal Hamlin,* p. 495.
[38] *Ibid.,* p. 496.   [39] *Autobiography of Thurlow Weed,* p. 622.
[40] New York *Herald,* March 10, 1865.

President by tendering him the desirable post of Collector of Customs of the Port of Boston. A year after Lincoln's death Hooper related:

> With that tender solicitude for the feelings of others which was so marked a trait in the character of the great magistrate, he [Lincoln] was anxious to make the change in such a way as to give the least offence [to the incumbent Collector of Boston, John Z. Goodrich], and consulted me in reference to it. I suggested that Mr. Goodrich might be glad to resign the duties and burdens of the office, if he was informed before hand of the wishes and intentions of the President in regard to it. The communication was accordingly made to Mr. Goodrich, as I suggested; and the Collectorship was offered to Mr. Hamlin.
>
> This occurred not long before the assassination of President Lincoln.[41]

Whether Hooper's contention that Lincoln offered Hamlin the Boston collectorship is true or not, must remain in doubt—at least until further evidence has been unearthed. When Andrew Johnson became President he appointed Hamlin to this profitable federal position—and Hamlin accepted.[42]

The possibility that Lincoln would reshuffle his Cabinet resulted in the most intense rivalry among the various factions of the Republican-Union party. The sixth resolution adopted at the Baltimore Convention, to which allusion has already been made, whetted the appetite of a number of ambitious party leaders who aspired to sit in the Cabinet or who wanted a particular friend or protégé to attain such a place of distinction and power. Indeed, the week following the election, impending changes in the President's Cabinet became a popular topic of gossip in Washington.[43] In particular, Senator Trumbull, representing Lincoln's home state in the upper chamber of Congress, was annoyed with many requests from those who aspired to a place in the President's inner council. Anson G. Henry, United States Surveyor General for

[41] Samuel Hooper, *A Defence of the Merchants of Boston against the Aspersions of the Hon. John Z. Goodrich, Ex-Collector of Customs*, pp. 3–4. The Boston collectorship in 1865 was "worth from $20,000 to $30,000 a year. The salary was $10,000, and the fees, commissions, and perquisites allowed on seizures and other things incidental to the customs service sometimes doubled or even trebled the salary." See C. E. Hamlin, *The Life and Times of Hannibal Hamlin*, p. 501.

[42] *U. S. Senate Executive Journal*, XIV, Part I (1864–66), 495.

[43] New York *Herald*, Nov. 17, 18, 1864.

Washington Territory and an old Illinois crony of Lincoln, was insistent that a Pacific Coast man receive a Cabinet seat.[44] Republicans of Michigan and other northwestern states were pressing James M. Edmunds, Commissioner of the General Land Office, for a Cabinet place.[45] Lincoln's old Illinois Whig friend, former Auditor Jesse K. Dubois, having been defeated for the Republican gubernatorial nomination, was presenting himself as a logical candidate for Secretary of the Interior.[46] And in another instance a candidate—probably Senator James H. Lane of Kansas—did not hesitate to recommend himself: ". . . [It] does seem to me that Mr. Lincoln could not find one west of the Mississippi whose appointment would give more general satisfaction than myself." [47]

Before his untimely death Lincoln was destined to make three changes in his Cabinet—the Attorney Generalship, the Secretaryship of the Treasury, and the Secretaryship of the Interior.

Attorney General Edward Bates, referred to as "that inoffensive old man" [48] by his enemies, had, indeed, never been quite happy in Washington. "In fact," he wrote one friend in 1863, "among strangers as I am, I begin to feel less self-reliant." [49] The hectic current of Washington politics seemed to move too swiftly for the comfort of his conservative nature, and by July, 1864, Bates was recording in his diary: "When the Whig party committed suicide, in 1856, and thereby left the nation without a *bodyguard*, I died with it. There are in fact, no parties now, united by any common principle." [50] In the heat of the campaign of 1864, Bates had made known to Lincoln his desire to retire to the more peace-

[44] A. G. Henry to Trumbull, Nov. 22, 1864, Trumbull Papers.

[45] A. Chester to Trumbull, Feb. 17, 1865, *ibid*.

[46] Jesse K. Dubois to Trumbull, Feb. 2, 1865, *ibid*. For Dubois's unsuccessful fight to secure the Republican nomination for governor of Illinois in 1864, see the Springfield *Daily Illinois State Journal*, May 26, 1864.

[47] Lane (probably J. H.) to L. U. Reavis of Beardstown, Ill., Dec. 8, 1864. Original manuscript in the Chicago Historical Society.

[48] New York *Herald*, June 9, 1864.

[49] Bates to James Eads, March, 1863, in Floyd A. McNeil, "Lincoln's Attorney General: Edward Bates," MS, Ph.D. Dissertation, State University of Iowa, 1930, p. 305.

[50] "Diary of Edward Bates, 1859–1866," ed. by Howard K. Beale, *Annual Report, American Historical Association*, IV (1930), 390. "Party ties are so weakened," Bates wrote, "that they no longer amount to an obligation, and party names are used only by crafty politicians, to juggle with, for electioneering purposes. Individuals seem bent only on the great work of taking care of themselves, and are ready to change sides, at short notice, and to enlist under any banner that promises higher pay and better hopes of plunder."

ful atmosphere of his Missouri home. On November 30—three weeks following Lincoln's reëlection—the Attorney General tendered his resignation to the President, which the latter accepted.[51] Immediately rivalry flared up among those who aspired to be his successor. "The resignation of Attorney General Bates has initiated more intrigues," noted Secretary of the Navy Welles at the time. "A host of candidates are thrust forward, or are thrusting themselves forward. Evarts, Holt, Cushing, Whiting, and the Lord knows who, are all candidates." [52]

Lincoln was of the opinion that since Bates was a Missourian, his successor should likewise come from a border state. The President accordingly offered the Justice portfolio to Judge Advocate General Joseph Holt, a Kentuckian. But Holt declined it, preferring his present position. Lincoln finally settled on James Speed, of Kentucky.[53] On December 1, the day following his acceptance of Bates's resignation, Lincoln telegraphed Speed: "I appoint you to be Attorney General. Please come at once." [54] Lincoln's selection of James Speed was for both political and personal reasons. Politically, Speed came from Kentucky, a pivotal border state, and was a staunch Unionist. Personally, Speed was the brother of Lincoln's closest friend in the early Springfield days, Joshua F. Speed, and was, like Lincoln, an old Henry Clay Whig.[55] James Speed, a conservative who was later to coöperate with the radicals, had throughout the war fought the political battle for Lincoln in Kentucky and had been a Kentucky delegate to the Baltimore Convention which renominated Lincoln.[56] Of his new Attorney General Lincoln said that he was "an honest man and a gentleman, and one of those well-poised men, not too common here, who are not spoiled by a big office." [57]

The second change in the Cabinet after Lincoln's reëlection

[51] "Diary of Edward Bates, 1859–1866," ed. by Howard K. Beale, *Annual Report, American Historical Association*, IV (1930), 428.

[52] *Diary of Gideon Welles*, II, 183.

[53] *Ibid.*, p. 187; Springer, "James Speed, the Attorney-General, 1864–1866," *The Filson Club History Quarterly*, XI (1937), 169.

[54] Lincoln to James Speed (Telegram), Dec. 1, 1864, in *Complete Works of Abraham Lincoln*, X, 278.

[55] Blaine, *Twenty Years of Congress*, II, 62; *President Lincoln's Cabinet by Honorable John P. Usher, Secretary of the Interior, January 7, 1863–May 15, 1865*, p. 29.

[56] Frankfort (Ky.) *Tri-Weekly Commonwealth*, May 27, 1864.

[57] Springer, "James Speed, the Attorney-General, 1864–1866," *The Filson Club History Quarterly*, XI (1937), 170.

was in the Treasury. Secretary Fessenden, as we have noted, was anxious to withdraw and return to the Senate. When in February (1865) definite word went out that Fessenden would leave the President's inner council, Lincoln was besieged with recommendations for succession to the Treasury portfolio. "Self-constituted delegations with long petitions," wrote a Washington correspondent in mid-February, "are daily arriving and soliciting the President to appoint to that position unheard-of men." [58] Lincoln called to Washington for consultation Thurlow Weed, political sponsor of Seward and one who had been of distinct service in the recent election. The outcome of the conference between Lincoln and Weed was the decision to tender the Secretaryship of the Treasury to United States Senator Edwin D. Morgan, of New York, and Weed was commissioned to sound Morgan on the subject. Morgan could not be persuaded and, on March 6, Lincoln's choice fell on Hugh McCulloch, conservative Indiana banker and Comptroller of the Currency—a most competent man, well versed in the national finances.[59]

The third and last change which Lincoln made in his Cabinet was that of Secretary of the Interior. Lincoln had long been dissatisfied with the administration of the Interior Department by Secretary John P. Usher. When this became known numerous candidates for the position entered the field. In January or February Lincoln held a conference at the White House with Governor Richard Yates, of Illinois, Senator Trumbull, and others regarding a successor to Usher. The name most prominently mentioned was that of United States Senator James Harlan, of Iowa.[60] Harlan received powerful backing for the Interior Department from the Iowa leader, Elijah Sells, then holding the position of Auditor in the Treasury Department.[61] Usher in March submitted his resignation to take effect on May 15, some two months hence. In early March Lincoln decided on Harlan for Secretary of the In-

[58] New York *World*, Feb. 18, 1865.
[59] This account of Morgan's refusal of the Treasury and its acceptance by McCulloch is based on *Autobiography of Thurlow Weed*, pp. 620–22; New York *World*, Feb. 14, 1865; New York *Herald*, Feb. 22, 1865; McCulloch, *Men and Measures of Half a Century*, pp. 193–95; Schell, "Hugh McCulloch and the Treasury Department, 1865–1869," *The Mississippi Valley Historical Review*, XVII (Dec., 1930), 404; *U. S. Senate Executive Journal*, XIV, Part I (1864–66), 221, 222.
[60] Jesse K. Dubois to Trumbull, Feb. 2, 1865, Trumbull Papers.
[61] J. M. Davis, "Elijah Sells," *Annals of Iowa*, Series III, II (1895–97), 520–21.

terior, sending his nomination to the Senate on March 9.[62] It was confirmed unanimously by the Senate, without previous reference to a standing committee, in accordance with the usage in cases in which the nominees were or had been members of the Senate.[63]

Harlan's selection to head the Interior Department was truly a personal appointment by Lincoln. During the war the friendship between Lincoln and Harlan had deepened, and on public occasions toward the end of the war the Iowan was usually in the presidential party: At the second inaugural Harlan was chosen as an escort for Mrs. Lincoln as the President took the oath for another term; and Harlan's daughter was often escorted by Lincoln's son Robert. Indeed, later Mary Harlan became Mrs. Robert Todd Lincoln. Harlan was also at Lincoln's side when the President made his last public utterance from the White House, on April 11, 1865.[64] In accepting a place in Lincoln's Cabinet—he did not take his seat, until one month following Lincoln's unfortunate death—Harlan wrote an intimate friend:

I now intend to accept the office of Secretary of the Interior if I find I can get the pack of thieves now preying on the Govt. under its auspices out of power, otherwise I will not. I do not deem it my duty to lend my name to plaster over their corruptions. The prospect of effecting this is not very good, for it happens that some of the worst of these people have the President's confidence.[65]

The changes made by Lincoln in his Cabinet during the period between his reëlection and assassination by no means made for unity at the start of his second administration, particularly in the colossal task of Reconstruction. His new Attorney General, James Speed, brother of his most intimate friend Joshua F. Speed, gave early evidence of opposing him in his attitude toward the "recovered" seceded states. As winter merged into spring in 1865 and the anaconda that was Grant's Army squeezed the Confederates out of Richmond, Attorney General Speed, contrary to his Kentucky background, leaned toward the radical members, Secretary of War Stanton and Postmaster General Dennison, who had little or no sympathy for the President's conciliatory

[62] U. S. Senate Executive Journal, XIV, Part I (1864–66), 256, 266.
[63] New York World, March 10, 1865.　　[64] Brigham, James Harlan, pp. 196–97.
[65] Harlan to James F. Wilson, March 24, 1865, in ibid., pp. 195–96.

or conservative policy toward the vanquished Confederate states. Lincoln had already set up reconstructed governments in Louisiana, Arkansas, and Tennessee, and meant to add other seceded states to the list. The Thirty-ninth Congress ended on March 4 (1865), and Lincoln would have a free hand until December 4. During the last week of his life—on April 10—he telegraphed the head of the rudimentary government in Virginia, Governor Francis H. Pierpont: "Please come up and see me at once." Pierpont came and spent three hours alone with Lincoln discussing the Virginia problem.[66] On the following day, April 11, Lincoln revealed to his Cabinet that he had given the legislature of Virginia a permit to restore Virginia to the Union. This meant that he would recognize the existing state government of Virginia as *de facto* until Congress could provide another. Speed joined Stanton and Dennison in attacking the plan—in fact, so strenuously that Lincoln confessed to Secretary of the Navy Welles that they were "annoying him greatly." [67] And the very day of Lincoln's death found Speed consulting with the radical Salmon P. Chase.[68]

At least as early as January, some three months before his death, Lincoln was being besieged by radicals and he apparently planned to curb them by utilizing his powers of patronage. During this month the Washington correspondent of one of the best-informed New York journals sent the following dispatch:

A Change From A Radical To A Conservative Course:

The signs of the times plainly indicate that the administration has determined to pursue a more conservative and conciliatory course from this time onward. In other words it is believed that the so-called Southern confederacy has reached that point in its downward career when the true policy of our government is to temper justice with mercy. It was necessary to be radical until the strength of the rebellion had become broken and so completely on the wane as to convince the people within its influence that its days were numbered. This having been accomplished additional strength can be secured by

[66] Nevins, "Lincoln's Plans for Reunion," *Abraham Lincoln Association Papers,* 1930, pp. 87–88.

[67] Springer, "James Speed, the Attorney-General, 1864–1866," *The Filson Club History Quarterly,* XI (1937), pp. 171–72.

[68] Schuckers, *The Life and Public Services of Salmon Portland Chase,* p. 519.

abandoning the radical or extreme policy, and adopting a conservative tone, as being more consonant with the new order of things.

The President apparently believes in the scriptural injunction
that there is a time for all things. A time to laugh and a time to cry,
a time to be radical and a time to be conservative. The time having
arrived to pursue the latter course, many of those who cannot appreciate the change in public events, and which renders that course
politic at this time, look on with amazement at the developments
here. There are more things than one involved in the removal of
Butler [General Benjamin F. Butler]. It will soon be found that he
is not the only person of the radical side that comes under the ban,
either of the government or public opinion.

The radicals, however, die hard . . . Ben Wade and his associates
have commenced their blowing again. . . . They are trying to create the impression that the President is willing to abandon his emancipation platform, and, as an offset, Senator Wade now declares that
the war shall go on for thirty years unless slavery is wiped out.[69]

This fight between conservatives and radicals over Reconstruction was made the more intense by quarrels over appointments
in various regions. The situation in New York is highly illustrative. During his campaign for reëlection Lincoln, it will be remembered, had removed from office two prominent friends of
Chase, Collector Hiram Barney of the Port of New York and
Surveyor Rufus F. Andrews. In their places Lincoln had appointed two Seward-Weed followers—Simeon Draper and Abram
Wakeman respectively. During the entire Congressional session—
from December, 1864, to March, 1865—the pro-Chase, or radical
members of the United States Senate opposed these nominations
and held up their confirmation. Weed journeyed to Washington
to clear the field for them. Not until the last day of the session—
March 3—did the Senate confirm them.[70]

Lincoln clearly indicated his opposition to the radicals two
days before his assassination by removing from office E. Delafield
Smith, United States Attorney for the Southern District of New
York, and putting in his place the conservative Daniel S. Dickin-

[69] New York *Herald*, Jan. 22, 1865.

[70] *U. S. Senate Executive Journal*, XIV, Part I (1864–66), 89, 96, 165, 215, 220;
New York *Herald*, Dec. 12, 1864; Feb. 10, 16, 19, 22, 25, March 3, 1865; New York
World, Feb. 13, 17, 1865.

son.[71] Smith had been hailed by New York radicals as "the only District Attorney that ever had the nerve to hang a slave-trader."[72] Dickinson, a Unionist conciliator of the South, expressed his views vigorously and clearly: "I hold further that the States are in the Union, as much as they ever were; that *individuals only* are *criminals*, whether few or many, it makes no difference; that the war can have but one object, putting down the rebellion; and when that end is attained, the prosecution of the war must cease."[73] "The appointment of Mr. Dickinson is creditable to the President,"[74] commented the anti-Lincoln "Copperhead" New York *World*.

The split in the New York Republican ranks between the Seward-Weed, or conservative faction and the Chase, or radical faction, made wider by quarrels over appointments, was evident in Lincoln's appointment of a successor to the late Chief Justice Roger B. Taney, of the United States Supreme Court. For Chase, who had been prominent in the radical cause throughout the war, was himself the leading contender for this loftiest of judicial positions.

Chase, however, was not the only one who aspired to this high office. In fact there was no dearth of candidates. Mr. Justice Noah H. Swayne was desirous of promotion to the Chief Justiceship and was vigorously urged by Lincoln's personal friend, Mr. Justice David Davis, and by Postmaster General Dennison.[75] Davis himself was being pushed editorially for the position by James Gordon Bennett in the columns of the New York *Herald*.[76] Judge William Strong, of Pennsylvania, had hopes. Secretary of War Stanton also had supporters. "I think that the President owes it to you,"[77] Mr. Justice Grier wrote Stanton. Mrs. Stanton enlisted the support of Lincoln's friend, United States Senator Orville H. Browning, of Illinois, in her husband's behalf.[78] Brown-

[71] New York *World*, April 13, 1865.   [72] New York *Evening Post*, Oct. 22, 1864.
[73] Dickinson to Rogers, July 31, 1864, in *Speeches, Correspondence, Etc., of the Late Daniel S. Dickinson, of New York*, II, 651–52.
[74] New York *World*, April 13, 1865.
[75] C. Warren, *The Supreme Court in United States History, 1935 edition*, II, 401.
[76] New York *Herald*, Dec. 4, 1864.
[77] Justice R. C. Grier to Stanton, Oct. 13, 1864, in *The Diary of Orville Hickman Browning, 1850–1864*, ed. by Pease and Randall, I, 688 n.
[78] *The Diary of Orville Hickman Browning, 1850–1864*, ed. by Pease and Randall, I, 687–88.

ing visited Lincoln, telling him the virtues of Stanton for the cherished Chief Justiceship. "He [Lincoln]," Browning recorded in his diary, "said nothing in reply to what I urged except to admit Stanton's ability and fine qualifications." [79] Lincoln further informed Browning that Attorney General Edward Bates had personally solicited the Chief Justiceship for himself. [80] Weed, representing the conservative faction of the party, strongly commended the legal light of the New York Republican organization, William M. Evarts. Many friends felt that Evarts was abundantly qualified for the high office. Unquestionably he was the best lawyer of them all. The New York court of appeals unanimously signed a petition to Lincoln, urging Evarts's appointment and declaring: "He is preeminent for his refinement, courtesy, and dignity of his manner, and these qualities are not undeserving of consideration in a man who is to occupy the place heretofore filled by a Jay, Ellsworth, Marshall and Taney." [81]

Naturally, Evarts wanted the appointment. To abandon a lucrative law practice for the salary of a Chief Justice would mean financial sacrifice, but the position was the highest goal of the legal profession. Evarts wrote Richard Henry Dana:

The Chief Justiceship is, it seems to me, for the next two years a place of great political importance over and above its simple judicial authority. . . . A good deal of interest has been spontaneously shown here to me in the place on public grounds, by persons of highest political influence. This has been gratifying to me, for public grounds are the only ones that I can for a moment justify myself in allowing any weight to. . . . Aside from Gov. Chase I am justified in thinking that many things concur to make me a very prominent, if not the most prominent candidate. [82]

But Chase felt himself the better qualified of the two. "Evarts," he wrote, "is a man of sterling abilities and excellent learning and a much greater lawyer than I ever pretended to be. The truth is, I always thought myself much overestimated. And yet I think I have more judgement than Evarts, and that tried by the Marshall standard [I] should make a better judge; while he might, tried by the Story standard." [83]

[79] The Diary of Orville Hickman Browning, 1850–1864, ed. by Pease and Randall, I, 688. 　　　　　　　　　[80] Ibid. 　　　　　　[81] Barrows, William M. Evarts, p. 125.
[82] Dyer, The Public Career of William M. Evarts, pp. 156–57.
[83] Hart, Salmon Portland Chase, pp. 320–21.

In Washington Evarts's nomination was urged by numerous persons including Richard Henry Dana, E. Rockwood Hoar, and Governor Andrew, of Massachusetts. The members of the Supreme Court, it was reported, were unanimously for him. Hoar wrote him that Taney just before his death had said that Evarts would be the best appointee. "What I want," Hoar confided to Evarts, "is to have Chase and Stanton, the Kilkenny cats [kill off each other], and have you come in as an innocent third person —on the grounds aside from politics." [84]

For a time Evarts's candidacy gave promise of success, but he lacked the large following of Chase. Not even Seward supported him. Sumner urged Chase's appointment in the Senate. Long before Taney's death Lincoln had declared he would appoint Chase if the opportunity arose. It was finally understood that Lincoln would select Chase, and, if he refused, Evarts would be second choice.[85]

Last, but by no means least, there were the conservative Blairs, hating Chase for his radicalism and because he had utilized the Treasury patronage to support Henry Winter Davis in Maryland. Commenting on this ubiquitous family group Lincoln said: "The Blairs have to an unusual degree the spirit of clan. Their family is a close corporation." [86] Former Postmaster General Montgomery Blair longed to be Chief Justice. His father, Francis P. Blair, Sr., nurtured a burning ambition to see his son wearing this most coveted of judicial robes. Shortly after Taney's death the elder Blair addressed a frank letter to Lincoln, under date of October 20, 1864, reminding him that for four years the Blairs had staunchly supported the Lincoln administration: "I think Montgomery's unswerving support of your administration in all its aspects coupled with his unfaltering attachment to you personally fits him to be your representative man at the head of that Bench." [87] Lincoln remained noncommittal, whatever may have been his innermost thoughts.

It was galling to the elder Blair to watch the pressure being

---

[84] Storey and Emerson, *Ebenezer Rockwood Hoar*, pp. 141–44.

[85] *The Diary of Orville Hickman Browning, 1850–1864*, ed. by Pease and Randall, I, 686–87; W. E. Smith, *The Francis Preston Blair Family in Politics*, II, 297; Barrows, *William M. Evarts*, p. 126; New York *World*, Oct. 18, 1864.

[86] Hay, *Lincoln and the Civil War in the Diaries and Letters of John Hay*, ed. by Dennett, p. 133.

[87] W. E. Smith, *The Francis Preston Blair Family in Politics*, II, 299.

exerted in Chase's behalf. On November 22, in a long letter, he enlisted the support of Simon Cameron, who had conducted Lincoln's campaign for reëlection in Pennsylvania. "Chase & his friends are moving all the powers of darkness to put him at the Head of the Supreme Court," Blair informed Cameron, "and I have intimated to the President that if he was [sic] (& as I hoped might be disposed to remember the service rendered him by the members of his Cabinet) I would be glad if his choice would fall on Montgomery." [88] The senior Blair appealed to Cameron: "If you would write me a letter of reply to this, which I could show to Lincoln as a manifestation of your opinion in favor of it, I would be extremely gratified—and if you could get some of your influential friends in Pa. also to back me, it would increase the many obligations I owe you personally." [89]

The pressure on Lincoln to select Chase as presiding judge of the Supreme Court during and following the election of 1864 was intense. Aside from many of Chase's friends in Ohio—such as G. Volney Dorsey, Republican state chairman [90]—the support for the former Secretary of the Treasury came largely from radical Republican members of the Senate, as for example, Massachusetts' two extremists, Charles Sumner and Henry Wilson.[91] Chase must be named, his radical partisans insisted, in order that the emancipation proclamation and the administration's financial and other policies be adequately safeguarded. Chase, they argued, having been identified with both the administration's emancipation and financial programs, was the logical man for Chief Justice.[92]

Montgomery Blair felt reasonably certain that he could outdistance Chase in the race for Chief Justice and rallied round him powerful foes of Chase.[93] One of these was Thurlow Weed, who, at the suggestion of Seward, himself a Blair supporter, rushed to Washington in an effort to block the Chase nomination. James Gordon Bennett, of the New York *Herald*, was said to

[88] F. P. Blair, Sr. to Cameron, Nov. 22, 1864, Cameron Papers.

[89] *Ibid.*

[90] G. Volney Dorsey to Lincoln (copy), Oct. 26, 1864, Chase Papers, Library of Congress.

[91] Hart, *Salmon Portland Chase*, p. 321; W. E. Smith, *The Francis Preston Blair Family in Politics*, II, 297-98.

[92] New York *Herald*, Dec. 10, 1864.

[93] W. E. Smith, *The Francis Preston Blair Family in Politics*, II, 297.

have likewise joined the anti-Chase group.[94] Only the alarming prospect of the radical Chase heading the Supreme Court could possibly have resulted in attempted concert of action by such traditional enemies as Seward and Blair, both of whom represented the conservative wing of the party despite their personal hostility.[95]

The efforts of the Blair-Seward or, better, the anti-Chase group, to check Chase were in vain. Lincoln apparently had made up his mind to appoint the Ohioan as Chief Justice after having been assured by Sumner that Chase had abandoned his ambitions for the presidency.[96] On December 6 (1864) the President sent the long-awaited message to the Senate: "I nominate Salmon P. Chase, of Ohio, to be Chief Justice of the Supreme Court of the United States, vice Roger B. Taney, deceased." [97] The Senate, true to its tradition of acting on nominations of present or former members of the Senate without referring such nominations to a committee, confirmed Chase on the same day.[98] Gideon Welles recorded in his diary that Chase's appointment was satisfactory to Sumner and a few others but not to the general public.[99]

Many and varied are the reasons suggested in explanation of Lincoln's action in appointing to one of the most esteemed positions his rival for the presidency in the preceding election. That he decided on Chase reluctantly is probable; one conservative Republican leader even maintained that he "would rather have swallowed his buckhorn chair than to have nominated Chase." [100] George S. Boutwell, one-time governor of Massachusetts and whom Lincoln had appointed United States Commissioner of Internal Revenue, maintained that the President told him at the time of Chase's appointment:

There are three reasons in favor of his appointment, and one very strong reason against it. First, he occupies the largest place in the

[94] *Independent*, Dec. 15, 1868, cited in C. Warren, *The Supreme Court in United States History*, II, 402 n.
[95] Senator Sumner wrote almost a year later: "Montgomery Blair . . . complained to Seward that he had not pushed him for the chief justiceship against Chase. Seward said that he had 'presented his papers,' and that Blair was 'his candidate.' Blair thought that if Seward had been much in earnest he could have prevented Chase's nomination." See Pierce, *Memoir and Letters of Charles Sumner*, IV, 255.
[96] Boutwell, *Reminiscences of Sixty Years in Public Affairs*, II, 29–30.
[97] *U. S. Senate Executive Journal*, XIV, Part I (1864–66), 1.
[98] *Ibid.* [99] *Diary of Gideon Welles*, II, 196. [100] *Ibid.*

public mind in connection with the office, then we wish for a Chief Justice who will sustain what has been done in regard to emancipation and the legal tenders. We cannot ask a man what he will do, and if we should, and he should answer us, we would despise him for it. Therefore we must take a man whose opinions are known. But there is one very strong reason against his appointment. He is a candidate for the Presidency, and if he does not give up that idea it will be very bad for him and very bad for me.[101]

Lincoln's fears that Chase had not shaken off the presidential fever were well founded. He worked for the presidential nomination in 1868 and was ready to accept it in 1872.[102] Indeed, no sooner did Lincoln pass away than the Chief Justice undertook a trip to Florida—during the late spring and early summer of 1865—to renew old acquaintances among the strong faction of special fiscal agents which he had built up while Secretary of the Treasury. Chase's activity following Lincoln's death was most obnoxious to the Blair family. From Florida Harrison Reed, chief postal agent in Florida and an appointee of Montgomery Blair while the latter served as Postmaster General, wrote to Blair two months after Lincoln's assassination:

I wish to bespeak your immediate and earnest assistance to rescue Florida from the hands of Chase and his corrupt agents now holding lucrative position under the Government. His late visit to this state was for no other purpose than to revive the efforts to secure this state for his future purposes and against the policy of the [Johnson] Administration. . . . He [Chase] has advised his friends here to organize the colored men and prepare them to vote, and their action will be sustained by the Supreme Court—holding that there is no legal power to deny suffrage to any citizen. . . .[103]

Chase's friend and biographer, Jacob W. Schuckers, later gave to the Chief Justice's southern trip a somewhat different slant: "Not long after the inauguration of President Johnson, Mr. Chase determined upon a visit to the Southern cities, with a view to

[101] Boutwell, *Reminiscences of Sixty Years in Public Affairs*, II, 29.
[102] Coleman, *The Election of 1868*, pp. 73–78; Hart, *Salmon Portland Chase*, pp. 362–68, 413.
[103] Harrison Reed to Montgomery Blair, June 26, 1865, in W. W. Davis, *The Civil War and Reconstruction in Florida*, pp. 351–52.

learn as much as possible, from actual observation, of the true condition of the country." [104]

Regardless of Chase's motives in making this extended tour through the South, it served to open wider the breach between the pro-Chase radicals and pro-Blair conservatives during the early days of President Johnson's administration. Nor should we overlook the fact that this struggle between conservatives and radicals within the Republican party, which proved to be a major factor in making such a debacle of Reconstruction during the Johnson administration, had taken deep root in the months preceding Lincoln's death. Not only was it a quarrel between Republican factions over the Reconstruction policy to be adopted toward vanquished Confederate states, but also over coveted federal appointments. This was clearly borne out in the struggle for control in Maryland between the conservative faction of Montgomery Blair and the radical faction of the fiery Congressman Henry Winter Davis.

Throughout the last two years of the war the feud between the two Maryland groups over the questions of patronage and Negro emancipation had continued with bitter intensity. In the November, 1863, election for comptroller and members to the state legislature the Davisites had triumphed on the issue of immediate emancipation as opposed to Blair's plan for gradual, "compensated" emancipation. Lincoln had declined to interfere.[105] The Blairites continued the fight, and in January, 1864, the Postmaster General himself, in company with his now ally, United States Senator Thomas H. Hicks, had addressed members of the legislature at Annapolis, alleging that Lincoln was favorable to their plan of compensated emancipation. Davis and his followers were furious over this statement.[106]

The approach of the presidential election of 1864 had opened wider the rift among the Maryland Unionists: The Davis forces, led by Congressman John A. J. Creswell and Collector Henry W.

---

[104] Schuckers, *The Life and Public Services of Salmon Portland Chase,* p. 519.

[105] *A Biographical Sketch of Hon. A. Leo Knott with a Relation of Some Political Transactions in Maryland, 1861–1867,* pp. 37–38. (Copy in Library of Congress.)

[106] Hugh L. Bond to Creswell, Jan. 19, 1864; George Earle to Creswell, Jan. 18, 28, 1864, John A. J. Creswell Papers.

Hoffman of the Port of Baltimore, secured control of the Union state convention that met in Baltimore on February 22 for the purpose of selecting delegates to the National Convention. The father of the Postmaster General, old Francis P. Blair, and the Blair lieutenant, Postmaster William H. Purnell, of Baltimore, were both defeated for delegate at large. The four delegates at large selected were Creswell, Collector Hoffman, and two other Davis followers, H. H. Goldsborough and A. C. Green. Moreover, after a stormy session the convention adopted a resolution declaring for "immediate" emancipation, over the opposition of the Blair forces.[107]

Political peace did not come to Maryland, nor to Lincoln, with the retirement of Blair from the Cabinet—particularly when, in October, Collector Hoffman heard that Blair's ally, Former Mayor Thomas Swann of Baltimore, on the stump for Lincoln's reëlection, declared that "Blair still had more influence with Lincoln than any man in the country." [108] Blair himself added fuel to the flames of discord by announcing that J. A. Leonard, a pro-Blair federal officeholder removed by Lincoln, would be reappointed.[109]

The victory of Lincoln over McClellan for another term in the White House seemed to add to the rivalry between Blairites and Davisites. Blair paid a visit to the White House and there gave vent to his hatred of Davis, charging that the radical Secretary of War Stanton had used the War Department patronage to aid Davis in Maryland and that the remnant of Chase officeholders in the Treasury had done likewise. Lincoln's private secretary, John Hay, who listened to Blair's complaints tolerantly, left this record: "November 9, 1864. . . . Montgomery Blair came in this morning. He . . . is very bitter against the Davis clique (what's left of it), and foolishly, I think, confounds the War Department and the Treasury as parties to the Winter Davis conspiracy against the President." [110] The disgruntlement of the

---

[107] Baltimore *Clipper*, Feb. 23, 1864; George Earle to Creswell, Feb. 24, 1864, Creswell Papers.

[108] Jas. W. Clayton to Creswell, Oct. 7, 1864, Creswell Papers.

[109] *Ibid.*

[110] Hay, *Lincoln and the Civil War in the Letters and Diaries of John Hay,* ed. by Dennett, p. 236.

Blairites continued, and on December 29 Blair's lieutenant, Senator Hicks, complained to Blair in a lengthy letter:

I write to say that if the Prest, Gov. Seward &c intend to let Hon. H. Winter Davis, Creswell, Bond &c that had brought us well nigh the brink of political ruin, control newspapers, appointments to office, &c in Maryland the sooner they let us know it the better; that we may cease to labor for naught. . . . I care nothing for men. I go for party and country— What sacrifice pecuniary has the Davis faction made, how many slaves did they vote from themselves in the new constitution for our State. I lost more than all of them. . . . Pardon this disjointed, but true epistle, drawn out at hearing that Davis & Co. are interfering to keep Judge Lewis [U. S. Commissioner of Internal Revenue Joseph J. Lewis] from appointing an assessor for my county and are striving with Hon. W. H. Seward to keep the printing by Govt. from the Cambridge Herald. . . . You will oblige me greatly, if you can see Gov. Seward, and say that the Herald is about to pass into other hands, and as the public printing has been divided between the Eastern & Western shore, to let it be so still if he can.[111]

Davis's followers took heart at Lincoln's appointment of the radical Chase as Chief Justice. Blair was soured that Lincoln had not given him this judicial prize.[112] In distress Blair called on his old friend, Secretary of the Navy Welles, a few days following Chase's selection. Of the visit Welles noted:

December 10, Saturday: Blair called on me in somewhat of a disturbed state of mind and wanted my advice. He had had one interview with the President since I last saw him, in which the President said he disliked to remove Hoffman from the collectorship of Baltimore, but that the Spanish mission would be vacant, and he would place that at Blair's disposal to arrange with Senator Hicks and Hoffman, as he pleased. Blair replied that he could go into no such arrangement; that he had no confidence in Hoffman, who is wholly unreliable, had deserted everybody and ought to be discarded. The appointment of Chase has brought the Maryland malcontents into

111 Thomas H. Hicks to Montgomery Blair, Dec. 29, 1864, Francis Preston Blair Papers.
112 Francis P. Blair, Jr. (Montgomery's brother) wrote him: "The thing that pains me most of all is that Chase's appointment *shakes my confidence in the President's integrity.*" See F. P. Blair, Jr. to Montgomery Blair, Jan. 17, 1865, Francis Preston Blair Papers.

position. . . . Blair fears the President is flinching and will succumb, and thought it advisable that he, or some one, should have an
explicit conversation with the President, and wanted my advice. I
told him that it seemed to me very important that such a conversation should take place, but no one could do this so well as himself.
. . . Blair . . . said he would see the President, and would boldly
and frankly express himself. Blair's present view is to go into the
Senate, in place of Hicks, who wishes to be made collector of Baltimore. Of course, Hoffman, the present collector, must be removed as
the initiatory step to this end.[113]

Hoffman, a Davis follower, was thus slated to go, and the Baltimore collectorship could then be filled by Senator Hicks; in that
event Blair might be elected to the Senate.[114] Lincoln was apparently reluctant to remove Hoffman lest he estrange further
the Davis radicals.[115] The President accordingly offered Blair
the post of Minister to Spain, which Blair promptly declined.[116]
The former Postmaster General shunned the Spanish mission, Senator Sumner related, with the "indignant" remark that he "had
refused the post when he was a young man during the administration of Polk." [117]

Before the President could make up his mind as to what action
to take regarding the Maryland impasse, Senator Hicks died in
mid-February (1865), thus throwing the patronage muddle in
this state into further confusion.[118] No sooner had Hicks been laid

[113] *Diary of Gideon Welles,* II, 195–96.

[114] "It is understood that Governor Hicks is to resign his seat in the Senate and be
appointed Collector of Customs at Baltimore, in the place of Hoffman, one of the
Davisites, and that Montgomery Blair is to have the Senatorship thus vacated"—so
wrote a Washington correspondent. See New York *Herald,* Dec. 3, 1864.

[115] On Dec. 18, 1864, Blair complained to John Hay that Lincoln was not favoring
his faction sufficiently, giving too much consideration to Davis's men. See Hay, *Lincoln and the Civil War in the Diaries and Letters of John Hay,* ed. by Dennett, pp.
243–44.

[116] W. E. Smith, *The Francis Preston Blair Family in Politics,* II, 331.

[117] Pierce, *Memoir and Letters of Charles Sumner,* IV, 255.

[118] Welles wrote: "The death of Governor Hicks has brought on a crisis of parties
in Maryland. Blair is a candidate for the position of Senator, and the President
wishes him elected, but Stanton and the Chase influence, including the Treasury, do
not, and hence the whole influence of those Departments is against him. Blair thinks
the President does not aid him as much as he had reason to suppose he would, and
finds it difficult to get an interview with him. I think he has hardly been treated as
he deserves, or as the President really wishes, yet the vindictiveness of the Chief
Justice and Stanton deter him, control him against his will." See *Diary of Gideon
Welles,* II, 243.

to rest than a mad tussle ensued between Blair and Congressman
John A. J. Creswell (Davis's chief lieutenant) for the vacant Senate seat. At Annapolis the Maryland legislature waxed warm
over the rival candidates, the conservative members supporting
Blair because he was "expected to favor compensation for the
slaves liberated," while the radical members (or extreme emancipationists) worked for Creswell's election.[119] Although Lincoln
was said to favor Blair, the War Department patronage in Maryland at the direction of the radical Secretary of War Stanton
and the pro-Chase officeholders in the Treasury Department
were utilized for Creswell.[120] The pro-Blair Baltimore *Clipper*
charged bitterly: "The purse and the sword, the Treasury of the
United States and all the patronage of the War Department
may elect him [Creswell]. . . . No person ever wished him to
be a candidate but Henry Winter Davis and his friends." [121] Despite all efforts in Blair's behalf, Creswell won the Senatorship.

The election of Creswell to the United States senate brought
no improvement in the Maryland scene as far as Lincoln was concerned, although the President tried valiantly to bring harmony
to the warring factions. The Blairs, stung by Montgomery's defeat, were in no mood for peace,[122] while Davis, apparently flushed
by Creswell's victory, resumed his baiting of the administration.
Indeed, on March 3 (1865), the last day of the expiring Congress,
Davis joined such radical leaders as Thaddeus Stevens, of Pennsylvania, in opposing Lincoln's conciliatory Reconstruction policy
toward Louisiana.[123] "Justice to all" was proving a difficult rule
for Lincoln to apply practically in Maryland.

Efforts by the Blair forces to remove the pro-Davis Hoffman
as Collector of the Port of Baltimore continued unabated. Creswell, as United States Senator, would, were the custom of Senatorial courtesy followed, have a powerful voice in the matter.
Nevertheless, the President apparently had made up his mind
to remove Hoffman and to reshuffle the entire Baltimore patronage

119 New York *Herald,* Feb. 18, 1865. For the relationship between Davis and Creswell, see Steiner, *Life of Henry Winter Davis,* pp. 65, 217, 297, 385–86.
120 *Diary of Gideon Welles,* II, 243.
121 Baltimore *Clipper,* March 6, 1865.
122 F. P. Blair, Jr., to Montgomery Blair, April 9, 1865, Francis Preston Blair
Papers.
123 McCarthy, *Lincoln's Plan of Reconstruction,* pp. 341–43.

in the interest of party harmony. In March (1865) Davis, knowing Lincoln's intention, advised Creswell sternly:

> I have been reflecting on the proposed Custom House arrangements & the more I think of it the more serious & dangerous it looks.
> I sounded Bond & Stirling. . . . B. & S. were unwilling to agree unless it were especially agreed the patronage should be disposed of *wholly* to our satisfaction you of course included. . . .
> I wish you to revise the ground & act prudently. Dont buy enemies nor pay allies from necessity at the expense of our best friends.
> Let the Custom House stand unless there is an absolute union of the head proposed with us & a dissolution of relations with Swann & Blair.
> A word for yourself in absolute confidence. Some of our friends think or are inclined to think you prefer to coalesce with our enemies too readily for temporary purposes. I have combated it sharply but you will understand how such a suspicion will impair your just influence.[124]

Creswell appears not to have been guided too rigidly by Davis's caution regarding the necessity of not coöperating with the Blair faction. At Lincoln's suggestion Creswell met with Thomas Swann, a Blair follower, for the purpose of drawing up a slate of appointments to the main federal positions in Baltimore. In April, 1865—the exact date cannot be determined—Creswell and Swann sent to the White House the following list of names on which they had agreed:

For Collector	Edwin H. Webster Bel-Air, Hartford Coy, Md.
Post Master	Genl Andrew W. Denison Baltimore, Md
Surveyor	Edington Fulton Baltimore, Md
Naval Officer	Samuel M. Evans Baltimore, Md
Marshal	James W. Clayton Baltimore, Md

[124] H. Winter Davis to Creswell, March, 1865, Creswell Papers. (No day is listed in this letter, but it is inserted after that of Floyd to Creswell, March 31, 1865.)

District Attorney   Wm J. Jones
                                     Elkton, Cecil County, Md

Navy Agent   Doctr Thomas King Carroll
                                     Cambridge, Md

Appraiser   Robert G. Proud
                                     Baltimore, Md

    "   Thomas A. Smith
                                     Urbana, Frederick Coy

    "   Ephraim F. Anderson
                                     Hagerstown,
                                     Washington County, Md [125]

Under this original list, dating it April 14, 1865, Lincoln wrote
the words:

Gov. Swann & Senator Creswell present the above to-day, which
they do on a plan suggested by me.
April 14, 1865.   [signed]   A. L.[126]

Several days later one Baltimore journal referred to Lincoln's
"selection" of the above officeholders for Maryland as "one of
the last official acts of the lamented President." [127] It is interest-
ing to note that at least one of these proposed selections—that
of Edwin H. Webster for Collector of Customs of the Port of
Baltimore—was appointed by Lincoln's successor, Andrew Johnson.[128]

The Maryland factional fight over patronage and the dual
issue of Negro emancipation and Reconstruction not having been
settled at the time of Lincoln's death, it remained to plague President Johnson. Although the radical Davis ended his service in
Congress, returned to the law, and died on the last day of the
year in which Lincoln passed to the Great Beyond,[129] the other
stormy petrel of Maryland politics, Montgomery Blair, attempted
to take a new lease on political life by becoming an adviser of

[125] A facsimile of this list is printed in Hertz, *Abraham Lincoln: A New Portrait,*
II, facing 900. This list, with only slight modification, appeared in the Baltimore
press two days after Lincoln passed away. See Baltimore *Clipper,* April 17, 1865.
[126] Hertz, *Abraham Lincoln: A New Portrait,* II, facsimile facing 900.
[127] Baltimore *Clipper,* April 17, 1865.
[128] *Biographical Directory of the American Congress, 1774–1927,* p. 1678.
[129] Steiner, *Life of Henry Winter Davis,* pp. 350–72.

Johnson and unsuccessfully endeavoring to persuade the new President to remove the radical Stanton as Secretary of War and to have first Grant and then Frank Blair appointed in his place.[130]

In addition to Maryland, there were other states in which the Republican (or "Union") party split into conservatives and radicals over reconstruction and patronage. One of these was Indiana. Lincoln's decision to appoint as Judge of the United States Court of Claims the Indiana leader, Richard W. Thompson, who had aided materially in selecting a pro-Lincoln delegation from the Hoosier State to the Baltimore Convention, was at once challenged. Thompson had always been a man of most conservative views and, while a strong Unionist, had intimate ties with the South.[131] In February Lincoln sent Thompson's nomination as Judge of the Claims Court to the Senate for confirmation.[132] Sitting in Congress from Indiana at this time was George Washington Julian, a radical of the radicals and a friend of many years' standing of Chase and Senator Charles Sumner.[133] The appointment of Thompson infuriated Julian, whose words in his diary constitute an illuminating commentary on the existence of the split between conservatives and radicals within the Republican party over the question of federal appointments. Wrote Julian:

Dick Thompson, an old pro-slavery fossil, has just been appointed judge of the Court of Claims. This is an outrage, but I learn from senators that nothing can be done to prevent his confirmation, for the reason that old Abe, through his patronage, is the virtual dictator of the country. I have tried to get Colfax [Speaker of the House of Representatives] and other Indiana congressmen to unite in a protest against the confirmation, but they decline, on the ground that they don't want any quarrel with Lincoln or Thompson. I am utterly sick of the every-day spectacles of moral cowardice. . . .[134]

Julian, an antislaveryite, had been affiliated with the pro-Chase or radical wing of the Republican party from the first. Early

[130] W. E. Smith, *The Francis Preston Blair Family in Politics,* II, 328–32, 334–35, 338.

[131] Roll, "Richard W. Thompson: A Political Conservative in the Fifties," *Indiana Magazine of History,* XXVII (Sept., 1931), 183–206.

[132] *U. S. Senate Executive Journal,* XIV, Part I (1864–66), 150.

[133] Clarke, *George W. Julian,* pp. 79, 101, 109, 122, 139, 182–83, 208 n.–9 n., 250.

[134] "George W. Julian's Journal," *Indiana Magazine of History,* XI (Dec., 1915), 328.

in January, 1861, he had journeyed to Springfield to see Lincoln, then President-elect, to remonstrate against the appointment of Caleb B. Smith and Simon Cameron to the Cabinet.[135] Julian's daughter related:

Smith he [Julian] knew as an old Whig who had opposed Free Soil principles in those early days when the struggle to secure for them a foothold in Indiana was desperate, and Cameron was distasteful from the fact that his name had already come to stand for political crookedness and trickery, as well as because he belonged to the conciliatory and temporizing wing of the Republican party. Cameron was backed by Seward and Thurlow Weed, who strongly opposed the appointment of Chase to a cabinet position.[136]

Julian, on the very day of Lincoln's death, April 15, 1865, met with Ben Wade, Henry Winter Davis, and other radicals, who had been at odds with Lincoln over federal appointments and a reconstruction policy, to urge the newly inaugurated Andrew Johnson to reorganize the Cabinet. Major General Benjamin F. Butler, it was planned, should supersede the conservative Seward as Secretary of State.[137] Butler, destined two years hence to be one of the House managers of the impeachment proceedings against Johnson, had only a few months before been dismissed by Lincoln from the command of the Army of the James. Immediately Butler became a favorite of the radicals in Congress and the close ally of such extremists as Henry Winter Davis, Wade, and Chandler.[138] Among the details of the conference Julian recorded the following:

I like the radicalism of the members of this caucus, but have not in a long time heard so much profanity. It became intolerably disgusting. Their hostility towards Lincoln's policy of conciliation and contempt for his weakness were undisguised; and the universal feeling among radical men here is that his death is a god-send.[139]

Naturally, Julian lost little time in opposing Johnson's conciliatory Reconstruction policy.[140] Indeed, the new President, im-

[135] Clarke, *George W. Julian*, p. 210.   [136] *Ibid.*, p. 211.
[137] "George W. Julian's Journal," *Indiana Magazine of History*, XI (Dec., 1915), 335.
[138] Clarke, *George W. Julian*, p. 210; *Diary of Gideon Welles*, II, 223–24, 226.
[139] "George W. Julian's Journal," *Indiana Magazine of History*, XI (Dec., 1915), 335.
[140] Bowers, *The Tragic Era*, pp. 5, 9–11, 15; Clarke, *George W. Julian*, pp. 273–74.

mediately on succeeding to the role of Chief Executive, was to find all too many of the key federal offices filled with radicals. And it was Johnson's inability to control the plums of patronage that was partly responsible for his failure to exert authority over the Republican party in Congress during the period of Reconstruction.[141]

Lincoln, considerably more than Johnson could or would do, had made officeholding dependent on loyalty to him. Just what Lincoln's fame would have been had the gods decided to shield him from Booth's bullet and had he been allowed to continue to tackle problems of patronage and reconstruction following Appomattox still remains a fruitful theme for conjecture.

[141] Beale, *The Critical Year*, pp. 117–21.

Chapter XII

IN SUMMARY AND RETROSPECT

ABRAHAM LINCOLN came to the presidency in the halcyon days of the spoils system and when pressure for a "clean sweep" on the part of the victor had never been more insistent. As far as is known, Lincoln prior to 1861 did not oppose this practice and, although he made no ante-nomination promises, once elected he operated along customary lines.[1] Indeed, the change in party control from Democrats to Republicans was the occasion for the most sweeping removal of federal officeholders up to that time in American history.[2] Of the 1,520 presidential officeholders no less than 1,195 were removed as a result of the Republican victory of 1860—an almost complete sweep if allowance is made for the vacancies in the South occasioned by the Secession.[3] Undoubtedly a few in office by President Buchanan's appointment continued to hold their jobs under Lincoln. They were primarily those whose efficiency raised them above party, such as William Hunter, retained in the Department of State; John J. Cisco, Sub-Treasurer at New York; James W. Taylor, Treasury Agent in Canada; and Elisha Whittlesey, Comptroller of the Treasury.[4]

Though changes in office under Lincoln were considerably more

---

[1] For Lincoln's attitude toward the spoils system prior to his elevation to the presidency, see Fish, "Lincoln and the Patronage," *American Historical Review,* VIII (1902), 55.

[2] Sellers, "James R. Doolittle," *The Wisconsin Magazine of History,* XVII (March, 1934), 296.

[3] On this point consult Fish, "Table of Removals," *Annual Report,* American Historical Association, I (1899), 82.

[4] With very few exceptions the Democrats accepted the dismissal of their party brethren with good grace. One leading Republican editor of Philadelphia made this comment a few days after Lincoln took office in March, 1861: "The Democrats have had more than a fair share of the spoils, and many of them are disposed to yield gracefully and to admit the claims of their opponents to recognition." See Philadelphia *North American and United States Gazette,* March 15, 1861. And one Republican appointee of Lincoln declared later: "The Democrats submitted to the turning-out with great good nature as a part of the game they had played and lost, and would have laughed at any scruples on the part of their opponents, as if one should jump in checkers and not take up his man." See Talbot, "James Shepherd Pike," *Collections and Proceedings of the Maine Historical Society,* Series II, I (1890), 251.

numerous than usual, they varied from department to department according to the disposition of those who administered the patronage. Seward, for example, did not make wholesale changes in the State Department; on the other hand, the master-spoilsman, Cameron, early intimated to War Department clerks "that most of them would be expected to retire, for others who had not enjoyed the flesh-pots." [5]

How many sinecure appointments existed during Lincoln's administration we do not know. Probably they could be found in every department. Under date of June 7, 1862, we find A. B. Mullett writing Chase as follows:

I have been assigned to a regular desk in your Bureau where I am engaged in keeping a book invented by Mr. Shannon, the chief merit of which is its utter uselessness for any other purpose than as an excuse for a Clerk. . . . The position is . . . one of the sinecures so abundant in the Department. And I am sure you should be astonished if you knew how little work is done by some, and how much useless work by other Clerks in the Department, as well as the cumbersome . . . methods that are in use generally.[6]

The preceding pages of this book leave little doubt that Lincoln distributed the patronage probably as wisely as any human could under the circumstances. No President of the United States, perhaps, was ever confronted by a more difficult situation. Not only did he face the task of keeping together a party composed of diverse elements, each thinking that its labors had been decisive in electing him to the nation's highest office, but he had to hold the allegiance of all those outside his party who loyally supported the Union. Furthermore, his renomination and reëlection for a second term could not be ignored.

Factionalism and wirepulling within his own party were especially vexatious. Notably was this true in New York, Illinois, Pennsylvania, and Indiana, where in 1861 the factions grouped themselves into a Seward-Weed-David Davis-Cameron-Caleb B. Smith alliance and a Barney-William Cullen Bryant-Judd-McClure-Colfax entente. In the formation of his Cabinet Lincoln was subjected

---

[5] New York *Daily Tribune,* March 23, 1861.

[6] A. B. Mullett to Chase, June 7, 1862, Salmon P. Chase Papers, Library of Congress.

to great pressure by both of these powerful groups. The former wanted Cameron in the Cabinet and Chase excluded; the latter wanted Chase appointed and Cameron excluded. To preserve harmony, Lincoln reluctantly took Cameron but refused to exclude Chase. This action was in keeping with his constant effort to balance or to adjust properly the claims of the various factions that made up the party.

For his initial Cabinet Lincoln brought together a heterogeneous group. In selecting his inner council he was governed by a variety of motives: recognition of rivals within the party, political antecedents, pivotal states, geographical regions, and pledges made by his managers. Yet his Cabinet was far from being a harmonious unit. Each member had been more or less of a political leader in his home state. Four of them—Seward, Chase, Cameron, and Bates—were defeated candidates for the elevated chair held by Lincoln. Moreover, both Whig and non-Whig or radical points of view were represented. It is a rather remarkable tribute to Lincoln that, with the exception of Chase, he increasingly gained the confidence and respect of his Cabinet members. Not immediately, but ultimately, they acquired the habit of turning to him, like quarreling children to their mother, to settle the questions that temporarily divided them.

In making appointments Lincoln followed practices that were in keeping with American political tradition. He consulted members of the upper house in making nominations for or from their states. Minor offices were generally given to those nominated by members of the House of Representatives. Lincoln also listened to governors, especially of important or pivotal states. Heads of departments and certain powerful nonofficeholding individuals, such as Thurlow Weed, were influential with Lincoln. Though he patiently gave ear to all requests irrespective of source, the President did not submit to dictation, unless the removal of Montgomery Blair from the Postmaster Generalship be so interpreted. Although Mrs. Lincoln on more than one occasion [7] tried to take a hand in

[7] See *supra, re* Judd, p. 30. When the Committee on the Conduct of the War was endeavoring to demolish McClellan, Zachariah Chandler wrote his wife that Mrs. Lincoln was "down upon Seward, McClelland [sic] & the whole crew & wants to see & talk with us." Zachariah Chandler to Mrs. Chandler, March 31, 1863, Zachariah Chandler Papers, Library of Congress.

politics, the evidence is not sufficient that her efforts were a controlling factor in influencing Lincoln's action. The attempt of Chase, as we have observed, to have his way in the matter of appointments made for unpleasantness and ultimately was a major reason for Lincoln's acceptance of Chase's resignation as Secretary of the Treasury.

Military appointments were made in much the same way as those in the civil service. In naming men to army posts, however, Lincoln found it desirable to call on Democrats. But in making civil appointments, the President almost invariably selected Republicans. Moreover, it would seem that Lincoln, except in a few cases, made no very searching effort to ascertain whether the persons appointed were those best fitted by talent and experience for the job. In other words, he followed the time-honored rule of political expediency. To friends—particularly those of long standing —he was inclined to show favoritism. Nepotism was not entirely absent.

In the slave regions Lincoln encountered a difficult situation. In the "loyal" border states of Missouri and Maryland patronage problems were acute, aggravated by the split of the Republican-Union party into conservatives and radicals. In distributing the federal jobs Lincoln endeavored, as we have noted, to appease both factions in these states, but not always did his maxim "Justice to All" prove practicable. In Missouri he found it more expedient to give the edge to the conservative Blair interests, but in Maryland he found it equally expedient to favor the Blairs' avowed enemies, the radical followers of Henry Winter Davis.

That Lincoln utilized the patronage for purely political ends is evident in the number of federal officeholders who participated in the movement to secure his renomination for the presidency in 1864. Professor James G. Randall succinctly summarizes the story:

Lincoln's managers had been active. They had the advantage of controlling the regular Republican (Union) party, in which they held the managerial positions; they had the patronage, including provost marshals, postmasters, and Federal employees the country over; they had the disposal of contracts; and they worked through state conventions in which delegates to the national convention were instructed for Lincoln. When the Republican Convention met at Baltimore on June 7 the effectiveness of organization and regularity in American politics was impressively demonstrated.[8]

During the campaign for reëlection in the summer and early fall of 1864, Lincoln found it necessary to make certain removals for the sake of victory in November. We need only remind the reader that to placate the radicals and to foster the movement for Frémont's withdrawal from the presidential race, Lincoln requested the conservative Montgomery Blair to give up the Postmaster Generalship. To conciliate the conservatives and bring greater harmony to his official family and to the party, he accepted Chase's proffered resignation from the Treasuryship.

Following Lincoln's reëlection in November, 1864, new troubles broke out within the party. In the creation of the complex, intricate, and bitter struggle between conservatives and radicals, rivalry for public office seemed at times to have been almost as potent a source of discord between the two main factions as difference of opinion over the Reconstruction policy to be adopted toward the crumbling states of the Confederacy.

The criticism that Lincoln gave too much time to patronage, especially during the early weeks of his administration—time that could have been utilized to effect a settlement with the South before the opening of hostilities—is perhaps not entirely justified.[9] Under the circumstances it is difficult to see how the matter could have been handled otherwise. To have entrusted it to an underling less astute politically than was Lincoln would have been unwise. The defense of Lincoln on this point by his Secretary of the Navy, Gideon Welles, is apt:

In striving to reconcile and bring into united action opposing views he [Lincoln] was accused of wasting his time in a great emergency on mere party appointments. Under the pressure and influence that were brought to bear upon him some things were doubtless done, which, under other circumstances and left to himself he would have

[8] Randall, *The Civil War and Reconstruction*, p. 612.

[9] On March 9, 1863, Richard Henry Dana in a letter to Charles Francis Adams made this statement: "He [Lincoln] seems to me to be fonder of details than of principles, of tithing the mint, anise and cummins of patronage, and personal questions, than of the weightier matters of empire." See C. F. Adams, *Richard Henry Dana*, II, 264.

ordered differently. Extensive removals and appointments were not only expected, but absolutely necessary, yet never under any administration were greater care and deliberation required. A host of ravenous partisans from Maine to California . . . who had participated in the election of Mr. Lincoln filled Washington and besieged the White House and Departments, demanding for themselves or their friends the local appointments, regardless of the patriotism or real merits of the incumbents. This crowd of active friends with their importunities at such a crisis was of course extremely embarrassing to the new administration, which commenced its labors with a demoralized government and crumbling Union that needed the vigilant attention of the wisest and most considerate statesmanship.[10]

Had Lincoln led a united party he might have utilized his time and effort somewhat differently. His wise use of the patronage in holding the party together was a necessary antecedent to the formulation of any statesmanlike policy concerning the nation. Many Lincoln admirers find it distasteful—perhaps unbelievable—to recognize in their hero the shrewd practical politician that he was. But to witness how, as a politician, he utilized the patronage in holding together diverse conflicting factions in common purposes—the preservation of the Union, the success of his administration, and the rewarding of the party faithful—is only to enhance the greatness of Lincoln. Essentially a practical man, reared in the realism of the frontier and educated in the old school of Whig politics, Lincoln recognized the necessity of patronage as a weapon in party leadership under the American system. In being a competent politician, he became a statesman. Had he not displayed his ability as a politician with such signal success, it is doubtful whether he would be regarded today as a statesman. Had he not wielded the patronage so skillfully—something that his predecessor James Buchanan and his successor Andrew Johnson did not do—probably his administration would not have been as successful. Certainly his task of holding the Union together would have been more difficult.

[10] "Two Manuscripts of Gideon Welles," ed. by Burnitt, *The New England Quarterly*, XI (Sept., 1938), 594.

APPENDIX

Delegates or Alternates to the Baltimore Convention of 1864 Who Were Subsequently Appointed by Lincoln to Army Posts or to Other Federal Jobs.[1]

Benjamin W. Norris, delegate from Maine, appointed paymaster in the Army.[2]

Joseph R. Hawley, delegate at large from Connecticut, appointed Brigadier General of Volunteers.[3]

William T. Minor, delegate at large from Connecticut, appointed Consul General at Havana.[4]

William A. Dart, delegate from New York, appointed United States Attorney for the Northern District of New York.[5]

Asahel C. Geer, delegate from New York, appointed Collector of Internal Revenue for the Fifteenth New York District.[6]

Cornelius Parmenter, delegate at large from Ohio, appointed Postmaster of Lima, Ohio.[7]

Winthrop W. Ketcham, delegate at large from Pennsylvania, appointed Solicitor of the United States Court of Claims.[8]

David P. Vinton, delegate from Indiana, appointed Associate Justice of the Supreme Court of New Mexico Territory.[9]

Peter Melendy, delegate from Iowa, appointed United States Marshal for Iowa.[10]

George S. Bangs, delegate from Illinois, appointed Postmaster of Aurora, Illinois.[11]

Harrison Dills, delegate from Illinois, appointed Postmaster of Quincy, Illinois.[12]

Clark E. Carr, delegate from Illinois, appointed Postmaster of Galesburg, Illinois.[13]

[1] The list of these delegates and alternates to the Baltimore Convention is taken from C. W. Johnson, *The First Three Republican National Conventions . . . 1856, 1860 and 1864*, pp. 248–55.

[2] *U. S. Senate Executive Journal*, XIV, Part I (1864–66), 132, 218.

[3] *Ibid.*, pp. 41, 163.   [4] *Ibid.*, pp. 85, 165.   [5] *Ibid.*, pp. 257, 287.

[6] *Ibid.*, pp. 193, 220.   [7] *Ibid.*, pp. 282, 296.   [8] *Ibid.*, pp. 175, 220.

[9] *Ibid.*, pp. 191, 194.   [10] *Ibid.*, pp. 213, 219.   [11] *Ibid.*, pp. 284, 296.

[12] *Ibid.*, pp. 292, 297.   [13] *Ibid.*, pp. 283, 296.

Thomas M. Bowen, delegate from Kansas, appointed Brigadier General by brevet.[14]

Joseph W. Edwards, alternate from Michigan, appointed Register of the Land Office at Marquette, Michigan.[15]

Martin L. Kimball, delegate from Wisconsin, appointed Postmaster of Berlin, Wisconsin.[16]

George D. Blakey, delegate from Kentucky, appointed Collector of Internal Revenue for the Second Kentucky District.[17]

James Speed, delegate from Kentucky, appointed Attorney General of the United States.[18]

John J. Anderson, delegate from Kentucky, appointed Collector of Internal Revenue for the Sixth Kentucky District.[19]

William E. Gleason, lone delegate from Dakota Territory, appointed Associate Justice of the Supreme Court of Dakota Territory.[20]

George M. Pinney, lone alternate from Dakota Territory, appointed United States Marshal for Montana Territory.[21]

[14] *U. S. Senate Executive Journal,* XIV, Part I (1864–66), 160, 194.
[15] *Ibid.,* pp. 252, 267.   [16] *Ibid.,* pp. 276, 296.   [17] *Ibid.,* pp. 14, 84.
[18] *Ibid.,* pp. 1, 7.   [19] *Ibid.,* pp. 14, 84.   [20] *Ibid.,* pp. 171, 194.
[21] *Ibid.,* pp. 161, 178.

BIBLIOGRAPHY

MANUSCRIPTS

John A. Andrew Papers, Massachusetts Historical Society, Boston.

Nathaniel P. Banks Papers, Essex Institute, Salem, Massachusetts.

Nathaniel P. Banks Papers, Illinois State Historical Library, Springfield, Illinois.

Edward Bates Papers, Missouri Historical Society, St. Louis.

John Bigelow Diary, MS, New York Public Library.

John Bigelow Papers, New York Public Library.

Austin Blair Papers, Burton Historical Collection, Detroit Public Library.

Francis Preston Blair Papers, Library of Congress.

James O. Broadhead Papers, Missouri Historical Society, St. Louis.

Bryant-Godwin Papers, New York Public Library.

Simon Cameron Papers, Library of Congress.

Henry C. Carey Papers, Historical Society of Pennsylvania, Philadelphia.

William E. Chandler Papers, Library of Congress.

Zachariah Chandler Papers, Library of Congress.

Chase-Hosea Papers, Widener Library, Harvard University.

Salmon P. Chase Papers, Historical Society of Pennsylvania, Philadelphia.

Salmon P. Chase Papers, Library of Congress.

Colfax-Orth Papers, Indiana State Library, Indianapolis.

John Covode Papers, Historical Society of Western Pennsylvania, Pittsburgh.

John A. J. Creswell Papers, Library of Congress.

Charles A. Dana Papers, Library of Congress.

David Davis Papers. Copies in possession of Dr. Harry E. Pratt, of Springfield, Ill.

Henry E. Dummer Papers (Photostats), Chicago Historical Society.

Jesse W. Fell Papers. Copies in possession of Dr. Harry E. Pratt, of Springfield, Ill.

William P. Fessenden Papers, Library of Congress.

Gibson, Charles, "Edward Bates," MS, Edward Bates Papers, Missouri Historical Society, St. Louis.

Joshua R. Giddings Papers, Ohio Archaeological and Historical Society, Columbus, Ohio.

Greeley-Colfax Papers, New York Public Library.

Horace Greeley Papers, Library of Congress.

Horace Greeley Papers, New York Public Library.

Emanuel Hertz Photostats, Library of Congress.

Jacob M. Howard Papers, Burton Historical Collection, Detroit Public Library.

George Jones Photostats. In the possession of Dr. Francis Brown of the New York *Times*.

George W. Julian Papers, Indiana State Library, Indianapolis.

Lincoln Cabinet Collection, Lincoln National Life Foundation, Fort Wayne, Indiana.

Lincoln Collection, John Hay Library, Brown University, Providence, Rhode Island.

Lincoln Collection, Illinois State Historical Library, Springfield, Illinois.

Lincoln Letters, Photostats, Library of Congress.

Manton Marble Papers, Library of Congress.

Miscellaneous Papers, Indiana State Library, Indianapolis.

Daniel D. Pratt Papers, Indiana State Library, Indianapolis.

Provost Marshal Papers, New York Historical Society, New York City.

Logan U. Reavis Papers, Chicago Historical Society.

William Schouler Papers, Massachusetts Historical Society, Boston.

William H. Seward Papers. In the possession of Mr. W. H. Seward, Auburn, N.Y.

Charles Perrin Smith, "Personal Reminiscences," MS, New Jersey State Library, Trenton, N.J.

John F. Snyder Papers, Missouri Historical Society, St. Louis.

Edwin M. Stanton Papers, Library of Congress.

Thaddeus Stevens Papers, Library of Congress.

Charles Sumner Papers, Widener Library, Harvard University.

Richard W. Thompson Papers, Lincoln National Life Foundation, Fort Wayne, Ind.

Lyman Trumbull Papers, Library of Congress.

Benjamin F. Wade Papers, Library of Congress.

Elihu B. Washburne Papers, Library of Congress.

Thurlow Weed Papers, Library of Congress.

Thurlow Weed Papers, University of Rochester Library, Rochester, New York.

Gideon Welles Papers, Library of Congress.

Gideon Welles Papers, New York Public Library.

Richard Yates Papers, Illinois State Historical Library, Springfield.

GOVERNMENT DOCUMENTS

Congressional Globe

"Execution of Treaty with Winnebagoes," Executive Document No. 229, 25th Cong., 3rd Sess., Serial no. 345.

Register of Officers and Agents, Civil, Military, and Naval, in the Service of the United States on the Thirtieth September, 1861. . . . Washington, 1862.

"Report of the Secretary of the Navy, 1861," Senate Executive Document no. 1, 37th Cong., 2nd Sess., Serial no. 1119.

Richardson, James D. (comp.), Messages and Papers of the Presidents, 1789–1897. Vol. VI. Washington, 1897.

"Ships For the Japanese Government," Senate Executive Document No. 33, 37th Cong., 3d Sess., Serial no. 1149.

U.S. Senate Executive Journal, Vol. XII, 1861–62; Vol. XIII, 1862–64.

War of the Rebellion: Official Records of the Union and Confederate Armies. Series III, Vols. I and II. Washington, D.C., 1899.

War of the Rebellion: Official Records of the Union and Confederate Navies. Series II, Vol. I. Washington, 1921.

NEWSPAPERS

Albany *Evening Journal*
Baltimore *Clipper*
Baltimore *Evening Patriot*
Baltimore *Sun*
Boston *Daily Advertiser*
Brooklyn *Daily Eagle*
Brooklyn *Daily Union*
Cincinnati *Daily Commercial*
Cincinnati *Daily Gazette*

Columbus *Daily Ohio State Journal*
Dawson's Fort Wayne *Daily Times*
Detroit *Daily Tribune*
Detroit *Free Press*
Dover *Delawarean*
Frankfort (Ky.) *Tri-Weekly Commonwealth*
Frankfort *Weekly Kentucky Yeoman*
Hartford *Daily Courant*
Indianapolis *Daily State Sentinel*
Leavenworth (Kansas) *Daily Conservative*
Manchester (N.H.) *Daily Mirror and American*
Milford (Del.) *Peninsular News and Advertiser*
New Haven *Morning Journal and Courier*
New Orleans *Times*
New York *Daily Times*
New York *Daily Tribune*
New York *Evening Post*
New York *Herald*
New York *World*
Philadelphia *Daily News*
Philadelphia *Inquirer*
Philadelphia *North American and United States Gazette*
Philadelphia *Press*
Philadelphia *Public Ledger*
Pontiac (Mich.) *Weekly Gazette*
Portsmouth (N.H.) *Journal of Literature and Politics*
Providence *Daily Journal*
St. Louis *Daily Missouri Democrat*
St. Louis *Daily Missouri Republican*
San Francisco *Daily Evening Bulletin*
Springfield (Ill.) *Daily Illinois State Journal*
Springfield (Mass.) *Republican*
Washington *National Intelligencer*
Wilkes' *Spirit of the Times*
Wilmington Delaware *State Journal and Statesman*
Worcester *Daily Spy*

BOOKS, PAMPHLETS, AND ARTICLES

Adams, Charles Francis, by His Son Charles Francis Adams. Boston and New York, 1900.
—— Richard Henry Dana. Vols. I–II. Boston and New York, 1891.
Aldrich, Charles, "At Lincoln's First Inauguration," *Annals of Iowa,* Series III, VIII (April, 1907), 43–50.
Ambler, Charles H., "The Cleavage between Eastern and Western Virginia," *The American Historical Review,* XV (July, 1910), 762–80.
—— Francis H. Pierpont: Union War Governor of Virginia and Father of West Virginia. Chapel Hill, N.C., 1937.
—— A History of West Virginia. New York, 1933.
—— West Virginia: Stories and Biographies. New York, 1937.
American Series of Popular Biographies: Maine Ed. Boston, 1903.
Andrew, John A., "Letters to Governor John A. Andrew in March, 1861," *Proceedings of the Massachusetts Historical Society,* LXII (June, 1929), 209–12.
Andrews, H. Franklin, The Hamlin Family. Exiro, Iowa, n.d.
Andrews, J. Cutler, Pittsburgh's Post-Gazette. Boston, 1936.
Andrews, Mathew P., Tercentenary History of Maryland, Vol. I. Chicago and Baltimore, 1925.
Angle, Paul M., Lincoln, 1854–1861: Being the Day-by-Day Activities of Abraham Lincoln from January 1, 1854, to March 4, 1861. Springfield, Ill., 1933.
—— (ed.), Herndon's Life of Lincoln, New York, 1930.
—— New Letters and Papers of Lincoln. Boston and New York, 1930.
Atwater, Edward E., History of the City of New Haven to the Present Time. New York, 1887.
Auchampaugh, Philip G., James Buchanan and His Cabinet on the Eve of Secession. Lancaster, Pa., 1926.
—— "John W. Forney, Robert Tyler and James Buchanan," *Tyler's Quarterly Historical and Genealogical Magazine,* XV (October, 1933), 71–89.
Badeau, Adam, Military History of Ulysses S. Grant from April, 1861, to April, 1865. Vol. I. New York, 1868.
Baehr, Harry W., "The American Mission to Rome," MS, M. A. Thesis, Columbia University, 1930. (Copy in Burgess Library, Columbia University.)
Bagley, Clarence B., History of King County, Washington. Vol. I. Seattle, 1929.
Baker's Biographical Dictionary of Musicians. 3d Edition.

Bancroft, Frederic, The Life of William H. Seward. Vols. I, II. New York and London, 1900.

Bancroft, Hubert H., History of Nevada, Colorado, and Wyoming. San Francisco, 1890.

—— History of Oregon. San Francisco, 1888.

—— History of the Life of William Gilpin. San Francisco, 1889.

—— History of Utah. San Francisco, 1889.

—— History of Washington, Idaho, and Montana. San Francisco, 1890.

Barbee, David R., "Hinton Rowan Helper," *Tyler's Quarterly Historical and Genealogical Magazine*, XV (January, 1934), 135–72.

Barclay, Thomas S., "The Liberal Republican Movement in Missouri," *The Missouri Historical Review*, XX (October, 1925), 3–78.

Baringer, William, "Campaign Technique in Illinois—1860," *Transactions of the Illinois State Historical Society*, 1932, pp. 229 ff.

—— Lincoln's Rise to Power. Boston, 1937.

Barnes, Thurlow W. (ed.), Memoir of Thurlow Weed. Boston, 1884.

Barrows, Chester L., William M. Evarts, Lawyer, Diplomat, Statesman. Chapel Hill, N.C., 1941.

Bartlett, Ruhl J., John C. Frémont and the Republican Party. Columbus, O., 1930.

Barton, William E., The Life of Abraham Lincoln. Vols. I and II. Indianapolis, 1925.

Baskin, O. L. (Publishers), History of the City of Denver and Arapahoe County, and Colorado. Chicago, 1880.

Bateman, Newton, and Paul Selby (eds.), Historical Encyclopedia of Illinois. Vol. I. Chicago, 1908.

[Bates, Edward] "The Diary of Edward Bates, 1859–1866," edited by Howard K. Beale. *Annual Report*, American Historical Association, Vol. IV, 1930.

Bates, Onward, Bates, et al., of Virginia and Missouri. Chicago, 1914.

Bay, W. V. N., Reminiscences of the Bench and Bar of Missouri. St. Louis, 1878.

Beach, Moses Y., The Wealth and Biography of the Wealthy Citizens of the City of New York. New York, 1846.

Beale, Howard K., The Critical Year. New York, 1930.

Beatty, Richmond C., Bayard Taylor. Norman, Oklahoma, 1936.

[Benedict, Charles L.] Proceedings of Meetings of Members of the Bar Held January 9 and 16, 1901, to Do Honor to the Memory of Honorable Charles L. Benedict. . . . Brooklyn, 1901.

Bennett, Frank M., The Steam Navy of the United States. Pittsburgh, 1896.

Beveridge, Albert J., Abraham Lincoln, 1809–1858. 4-Volume Edition. Boston and New York, 1928.

Biesele, Rudolph L., The History of the German Settlements in Texas, 1831–1861. Austin, 1930.

—— "The Texas State Convention of Germans in 1854," *The Southwestern Historical Quarterly*, XXXIII (April, 1930), 247–61.

Bigelow, John, Retrospections of an Active Life. Vols. I and II. New York, 1909.

Biographical Directory of the American Congress, 1774–1927. Washington, 1928.

Biographical Encyclopaedia of Maine of the Nineteenth Century. Boston, 1885.

A Biographical History of Eminent and Self-made Men of the State of Indiana. Vol. II. Cincinnati, 1880.

A Biographical Sketch of Hon. A. Leo Knott with a Relation of Some Political Transactions in Maryland, 1861–1867. Baltimore, n.d.

Black, John R., Young Japan. Vol. II. London, 1880.

Blaine, James G., Twenty Years of Congress. Vol. II. Norwich, Conn., 1886.

Blanchard, Charles, The Progressive Men of the Commonwealth of Pennsylvania. Vol. II. Logansport, Indiana, 1900.

Blegen, Theodore C., "Campaigning with Seward in 1860," *Minnesota History*, VIII (June, 1927), 150–71.

—— "James Wickes Taylor: A Biographical Sketch," *Minnesota History Bulletin*, I (November, 1915), 155 ff.

Bonney, Catharine V. R., A Legacy of Historical Gleanings. Albany, 1875.

Boughter, I. F., "Internal Improvements in Northwestern Virginia: A Study of State Policy Prior to the Civil War," MS, Ph.D. Dissertation, University of Pittsburgh, 1930. (Copy in University of Pittsburgh Library, Pittsburgh.)

Boutwell, George S., Reminiscences of Sixty Years in Public Affairs. Vol. II. New York, 1902.

Bowers, Claude G., The Tragic Era. Cambridge, Mass., 1929.

Bradsby, H. C., History of Vigo County, Indiana. Chicago, 1891.

Brand, Carl F., "History of the Know Nothing Party in Indiana," *Indiana Magazine of History*, XVIII (1922), 204 ff.

Brigance, William N., Jeremiah Sullivan Black: A Defender of the

Constitution and the Ten Commandments. Philadelphia, 1934.

Briggs, John E., "The Enlistment of Iowa Troops during the Civil War," *The Iowa Journal of History and Politics*, XV (July, 1917), 323–92.

Brigham, Johnson, James Harlan. Iowa City, Iowa, 1913.

Brillhart, Norman C., "The Election of 1864 in Western Pennsylvania," *Western Pennsylvania Historical Magazine*, Vol. VIII (1925), 26–36.

[Browning, Orville Hickman] The Diary of Orville Hickman Browning, 1850–1864, edited by Theodore C. Pease and James G. Randall. Vol. I. "Collections of the Illinois State Historical Society," Vol. XX.

Brummer, Sidney D., Political History of New York State during the Period of the Civil War. New York, 1911.

Bruncken, Ernest, "German Political Refugees in the United States during the Period from 1815–1860," *Deutsch-amerikanische Geschichtsblätter*, IV (January, 1904), 33–59.

[Buchanan, James] The Works of James Buchanan, edited by John Bassett Moore. Vol. XI. Philadelphia and London, 1910.

Buell, Walter, "Zachariah Chandler," *Magazine of Western History*, IV (1886), 437–38.

[Butler, Benjamin F.] Private and Official Correspondence of Gen. Benjamin F. Butler during the Period of the Civil War. Vols. I, V. Norwood, Mass., 1917.

Campbell, James E., "Sumner-Brooks-Burlingame, or the Last of the Great Challenges." *Ohio Archaeological and Historical Quarterly*, XXXIV (October, 1925), 435–73.

Carey, Charles H., History of Oregon. Vol. I. Portland, 1922.

Carman, Harry J., and Reinhard H. Luthin, "Some Aspects of the Know Nothing Movement Reconsidered," *The South Atlantic Quarterly*, XXXIX (April, 1940), 213–34.

Carpenter, Francis B., Six Months at the White House with Abraham Lincoln. New York, 1866.

Carr, Clark E., My Day and Generation. Chicago, 1908.

Carroll, Howard, Twelve Americans. New York, 1883.

Case, Lafayette W., The Goodrich Family in America. Chicago, 1889.

Chandler, P. W., Memoir of Governor Andrew. N.p., 1880.

[Chase, Salmon P.] "Diary and Correspondence of Salmon P. Chase," *Annual Report*, American Historical Association, Vol. II (1902).

Chittenden, L. E., Recollections of President Lincoln and His Administration. New York, 1891.

Clark, George T., Leland Stanford. Stanford University, 1931.

Clarke, Grace Julian, George W. Julian. Indianapolis, 1923.

[Clay, Henry] The Private Correspondence of Henry Clay, edited by Calvin Colton. New York, 1855.

Clephane, Walter C., "Lewis Clephane: A Pioneer Washington Republican," *Records of the Columbia Historical Society*, XXI (Washington, 1918), 263–77.

Cochrane, John, The American Civil War. New York, 1879.

Cole, Arthur C., The Era of the Civil War, 1848–1870. Vol. III of The Centennial History of Illinois. Springfield, Ill., 1919.

—— "Lincoln and the Presidential Election of 1864," *Transactions of the Illinois State Historical Society*, 1917, pp. 130–38.

[Cole, Cornelius] Memoirs of Cornelius Cole. New York, 1908.

Coleman, Charles H., The Election of 1868. New York, 1933.

Collins, Richard H., The History of Kentucky. Vols. I and II. Covington, Ky., 1874.

Conkling, Alfred R., The Life and Letters of Roscoe Conkling, Orator, Statesman, Advocate. New York, 1889.

Connelly, William E., and E. M. Coulter, History of Kentucky. Vol. II. Chicago and New York, 1922.

Corning, Charles R., Amos Tuck. Exeter, N.H., 1902.

Coulter, E. Merton, The Civil War and Readjustment in Kentucky. Chapel Hill, N.C., 1926.

Cox, Jacob D., Atlanta. New York, 1898.

—— The Battle of Franklin, Tennessee. New York, 1897.

—— Military Reminiscences of the Civil War. Vols. I and II. New York, 1900.

Crandall, Andrew W., The Early History of the Republican Party, 1854–1856. Boston, 1930.

Cranmer, Gibson L., History of Wheeling City and Ohio County, West Virginia. Chicago, 1902.

Craven, Avery, The Coming of the Civil War. New York, 1942.

Cunz, Dieter, "The Maryland Germans in the Civil War," *The Maryland Historical Magazine*, XXXVI (December, 1941), 407 ff.

Curran, Ruth Gertrude, "David Kellogg Cartter," *Ohio Archaeological and Historical Quarterly*, XLII (January, 1933), 105–15.

Curtis, Francis, The Republican Party. Vol. I. New York and London, 1904.

Dana, Charles A., Recollections of the Civil War. New York, 1899.

Darling, Arthur B., Political Changes in Massachusetts, 1824–1848. New Haven, 1925.

Davis, John M., "Elijah Sells," *Annals of Iowa*, Series III, II, (1895–97), 518–30.

Davis, Stanton L., Pennsylvania Politics, 1860–1863. Cleveland, Ohio, 1935.

Davis, William W., The Civil War and Reconstruction in Florida. New York, 1913.

Dennett, Tyler, Americans in Eastern Asia. New York, 1922.

—— John Hay: From Poetry to Politics. New York, 1933.

—— "Lincoln and the Campaign of 1864," Abraham Lincoln Association Papers, 1935, pp. 31–58.

Dent, Thomas, "David Davis—A Sketch," *The American Law Review*, LIII (1919), 545 ff.

Derby, J. C., Fifty Years among Authors, Books and Publishers. New York, 1884.

Detroit Post and Tribune, Zachariah Chandler: An Outline Sketch of His Life and Public Services by the Detroit Post and Tribune. Detroit, 1880.

"The Diary of a Public Man," *The North American Review*, CXXIX (1879), 125–40, 259–73.

Dickins, F. V., and S. Lane-Poole, Life of Sir Harry Parkes. Vol. II. New York and London, 1894.

[Dickinson, Daniel S.] Speeches, Correspondence, etc., of the Late Daniel S. Dickinson, of New York, edited by John R. Dickinson. Vol. II. New York, 1867.

Dictionary of American Biography, edited by Allen Johnson and Dumas Malone. 20 vols. New York, 1928–36.

Donner, Barbara, "Carl Schurz as Office-Seeker," *The Wisconsin Magazine of History*, XX (December, 1936), 127–42.

Dudley, Harold M., "The Election of 1864," *The Mississippi Valley Historical Review*, XVIII (March, 1932), 500–18.

Dunning, William A., "The Second Birth of the Republican Party," *The American Historical Review*, XVI (October, 1910), 56–63.

[Durell, Edward H.] "Hon. Edward Henry Durell," *The Granite Monthly*, April, 1888, pp. 115–29.

Dwight's Journal of Music.

Dyche, Grace L. S., "John Locke Scripps, Lincoln's Campaign

Biographer," *Journal of the Illinois State Historical Society,* XVII (1924–25), 333–51.

Dyer, Brainerd, The Public Career of William M. Evarts. Berkeley, Calif., 1933.

[Edmunds, James M.] Memorial Discourse Delivered by Rev. Byron Sunderland, at the Funeral of Hon. James M. Edmunds, Tuesday, December 16, 1879. Washington, 1880.

Edwards, Arthur, Sketch of the Life of Norman B. Judd. N.p., n.d.

Egle, William H., Histories of the Counties of Dauphin and Lebanon in the Commonwealth of Pennsylvania. Philadelphia, 1883.

Eiselen, Malcolm R., The Rise of Pennsylvania Protectionism. Philadelphia, 1932.

Eliot, Charles W., "Robert Samuel Rantoul," *Essex Institute Historical Collections,* LVIII (1922), 265–69.

Ellison, Joseph, California and the Nation, 1850–1869. Berkeley, Calif., 1927.

Elmer, Lucius Q. C., The Constitution and Government of New Jersey . . . and Reminiscences of the Bench and Bar. Newark, 1872.

Fahrney, Ralph R., Horace Greeley and the *Tribune* in the Civil War. Cedar Rapids, Iowa, 1936.

Fairman, Charles, Mr. Justice Miller and the Supreme Court, 1862–1900. Cambridge, Mass., 1939.

Farwell, John D., The Farwell Family. Vol. I. Rutland, Vt., 1929.

Farwell, Willard B., "Brief Biography of Willard Brigham Farwell," *Quarterly of the Society of California Pioneers,* I (1924), 28–29.

Faust, Albert B., The German Element in the United States. Vol. II. New York, 1927.

Fessenden, Francis, Life and Public Services of William Pitt Fessenden. Vols. I and II. Boston and New York, 1907.

Ficklen, John R., History of Reconstruction in Louisiana through 1868. Baltimore, 1910.

Field, Henry M., The Life of David Dudley Field. New York, 1898.

Field, Maunsell B., Memories of Many Men and of Some Women. New York, 1874.

Fish, Carl Russell, The Civil Service and the Patronage. New York, 1905.

—— "Lincoln and the Patronage," *The American Historical Review,* VIII (October, 1902), 53–69.

Fish, Carl Russell, "Table of Removals," *Annual Report*, American Historical Association, I (1899), 67–86.

Fite, Emerson D., The Presidential Campaign of 1860. New York, 1911.

Fleming, Walter L., Civil War and Reconstruction in Alabama. New York, 1905.

Flower, Frank A., Edwin McMasters Stanton. Akron, Ohio, 1905.

[Fogg, George G.] A Memorial of George Gilman Fogg: The Address of Rev. Augustus Woodbury, at the Funeral Services, Oct. 8, 1881. Concord, N.H., 1882. (Copy in the New York Public Library.)

Folwell, William W., A History of Minnesota. Vol. III. St. Paul, Minnesota, 1926.

[Forbes, John Murray] Letters and Recollections of John Murray Forbes, edited by Sarah F. Hughes. Vol. I. Boston and New York, 1899.

Forney, John W., Anecdotes of Public Men. Vol. I. New York, 1873.
—— Forty Years of American Journalism: Retirement of Mr. J. W. Forney from the Philadelphia "Press." Philadelphia, 1877.

Foulke, William D., Life of Oliver P. Morton. Vol. I. Indianapolis and Kansas City, 1899.

[Fox, Gustavus Vasa] Confidential Correspondence of Gustavus Fox, Assistant Secretary of the Navy, 1861–1865, edited by Robert M. Thompson and Richard Wainwright. Vols. I and II. New York, 1898–99.

Freeze, John G., A History of Columbia County, Pennsylvania. Bloomsburg, Pa., 1883.

Gallaher, Ruth A., "Samuel Ryan Curtis," *The Iowa Journal of History and Politics*, XXV (July, 1927), 331–58.

Geary, Sister M. Theophane, A History of Third Parties in Pennsylvania, 1840–1860. Washington, 1938.

"The Genesis of the Republican Party in Minnesota," *Minnesota History Bulletin*, II (February, 1917), 24–30.

Gentry, North Todd, "William F. Switzler," *The Missouri Historical Review*, XXIV (January, 1930), 161–76.

Gilmore, James R., Personal Recollections of Abraham Lincoln and the Civil War. Boston, 1898.

Ginsberg, Sanford J., "Corruption and Fraud in Government Contracts during the Civil War," MS, M. A. Thesis, Columbia University, 1940.

Godwin, Parke, A Biography of William Cullen Bryant. Vol. II. New York, 1883.

Goebel, Dorothy Burne, William Henry Harrison. Indianapolis, 1926.

Gorham, George C., Life and Public Services of Edwin M. Stanton. Vol. I. Boston and New York, 1899.

Grant, U. S., Personal Memoirs of U. S. Grant. Vol. I. New York, 1885.

Gray, Wood, The Hidden Civil War. New York, 1942.

Gregory, Charles N., Samuel Freeman Miller. Iowa City, Iowa, 1907.

—— "Samuel Freeman Miller: Associate Justice of the Supreme Court of the United States," *Yale Law Journal*, XVII (April, 1908), 422–42.

Gresham, Matilda M., Life of Walter Quintin Gresham. Vols. I and II. Chicago, 1919.

Griswold, B. J., The Pictorial History of Fort Wayne, Indiana. Vol. I. Chicago, 1917.

Gue, Benjamin F., History of Iowa. Vol. IV. New York, 1903.

[Gurowski, Adam] Diary of Adam Gurowski. Vol. I. Boston, 1862.

Hall, Clifton R., Andrew Johnson, Military Governor of Tennessee. Princeton, 1916.

Hall, Granville D., The Rending of Virginia. Chicago, 1901.

Halstead, Murat, Caucuses of 1860: A History of the National Political Conventions of the Current Presidential Campaign. Columbus, 1860.

Hamilton, J. G. de R., Reconstruction in North Carolina. New York, 1914.

Hamlin, Charles E., The Life and Times of Hannibal Hamlin. Cambridge, Mass., 1899.

Hansen-Taylor, Marie, and Horace E. Scudder, Life and Letters of Bayard Taylor. Vol. I. Boston, 1885.

Harbison, Winfred A., "Indiana Republicans and the Re-Election of President Lincoln," *Indiana Magazine of History*, XXXIV (March, 1938), 42–64.

—— "Lincoln and Indiana Republicans, 1861–1862," *Indiana Magazine of History*, XXXIII (September, 1937), 277–303.

—— "Zachariah Chandler's Part in the Reëlection of Abraham Lincoln," *The Mississippi Valley Historical Review*, XXII (September, 1935), 267–76.

Harlan, Alpheus H., History and Genealogy of the Harlan Family. Baltimore, 1914.

Harrington, Fred Harvey, "Nathaniel Prentiss Banks: A Study in Anti-Slavery Politics," *The New England Quarterly*, IX (December, 1936), 626–54.

Hart, Albert Bushnell, Salmon Portland Chase. Boston and New York, 1899.

Hartley, Isaac S., "General Francis E. Spinner, the Financier," *Magazine of American History*, XXV (March, 1891, 185–200).

Hatch, Louis C., Maine: A History. Vol. II. New York, 1919.

Hay, John, "Life in the White House in the Time of Lincoln," *The Century Magazine*, November, 1890, pp. 33 ff.

—— Lincoln and the Civil War in the Diaries and Letters of John Hay, edited by Tyler Dennett. New York, 1939.

Herriott, F. I., "Iowa and the First Nomination of Abraham Lincoln," *Annals of Iowa*, Series III, VIII (July, 1907), 96 ff.

—— "The Conference at the Deutsches Haus, Chicago, May 14–15, 1860," *Transactions of the Illinois State Historical Society*, 1928, pp. 101–191.

—— "The Premises and Significance of Abraham Lincoln's Letter to Theodore Canisius," *Deutsch-amerikanische Geschichtsblätter*, XV (1915), 181–254.

Hertz, Emanuel, Abraham Lincoln: A New Portrait. Vol. II. New York, 1931.

—— The Hidden Lincoln. New York, 1938.

Hewitt, Warren F., "The Know Nothing Party in Pennsylvania," *Pennsylvania History*, II ,(April, 1935), 69–85.

Higginson, T. W., "Regular and Volunteer Officers," *The Atlantic Monthly*, XIV (September, 1864), 354 ff.

Hill, Lawrence F., Diplomatic Relations between the United States and Brazil. Durham, N.C., 1932.

Holbrook, Franklin F., "The Early Political Career of Ignatius Donnelly, 1857–1863," MS, M. A. Thesis, University of Minnesota, 1916.

Hollister, O. J., Life of Schuyler Colfax. Chicago and New York, 1887.

Holmes, Oliver Wendell, John Lothrop Motley: A Memoir. Boston, 1888.

Hooper, Samuel, A Defence of the Merchants of Boston against the Aspersions of the Hon. John Z. Goodrich, Ex-Collector of Customs. Boston, 1866. (Copy in the New York Public Library.)

Hosmer, James K., Outcome of the Civil War, 1863–1865. New York and London, 1907.

[Howard, William A.] "The Death of Governor William A. Howard," *Michigan Pioneer Collections*, IV (1881), 128 ff.

Howe, M. A. de Wolfe, The Life and Letters of George Bancroft. Vol. I. New York, 1908.

Howell, George R., and Jonathan Tenney (eds.), History of the County of Albany, N.Y. Albany, 1886.

[Howells, William Dean] "Letters of William Dean Howells, 1857–1867," *The Bookman*, LXVII (May, 1928), 267 ff.

—— Years of My Youth. New York and London, 1916.

Hudson, Charles, "Life, Services and Character of Levi Lincoln," MS, American Antiquarian Society, Worcester, Mass.

Hudson, Frederic, Journalism in the United States from 1690 to 1872. New York, 1873.

Hunt, Herbert, and Floyd C. Kaylor, Washington: West of the Cascades. Vol. III. Chicago, 1917.

Hyde, William, and Howard L. Conard (eds.), Encyclopedia of the History of St. Louis. Vols. I and III. St. Louis, 1899.

Ingersoll, L. D., Iowa and the Rebellion. Philadelphia, 1867.

[Jayne, William] "Dr. William Jayne," *Journal of the Illinois State Historical Society*, IX (1916–17), 82–94.

—— "Doctor William Jayne, First Governor," *South Dakota Historical Collections*, I (1902), 118 ff.

Johnson, Charles W., The First Three Republican National Conventions . . . 1856, 1860, and 1864. n.d.

Johnson, Franklin, "Nominating Lincoln," *The Companion*, February 8, 1917.

Jones, Samuel, "The Battle of Olustee, or Ocean Pond, Florida," in Robert U. Johnson and Clarence C. Buel (eds.), Battles and Leaders of the Civil War. Vol. IV. New York, 1884.

Journal of the Convention Assembled at Wheeling, on the 11th of June, 1861. Wheeling, Va., 1861.

[Julian, George W.] "George W. Julian's Journal," *Indiana Magazine of History*, XI (December, 1915), 324–37.

—— Political Recollections, 1840 to 1872. Chicago, 1884.

[Kasson, John A.] "John A. Kasson, an Autobiography," *Annals of Iowa*, Series III, XII (July, 1920), 346–58.

Kennedy, Elijah R., The Contest for California in 1861; How Colonel E. D. Baker Saved the Pacific States to the Union. Boston and New York, 1912.

King, Charles, "Rufus King: Soldier, Editor and Statesman," *The Wisconsin Magazine of History*, IV (1920–21), 371–81.

[Kinney, John F.] "John Fitch Kinney," *Annals of Iowa*, Series III, XVI (October, 1927), 145–50.

Kirkland, Edward C., The Peacemakers of 1864. New York, 1927.

Knapp, Charles M., New Jersey Politics during the Period of the Civil War Reconstruction. Geneva, N.Y., 1924.

Koerner, Gustave, Memoirs of Gustave Koerner. Vol. II. Cedar Rapids, Iowa, 1909.

Lamon, Ward H., Recollections of Abraham Lincoln, 1847–1865. Chicago, 1895.

Lanman, Charles, Biographical Annals of the Civil Government of the United States. Washington, D.C., 1876.

Laughlin, Sceva B., "Missouri Politics during the Civil War," *The Missouri Historical Review*, XXIV (1929–1930), 87–113, 261–84.

"Colonel Timothy Bigelow Lawrence," *Proceedings of the American Antiquarian Society* (1869).

Lawrence, Robert M., The Descendants of Major Samuel Lawrence of Groton, Massachusetts. Cambridge, Mass., 1904.

Leonard, L. O., "Norman B. Judd," *Rock Island Magazine*, May, 1926, pp. 33–34.

Lewis, Lloyd, Sherman, Fighting Prophet. New York, 1932.

"Lincoln's Faith in Greeley," *The Magazine of History* (1930), XL, No. 1, pp. 3–8.

Linder, Usher F., Reminiscences of the Early Bench and Bar of Illinois. Chicago, 1879.

Linn, William A., The Story of the Mormons. New York and London, 1902.

Lonn, Ella, Reconstruction in Louisiana After 1868. New York and London, 1918.

Lore, Charles P., "The Life and Character of George P. Fisher," *Papers of the Historical Society of Delaware*, No. 36 (1902), 3–16.

Lunt, George, The Origins of the Late War. New York, 1866.

Luthin, Reinhard H., "Abraham Lincoln and the Massachusetts Whigs in 1848," *The New England Quarterly*, XIV (December, 1941), 619–32.

Lyford, James O., History of Concord, New Hampshire. Concord, N.H., 1903.

Lyman, Horace S., History of Oregon. Vol. IV. New York, 1903.

Mack, Effie M., Nevada: A History of the State from the Earliest Times through the Civil War. Glendale, Calif., 1936.

Mackenzie, George N., Colonial Families of the United States of America. Vol. V. Baltimore, 1915.

Manning, John W., "Reconstruction in Kentucky," MS, M. A. Thesis, University of Louisville, 1926. (Copy in Library of the University of Louisville, Louisville, Ky.)

Marsh, Caroline C. (compiler), Life and Letters of George Perkins Marsh. Vol. I. New York, 1888.

Martyn, Carlos, William E. Dodge: The Christian Merchant. New York and London, 1890.

McCarthy, Charles H., Lincoln's Plan of Reconstruction. New York, 1901.

McClure, Alexander K., Abraham Lincoln and Men of War-Times. Philadelphia, 1892.

—— Old Time Notes of Pennsylvania. Vol. I. Philadelphia, 1905.

McCulloch, Hugh, Men and Measures of Half a Century. New York, 1888.

McDougal, H. C., "A Decade of Missouri Politics—1860 to 1870: From a Republican Viewpoint," The Missouri Historical Review, III (January, 1909), 126–53.

McLean, John, Reports of Cases . . . in the Circuit of the United States for the Seventh Circuit, VI (1856).

McMaster, John Bach, A History of the People of United States during Lincoln's Administration. New York and London, 1927.

McNeil, Floyd A., "Lincoln's Attorney General: Edward Bates," MS, Ph.D. Dissertation, State University of Iowa, 1933. (Copy in the Library of the State University of Iowa, Iowa City.)

Meany, Edmond S., Governors of Washington, Territorial and State. Seattle, 1915.

—— History of the State of Washington. New York, 1909.

Meneely, A. Howard, The War Department, 1861. New York, 1928.

Merriam, George S., The Life and Times of Samuel Bowles. Vol. I. New York, 1885.

Miller, Thomas C. and H. Maxwell, West Virginia and Its People. Vol. II. New York, 1913.

Milton, George Fort, The Eve of Conflict: Stephen A. Douglas and the Needless War. Boston and New York, 1934.

—— Abraham Lincoln and the Fifth Column. New York, 1942.

—— Conflict; The American Civil War. New York, 1941.

Monteiro, Margaret K., "The Presidential Election of 1860 in Virginia," Richmond College Historical Papers, I (June, 1916), 222–58.

Morrow, Josiah, Life and Speeches of Thomas Corwin. Cincinnati, 1896.

[Motley, John Lothrop] The Complete Works of John L. Motley, edited by George W. Curtis. De luxe edition, Vol. XVI. New York, n.d.

—— John Lothrop Motley and His Family: Further Letters and Records Edited by His Daughter and Herbert St. John Mildmay. New York and London, n.d.

Mueller, Henry R., The Whig Party in Pennsylvania. New York, 1922.

Myers, Gustavus, History of the Supreme Court of the United States. Chicago, 1912.

Myers, William Starr, The Maryland Constitution of 1864. Baltimore, 1901.

The National Cyclopædia of American Biography. 29 vols. New York, 1892–1938.

Nelson, S. B. (Publisher), History of Baltimore, Maryland. Baltimore, 1898.

Nettels, Curtis, "The Overland Mail Issue during the Fifties," The Missouri Historical Review, XVIII (July, 1924), 521–34.

Nevins, Allan, Frémont: Pathmarker of the West. New York and London, 1939.

—— Frémont: The West's Greatest Adventurer, Vols. I, II. New York and London, 1928.

—— Hamilton Fish: The Inner History of the Grant Administration. New York, 1936.

—— "Lincoln's Plans for Reunion," Abraham Lincoln Association Papers, 1930, pp. 51–92.

Nichols, Roy F., The Democratic Machine, 1850–1854. New York, 1923.

Nicolay, John G. and John Hay, Complete Works of Abraham Lincoln. Gettysburg Edition, Vols. V–XII. New York, 1894.

Noonan, Carroll J., Nativism in Connecticut, 1829–1860. Washington, 1938.

Oberholtzer, Ellis P., Jay Cooke, Financier of the Civil War. Vol. I. Philadelphia, 1907.

Owen, Thomas M., History of Alabama and Dictionary of Alabama Biography. Vol. III. Chicago, 1921.

[Palfrey, John G.] "John Gorham Palfrey," Report of the Numismatic and Antiquarian Society of Philadelphia, 1881.

Palmer, John M., The Bench and Bar of Illinois. Vol. II. Chicago, 1899.

—— Personal Recollections of John M. Palmer. Cincinnati, 1901.

[Palmer, Robert M.] Washington and the Union: Oration Delivered by Hon. Robert M. Palmer, Speaker of the Senate of Pennsylvania, at the Reception of President Lincoln at Harrisburg . . . on the 22d Day of February, 1861. N.p., n.d.

Paullin, Charles O., "The Navy Department during the Civil War," *Proceedings of the United States Naval Institute*, XXXIX, 119 ff.

—— "President Lincoln and the Navy," *The American Historical Review*, XIV (January, 1909), 284–303.

Pearson, Henry G., James S. Wadsworth of Geneseo. New York, 1913.

—— The Life of John A. Andrew. Vol. I. Boston and New York, 1904.

Pelzer, Louis, "The History of Political Parties in Iowa from 1857 to 1860," *The Iowa Journal of History and Politics*, VII (April, 1909), 179–229.

Perrin, William H., The Pioneer Press of Kentucky. Louisville, 1888.

Phelps, Alonzo, Contemporary Biography of California's Representative Men. San Francisco, 1882.

Phillips, Ulrich B. (ed.), "The Correspondence of Robert Toombs, Alexander H. Stephens and Howell Cobb," *Annual Report*, American Historical Association, Vol. II, 1911.

Pierce, Edward L., Memoir and Letters of Charles Sumner. Vols. II, III, IV. Boston, 1893.

[Pike, James S.] "The Notebooks of James S. Pike, 1861–1862," edited by Harold A. Davis, MS, M. A. Thesis, Columbia University, 1937.

Pitkin, Thomas M., "The Tariff and the Early Republican Party," MS, Ph.D. Dissertation, Western Reserve University, 1935.

Porter, George H., Ohio Politics during the Civil War Period. New York, 1911.

Potter, David M., Lincoln and His Party in the Secession Crisis. New Haven, 1942.

Potter, Marguerite, "Hamilton R. Gamble, Missouri's War Governor," *The Missouri Historical Review*, XXXV (October, 1940), 25–71.

Potts, William J., "Biographical Sketch of the Hon. Thomas H. Dudley, of Camden, N.J.," *Proceedings of the American Philosophical Society*, XXXIV (1895), 102–28.

Pratt, Harry E., "David Davis, 1815–1886," MS, Ph.D. Dissertation, University of Illinois, 1930.

—— "David Davis, 1815–1886," *Transactions of the Illinois State Historical Society*, 1930, pp. 168 ff.

Pratt, Harry E., "Simon Cameron's Fight for a Place in Lincoln's Cabinet," *Bulletin of the Abraham Lincoln Association*, No. 49, September, 1937.

Putnam, Eben, The Putnam Lineage. Salem, Mass., 1907.

[Putnam, James O.] "James O. Putnam Memorial Evening," *Publications of the Buffalo Historical Society*, VI (1903), 632 ff.

Randall, James G., The Civil War and Reconstruction. Boston and New York, 1937.

Rantoul, Robert S., Personal Recollections. Cambridge, Mass., 1916.

Rayback, Joseph, "Land for the Landless: The Contemporary View," MS, M. A. Thesis, Western Reserve University, 1935.

Raymond, Henry J., The Life and Public Services of Abraham Lincoln. New York, 1865.

Reid, Whitelaw, Ohio in the War. Cincinnati, 1868.

Reizenstein, Milton, The Economic History of the Baltimore and Ohio Railroad, 1827–1853. Baltimore, 1897.

Representative Men and Old Families of Rhode Island. Vol. III. Chicago, 1908.

Reynolds, John H., "Presidential Reconstruction in Arkansas," *Publications of the Arkansas Historical Association*, I (1906), 352–61.

Rhodes, James Ford, History of the Civil War. New York, 1917.

—— History of the United States from the Compromise of 1850. Vol. III. New York, 1895.

Rice, Allen Thorndike (ed.), Reminiscences of Abraham Lincoln by Distinguished Men of His Time. New York, 1886.

Rice, Franklin P., "The Life of Eli Thayer," MS, Widener Library, Harvard University.

Riddle, Albert G., Life of Benjamin F. Wade. Cleveland, 1888.

—— Recollections of War Times, 1860–1865. New York and London, 1895.

Robertson, James R., A Kentuckian at the Court of the Tsars: The Ministry of Cassius Marcellus Clay to Russia, 1861–1862, and 1863–1869. Berea, Ky., 1935.

Robinson, Elwyn B., "The North American: Advocate of Protection," *The Pennsylvania Magazine of History and Biography*, LXIV (July, 1940), 345 ff.

—— "The Public Press of Philadelphia during the Civil War," MS, Ph.D. Dissertation, Western Reserve University, 1936.

Roll, Charles, "Richard W. Thompson: A Political Conservative in the Fifties," *Indiana Magazine of History*, XXVII (September, 1931), 183–206.

Salmon, Lucy M., "History of the Appointing Power of the President," *Papers of the American Historical Association*, I (1886), 84 ff.

Salter, William, The Life of James W. Grimes. New York, 1876.

Sandburg, Carl, Abraham Lincoln: The War Years. Vol. III. New York, 1939.

Sandburg, Carl, and Paul M. Angle, Mary Lincoln, Wife and Widow. New York, 1932.

Sanford, Carlton E., Thomas Sanford, the Emigrant to New England. Vol. I. Rutland, Vt., 1911.

Schafer, Joseph, "Who Elected Lincoln?" *The American Historical Review*, XLVII (October, 1941), 51–63.

Scharf, J. Thomas, History of Western Maryland. Vol. II. Philadelphia, 1902.

Scharf, J. Thomas, and Thompson Westcott, History of Philadelphia, 1609–1884. Vol. I. Philadelphia, 1884.

Schell, Herbert S., "Hugh McCulloch and the Treasury Department, 1865–1869," *The Mississippi Valley Historical Review*, XVII (December, 1930), 404–21.

Schneider, George, "Anti-Nebraska Republican Convention at Bloomington, Illinois, May 29, 1856," *Transactions of the McLean County Historical Society*, III (1900), 87–94.

Schofield, John M., Forty-Six Years in the Army. New York, 1897.

Schuckers, J. W., The Life and Public Services of Salmon Portland Chase. New York, 1874.

[Schurz, Carl] Intimate Letters of Carl Schurz, 1841–1869, edited by Joseph Schafer. *Collections of the State Historical Society of Wisconsin*, Vol. XXX.

—— Speeches, Correspondence and Political Papers of Carl Schurz, edited by Frederic Bancroft. Vol. I. New York and London, 1913.

Scott, Eben G., Reconstruction during the Civil War. Boston and New York, 1895.

Scott, Franklin W., Newspapers and Periodicals of Illinois, 1814–1879. Springfield, Ill., 1910.

Seeds, Russel M., History of the Republican Party of Indiana. Vol. I. Indianapolis, 1899.

Seitz, Don C., Horace Greeley, Founder of the New York *Tribune*. Indianapolis, 1926.

—— The James Gordon Bennetts: Father and Son. Indianapolis, 1928.

Sellers, James L., "James R. Doolittle," *The Wisconsin Magazine of History*, XVII (March, 1934), 277–306.

Seward, Frederick W., Reminiscences of a War-Time Statesman and Diplomat, 1830–1915. New York and London, 1916.

—— Seward at Washington as Senator and Secretary of State. Vol. II. New York, 1891.

Shanks, Henry T., The Secession Movement in Virginia, 1847–1861. Richmond, 1934.

Shannon, Fred A., The Organization and Administration of the Union Army, 1861–1865. Vols. I and II. Cleveland, 1928.

Shaw, William H. (Comp.) History of Essex and Hudson Counties, New Jersey. Vol. I. Philadelphia, 1884.

Shutes, Milton H., "Colonel E. D. Baker," *California Historical Society Quarterly*, XVII (December, 1938), 291–324.

Smalley, E. V., A History of the Republican Party. . . . To which Is Added a Political History of Minnesota from a Republican Point of View. St. Paul, 1896.

Smith, Donnal V., Chase and Civil War Politics. Columbus, O., 1931.

—— "The Influence of the Foreign-born of the Northwest in the Election of 1860," *The Mississippi Valley Historical Review*, XIX (September, 1932), 192–204.

—— "Salmon P. Chase and the Election of 1860," *Ohio Archaeological and Historical Quarterly*, XXXIX (1930), 515–607.

Smith, Edward C., A History of Lewis County, West Virginia. Weston, W.Va., 1920.

Smith, Joseph P., History of the Republican Party in Ohio, Vol. I. Chicago, 1898.

Smith, Theodore C., The Life and Letters of James Abram Garfield. Vols. I and II. New Haven, 1925.

Smith, William E., The Francis Preston Blair Family in Politics. 2 vols. New York, 1933.

Smith, W. H., "Schuyler Colfax: Whig Editor, 1854–1855," *Indiana Magazine of History*, XXXIV (September, 1938), 262–82.

Smithers, William T., "Memoir of Nathaniel B. Smithers," *Papers of the Historical Society of Delaware*, No. 23 (1899), pp. 5–39.

Sorenson, Alfred, The Story of Omaha. Omaha, 1923.

Speed, Thomas, The Union Cause in Kentucky, 1860–1865. New York and London, 1907.

Springer, Helen L., "James Speed, The Attorney General, 1864–1866," *The Filson Club History Quarterly*, XI (1937), 169–88.

Stackpole, Everett S., History of New Hampshire, Vol. III. New York, 1916.

Stanton, Henry B., Random Recollections. 3d edition, New York, 1887.

Staples, Thomas S., Reconstruction in Arkansas, 1862–1874. New York, 1923.

Steiner, Bernard C., Life of Henry Winter Davis. Baltimore, 1916.

Stephenson, George M., The Political History of the Public Lands from 1840 to 1862, Boston, 1917.

Stevens, Walter B., "Lincoln and Missouri," *The Missouri Historical Review*, X (January, 1916), 63–119.

Stevenson, Daniel, "General Nelson, Kentucky, and Lincoln Guns," *The Magazine of American History*, X (August, 1883), 114–39.

Stillman, William J., Autobiography of a Journalist. Vol. I. Boston and New York, 1901.

Stock, Leo F., "The United States at the Court of Pius IX," *The Catholic Historical Review*, New Series, III (April, 1923), 114 ff.

—— (ed.), United States Ministers to the Papal States: Instructions and Despatches, 1848–1868. Washington, 1933.

Stocking, William (ed.), Under the Oaks: Commemorating the Fiftieth Anniversary of the Republican Party at Jackson, Michigan, July 6, 1854. Detroit, 1904.

Stoler, Mildred C., "The Influence of the Democratic Element in the Republican Party in Illinois and Indiana, 1854–1860," MS, Ph.D. Dissertation, Indiana University, 1938.

Stone, Candace, Dana and the Sun, New York, 1938.

Storey, Moorfield, and Edward W. Emerson, Ebenezer Rockwood Hoar, Boston and New York, 1911.

Storke, Elliott G., and James H. Smith, History of Cayuga County, New York. Syracuse, 1879.

Street, Ida M., "The Simon Cameron Indian Commission of 1838," *Annals of Iowa*, VII (1905), 115–39, 172–95.

Strevey, Tracy E., "Joseph Medill and the Chicago *Tribune* during the Civil War Period," MS, Ph.D. Dissertation, University of Chicago, 1930.

Strong, Henry, "Justice Samuel Freeman Miller," *Annals of Iowa*, Series III, I (January, 1894), 241–57.

Sulgrove, B. R., History of Indianapolis and Marion County, Indiana. Philadelphia, 1884.

—— "John D. Defrees," *Indiana Magazine of History*, II (1905), 147–50.

Swasey, W. F., The Early Days and Men of California. Oakland, Calif., 1891.

Swisher, Carl B., Roger B. Taney. New York, 1935.

—— Stephen J. Field: Craftsman of the Law. Washington, 1930.

Talbot, George F., "James Shepherd Pike," *Collections and Proceedings of the Maine Historical Society*, Series II, I (1890), 225–60.

Tarbell, Ida M., The Life of Abraham Lincoln. Vol. II. New York, 1917.

Taylor, E. L., Sr., "Richard Plantaganet Llewellyn Baber," *Ohio Archaeological and Historical Publications*, XIX (1910), 370–81.

Thayer, William R., The Life and Letters of John Hay. Vol. I. Boston and New York, 1916.

"The 1860 Presidential Campaign," *The Moorsfield Antiquarian*, I (August, 1937), 104–10.

Thomas, Benjamin P., "Lincoln and the Courts, 1854–1861," *Abraham Lincoln Association Papers*, 1933, pp. 47–103.

Thompson, A. M., A Political History of Wisconsin. Milwaukee, 1900.

Tilton, Clint C., "Lincoln and Lamon: Partners and Friends," *Transactions of the Illinois State Historical Society*, 1931, pp. 175–228.

Tracy, Gilbert A. (comp.), Uncollected Letters of Abraham Lincoln. New York, 1917.

Treat, Payson J., The Early Diplomatic Relations between the United States and Japan, 1853–1865. Baltimore, 1917.

Tribune Almanac, 1861. New York, 1862.

Trumbull, J. Hammond, The Memorial History of Hartford County, Connecticut, 1663–1884, Vol. I. Boston, 1886.

Tullidge, Edward W., History of Salt Lake City. Salt Lake City, 1886.

Twain, Mark, Mark Twain's Autobiography. Vol. II. New York and London, 1924.

Twitchell, Ralph E., "Kirby Benedict," *Old Santa Fe*, I (July, 1913), 3–49.

—— Leading Facts of New Mexico History. Vols. II and V. Cedar Rapids, Iowa, 1912.

The United States vs. Richard Busteed: Argument of H. C. Semple before the Committee on the Judiciary of the House of Representatives.

[Usher, John P.] President Lincoln's Cabinet, by Honorable John P. Usher, Secretary of the Interior, January 7, 1863-May 15, 1865.

With a Foreword and Sketch of the Author by Nelson H. Loomis. Omaha, 1925.

[Villard, Henry] Memoirs of Henry Villard. Vol. I. Boston and New York, 1904.

Warner, G. E., and C. M. Foote, History of Hennepin County and the City of Minneapolis. Minneapolis, 1881.

Warren, Charles, The Supreme Court in United States History. Vol. III. Boston, 1935.

Warren, Louis A., "Cabinet Building in 1861," *Lincoln Lore*, No. 464 (February 28, 1938).

—— "Lincoln and Patronage," *Lincoln Lore*, No. 290 (October 29, 1934).

Washburn, Julia Chase, Genealogical Notes of the Washburn Family. Lewiston, Me., 1898.

[Weed, Thurlow] Autobiography of Thurlow Weed, edited by Harriet A. Weed. Boston, 1883.

[Welles, Gideon] Diary of Gideon Wells. Vols. I and II. Boston and New York, 1911.

—— "Letters of Gideon Welles, 1860–1871," *The Magazine of History*, Extra No. 105 (1924), pp. 7–37.

—— "Three Manuscripts of Gideon Welles," edited by A. Howard Meneely, *The American Historical Review*, XXI (April, 1926), 484–94.

—— "Two Manuscripts of Gideon Welles," edited by Muriel Burnitt, *The New England Quarterly*, XI (September, 1938), 576–604.

[Wells, Hezekiah G.] "Memorial of Hezekiah G. Wells," *Michigan Pioneer Collections*, VIII (1885), 170–71.

White, Horace, The Life of Lyman Trumbull. Boston and New York, 1913.

Whitney, Henry C., Lincoln the President, New York, 1909.

Wilder, Daniel W., Annals of Kansas. Topeka, 1875.

Willey, William P., An Inside View of the Formation of the State of West Virginia. Wheeling, W.Va., 1901.

Williams, Frederick W., Anson Burlingame and the First Chinese Mission to Foreign Powers. New York, 1912.

Williams, J. Fletcher, A History of the City of Saint Paul and of the County of Ramsey, Minnesota. St. Paul, 1876.

Williams, T. Harry, "The Committee on the Conduct of the War," *Journal of the American Military History Institute*, III, 139–56.

Williams, T. Harry, Lincoln and the Radicals. Madison, Wis., 1941.

Wilmer, Lambert A., Our Press Gang. Philadelphia, 1859.

Wilson, Charles R., "New Light on the Lincoln-Blair-Frémont 'Bargain' of 1864," *The American Historical Review*, XLVI (October, 1936), 71–78.

—— "The Original Chase Organization Meeting and *The Next Presidential Election*," *The Mississippi Valley Historical Review*, XXIII (1936), 64–76.

Winslow, Stephen N., Biographies of Successful Philadelphia Merchants. Philadelphia, 1864.

Woodward, Walter C., The Rise and Early History of Political Parties in Oregon, 1843–1868. Portland, 1913.

Woollen, William W., Biographical and Historical Sketches of Early Indiana. Indianapolis, 1883.

Yager, Elizabeth F., "The Presidential Campaign of 1864 in Ohio," *Ohio Archaeological and Historical Quarterly*, XXXIV (October, 1925), 548–89.

Young, Jessie Emilie, "Some Unpublished Letters of Salmon P. Chase," MS, M. A. Thesis, Columbia University, 1922.

" 'Your Tired Friend': A Newly Published Lincoln Letter," *The Abraham Lincoln Quarterly*, June, 1940, pp. 101–5.

"Zachariah Chandler in Lincoln's Second Campaign," *The Century Magazine*, New Series, XXVIII (July, 1895), 476–77.

Zimmerman, Charles, "The Origin and Rise of the Republican Party in Indiana from 1854 to 1860," *Indiana Magazine of History*, XIII (1917), 260 ff., 349–412.

INDEX